Rhetorical and Critical Approaches to Public Relations

COMMUNICATION TEXTBOOK SERIES

Jennings Bryant—Editor

Public Relations
James E. Grunig—Advisor

TOTH/HEATH • Rhetorical and Critical
Approaches to Public Relations
GRUNIG • Excellence in Public Relations
and Communication Management

Rhetorical and Critical Approaches to Public Relations

Edited by

Elizabeth L. Toth
Syracuse University

Robert L. Heath
University of Houston

LEA LAWRENCE ERLBAUM ASSOCIATES, PUBLISHERS
1992   Hillsdale, New Jersey   Hove and London

Lawrence Erlbaum Associates, Inc., Publishers
365 Broadway
Hillsdale, New Jersey 07642

Library of Congress Cataloging-in-Publication Data

Rhetorical and critical approaches to public relations / edited by
    Elizabeth L. Toth, Robert L. Heath.
        p.   cm.
    Includes bibliograhical references and indexes.
    ISBN 0-8058-0470-6
    1. Public relations—Moral and ethical aspects.   2. Public
relations—Corporations—Moral and ethical aspects.   I. Toth,
Elizabeth L.   II. Heath, Robert L. (Robert Lawrence), 1941-
HM263.R46   1992
659.2—dc20   91-20591
                                                         CIP

Printed in the United State of America
10 9 8 7 6 5 4 3 2 1

Dedicated to the Memory of

RON PEARSON

Ron Pearson was a professor at Mount Sant Vincent University, Halifax, Nova Scotia, Canada, until his death in 1990. His rhetorical and critical scholarship in public relations inspired us all. We miss his brilliant challenges to the public relations profession and its body of knowledge.

Contents

Preface

Addressing the relationship between ethics, corporate actions, and public relations, Ron Pearson (1989) reasoned:

> Dialogue is a precondition for any legitimate corporate conduct that affects a public of that organization. The prime concern of those departments is the constitution and maintenance of communication systems that link the corporation with its publics—those organizations and groups affected by corporate actions. The goal of public relations is to manage these communication systems such that they come as close as possible to the standards deduced from the idea of dialogue. This is the core ethical responsibility of public relations from which all other obligations follow. (p. 128)

This observation sets the tone for the analysis of the rhetoric and criticism of public relations. Rhetoric is used to advance interests by expressing and challenging ideas. It entails the assertion of many interests, some competing and some compatible.

Rhetoric can be thought of as a one-way flow of information, argument, and influence whereby one entity persuades and dominates another. It can be used on behalf of one interest and against others. It is sometimes used to distort and avoid truth and wise policy rather than champion them. That view may capture what happens at times, but interests do not remain imbalanced for long.

In the best sense, rhetoric should not be thought of as monologue, but dialogue. By featuring dialogue, we opt to emphasize the dynamics of rhetorical exchange by which interested parties seek to induce agreement and action. Each side in a dialogue is privileged to assert its interest and listen to the expression of interest by other sides. Each party in this exchange may agree or disagree. Through rhetorical dialogue, parties form opinions and negotiate the limits and obligations that are basic to their relationships—their mutual interests.

A vivid lesson learned by all organizations in recent decades is the need for public approval and successful relationships. The American Heart Association, for example, responded to losses in financial support by providing its public with information that encourages leading a healthy life. The makers of Tylenol believed that if they put public safety first their customers would respond favorably. President George Bush needed to create a coalition and gain United Nations sanctions before bringing military force to bear on Iraq. The U.S. Council on Energy Awareness realizes that the future use of nuclear fuel to generate electricity depends on public approval.

For these reasons, a premium is placed on building successful relationships between organizations and their public interests. This confluence of interests has produced a surge in the practice and study of public relations.

Public relations receives scrutiny from all directions because it plays a pivotal role in helping organizations to be more in harmony with communities that support *and* rely on them. Critics can point to instances where public relations has been based on deceit, misinformation, and distortion.

Reporters and the lay public criticize public relations practices. Public relations practitioners are criticized by executive management teams who expect them to work miracles. Few professions have so many pejorative terms (such as *flacks*) associated with them. Public relations practitioners criticize one another, seeking ever more effective methods and higher ethical standards.

Some observers may believe that this extensive scrutiny will damage public relations. But if we are to understand and appreciate how relationships between organizations and communities of individuals are shaped and exploited, we must examine critically the rhetoric of public relations.

The profession is no different in regard to the criticism it suffers than is the legal profession (ambulance chasers) or physicians (quacks). Unlike other professions, public relations has not established itself, but is making strides toward that end. As Pavlik and Salmon (1984) observed, "lack of a systematic body of knowledge is particularly significant, as it remains a hindrance in the development of public relations from a 'practice' to a "profession" (p. 40).

Rhetorical criticism offers a useful means for such examination because of the long history of critical thought that has surrounded informative and suasive discourse. As has public relations, rhetoric has been maligned but it persists because it is a vital means for seeking and sharing information and arguing the wisdom of opinions, actions, and policies. In this sense, public relations draws on the tradition of rhetoric as the rationale for persuasive discourse. As we know the term today, *rhetoric* has come to us over thousands of years of development and refinement. It has been used to enslave and lie. It has been employed to achieve freedom and to argue for truth.

Critics of rhetoric are interested in the goals and strategies individuals and organizations employ to influence each others' opinions and actions. This criticism looks beyond strategies to disclose patterns of thought and judgment that speakers and writers use in their efforts to influence one another. At the heart of this study, meaning, thought, ideas, ideology, and perspectives have special relevance. These concepts have to do with human relations and society. What people believe affects their individual lives as well as the character of society.

For this reason, rhetoric has to do with relationships—how they are shaped—typically between organizations and individuals. Sometimes these relationships are constructive, based on fact, trust, and cooperation. Sometimes they are destructive, resulting in a clash of base interests and narrow perspectives. At what point is public relations functional—serving to produce harmony—and at what times is it dysfunctional—leading to unsound ends? This question, which runs throughout this book, is profoundly affecting the study of public relations. In this vein, Olasky (1987) indicted public relations when it creates regularity in the marketplace and destroys competition. Dionisopoulos and Crable (1988) advised constant awareness of the rhetoric of definition because any entity in a public controversy that can define the key aspects of that controversy has disproportionate power over how events will be perceived and issues decided. Interests are often at odds with one another, not because of misunderstanding or the need for information, but because they have different opinions of what practices are right or wrong. Consequently, public relations often is confronted with seeking a balance between competing interests. Peterson (1988) demonstrated this point by discussing the conflict between preservationists and conversationists over the use of national forests. Such conflicts are brought into focus by Kruckeberg and Starck (1988) who challenge public relations practitioners to foster a sense of community between the entities that they represent and the persons who are affected. In these ways, critics present public relations as inseparable from citizenship—serving society through open discussion of vital points of view, the role rhetoric has performed for over 2,000 years.

What is that citizenship and how well does it serve society? In the answer to that question rests the future of public relations. As Kenneth Burke (1966) observed, "I assume that rhetoric was developed by the use of language for purposes of cooperation and competition. It served to form appropriate attitudes that were designed to induce corresponding acts" (p. 296). In keeping with this point of view, rhetoric is the use of discourse by competing interests seeking to induce one another to accept a mutually harmonious point of view. This dialogue has the potential of improving society by bringing each statement of fact, each policy claim, and values of our society into close scrutiny.

This challenge requires reexamination of the principles and assumptions on which public relations rests. One of those assumptions is that objectivity is inherently superior to persuasion, as if persuasion cannot be objective and information unobjective. Examining this issue, McBride (1989) pointed to the false sense of objectivity journalists enjoy which they operationalize by citing sources from each side of a controversy, a model often used as the standard for public relations communication. McBride put the issue this way: "Public relations must accept a commitment to the ethics of persuasion in order to reduce a crippling inferiority complex and advance understanding of the profession by its practitioners as well as the public" (p. 5). In this spirit, this book engages issues central to the foundation of the public relations process. How well public relations practitioners and scholars perform their roles will determine what they contribute to society and the organizations that sponsor those activities in coming years.

Toward that end, this book is divided into four sections. Part I reviews the rhetoric of public relations and sets forth critical perspectives that establish the foundation for examinations developed in Parts II and III. Part II starts by offering a philosophy of public relations (chapter 4). Chapter 5 seeks to define crisis management by examining several leading cases of how companies respond to events that catch them off guard and demand candid responses under emergency circumstances. Chapter 6 evaluates conflicting views of the role of public relations that become apparent by comparing historical interpretations of Ivy Lee, a leading figure in the development of public relations. Chapter 7 explains how public relations participates in the creation of viewpoints that eventually become sufficiently well established and widely held that they justify the power structures that sponsored those public relations efforts. Chapter 8 discusses problems that arise from the emerging trend of corporations to be image without substance. The theme of this section restates the need for public relations but attempts to set standards of responsible performance that can make it even more of a positive social, economic, and political force.

Public relations transpires on behalf of organizations trying to inform and influence other organizations and key audiences. As such, public relations activities range from publicity and press agentry to those required to foster policy relationships with stakeholders. How this is done satisfactorily or dysfunctionally can be understood by examining selected case studies, which address the rhetorical efforts of organizations.

Part III is devoted to case studies of the practice of public relations.

Chapter 9 considers how companies attempt to maintain an illusion of efficacy in their annual reports by taking credit for business decisions that produce positive outcomes and by blaming external conditions when business difficulties occur and profits fail. Chapter 10 investigates the clumsy rhetorical efforts that transpired when a public relations campaign by the nuclear generating industry attempted to target women in an effort to persuade them to accept nuclear power. Chapter 11 discusses the role of trade association public relations, in this case the promotional efforts of the glass industry. Chapter 12 argues that anti-smoking advocates have incrementally eroded attitudinal and public policy support for the tobacco industry by raising health claims about the effects of cigarette smoking. Chapter 13 discusses the drama created by competing interests who sought to influence the sale of a professional baseball team, specifically the Texas Rangers. Chapter 14 offers insight into how Chevron Oil Company has attempted to attract customers by using its "People Do" campaign to present itself as being environmentally responsible. Chapter 15 examines good character (source credibility) as a factor in the debate over planned parenthood.

The final section sums up the discussion by taking the view that public relations will continue to make strides toward establishing itself as a profession by constantly undergoing close scrutiny of its role in society. Few professions have so many skilled and talented individuals contributing to the thoughts, actions, and policies of our nation. This point becomes focused as we note how the last three decades have witnessed a careful and widespread critical examination of the ideology that guides how companies do business, and how people regulate the private sector through public policy.

To understand this process requires that public relations practices and philosophies not be dismissed as flackery. Rather, scrutiny can improve the practice of public relations and thereby help us better understand and improve our society. The voices expressed through public relations are unlikely to be stilled, but can be guided toward ever more constructive and socially responsible ends through close examination and refined standards of performance.

REFERENCES

Burke, K. (1966).*Language as a symbolic action.* Berkeley: University of California Press.

Dionisopoulos, G. N., & Crable, R. E. (1988). Definitional hegemony as a public relations strategy: The rhetoric of the nuclear power industry after Three Mile Island. *Central States Speech Journal, 39,* 134–145.

Kruckeberg, D., & Starck, K. (1988). *Public relations and community: A reconstructed theory.* New York: Praeger.

McBride, G. (1989). Ethical thought in public relations history: Seeking a relevant perspective. *Journal of Mass Media Ethics, 4,* 5–20.

Olasky, M. N. (1987). *Corporate public relations: A new historical perspective.* Hillsdale, NJ: Lawrence Erlbaum Associates.

Pavlik, J. V., & Salmon, C. T. (1984). Theoretic approaches in public relations research. *Public Relations Research and Education, 1*(2), 39–49.

Pearson, R. (1989). Business ethics as communication ethics: Public relations practice and the idea of dialogue. In C. H. Botan and V. Hazelton, Jr. (Eds.), *Public relations theory* (pp. 111–131). Hillsdale, NJ: Lawrence Erlbaum Associates.

Peterson, T. R. (1988). The meek shall inherit the mountains: Dramatistic criticism of Grand Teton National Park's interpretive program. *Central States Speech Journal, 39,* 121–133.

I

An Overview

The Case for Pluralistic Studies of Public Relations: Rhetorical, Critical, and Systems Perspectives

ELIZABETH L. TOTH
Syracuse University

Looking to strengthen the body of knowledge in public relations, "the management of communication between an organization and its publics" (J. Grunig & Hunt, 1984, p. 6), rhetorical and critical scholars of public relations are creating a body of literature that conceives of public relations as a potent force in society. Rhetorical and critical scholars have taken a global approach that considers the organization as speaker, with messages that influence social development and change. Rhetorical and critical scholars believe that the symbolic properties of communication shape our world views; as for example, Mobil Oil seeking "to portray itself as a champion of the public interest" (Smith & Heath, 1990, p. 49), or Planned Parenthood seeking to define the issue of abortion rights with its "The Decision is Yours" campaign (Bostdorff, see chapter 15).

Although the communication concept is part of the dominating systems theory of public relations, public relations scholars who use the systems paradigm have developed much more fully such concepts as the two continua of public relations practice (J. Grunig & L. Grunig, 1990), the environment, and the dominant coalition (J. Grunig & Hunt, 1984). *Communication* has been defined as "some evidence that your message has moved to and been received by target publics" (J. Grunig & Hunt, 1984, p. 192). Such a definition focuses on the transfer of information, as opposed to the more global rhetorical sense that with communication we transform our culture.

Systems scholars, such as J. Grunig (1989b), argue for a world view of public relations concerned with the solving of problems of the domain; that is, the "items that have deeper unity: phenomena to be explained, facts and observations that have been made about these phenomena and theories that have been used to explain them" (J. Grunig 1989b, p. 20). This problem-solving focus has meant that J. Grunig's studies and others (see Dozier, 1990; J. Grunig & L. Grunig, 1989; J. Grunig & L. Grunig, 1990) have presented findings that seek to explain and improve how public relations functions in organizations. J. Grunig and Hunt (1984) and J. Grunig and L. Grunig (1990) have established models that explain why public relations is practiced dif-ferently in each situation or problem presented and also have argued for the ideal practice of public relations (J. Grunig, 1989b).

This systems world view and the distinct rhetorical and critical world views of public relations practice have been extensively contrasted by Trujillo and Toth (1987). However, recently, systems and rhetorical/critical scholars of public relations have begun finding complementary contribu-tions to an understanding of public relations. This chapter describes the rhetorical/critical and systems perspectives of public relations—their defini-tions, units of analysis, and research directions. There is a discussion of how they provide complementary understandings and develop the body of knowl-edge in public relations. Finally, there are proposed new research directions to be taken up.

RHETORICAL PERSPECTIVES OF PUBLIC RELATIONS

Perhaps one way of defining *rhetoric* that connects most clearly to the field of public relations, is to use Sproule's (1988) description of the "new managerial rhetoric." Sproule drew attention in his historical perspective on rhetoric to its use, not by individuals, but by institutions such as the U.S. government in World War I, that prepared "pamphlets, leaflets, posters, and other media in collaborative fashion, causing rhetors to take on the homogenized persona of spokespersons, purveyors of a settled ideology" (p. 469).

Sproule argued that managerial rhetoric focused more greatly, but not exclusively, on the use of media to reach mass audiences, rather than attempting to persuade individuals—"the eyes of managerial communicators are ever focused on the mass audience; this may be contrasted to the tendency of the old rhetoric to move society by first focusing on the social-political elite" (p. 469). The use of mass media channels was featured as well in Crable and Vibbert's (1983) landmark rhetorical work applied to public relations activity.

Clearly, rhetoric concerns itself principally with the phenomena of com-munication. Rhetorical scholars believe that symbolic behavior creates and influences relationships between organizations and publics, through what Heath (see chapter 2) calls "the wrangle in the marketplace"—people who use words and visual symbols to "share and evaluate information, shape beliefs, and establish norms for coordinated collective action." Rhetorical scholars Cheney and Dionisopoulos (1989), argued for the centrality of communication, in that symbolism "must be considered as the substance of organization" (p. 138); and in summary:

> corporate communications must be self-conscious about its role in the organizational process (which is fundamentally rhetorical and symbolic) in responding to and in exercising power (in public discourse), and in shaping various identities (corporate and individual). (p. 140)

Crable and Faulkner's (1988) efforts, to examine the life cycle of the deadly force issue, are to study the parts of the communication process—"to isolate past and future critical events, important publics, and influential agents in any issue's development" (p. 120).

Rhetorical research in public relations, illustrating how symbolic strategies work, has concerned primarily the areas of "corporate advocacy" and "issues management." Early writings by Lerbinger (1975), Crable and Vibbert (1983), and Heath (1980) argued that corporate symbolic actions reach and influence publics (e.g., Mobil's use of the Sunday newspaper to "become part of America's afternoon; Crable & Vibbert, 1983, p. 380). Issues management studies, such as those by Crable and Vibbert (1985), Vibbert (1987), Heath and Nelson (1986), posited that issues can be created by institutional rhetors, and that through the use of symbolic strategies, communication can influence the public policy debate.

According to Crable and Vibbert (1985), issues have a life cycle of growth and decline that can be affected by symbolic strategies. Crable and Faulkner (1988), for example, detail the demise of issues if they're not refueled or given additional impetus from organizational efforts:

> simply put, issues managers deal with a world in which news becomes old news rapidly. An issue—even a nationally prominent issue—needs re-fueling to keep it at the status of currency. It needs renewed impetus from local events and organizational efforts to maintain its currency. (p. 114)

The unit of analysis most often used by scholars of "managerial" rhetoric is the "public record," of reports of such rhetoric as distributed by the mass media. Crable and Faulkner (1988) traced the growth and development of deadly force as an issue from 1978 to 1985 through an examination of newspaper articles, magazines, academic journals, and public documents. This unit of analysis may trouble those who believe that what is reported through the mass media is filtered by such gatekeepers as reporters, editors, and producers of news. However, what is said by an organization or about an organization as a matter of public record becomes part of the rhetorical debate, despite its filtered properties. Today, public relations professionals argue for clarifications to be run if stories are interpreted as "incorrect," or "unfair," because the messages of the mass media create the public record and the agenda for public discussion (Pavlik, 1987, pp. 94–100).

What are the research directions of rhetorical scholars of public relations? Although not all rhetorical studies of organizational communication have relied on mass mediated messages (see Conrad's use of annual reports in chapter 9; Geisler's use of books, 1987; Measell's use of trade journals and newsletters in chapter 11; and Dionisopoulos and Goldzwig's use of promotional materials in chapter 10), the research direction of rhetorical studies of public relations seems firmly committed to basing rhetorical analyses of organizational speech on mass media accounts. Also, rhetorical scholars have directed their research toward that of corporate speech, because corporate stances will be reported on publicly—or if publicly owned, a corporation's messages will be more likely to be part of the public record.

Rhetorical studies rely heavily on the work of Kenneth Burke (1945/1969a, 1950/1969b), who argued for the dialectic process, in which rival parties use symbolic exchange to come to agreements about cultural structures, events, and actions. Based on Burke's work, Heath (in chapter 2) stated that this dialectic process is based on such factors as a situation, a problem, one or more audiences, messages, message sources, images, channels, and the opinion environment:

> It (rhetoric) seeks to explain the dynamics among many factors: a situation that requires or allows a strategic response, a problem that arises from that situation, one or more audiences, messages, message sources, images or opinions participants in the event have of the sources, channels, and the opinion environment surrounding each statement. (see chapter 2).

Heath (see chapter 2) argues against one-way rhetoric, intended to persuade and dominate the opposition:

> Rhetoric can be thought of as a one-way flow of information, argument, and influence whereby one entity persuades and dominates another. It can be used in behalf of one interest and against others. It is sometimes used to distort and avoid truth and wise policy rather than champion them. That view may capture what happens at times, but interests do not remain imbalanced for long. (see chapter 2)

Finally, the rhetorical enterprise is to evaluate or criticize the effectiveness of organizational messages as successfully advocating organizational stances. These rhetorical messages will be evaluated on their ethical value to the public interests (Trujillo & Toth, 1987). For example, Condit and Condit (see chapter 12) used a rhetorical balance sheet to assess the symbolic strategies of the tobacco industry and anti-smoking groups. They concluded that both the tobacco industry and the anti-smoking activist groups will have differing advantages in the political arena:

> As the battle over Premier shows, the strategy of incremental erosion, although it is a long term effort, can provide a particularly well-adapted approach to meet the constraints faced by public interest groups. Further, even when such regulatory initiatives are not fully successful, the threat of regulatory initiatives may limit the rhetorical options of industries dependent on successful marketing and so constrain their expansion. (see chapter 12)

CRITICAL PERSPECTIVES OF PUBLIC RELATIONS

Critical perspectives of public relations also focus on the symbolic processes of organizational behavior. However, critical scholars of public relations approach organizations and their messages, not to improve on their efforts to advocate positions or reach audiences, but to disrupt our beliefs about organizations. Kelly (1990) used Hall's (1980) definition of *critical studies* as focusing on "significant breaks—when old lines of thought are disrupted, older constellations displaced, and elements, old and new, are regrouped around a different set of premises and themes" (p. 57). The purpose of the critical perspective is to be confrontational. That is, rather than looking at the ways communication assists the organization's management function, the critical scholar would be intent on learning such questions as those posed by Deetz and Kersten (1983): "Whose interests are served by organizational goals? What role do they play in creating and maintaining structures of power and domination?" (p. 155).

Critical studies of public relations have used written messages as the unit of analysis—such as Conrad's analysis of the annual reports of the Big Three automakers (see chapter 9). Based on these reports, Conrad argues that what is revealed in times of organizational decline and potential threats from stockholders is to turn to the use of myths, such as the American Cooperative Dream and the Redemptive Power of Technical Reason to maintain control over stockholders. Critical scholar Conrad concludes that by using such powerful myths, the managers of the Big Three automakers reassure themselves that they will stay in charge, because such myths are not likely to be disputed by those who actually own the company.

Critical scholars of public relations have used organizational values as well as written messages as the unit of analysis in examining the practice of public relations. Rakow (1989) argued that organizations most commonly value public relations that is "masculine," yet there are tendencies for public relations to swing back and forth between ideologies of "masculinity" and "femininity." Rakow called the entrance of substantial numbers of women into the field of public relations nothing "less than an gender crisis, a crisis triggered by women but also fed by a long-standing conflict over these ideologies" (p. 295). Women entering public relations will have the opportunity to favor the "symmetrical, relational, cooperative forms of public relations" (pp. 294–295). However, if organizations continue to be "macho"—that is desire such masculine values as "efficiency, rationality, individualism, and competition," (p. 291), then only their vested interests will be served.

Because critical scholars do examine organizations as arenas of power (Trujillo & Toth, 1987), one research direction becoming recognized in the body of knowledge is that concerned with the feminization of the field. Perceptions of public relations practitioners are that the increasing numbers of women will drive down the salaries and influence of the profession, that women are not "good" managers because they do not have "masculine" managerial traits (Toth & Cline, 1989). In 1988, L. Grunig posed a research agenda for women in public relations and there has been a substantial response to this call (see Creedon, 1989 and Grunig, 1988).

SYSTEMS PERSPECTIVE OF PUBLIC RELATIONS

This chapter began by depicting the systems theory of public relations as having more fully dealt with the concepts of the models of public relations, the environment, and the dominant coalition. The notion of systems, from organizational theory, is that for organizations to be effective they must concern themselves with the environment if they are to survive. The systems focus is on the means, rather than the ends, to achieving ends, such as the input, throughput, and outputs that will maintain the organization (Robbins, 1990, p. 58).

Public relations is, according to J. Grunig and Hunt (1984), a subunit of the management function of organizations, defined as the subsystem that controls and integrates the other subsystems. "They (the managers) must control conflict and negotiate between the demands of the environment and the need for the organization to survive and prosper (Grunig & Hunt, 1984, p. 9).

J. Grunig and L. Grunig (1989, 1990) have developed a substantial body of knowledge for public relations about the environment, as a concept that considers all of the elements outside the boundary of organizations. Organizations seek to maintain an equilibrium with their environment, but as Grunig and Hunt (1984) described this equilibrium, it is a "moving equilibrium" (p. 139), moving in the sense that organizations must adapt in some situations and control in others the potential consequences of the environment on organizational objectives.

J. Grunig and L. Grunig (1990) argued that the ideal model for public relations is that it be symmetrical, the management of communication for the organization based on professional two-way communication. Symmetrical public relations:

> provides a forum for dialogue, discussion, and discourse on issues for which people with different values generally come to different conclusions. As long as the dialogue is structured according to ethical rules, the outcome should be ethical—although not usually one that fits the value system of any competing party perfectly. (J. Grunig & L. Grunig, 1990, p. 177)

J. Grunig and L. Grunig (1990) admitted that the symmetrical model is the ideal way to practice public relations (although J Grunig, 1989b, has argued also that the ideal model is also most effective). Therefore, professional public relations, that which is strategically driven by the public relations function, "to manage conflict and build relationships with strategic publics that limit the autonomy of the organization" (J. Grunig & L. Grunig, 1990, p. 192) will be conducted on a continuum between asymmetrical (compliance-gaining) and symmetrical (problem-solving) tactics.

When Grunig and Hunt (1984) introduced systems theory as the paradigm to understand public relations as it is practiced in organizations, they did recognize the dominant coalition, the overall policymaking group in an organization, as a concept of the systems perspective. However, Dozier and L. Grunig (1990) and J. Grunig and L. Grunig (1990) have begun to emphasize the power control imperative, as an explanation for why organizations do not create appropriate structures or practice public relations as they should. Instead organizations create structures and make decisions based on what the dominant coalition, those most powerful people in the organization, choose to do.

Communication, according to J. Grunig and L. Grunig as recently as 1990, "is not a magical solution to conflict" (p. 38). Communication remains undefined by J. Grunig and L. Grunig in their most recent review (1990). They do, however, elaborate on three concepts studied by communication scholars: negotiation, collaboration, and mediation (p. 39). Citing Conrad (1985), *collaboration* is defined as: "All parties believing that they should actively and assertively seek a mutually acceptable solution and be willing to spend large amounts of time and energy to reach such an outcome" (p. 243).

J. Grunig and L. Grunig (1990) used Wilson and Putnam's (1990) definition of *negotiation*—"a process whereby two or more parties who hold or believe they hold incompatible goals engage in a give-and-take interaction to reach a mutually accepted solution" (p. 375). *Mediation* is defined, using Keltner's

(1987, p.8) definition, as that which "occurs when a neutral third party enters the process of negotiation" (J. Grunig & L Grunig, 1990, p. 187).

Those who use the systems paradigm to study public relations have generally used individual interviews or surveys of individuals who are asked to report on their activities and beliefs about the practice of public relations. L. Grunig (1987) asked practitioners in 48 organizations to describe the structure of the public relations unit. There are instances in which, along with such surveys, qualitative data are gathered (see Schneider, aka L. Grunig, 1985). L. Grunig (1990) conducted in-depth personal interviews with public relations managers and used a self-administered questionnaire. However, she prefaced her report of this data collection by stating that the historical-critical method contributed the bulk of the data (p. 130). She reported analyzing such internal media and mass media as company newsletters, annual reports, memoranda, organization charts, news releases, and public service announcements (p. 131).

J. Grunig's most recent writings on public relations suggest that his research direction has turned more greatly toward the presuppositions by which public relations is practiced. He maintains his focus on "solving the important problems of the domain;" however, J. Grunig and White (1990) have developed presuppositions that guide the activities of public relations, "as part of the social structure and culture that integrates the organization" (p. 15). J. Grunig (1989b) listed such symmetrical sets of assumptions as: interdependence, open system, moving equilibrium, equity, autonomy, innovation, decentralization of management, responsibility, conflict resolution, and interest group liberalism (pp. 38–39).

THE COMPLEMENTARY UNDERSTANDINGS

Given the definitions, units of analysis, and directions of research for rhetorical, critical, and systems perspectives of public relations, there appear now to be three complementary understandings that each share to some extent with one another. First, the purposes of each appear to be spread along a continuum between persuasion (or assymmetrical) and consensus (symmetrical). Although the critical theorists may be the most set on depicting the organization as bent on dominating those with lesser power, Rakow (1989) at least suggested that there is some movement or interest in competing ideologies—between competition and cooperation, to put it much too simply. More clearly, Heath (see chapter 2) argued that rhetoric concerns dialogue. Heath (see chapter 2) stated that "rhetoric can be thought of as a one-way flow of information argument and influence whereby one entity persuades and dominates another." However, he argued also that in the best sense, rhetoric is a "dynamic exchange by which interested parties seek to induce agreement and action." J. Grunig and L. Grunig (1990) also recognized the movement of public relations activity between compliance gaining and consensus; whereas again, the best public relations would be conducted to obtain consensus between the organization and its publics.

A second complementary understanding to be gleaned in the study of rhetorical and systems approaches to public relations is in the cross-over research that has been done. L. Grunig's (1990) report on power in the public relations department acknowledged the importance of comparative research, the use of the historical-critical method, in addition to the quantitative portion of the research. Kelly (1990) sought to build a theory of donor relations through the use of critical methodology. Finally, in an intriguing advance in rhetorical studies, Ice (1991) examined the role of rhetorical strategies in repairing damaged corporate relations resulting from Union Carbide's Bhopal gas leak tragedy, through the use of Grunig and Hunt's (1984) systems conceptual scheme of organizational linkages. These three studies were not confined to one or another perspective; but, took from each what advanced their understanding of their research problems.

Finally, what appears to be complementary in the rhetorical, critical, and systems approaches to public relations is the critical stance. The respective critical intentions may differ. That is, critical theorists concern themselves with power and domination; whereas systems theorists seem to use criticism to search for excellence in public relations. For example, critical scholar Gandy (see chapter 7) concludes that the practices of public relations so advantage the players that citizens/consumers can only learn more clearly how their power is being diminished. Systems scholar J. Grunig (1989a) believes that communication systems and organization may be captives of societal culture; however, they are also a "critical tool for the recreation of culture" (p. 25). He proposed a strategy for intervening in this "circle of relationships" (p. 25).

All three perspectives do seek more global positions on the causes, influences, and contributions to society of the practice of public relations. The body of knowledge in public relations cannot help but be enriched by such scrutiny.

TWO NEW DIRECTIONS

Until now, what may have kept those engaged in rhetorical, critical, and systems approaches to public relations apart is merely their lack of opportunity to interact. The evidence of such interaction is that there is a sharing of commonalities and dialogue that will strengthen our understanding of public relations. Initially, this chapter was to have been entitled "Betting on

All the Horses" because there looked to be such invigorating advances being reported that all those engaged should be encouraged and rewarded.

However, such contributions to the body of knowledge are not in competition. Nor, do I wish to suggest in this review that I favor one perspective over another. Rather, I propose two new directions that could make use of the rhetorical, critical, and systems perspectives. First, I believe that rhetorical and critical scholars must make clearer on what theoretical foundations their criticisms rest. Those who begin their work with full explanations for such theoretical work as that of Burke, Black, and Simon (see Sproule's 1988 review of their contributions), as a preface to their analyses and criticisms of specific messages assist greatly in bridging the gap between perspectives. Rhetorical and critical scholars must at least define what they mean by rhetoric and public relations; and, at best argue how their findings contribute to our theoretical understanding of the domain. Perhaps Pearce (1985) argued best, when discussing speech communication scholars, that they have not been nearly fundamental enough in critiquing their own assumptions, and not nearly radical enough in the construction of theories and models to be convincing (pp. 225–281). Those who wish to be read and understood by public relations researchers must be more fundamental and radical in their construction of rhetorical and critical theories for public relations.

Second, the most obvious contribution to be made by rhetorical and critical scholars to the research of the systems perspective is the much richer delineation of what is meant by communication. If rhetorical and critical scholars will elaborate on how organizing and communicating are "inextricably interwoven dimensions of social life" (Cheney & Dionosopoulis, 1989, p. 136), they will provide very new dimensions to one of the key concepts of the definition of public relations—the concept of communication. They have started, with the recognition that "myths," for example, carry with them societal as well as more surface meanings (in Conrad, chapter 9). It is this powerful view of the potential effects of public relations that should engage us all.

CONCLUSIONS

This chapter was intended to depict the complementary nature of three research perspectives becoming apparent in the body of knowledge in public relations. Rhetorical, critical, and systems scholars have brought much to an understanding of the nature of public relations. Rather than simply accepting one research perspective or arguing for one approach, it is because there are differing approaches with different assumptions and directions that our understanding of public relations is enriched.

Social scientist Ferguson (1984) expressed a preference for mapping out areas likely to yield information: prospecting through scree, rubble, and dirt, to find the ore-bearing rock (pp. 19–20). Others, according to Campbell, Daft, and Hulin (1982) "throw mud against a wall."

> The mud that sticks to the wall is knowledge and should be retained. That which falls off is indeed mud and should be discarded. This theory of knowledge accumulation suggests that the more individuals there are throwing different kinds of mud, the more likely it is that some of them will throw something that sticks. (pp. 19–20)

Happily, the research to understanding public relations includes such a diversity of approaches.

REFERENCES

Burke, K. (1969a). *A grammar of motives*. Berkeley: University of California Press. (Original work published 1945)

Burke, K. (1969b). *A rhetoric of motives*. Berkeley: University of California Press. (Original work published 1950)

Campbell, J.P., Daft, R.L., & Hulin, C.L. (1982). *What to study: Generating and developing research questions studying organizations*. Beverly Hills: Sage.

Cheney, G., & Dionisopoulos, G.N. (1989). Public relations? No, relations with publics: a rhetorical–organizational approach to contemporary corporate communications. In C.H. Botan & V. Hazelton (Eds.), *Public relations theory* (135–158). Hillsdale, NJ: Lawrence Erlbaum Associates.

Conrad, C. (1985). *Strategic communication: Cultures, situations, and adaptation*. New York: Holt, Rinehart & Winston.

Crable, R.E., & Faulkner, M. (1988). The issue development graph: A tool for research and analysis. *Central States Speech Journal. 39*(2), 110–120.

Crable, R.E., & Vibbert, S.L. (1983). Mobil's epideictic advocacy: 'observations' of prometheus-bound. *Communication Monographs, 50*(4), 380–394.

Crable, R.E., & Vibbert, S.L. (1985). Managing issues and influencing public policy. *Public relations review, 11*, 3–16.

Creedon, P.J. (Ed.). (1989). *Women in mass communication: Challenging gender values*. Newbury Park, CA: Sage.

Deetz, S.A., & Kersten, A. (1983). Critical models of interpretive research. In L.L. Putnam & M. Pacanowsky (Eds.), *Communication and organization: An interpretive approach* (pp.). Beverly Hills, CA: Sage.

Dozier, D.M. (1990). The innovation of research in public relations practice: Review of a program of studies. In L.A. Grunig & J.E. Grunig (Eds.), *Public relations research annual* (Vol. 2, pp. 3–28). Hillsdale, NJ: Lawrence Erlbaum Associates.

Dozier D.M., & Grunig, L.S. (1990). *The organization of the public relations function*. Manuscript submitted for publication.

Ferguson, M.A. (1984,). *Building theory in public relations: Interorganizational relationships as a public relations paradigm*. Paper presented to the Association for Education in Journalism and Mass Communication, Gainesville.

Geisler, D.M. (1987, May). *Power politics and special interests groups: The dramatism of the liturgy of abortion.* Paper presented to the International Communication Association, Honolulu.

Grunig, J.E. (1989a, November). *A symmetrical communication system: A necessary component of an excellent development organization.* Paper presented to the Association for the Advancement of Policy, Research, and Development in the Third World, San Juan, Puerto Rico.

Grunig, J.E. (1989b). Symmetrical presuppositions as a framework for public relations theory. In C. Botan & V. Hazelton (Eds.), *Public relations theory* (pp. 17–44). Hillsdale, NJ: Lawrence Erlbaum Associates.

Grunig, J.E. (1990, December). *The development of public relations research in the United States and its status in communication science.* Paper presented to the Professional Conference of the Herbert Quandt Foundation Communication Group, Salzburg, Austria.

Grunig, J.E., & Grunig, L.A. (1989). Toward a theory of public relations behavior of organizations: Review of a program of research. In J.E. Grunig & L.A. Grunig (Eds.) *Public relations research annual* (Vol. 1, pp. 27–63). Hillsdale, NJ: Lawrence Erlbaum Associates.

Grunig, J.E., & Grunig, L.A. (1990, August). *Models of public relations: A review and reconceptualization.* Paper presented to the Association for Education in Journalism and Mass Communication, Minneapolis.

Grunig, J.E., & Hunt, T. (1984). *Managing public relations.* New York: Holt, Rinehart & Winston.

Grunig, J.E., & White, J. (1990). *The effect of world views on public relations theory and practice.* Manuscript submitted for publication.

Grunig, L.A. (1987). Variation in relations with environmental publics. *Public Relations Review,* 13(3), 46–58.

Grunig, L.A. (1988). A research agenda for women in public relations. *Public Relations Review,* 14(3), 48–57.

Grunig, L.A. (1990). Power in the public relations department. In L.A. Grunig & J.E. Grunig (Eds.), *Public relations research annual* (Vol. 1, pp. 115–156). Hillsdale, NJ: Lawrence Erlbaum Associates.

Hall, S. (1980). Cultural studies: two paradigms. *Media, culture, and society, 2,* 57–72.

Heath, R.L. (1980). Corporate advocacy: An application of speech communication perspectives and skills—and more. *Communication Education, 29,* 370–377.

Heath, R.L., & Nelson, R.A. (1986). *Issues management: corporation public policymaking in an information society.* Newbury Park, CA: Sage.

Ice, R. (1991). Corporate publics and rhetorical strategies: the case of union carbide's bhopal crisis. *Management Communication Quarterly, 4*(3), 341–362.

Kelly, K.S. (1990, August). *Shifting the public relations paradigm: A theory of donor relations.* Paper presented to the Association for Education in Journalism and Mass Communication, Minneapolis.

Keltner, J.W. (1987). *Mediation: Toward a civilized system of dispute resolution.* Annandale, VA: Speech Communication Association.

Lerbinger, O. (1975). How far toward the social audit? *Public relations review, 1,* 38–52.

Pavlik, J.V. (1987). *Public relations: What research tells us.* Newbury Park, CA: Sage.

Pearce, W.B. (1985). Scientific research methods in communication studies and their implications for theory and research. In T.W. Benson (Ed.), *Speech communication in the 20th century.* Carbondale, IL: Southern Illinois University Press.

Rakow, L. (1989). From the feminization of public relations to the promise of feminism. In E.L. Toth & C.G. Cline (Eds.), *Beyond the velvet ghetto* (pp. 287–298). San Francisco, CA: IABC Foundation.

Robbins, S.P. (1990). *Organizational theory* (3rd ed.). Englewood Cliffs, NJ: Prentice-Hall.

Schneider, L.A. (1985). The role of public relations in four organizational types. *Journalism Quarterly, 62*(3), 567–576.

Smith G.L., & Heath R.L. (1990). Moral Appeal in Mobil Oil's Op-Ed Campaign. *Public Relations Review, 16*(4), 48–54.

Sproule, J.M. (1988). The new managerial rhetoric and the old criticism. *Quarterly Journal of Speech, 74*, 468–486.

Toth, E.L., & Cline, C.G. (1989). *Beyond the velvet ghetto*. San Francisco, CA: IABC Research Foundation.

Trujillo, N., & Toth, E.L. (1987). Organizational paradigms for public relations research and practice. *Management Communication Quarterly, 1*(2), 199–281.

Vibbert, S.L. (1987, May). *Corporate communication and the management of issues*. Paper presented to the International Communication Association, Montreal.

Wilson, S.R., & Putnam, L.L. (1990). Interaction goals in negotiation. In J.A. Anderson (Ed.), *Communication yearbook 13* (pp. 374–406). Newbury Park, CA: Sage.

The Wrangle in the Marketplace: A Rhetorical Perspective of Public Relations

ROBERT L. HEATH
University of Houston

Rhetoric is vital to society. Society could not exist if people did not use words and visual symbols to share and evaluate information, shape beliefs, and establish norms for coordinated collective action. Through rhetoric, people—individually and on behalf of organizations—influence opinions, understanding, judgment, and actions. Negotiation and conflict resolution involve rhetorical exchanges of opinions, facts, and resources. Policies by which people live together often require extensive debate and consideration.

Corporations, as well as other organizations, have used rhetoric to help form our society for the past century (Heath & Nelson, 1986; Raucher, 1968). Such has been the case whether this rhetoric contained lies and distortions or presented facts and arguments that enlightened audiences to important points of view. A significant part of the voice of organizations, public relations is a vital political, social, and economic force in conjunction with marketing, strategic planning, consumer and environmental activism, governmental operations, and charitable fund raising—to list but a few. Organizations, especially those of the private sector, contribute to perceptions and judgments by creating an idiom that subtly filters into thoughts about those organizations and their activities. In this way, Tedlow (1979) concluded, public relations practitioners, by the 1950s, "had helped to alter permanently the public vocabulary of business" (p. 163).

Mass society has made the individual voice less easily heard. For this reason, paid professional public relations efforts continue to increase in importance. They arise in response to the needs and desires of private,

17

public, and activist group efforts to exert self-interest. Paid for their services, public relations professionals employ a vast array of technical and social scientific methods to reach and influence their audiences.

A rhetoric paradigm for the study of public relations is made meaningful by acknowledging that it assumes the assertion of self-interest. People and the organizations for which they work use rhetoric to achieve compliance, good will, understanding, appreciation, and action. They use rhetoric to create images and to manage reputations.

In the narrow sense, the rhetoric of public relations can be employed to "put an organization's best foot forward" or "make the best of an otherwise negative situation." These typical public relations activities, along with interpretation of facts, are executed by organizations or individuals.

The discussion that is undertaken in this book acknowledges these rhetorical efforts, but suggests that the real action is broader in scope. Interest in the rhetoric and criticism of public relations focuses on symbolism and interpretation, how a society comes to think of itself, as well as how persons in that society think of themselves and their actions as well as organizations that are dominant social, political, and economic forces.

Even though they do not always create the ideas they disseminate, public relations professionals are influential rhetors. They design, place, and repeat messages in behalf of sponsors on an array of topics that shape views of government, charitable organizations, institutions of public education, products and consumerism, capitalism, labor, health, and leisure. These professionals speak, write, and use visual images to discuss topics and take stances on public policies at local, state, and federal levels.

This rhetoric occurs in many ways. Public relations specialists create identity for organizations and products as well as publicize business and special interest events. Words these practitioners write and images they create invite young men and women to join the military forces. Reputations of many organizations—whether private or public sector—are shaped by public relations. A logo may be used to differentiate one company from another, such as the use of blimps to distinguish tire companies. Company slogans such as "At Ford, quality is job one!" may attract customers and investors, as well as raise employees' pride and spur them to produce high quality work. In conjunction with advertising and marketing experts, public relations practitioners help form opinions people use in their daily product selection and buying activities.

Through rhetoric, individuals and organizations negotiate their relationships. To do so, they form opinions of one another, decide on actions, set limits, and express obligations that influence how each is to act toward the other. From the company point of view, for instance, public relations is used to establish the visibility and identity of products and services. Customers are attracted to one company instead of its competitors. Companies use public relations to build customer and community relations. They use financial support and employee good works to demonstrate their community stewardship. They argue for some public policies and against others.

Rhetoric serves individuals as well as organizations. To counterbalance the power of large organizations, such as corporations, individuals band together. Two important instances of this effort have been unionization and environmentalism. Disturbed by timber company claims that clear cutting is a wise policy, environmentalists can use rhetoric to condemn such measures and the companies that engage in them. In such instances, rhetoric is used to exert influence.

Ability to create opinions that influence how people live is the focal aspect of the rhetoric of public relations. In the process of establishing product, service, or organizational identity as well as improving relationships with people whose lives are affected by organizations' actions and policies, public relations practitioners help establish key terms—especially slogans, axioms, and metaphors—by which people think about their society and organizations. These terms shape the way people view themselves as consumers, members of a community, contributors to the arts, and myriad other ways. Opinions that are formed set standards of ethical performance to which organizations are expected to adhere, and they foster understanding of public policy issues, such as the impact manufacturing processes have on the environment.

The prominence of these organizations requires sustained examination of the symbols and rhetorical tactics they employ. Similar interests have led critics to examine rhetoric over the centuries to scrutinize the strategies and appeals used to shape society and induce action. Critics examine the rhetorical strategies that are employed, the ends pursued by those who use rhetoric, and the ideas they advocate. Critics want to know what strategies are used, whether they are used ethically, and whether the ideas advocated lead society in proper directions.

The authors who contributed to this book have a collective interest in the impact public relations has on society and the people in it. To make useful assessments of public relations demands that the rationale of the profession be scrutinized systematically. To accomplish this end involves two broad activities that are central to this book: to understand how public relations is rhetorical and to decide how that rhetoric should be critically assessed.

The concept of rhetoric itself is important to this critical process. How the influence of public relations is studied differs if critics believe that rhetoric is used only by sources to dominate receivers, if it is used to manipulate audiences, or if it is used to control thought. A vital ingredient in this critical process, as Larissa Grunig argues in chapter 4, is to lead practitioners to think seriously about the rationale for their profession. In this sense, the view of rhetoric that serves as a launching pad for the studies conducted in the book is that rhetoric is best when it is used dialogically to search for truth, examine symbols that dominate society and individual lives, and foster wise and just public policy.

ROBUST CONTEST OF IDEAS

Professional communicators have a major voice in the marketplace of ideas— the dialogue in behalf of various self-interests. What is this marketplace? Kenneth Burke (1945/1969a) called it "the Scramble, the Wrangle of the Marketplace, the flurries and flare-ups of the Human Barnyard, Give and Take, the wavering line of pressure and counterpressure, the Logomachy, the onus of ownership, the War of Nerves, the War" (p. 23).

Those metaphors aptly capture the advice given by former Mobil Oil vice president of public relations, Herbert Schmertz (1986). Believing that the press does not always accurately understand key facts or report them fairly, he engaged in a campaign to demonstrate the foibles of journalists. He challenged public relations practitioners to put media reporters on the defensive, making them justify their professional practices.

The metaphor of the wrangle is not flattering, but then, at times, neither are the voices involved in it. They may inspire audiences to high aspirations and fill them with noble thoughts. But the voices can lie and appeal to base and unwholesome opinions and motives. Witnessing this kind of behavior, Burke (1946) asked, "How can a world with rhetoric stay decent, how can a world without it exist at all?" One answer to this question is that interpretation of facts, soundness of arguments, and accuracy of conclusions can only be hammered out on the anvil of public debate. Our form of government and free enterprise prescribe that ideas be forged by debate, not imposed by tyrants—even organizational ones. Critics challenge those who use rhetoric to execute the art responsibly.

Voices compete to achieve cooperation—the collective and coordinated actions of people in society. Reflecting on this point, Burke (1941/1973) concluded that our form of government is "a device for institutionalizing the dialectic process, by setting up a political structure that gives full opportunity for the use of competition to a cooperative end" (p. 444).

Rhetoric deals with "the ways in which the symbols of appeal are stolen back and forth by rival camps" (Burke, 1937, p. 365). An example of this tactic is provided by companies that are reluctant to comply with regulatory controls to prevent pollution or install seat belts. If forced to adopt these measures, they "steal" the rhetorical stance of the advocates of automobile safety and trumpet how well the newly designed automobiles abate pollution and lessen fatal automobile accidents. If they convince the public that they have solved the pollution or auto safety problem, will the public allow regulatory restrictions to be eased? In this way, rhetoric can be viewed as a form of "courtship" whereby suitors attempt to woo key publics and make allies of critics. As Burke (1950/1969b) concluded, "There can be courtship only insofar as there is division" (p. 271).

What does the term *rhetoric* mean? As Aristotle (1954) conceived of it 2,000 years ago, rhetoric is the ability to observe in any given case the available means of persuasion—what needs to be said and how it should be said to achieve desired outcomes. It entails the ability and obligation to demonstrate to an audience facts and arguments available to bring insight into an important issue.

Aristotle's view of rhetoric focused on the individual speaker, the lone person. For this reason, rhetoric has often been associated with public speaking or oratory. But it can refer to the entire range of discourse including nonverbal and visual tactics. During the middle ages, rhetoric became associated with the art of writing. Now rhetoric occurs in all media: film, television, radio, painting, sculpture, and architecture. It is inseparable from corporate and product names, as well as nonverbal components of corporate image, including logos. The Texaco star continues to be featured in product and service advertisements—"The man who wears the star." "Mr. Goodwrench" is asserted as the symbol of excellence in automobile repairs, and "Ronald MacDonald" signifies having fun.

Throughout the ages, rhetoric has been thought of as a useful art. Society cannot function without the analysis made possible by argument and counterargument. For this reason, rhetoric has been considered vital to the education of responsible and effective citizens, at least since the age of ancient Greece when this point was voiced by Isocrates (1928) 400 years BC. As ancient Rome moved toward the apex of its influence as a law-governed republic, Quintilian (1920–1922) prescribed how citizens should be schooled in the art of rhetoric to prepare them to participate in society.

These and other champions of rhetoric had laid out the rationale for its study long before the First Amendment of the U.S. Constitution proclaimed the importance of people speaking freely. Not only does the Supreme Court support speech because people should be allowed to advocate their ideas, but the Court supports speech because it believes that people are entitled to hear different points of view.

For hundreds of years, people have studied rhetoric to learn how to speak effectively, to become an effective rhetor—a privilege and responsibility of each citizen. Is the practice of public relations part of that tradition? Are the claims of practitioners worth considering by applying methods and standards originated to judge significant public addresses?

THE PRESENCE OF PUBLIC RELATIONS

If for no other reason, the vast and deep presence of public relations in our society demands that its practices be given careful and thorough critical consideration. In place of the lone speaker or writer stating his or her case on significant issues, the 20th century spawned thousands of professional communicators who serve a vast array of sponsors in the private and public sectors. Massive public relations firms work in conjunction with mammoth advertising agencies to represent the interests of huge corporations, activist groups, and public sector agencies, such as the Department of Defense effort to recruit young men and women to military service by claiming that they will learn useful job skills while seeing the world. Universities and colleges have increasingly turned to professional communicators to help them attract the best students and generous benefactors.

Billions of dollars go into public relations efforts. This expenditure is footed by private sector businesses, public sector agencies, and activist groups; its costs are passed on to those who buy products, pay taxes, purchase newspapers, or hold memberships in activist groups. *O'Dwyer's PR Directory* lists nearly 1,700 public relations firms. S. Prakesh Sethi (1986) estimated that $2 billion are spent each year on issue advertising. Public relations is growing at a rate projected to require 1 million practitioners by the turn of the century (Kendall, 1984). Numbers of this magnitude argue loudly for sophisticated methods and high standards by which to assess the impact the profession has on our lives.

Professional communicators put words into the mouths of U.S. presidents as well as members of congress. They make White House proclamations and conduct political campaigns shaped by that new breed of politico, the "spinster" who tells the media and the public what the candidate or governmental official "actually" said, what the implications of the statement are, and how it should be reported and understood. Governors and mayors speak words prepared by public relations practitioners. Practitioners lobby legislators and regulators in regard to their sponsors' positions on public policy issues.

Through public relations, ruthless corporate leaders have been made to seem humane and kind, dripping with philanthropy and public interest (Olasky, 1987). Musicians and actors may depend on their talents to make their careers, but publicists assist in vital ways to give them competitive advantage—sometimes over people with more talent but less publicity. Activist groups, which have grown large enough to pressure major corporations and governmental agencies, employ skilled public relations assistance. In the past few years, crude publications and unsophisticated environmental issue campaigns have been replaced by carefully orchestrated events, strategically selected comments, slick publications, and targeted fund raising through sophisticated telemarketing and direct mail.

Public relations practitioners make statements that add to the culture of opinions inside organizations. Organizational culture consists of values and judgments unique to each organization. As a new member enters an organization, he or she is likely to be given materials that explain and tout the organization. Such materials may describe how old and esteemed a company is—"Solid as a rock." Or the literature may feature the organization as new, sleek, and innovative—"Taking off like a rocket." Publications feature key members of the organization, ranging from top brass to those who have worked for "25 years," as revered people who set the tone for the organization. As Deetz (1982) concluded, "An organizational culture consists of whatever a member must know or believe in order to operate in a manner understandable and acceptable to other members and the means by which this knowledge is produced and transmitted" (p. 133). Each organization needs to make sense of what it does and how that is accomplished. This sense making is done through communication, part of which is created by public relations specialists. An organization's culture is created as "people go about the business of construing their world as sensible—that is, when they communicate" (Deetz, 1982, p. 123).

Careful attention reveals that through their statements public relations practitioners help define standards by which public and private sector organizations are judged. (These points are amplified by Grunig in chapter 4, Pearson in chapter 6, and Gandy in chapter 7.) Whereas communication has helped many companies get their points across and ease public criticism, as Sethi (1977) reported, some companies that have complained loudest against environmental regulation were irresponsible and deserved regulation most.

If public relations practitioners did nothing but use stunts to call attention to products, businesses, and services, the claim that the activity is benign would be justified and this book would not be needed. But as they work with the press, public relations practitioners help create and disseminate vital information and judgment that are presented as news. Through statements made in behalf of products and services, public relations adds to the social reality that fosters buying behavior and defines lifestyles. Corporate images are massaged by public relations experts; these images and the criteria that define them become the heart of the free enterprise system. Practitioners play key roles in the design and execution of public health campaigns. Employees think of themselves and their work in part because of the publications and other organizational communication media used by practitioners to foster a productive and harmonious labor force. Public policies are contested through facts presented and values discussed by paid professional communicators. The extensiveness of its presence demands that systematic, critical attention be given to the public relations process.

A PERSPECTIVE ON RHETORIC

What is to be made of this "wrangle" of voices—both inside and outside of organizations? First, these voices should be studied as rhetoric and subjected to appropriate critical methods and standards. Such judgments require an accurate understanding of rhetoric. "Nothing but rhetoric" is an expression designed to blast vacuous comments—often those with which the critic disagrees. For some, rhetoric implies slick and hollow statements, whereas others think of it as valuable discourse people use to appeal to one another and work out differences regarding which policies are needed for an orderly and harmonious society. A rationale for rhetoric is this: Because differences of opinion and action occur, rhetoric is employed to achieve sufficient agreement that activities can be coordinated.

Rhetoric can be viewed as one-way, manipulative communication, but it can also be understood as contested examination of issues and action—as dialogue. A very subtle view of rhetoric focuses on the opinions that result from messages that create ways of thinking about activities and policies of organizations. As is true of all other kinds of human behavior, ethical examination of rhetoric can focus on means and ends.

Donald C. Bryant (1953) supplied an enduring definition of rhetoric by stressing its usefulness for giving effectiveness to truth. He concluded that because "rhetoric is the rationale of informative and suasory discourse, it operates chiefly in the areas of the contingent, its aim is the attainment of maximum probability as a basis for public decision, it is the organizing and animating principle of all subject-matters which have a relevant bearing on that decision" (p. 408). He continued, "Though it is instrumental in the discovery of ideas and information, its characteristic function is the publication, the publicizing, the humanizing, the animating of them for a realized and usually specific audience" (pp. 412–413). He claimed that rhetoric "is the *function of adjusting ideas to people and of people to ideas*" (p. 413). This view of rhetoric makes a commitment to discover truth and acknowledges the organic interaction between people and ideas. A timeless theme throughout the study of rhetoric is that it is "the use of symbols to influence thought and action" (Foss, 1989, p. 4). The domain of rhetoric is "enlightened choice" (Nichols, 1963, p. 6).

Bryant's definition of rhetoric served as a foundation for Crable and Vibbert's (1986) view of corporate discourse as "the art of adjusting organizations to environments and environments to organizations" (p. 394). This approach to public relations emphasizes the situational fluidity of fact, opinion, value, and policy. If views held by key publics change, so does the opinion environment in which corporations and other organizations operate. The response to this change can be either to conform organizational practices to fit new standards or to attempt to change or mitigate formation of opinion and value that is thought to be unwise and harmful to the interests of the organizations and their stakeholders. This paradigm features the view that through rhetoric people and organizations negotiate their relationships.

A view of rhetoric sufficient to understand public relations must acknowledge that advocates who are trying to adjust ideas to people and people to ideas fall into several categories. They are not just the organizations who are using public relations to defend and assert their self-interests. Advocates include individuals, activist groups, legislators, regulators, other businesses (inter- and intra-industry), journalists, editorialists, and the judiciary. This rich mix of voices constitutes the wrangle in the marketplace of ideas.

Rhetoric is the rationale for explaining how people and organizations strategically manage their relationships through words, interests, opinions, and action. It seeks to explain the dynamics among many factors: a *situation* that requires or allows a strategic response, a *problem* that arises from that situation, one or more *audiences*, *messages*, message *sources*, *images* or opinions participants in the event have of the sources, *channels*, and the *opinion environment* surrounding each statement. This opinion environment influences which facts and arguments are relevant. It constrains what can be said and how it can be phrased.

Attention to these factors gives insight into where to look for success or failure. A public relations campaign can fail because it makes the wrong statements to the wrong audience at the wrong time with the wrong purpose. Or the campaign can fail even if all of these factors are "right" but one. A campaign can fail because the right statements are made, but to the wrong audience. The right audience may be addressed, but with the wrong statements or by the wrong person.

Some critics of rhetoric in general, and public relations in particular, attempt to cut through this strategic quandary by saying that the only right statements are those that tell the truth. For instance, most people would agree that a company should admit the truth if it is caught knowingly discharging toxic wastes. (The public relations staff might plead for openness in such circumstances only to be vetoed by a company's legal staff, and the company should not have been discharging toxic wastes.) According to this lore, if the truth is told, it makes no difference what the audience is or when the statement is made. Without doubt, no standard other than truth can serve as a rationale for rhetoric because falsehood leads to misinformed judgments—the opposite of what is needed for people to use rhetoric to achieve useful judgments.

This viewpoint, however, can assume that "truth" never requires interpretation. Indeed, "facts" demand interpretation as to their accuracy, relevance, and meaning. Not only do people argue about facts, but they also contest the accuracy of conclusions drawn from them. For example, the timbering policy of clear cutting is a fact, but is it wise management of resources? In any situation, participants are prone to ask what the facts are and what they mean. What criteria and perspectives should be used to interpret the facts? Which interpretive perspective is best? How facts are interpreted makes the difference between good and wise choices or bad and unsound ones.

As well as contesting facts, an important function of rhetoric is to debate which interpretive frames are best to use to judge what the facts are and what they mean. Looking at this issue from the vantage point of public relations history in chapter 6, Pearson discusses how facts become meaningful only in light of the interpretative frameworks of the observers. Interpretations of fact, Trujillo argues in chapter 13, may be shaped by the motives of persons enjoined in a controversy surrounding ownership of a major league baseball franchise.

For this reason, circumstances that demand public relations do not entail merely "telling the truth." Because of the uncertainty that often abounds in situations requiring public relations, interpretations are needed to define and evaluate facts. For example, it is true—a fact—that drinking water supplied through most municipal or private water works could be more pure, but are citizens willing to pay the taxes needed to increase its purity? The air of most major cities and even many rural locations could be cleaner, but judgment prevails when we ask what the costs of clean air would be in dollars and lifestyle. Is the use of nuclear energy to generate electricity safe— safe enough? Should this fuel source be used to lessen dependence on foreign oil and reduce balance of payments deficits? What should the lifestyle be for the citizens of this nation? In this regard, why should they have high regard for certain products, services, and organizations? Existence assumes judgment. And judgment is made public through rhetoric.

Rhetoric involves positioning an organization or an issue to gain advantage without distorting the debate. Advising companies on strategies to employ in defense against activist groups, Philip Lesly (1984) demonstrated the rhetorical nature of public relations. He observed how activist groups attempt to moralize issues in such a way that companies are "bad" whereas activists are "good" because they are protecting some vital interest. If they can, Lesly believed, activists will shift the cost and responsibility for solving problems.

Exploring the implications of this strategy leads to some interesting questions. Can a product be made so safe that it cannot hurt its user, no matter how irresponsible that person is? Should corporations solve social issues that they did not create? The irony of Lesly's book is that the tactics he discussed are not only worth considering when speaking on behalf of companies but can be used for a wider range of clients. Companies also moralize issues. They shift the cost and responsibility of solving problems, sometimes to the government but also to other industries. In this way, the insurance industry has been an effective advocate for car safety measures, much to the discomfort of the automobile industry.

If the goal of organizations is to persuade others to hold their views of reality, they are faced with many challenges—all of which relate to rhetoric. The first is acknowledging honest difference of opinion. Since at least the time of Aristotle, writers have acknowledged that rhetoric is necessary because people attack one another and defend themselves with words. The true meaning of this notion is best appreciated by thinking that all statements can affect opinions and shape views of reality. Even ostensibly objective news reports contain shades of opinion which if accepted by audiences create a favorable or unfavorable view of the object or issues of discussion.

This analysis demonstrates the role rhetoric plays in establishing truth and knowledge. During a time of increasing relativism, writers such as Cherwitz and Hikins (1986) argued that rhetoric is valuable to the search for knowledge because it is by this means that people assert and challenge claims about the nature of events. In this vein, they defined *rhetoric* as *"the art of describing reality through language"* (p. 62).

This conception of rhetoric goes beyond the notion that it is a means to embellish and make truth known. This view proposes that each statement expresses a perspective. Each perspective interprets reality in a different way. Fact: An oil tanker hits a reef and spills oil into pristine waters. The interpretation based on the oil industry's perspective is that such an incident is an unfortunate but inevitable outcome of a massive effort to supply gasoline and other oil related products to a nation demanding large quantities of such products. A contrasting interpretation based on an environmentalist perspective is that the spill rapes the environment. Which interpretation is correct? Both evaluations reflect competing perspectives.

Any discussion of rhetorical and critical approaches to public relations would be remiss if it did not re-assert the premise that discourse is valuable because it allows people to assert and contest truth and knowledge. Rather than making truth effective, rhetoric can be thought of as *"a way of knowing not the way"* (Scott, 1976, p. 259). This means that through the contest of ideas people sort and judge those facts and claims that seem most veridical and vital to their collective self-interests. The problem with this view, that "reality is socially constructed" (Scott, 1976, p. 261), is the tendency to conclude that no ideas or claims based on facts are superior to others. But ideas are organic. Times change. New eras produce different sets of opinion and criteria by which the performance of organizations is measured. The temper of the times determine which interpretations are best for the people involved.

To establish this point, recall the case for pesticides. Once many pesticides, especially DDT, were thought to be blessings; now they are avoided because they have been found to be carcinogenic. Another example: Years were required to gain popular support for the claim that air pollution and other forms of pollution are harmful as well as unsightly. One more example: Standards of corporate social responsibility have slowly evolved so that, for instance, laborers are treated quite differently now than they were at the turn of the century.

Rhetoric is a means by which powerful forces in society create perspectives that they seek to have become routine patterns of thought leading to accepted standards of behavior. A critical orientation has developed to discuss the discourse of power "as it serves in the first case to maintain the privilege of the elite" and "to maintain social relations across a broad spectrum of human activities" (McKerrow, 1989, p. 91). Power and knowledge must be integrated, not at odds with one another for the benefit of society. Gandy, in chapter 7, demonstrates how rhetorical perspectives become ingrained into ideology and policy. On the other hand, in chapter 12, Condit and Condit argue that anti-smoking factions have eroded the popular appeal for smoking.

One prescription to avert undue influence of the power organizations can wield is for them to "tell the truth." Such prescriptions work to achieve understanding as long as audiences use the same interpretive frameworks. Another problem with this advice is that organizations can believe that audiences will accept the truth as it is presented. This view of rhetoric can have an "imperial" quality that assumes that some know the truth and use rhetoric to tell others who are expected to accept it.

Critiquing this view of public relations, Gaudino, Fritch, and Haynes (1989) captured its weakness by indicting the assumption that "If you knew what I know, you'd make the same decision" (p. 299). That model of discourse is heavily sender-oriented, whereas the formation of opinions among those who have a stake in organizations is receiver-oriented. Knowledge is not necessarily what people believe or can be led to believe, but a prevailing view will guide judgments until competing claims come along, displace them, and prevail in turn.

For this reason, the view of rhetoric used to understand public relations can never lose sight of the need to know and tell the truth. This challenge is relevant not only because if people do not have the truth they will make false judgments but also because others will satisfactorily contest the facts presented, claims drawn, and policies recommended. The challenge before those who intend to criticize the practice of public relations is to develop methods and standards that can sensitively accommodate this fluidity. A provocative perspective on rhetoric is that suggested by Cherwitz and Hikins (1986) who concluded that "*the process of striving for knowledge systematically is more important than the attainment of knowledge itself*" (p. 166).

Public relations practitioners often lack the technical or legal expertise to know the accuracy of conclusions they are called on to present. In this regard, they are uneasy partners in the public relations process. They are often given information regarding managerial or operating decisions or practices that they are expected to report as though it were true and just.

The problem of reporting information that they cannot personally verify does not excuse them from being responsible communicators. Their responsibility is to demand that the most accurate information be provided and the evaluations be the best available.

Their discourse requires candor and openness, without the masking or shading of what they think others will believe to be the truth. Their responsibility is to know what conclusions society is attempting to draw for a wise and insightful understanding of key issues. Information and its interpretations should be couched in terms of the overriding issue rather than shaded to the narrow self-interest of those making the claims. The rhetorical standard of public relations is to use discourse to guide key publics' judgment on issues leading to interpretations that foster fair and candid understanding as well as supporting responsible conclusions. Without such understanding organizations will soon find themselves at odds with their stakeholders. As Cheney and Vibbert (1987) concluded, organizations need to participate in the creation of the opinion environment to lessen the extent to which they find themselves at odds with it.

Addressing this issue, Olasky (1987) concluded:

> The history of corporate public relations has been dominated by the grab for the big brass ring. Instead of trying to communicate information that folks outside companies need to know, many public relations workers have seen their role as one of furthering corporate activities in nonbusiness areas. (p. 148)

Why is this so? He answered that public relations people attempt to do their job in the "public interest." Olasky focused on the crisis facing those who have the power and responsibility of speaking on policy issues. Thus, he indicted public relations practice: "If companies live by opinion polling during this age of philosophical confusion, then public relations becomes merely the tail of a potentially rabid dog. If companies bow to politicians or media stars, the door is open for demagoguery and the arrogance of self-professed messiahs" (p. 148).

Although this jab is directed at public relations superstars, such as Edward L. Bernays and Ivy J. Lee, it also reasons that a profession cannot be vital if it only aspires to tell audiences what they want to know or what they will accept. Corporations enjoy the status of an individual and are protected as such by law. In consequence of this privilege, they are duty bound to shoulder the stewardship expected of other individuals.

PUBLIC RELATIONS AND THE CREATION OF PERSPECTIVES

A theme that runs throughout the practice and criticism of public relations is its ability to influence what people think and how they act. Even when practitioners' efforts fail to establish their point of view or to foster the interests of their sponsors and influence stakeholders, their comments become part of the fabric of thought and over time add to societal beliefs and actions. Practitioners create opinions, reinforce them, or draw on them to advocate new opinions and actions.

As Cheney and Dionisopoulos (1989) concluded, "corporate discourse seeks to establish public frames of reference for interpreting information concerning issues deemed important by Corporate America" (p. 144). This observation extends beyond corporations to environmental groups, consumer activists, unions, nonprofit community service organizations, and governmental agencies. Through the organizations they form, people create and respond to meanings of words that dominate their symbolic environment.

Public relations has been instrumental in establishing the unique ideology of this country. Each practitioner labors on behalf of some specific interest, but collectively these statements add to and improve or weaken the standards by which activities—corporate, nonprofit, and governmental—are evaluated. Chapters that follow, for instance, examine public relations efforts such as those in behalf of the tobacco industry, oil company environmentalism, trade associationism, nuclear generation of electricity, professional baseball, and planned parenthood. Such discussions are interesting not only because of what they say about messages and opinions unique to each case, but also because each case is part of encompassing points of view. To critique the rhetoric of public relations, we need to balance our attention between individual cases and ideologies that practitioners help to establish and from which they draw as they differentiate between organizations and products, advocate or contest public policies, and speak to the interests of stakeholders.

Some examples will demonstrate how these opinions become part of the rhetoric of public relations. In a 1989 corporate image/product identity ad, United Technologies employed a theme that runs through all of its internal and external communication as it touted its Carrier window air conditioners. Using graphics to claim that they are so quiet a musician can practice while sitting beside one, the caption read, "Cool should whisper. We don't think you should hear it. It's just meant to be *felt.*" At first glance this ad seems to be designed to enhance one product's reputation and to differentiate it from its competitors. Of special note, the ad builds product and corporate identity by reinforcing and drawing veracity from a cultural truism that better living can be achieved through technology. This powerful belief underpins the commitment to technological innovation, but it also suffers criticism by persons who argue that technology does not always produce a better lifestyle. Technology has brought harmful side effects such as pollution, toxic waste, and cancer producing substances.

In addition to comments on products and company image, public relations takes stances on broad issues. For instance, as a part of its advocacy campaign, a 1989 op-ed sponsored by Mobil Oil Corporation read, "The powerful U. S. economy continues to amaze." This strong economy increased median family income by 11.8% between 1982 and 1987. What has produced this robust economy? Mobil's answer: Lower taxes, deregulation, a government climate promoting growth, investment, technology, and workers "who keep the American dream very much alive, and in fact, translate it into reality." Mobil wants to keep conditions right for corporate growth and economic expansion. In this way, corporate voices champion governmental policies that favor their economic interests. However, such discussions can be faulted for their narrow view of conditions in society. In contrast to applause for a robust economy is the growing number of homeless people. All is not rosy, even though Mobil seeks to increase support for economic measures that allegedly lead to prosperity.

Events occur that demand organizational response. Out of such events come a new, or renewed, sense of public stewardship. For example, on April 3, 1989, the chairman of Exxon Corporation apologized in an open letter for the accident of its tanker, the Exxon Valdez, which spilled crude oil off the coast of Alaska. He pledged, "We will meet our obligations to all those who have suffered damage from the spill." He expressed sympathy "to the residents of Valdez and the people of the State of Alaska. We cannot, of course, undo what has been done. But I can assure you that since March 24, the accident has been receiving our full attention and will continue to do so."

While Exxon's chairman hoped to mitigate environmentalist and public backlash, he also sought to soften criticism of oil industry operations in Alaska—particularly at a time when the industry was deeply involved in the controversy of seeking to open the Arctic National Wildlife Refuge (ANWR) to oil exploration.

The statement echoed the prevailing belief that people and corporations should be responsible to the people, animals, and countryside affected by their actions. This is a noble theme, but merely saying it did not convince many publics that Exxon was environmentally responsible. The difficulty Exxon had with its oil spill became a cliché for failed public relations. The stance assumed by Exxon was, in the view of many, not very different from that of generations of strip miners, sweat shop operators, and industrial giants indifferent to any value other than profit. Exxon tried to diffuse a crisis by making a public commitment to values and actions expected of a steward of the public trust.

Corporations are not the only entity to use public relations in time of crisis. Environmentalists seized the Exxon oil spill as an opportunity to promote stronger environmental protection policies. By exploiting this disaster, environmental groups worked to increase their membership power base as well as their financial resources through fund raising and to galvanize legislators and regulators against those who harm the environment. Using the occasion of the Exxon tanker spill, environmental groups championed new standards for the transportation of crude oil and clean up procedures. Coincidental to this disaster, the Natural Resources Defense Council featured the issue of exploring for oil in ANWR in a direct mail appeal for membership and financial support of its environmental efforts in Alaska, specifically to keep ANWR free from oil exploration.

Public relations campaigns address themes that are fundamental to the mentality of society. One of these, the public information campaign by the U. S. Council for Energy Awareness, draws on several established opinions—energy independence, environmentalism, and advances through technology—to advocate a highly contested opinion. The Council has battled for many years to create an informed and favorable opinion environment for the construction and operation of nuclear generating plants. The Council's theme is reflected in one of its ads: "The 110 nuclear electric plants in the U. S. have cut our foreign oil dependence by over three billion barrels since the first Arab oil embargo. And they have cut foreign oil payments by over 100 billion dollars." Shortly after the Chernobyl nuclear generating plant accident occurred in the U.S.S.R., the Council described the differences between that plant and ones built in the United States. The ad showed that U. S. plants are safer because their containment domes would hold radiation in the event of an accident.

Car companies associate their products with widely held opinions, thereby drawing on and reinforcing those opinions as well as creating favorable product identity and customers' willingness to buy. In this vein, Chrysler Motors proclaimed "The Car Buyer's Bill of Rights." This "Bill" asserted the buyer's right to a quality car, long-term buyer protection, friendly treatment, honest service, competent repairs, safety, ability to address grievances, and satisfaction.

Safety is an important issue. This value has underpinned ads by General Motors that combined corporate image and public service by offering advice on how to stop drunk driving—because 25,000 people die each year in alcohol-related accidents. If ads such as this lessen traffic accidents, they can mitigate efforts to strengthen automobile safety regulations. However, at a time when safety is a major issue, General Motors did not call on its industry to manufacture "drunk-proof" automobiles. How "safe" is a safe automobile? How "glittering" is a glittering generality?

These samples highlight the variety of topics that public relations practitioners discuss and how they reinforce, create, and draw on beliefs to advance some interest. Each statement is sponsored by an organization with a vested interest; each organization is seeking to influence its stakeholders.

A PERSPECTIVE ON CRITICISM

If irresponsible and empty communication becomes the norm, audiences become sceptical. They come to doubt the value of using words to solve problems and to create a reasonable and sound society. Slick and facile discourse cannot displace insightful, well-informed statements without harming a society that assumes that thoughts and policies should be shaped through informed discussion. Part of the correction against such occurrences is the response by other advocates in the marketplace of ideas. Another means for correcting such problems is to engage in critical judgment of rhetoric.

Critical judgment is needed to improve skills and to insure that a profession is responsible and sound. Public relations is no exception. It is strengthened if critical standards and methods are used to probe its depths. Such analysis requires judgments regarding what is said as well as how and when statements are made. Criticism assumes that it is essential to have something important to say and to say it to foster harmony and trust.

"Every living thing is a critic," so said Kenneth Burke (1935/1965, p. 5). If such is the case, criticism is an activity in which people make choices and express preferences. Some things they like, and others they do not. For instance, movie critics help us be discriminating viewers and pressure filmmakers to strive for excellence. We can be forewarned by a critic that a movie is not suspenseful or funny, but we all know that our judgment of the event may differ from that of the critic. We may like it more or less than the critic does. When that occurs is the critic incompetent? Perhaps. Does it mean that criticism is of no value? Hardly. Differences of judgment abound, but without critical standards, all would be the same.

The key to making good judgments is knowing what insights criticism can offer. This view is helpful for understanding how rhetorical criticism can serve to improve the practice of public relations. As the substance, forms, and tactics of its communication are better explained, the rationale and practice of public relations should become clearer and improved.

Critics shoulder the responsibility of being involved in society; their observations should not be trivial. The critic is "the interpreter, the teacher, the social actor." A critic can be "a moral participant, cognizant of the power and responsibility that accompanies full critical participation in his/her society" (Klumpp & Hollihan, 1989, p. 94).

Criticism is an art that requires critics to be rhetors who must present arguments to support their judgments (Brockriede, 1974). Each critic is responsible for selecting and applying criteria to make judgments and to produce evidence to justify evaluations of the object of criticism. Critics must explain and justify assumptions supporting their criticism.

In this vein, Brockriede (1974) challenged critics to improve their methods of criticism. Standards and methodologies are not equal; some are better than others. Criticism should not merely reflect individual taste whereby one person's judgment is as good as another's. The point of developing critical standards is to strive for critical insights that are so well developed and useful that they become widely adopted. Once they reach that point, they are likely to be incorporated into the practice of rhetorical communication, including public relations.

Criticism requires standards and techniques by which insight can be gained into the object of criticism. Toward this end, three activities are central: description, classification, and explanation (Brockriede, 1974). Description and classification tell us the nature of each rhetorical act, but do not give detailed insight or evaluate its quality. Explanation "can involve the use of knowledge about a concrete rhetorical experience as a way of learning something about concepts of rhetoric" (p. 171).

Critics must *define and describe* the act or object being criticized. Different forms and media of communication require different critical standards. For instance, public relations activities in behalf of product publicity may differ from those required to foster a positive corporate image. Either of these may be different in harmonious times when public scrutiny does not doubt the quality of the product or good will of a corporation. Reasoning that conditions surrounding each crisis are crucial to how well a company executes crisis communication, Berg and Robb (chapter 5) examine crises to determine the requirements of this form of public relations. Analyzing statements made about a company in its annual reports might require different assumptions than would the criticism of its corporate image advertising. Annual reports are not designed for general readership, but for a select audience comprised of financial analysts, stockbrokers, and investors. Content of annual reports is regulated by the Securities Exchange Commission which governs what must and can be said and how it can be said. Conrad, in chapter 9, explains why companies take credit in their annual reports for good news and blame external forces for adverse financial reports.

Critics must *erect and apply* standards to judge each rhetorical act. Standards must be sensitive to the uniqueness of each rhetorical act set in the context of the rhetorical problem it is designed to solve.

REFERENCES

Aristotle. (1954). *Rhetoric* (W. R. Roberts. Trans.). New York: Modern Library.

Brockriede, W. E. (1974). Rhetorical criticism as argument. *Quarterly Journal of Speech, 60,* 165–174.

Bryant, D. C. (1953). Rhetoric: Its function and its scope. *Quarterly Journal of Speech, 39,* 401–424.

Burke, K. (1937). Synthetic freedom. *New Republic, 89,* 365.

Burke, K. (1946, October 22). Letter to Malcolm Cowley, Burke File, Pennsylvania State University.

Burke, K. (1965). *Permanence and change.* Indianapolis: Bobbs-Merril. (Original work published 1935)

Burke, K. (1969a). *A grammar of motives.* Berkeley: University of California Press. (Original work published 1945)

Burke, K. (1969b). *A rhetoric of motives.* Berkeley: University of California Press. (Original work published 1950)

Burke, K. (1973). *The philosophy of literary form* (3rd ed.). Berkeley: University of California Press. (Original work published 1941)

Cheney, G., & Dionisopoulos, G. N. (1989). Public relations? No, relations with publics: A rhetorical-organizational approach to contemporary corporate communications. In C. H. Botan & V. Hazelton, Jr. (Eds.), *Public relations theory* (pp. 135–157). Hillsdale, NJ: Lawrence Erlbaum Associates.

Cheney, G., & Vibbert, S. L. (1987). Corporate discourse: Public relations and issue management. In F. M. Jablin, L. L. Putnam, K. H. Roberts, & L. W. Porter (Eds.), *Handbook of organizational communication: An interdisciplinary perspective* (pp. 165–194). Newbury Park, CA: Sage.

Cherwitz, R. A., & Hikins, J. W. (1986). *Communication and knowledge: An investigation in rhetorical epistemology.* Columbia, SC: University of South Carolina Press.

Crable, R. E., & Vibbert, S. L. (1986). *Public relations as communication management.* Edina, MN: Bellweather Press.

Deetz, S. A. (1982). Critical interpretive research in organizational communication. *Western Journal of Speech Communication, 46,* 131–149.

Foss, S. K. (1989). *Rhetorical Criticism: Exploration & Practice.* Prospect Heights, IL: Waveland Press.

Gaudino, J. L., Fritch, J., & Haynes, B. (1989). "If you knew what I knew, you'd make the same decision": A common misperception underlying public relations campaigns? In C. H. Botan & V. Hazelton, Jr. (Eds.), *Public relations theory* (pp. 299–308). Hillsdale, NJ: Lawrence Erlbaum Associates.

Heath, R. L., & Nelson, R. A. (1986). *Issues management: Corporate public policymaking in an information society.* Newbury Park, CA: Sage.

Isocrates. (1928). *Isocrates* (G. Norlin, Trans., Vols 1–2; L. R. Van Hooks, Trans., Vol 3). Cambridge: Harvard University Press.

Kendall, R. (1984). Public relations employment: Huge growth projected. *Public Relations Review, 10*(3), 13–26.

Klumpp, J. F., & Hollihan, T. A. (1989). Rhetorical criticism as moral action. *Quarterly Journal of Speech, 75,* 84–97.

Lesly, P. (1984). *Overcoming opposition: A survival manual.* Englewood Cliffs, NJ: Prentice-Hall.

McKerrow, R. E. (1989). Critical rhetoric: Theory and praxis. *Communication Monographs, 56,* 91–111.

Nichols, M. H. (1963). *Rhetoric and criticism.* Baton Rouge: Louisiana State University Press.

Olasky, M. N. (1987). *Corporate public relations: A new historical perspective.* Hillsdale, NJ: Lawrence Erlbaum Associates.

Quintilian. (1920–1922). *The institutio oratorio* (H. E. Butler, Trans., Vols 1–4). Cambridge: Harvard University Press.

Raucher, A. R. (1968). *Public relations and business: 1900–1929.* Baltimore, MD: Johns Hopkins University Press.

Schmertz, H. (1986). *Good-bye to the low profile: The art of creative confrontation.* Boston: Little, Brown.

Scott, R. L. (1976). On viewing rhetoric as epistemic: Ten years later. *Central States Speech Journal, 27,* 258–266.

Sethi, S. P. (1977). *Advocacy advertising and large corporations: Social conflict, big business image, the news media, and public policy.* Lexington, MA: D. C. Heath.

Sethi, S. P. (1986, August 10). Beyond the Fairness Doctrine: A new war on corporate "propaganda." *New York Times,* p. F3.

Tedlow, R. S. (1979). *Keeping the corporate image: Public relations and business: 1900–1950.* Greenwich, CT: JAI Press.

Critical Perspectives on Public Relations

ROBERT L. HEATH
University of Houston

Criticism, Nichols (1965) argued, "involves a judicial act of determining what is better or worse" (p. 4). The critic's "aims are to evaluate rhetorical effort or to account for effectiveness or ineffectiveness in rhetorical situations" (p. 22). Especially in public relations, effect is a vital dimension to consider, but it is difficult to determine even when a well-executed public relations campaign involves measurable outcomes. Not limited to effect, criticism involves judicious examination of how rhetorical acts are performed and contribute to the opinions that support society. An important critical objective is to observe the perspectives embedded in what is said, a search for the interpreting functions of language (McKerrow, 1989).

Criticism must be sensitive to rhetorical problems that lead to each instance of rhetoric. Each type of rhetorical response should be treated uniquely as is done in the case studies in this book. The objective is to employ critical approaches that isolate and examine different critical problems. For instance, when public relations personnel handle a crisis, they use different techniques than if they are generating publicity, fostering a positive corporate image, or seeking to differentiate between competing products or services. The rhetorical problem of correcting misperceptions created by misreported information is different than encouraging an audience to prefer one set of values in place of another to support or oppose a public policy stance.

A creative process, criticism entails (a) laying out assumptions that will be used to make judgments, (b) justifying those assumptions, (c) applying them to the object of criticism, and (d) drawing conclusions. The ends of this effort, Andrews (1983) believed are "illumination and evaluation" (p. 4). Criticism can give insight into the object of criticism, as well as allow enlightened judgments regarding the rhetorical technique employed and the social worth of the ideas presented.

The critic engages the rhetorical act at key points, especially those where meanings become important to the quality of relationships and to the wisdom of policies and actions. The critic looks for artifacts that can be isolated for analysis. Artifacts include what is said or presented visually. They may be what is done; actions of the organization affect public relations.

Several options are available to critics. First, if standards have been developed specific to the genre of an object of criticism, they can be employed to compare it to others of its type. Second, criticism implies that the object of criticism be scrutinized according to something other than itself. This could involve comparisons against other objects of its genre, or it might involve tests such as factuality, candor, veracity, wisdom, or expedience. Third, a critic can give insight into the object of criticism by illuminating and scrutinizing the tactics employed; once the object is illuminated, persons who read the criticism employ their own perspectives to evaluate the object being criticized. Insight can be achieved by examining the relationship between a source and its statements, between statements and targeted audiences' opinions and interests, or by looking at one artifact or an entire campaign.

Rhetoric is the art of skillful adaptation of arguments, facts, appeals, and interpretations to unique circumstances of each rhetorical situation. For this reason, criticism draws on an understanding of rhetoric to form critical methods and assumptions to yield insight into strategic choices and skilled execution of each rhetorical act. The critic selects or creates an approach to illuminate and assess the object of criticism.

Critics have not fulfilled their responsibility until they have gone beyond describing or chronicling a set of rhetorical efforts; the full value of criticism results when a critic provides useful insights and judgments about the discourse, the source that supplied it, or the audience for which it was intended. The focal point of criticism is consideration of the value of what is said and done in light of needs and interests of the people involved in the rhetorical situation. Critics focus on the rhetor's selection of supporting material and the worth of the statement in light of the needs of the persons in the situation.

This focus is even more important now that our age has a renewed awareness of lying—the modern term is *disinformation*. Message—what is said—deserves special scrutiny. Coupled to efforts to determine the veracity of what is said is the need to determine whether the statements lead to wise judgments. Criticism addresses a key issue: Does the statement contribute insights, understanding, and judgment that support individual and collective self-interest? Will acceptance of a rhetor's statements lead to wise decisions for the persons involved in the rhetorical situation? As McKerrow (1989) concluded, "To consider ideology in terms of truth and falsity is to focus attention on its character and to typify it as a product rather than a process" (p. 100).

Because the value of what is said is crucial to criticism, the critic may fault or argue against the statements being analyzed. Or, the critic may praise the efforts of a rhetor, a public relations practitioner. Criticism entails not only examination of tactics associated with influence but also standards and judgments regarding the worth of statements in their service to society at large not merely the interest of the sponsor of those statements.

THE PERSONA OF ORGANIZATIONS

While communicating, a rhetor presents its "voice" or "personality," an image or *persona* (Campbell, 1982). What is said and how it is said through public relations conveys an organization's persona. Organizations also convey their persona through their operations. These points are central to the chapters that follow. For instance, Grunig, in chapter 3, challenges public relations to take on the persona of "meliorism," to make society better. Gandy, in chapter 7, argues that public relations gives voice to a power elite in ways that make its views the accepted perspective of society. Cheney, in chapter 8, points out that companies have come to be only so much image that society suffers the loss of responsible persons who are willing to be accountable for their actions; in this sense, corporations' personae are nothing more than image. Conrad, in chapter 9, compares annual reports in good and bad times to conclude that companies attempt to convey an illusion of efficacy. Trujillo, in chapter 13, compares the persona the media presented of suitors who competed in the drama to purchase the Texas Rangers baseball team. The collective "we" is important to marketing efforts of Chevron, concludes Porter in chapter 14.

Persona is a useful concept to focus on the source of messages as a starting point for criticism. This focal point is especially important in the critical analysis of public relations that is called on to put forward the best foot possible for organizations it represents. It is an image-building activity. Even in the midst of bad times, the objective is to present the organization in the best way possible.

Whether an audience accepts a persona has a lot to do with the rhetorical skills of the organization, interpretations that compete with the persona, and the willingness of each stakeholder to accept the organization's persona.

Carefully crafted and wisely developed, a persona can enhance an organization's communication efforts. Poorly handled, persona is a liability.

Personae of organizations can be captured in commonplace phrases that describe business practices (Heath, 1988). "Not-our-problem" companies, for example, blame their woes on others and discredit customers' concerns. Some organizations have a "fly-by-night" or "check-is-in-the-mail" persona. Some businesses present themselves as "can't make an omelet without breaking an egg." Others offer the persona "trust us, we have your best interest in mind." Companies like to associate themselves with the persona of goodness: "You're in good hands with Allstate" or "Mr. Goodwrench."

Personae can be quite different. A bank might present itself as a community pillar by providing loans that drive the economy of its city or as a friendly banker lending to its neighbors who want to build cottages with white picket fences. Trying to lessen the stigma of being an oil company, Phillips Petroleum stressed its other product lines such as those used in medical care or for solving communities' needs for durable and inexpensive paving materials. Environmental organizations present a "save the planet" persona. Government agencies often have a persona that corresponds to their mission. For example, Surgeon General Koop presented a persona of a medical expert who was aggressively responsive to the health needs of the nation.

Few companies, if any, have tried harder than Mobil Oil Corporation to establish a persona of enlightened assertiveness. As the result of its public relations efforts, some people might see Mobil as a "teacher" attempting to educate the U. S. public through its "Observations" ads. Others might see Mobil as a champion of truth and fairness for battling journalists who, at least according to Mobil's op-eds, are not as responsible as they should be and, therefore, should not enjoy public trust. Examining Mobil's use of fairness and democratic capitalism to establish its persona, Simons (1983) cautioned that it is a "bowerbird" luring an innocent public into its bower with appeals.

Examining a different persona, Crable and Vibbert (1983) compared Mobil to Prometheus. As a modern Prometheus, reasoned Crable and Vibbert, Mobil communicates in defense of itself and its industry. Part of Mobil's campaign was a series of "Observations," which were placed in Sunday supplements of major newspapers. These "Observations" supplied information on technical aspects of the oil industry, unfair treatment of the oil industry by journalists, and unwise regulatory decisions of government. Crable and Vibbert treated these "Observations" as discourse designed to establish premises or warrants that could subsequently be used as the basis of arguments in public relations campaigns. Such premises are typical of the axioms in "Fourth of July" speeches that people accept without reservation. In its endeavor, Crable and Vibbert believed, Mobil adopted the persona of

Prometheus, the Greek god who symbolizes rebellion against a superior controlling power. Prometheus gave fire to humans against the order of Zeus. As Prometheus opposed Zeus, so Mobil challenges those who would unwisely control it.

An interesting change in persona has been that by IBM which for years featured its high-tech competence and precision. That persona apparently was part of IBM's success in dominating the market for huge computers used by major companies and universities. But that persona was inappropriate when selling personal computers to novices who fear them. In place of product representatives in corporate blue suits, IBM hired the cast from "M*A*S*H," put them in casual clothing, and had them portray the friendly aspects of personal computers.

Another interesting example of persona is apparent in the problems Exxon faced with its cleanup of Prince William Sound following the Exxon Valdez oil spill. Many entities—such as the governor of Alaska, Coast Guard, various federal agencies, environmentalists, and the media—vied to assert the persona of an authority regarding the cleanup effort. Exxon was portrayed as a villain, even though it alleged that governmental agencies prevented it from using its superior cleanup technology. Even the location where the tanker ran aground became a factor in defining Exxon's persona. Had the tanker broken up on some barren coastline of an Arab country, the outcry would have been minimal. The situation was ripe for the attention of critics who associated the spill with drilling activities in the Arctic National Wildlife Refuge (ANWR) region of Alaska. The truth is that drilling and transportation have nothing to do with one another. No massive outcry called for the U. S. public to conserve by driving less and using fewer products made from petrochemicals. Exxon became synonymous with oil stained seals, birds, and sea otters. When it did good deeds, such as paying to fly sea otters to a reserve in California, it was not given credit by the media. Because of the way it managed the cleanup, its persona became that of a blundering giant whose thrashing around damaged the environment. The persona Exxon tried to establish was that of an environmentally sensitive company that was betrayed by a key employee who had received treatment and been encouraged by the company to recover from a drinking problem.

An industry can have a persona. In the minds of many people, the persona of the oil industry is ruthless, bottom-line self-interest. Thus, it was not surprising that an outcry occurred when gasoline prices went up coincidental to the Valdez oil spill. In the minds of many of the public and journalists, this correlation became causation. Whether a bowerbird or not, Mobil Oil Corporation spoke for its sisters in the oil industry to explain that the price rise reflected the dramatic worldwide increase in crude oil costs and had nothing to do with opportunism or the oil spill. In an op-ed piece of April 27, 1989, Mobil cited the testimony John H. Lichtblau of the Petroleum

Industry Research Foundation made to a U. S. Senate subcommittee. The point: "Crude oil prices were rising even before the Valdez spill, but retail prices didn't follow immediately. Gasoline prices eventually do reflect the price of crude, but there's almost always a time lag." This is an important perspective on a topic of general interest; it may, for some, correct the widely held persona of the oil industry. For others, the ruthless and dishonest persona will only be reinforced by statements such as this that smack of oil industry self-interest.

One inescapable issue in regard to public relations is that its sponsor always has a vested interest in the outcome. If apparent self-interest leads a source's credibility to be questioned, then that self-interest may be lessened if the persona speaks to the honest, candid, and idealized self-interest of the audience. Thus, how the organization presents itself and asks its audience to think about itself can be crucial to the impact of a public relations campaign.

How the audience thinks of itself, at least insofar as the source of the rhetorical message attempts to get the audience to think of itself, is called the *second persona*, the "implied auditor" (Black, 1970, p. 111). If the audience thinks of itself in a particular way, the arguments presented are likely to be more persuasive because they are "adapted" to the audience. The equation goes like this. One person might say to another, "Because you are such a nice person, I'm going to give you a bargain." If the second person thinks of him or herself as a nice person who deserves a bargain, he or she has accepted the second persona the rhetor intended—and may "fall for" a "sales pitch." (This kind of strategy occurs in commonplace activities. A parent might say, "Big children don't cry," or "Good kids get treats." Each of these statements is designed to get the child to accept a particular second persona.)

Each statement made contains some sense of what the source wants the audience to think of itself. If the audience adopts that second persona, it becomes prone to accept the statements being made to it. Mobil presented its criticism of irresponsible journalists, those who hide behind First Amendment privileges instead of telling the truth, by saying to the audience, "Imagine what you would feel if you had been treated unfairly." The product publicity tactic of IBM had this kind of second persona: "Think of yourself as a nice, warm, and friendly person who wants but fears a personal computer; you like nice, warm, and friendly people; you will like us because we are nice, warm, and friendly and sell personal computers." If the rhetor successfully gets the audience to accept the second persona, the audience will think of itself is a particular way—one that fosters the ends of the public relations effort.

Several of the chapters that follow give attention to how sources want their audiences to think of themselves as they receive and think about the messages. Dionisopoulos and Goldzwig (chapter 10) demonstrate the errors made by pro-nuclear generation advocates who wanted women to think of themselves as having to choose between labor-saving appliances or adopting a favorable attitude toward nuclear energy. Porter (chapter 14) provides evidence that Chevron employs pro-environment statements to attract customers who desire to buy products from environmentally responsible companies. Bostdorff (chapter 15) argues that good character is a primary rhetorical dimension in the planned parenthood campaign.

Public relations is short for public relationships. Criticism of public relations can focus on this relationship. It is subject to what the source does and says. Is the persona accurate and appropriate to the particular rhetorical problem? What second persona is implied in what the public relations campaign says? Is the second persona constructive to resolving the issues that emerge from the rhetorical problem? Questions such as these focus critical judgments related to images of the source and audience in a public relationship.

RHETORICAL PROBLEM: THE NEED TO RESPOND

Each rhetorical statement comes in response to a rhetorical problem that arises from differences of opinion brought about by individuals, media reporters, governmental agencies, activists, or other companies (inter- or intra-industry). A rhetorical problem results from an actual or contrived situation in which an organization experiences the need to communicate with key audiences to erase doubt or to reconcile differences of understanding or judgment. Public relations responses to such problems range from "no comment" to a series of statements designed to explain and justify actions taken and positions held. One objective *"is to take an issue through its life cycle so that it is resolved in directions favorable to an organization"* (Crable & Vibbert, 1985, pp. 11–12).

Rhetoric deals with differences of opinions and divisions between groups created by conflicting interests. Viewed this way, issues are contestable points of difference that are important because they affect the interests of the parties involved. Regardless of the philosophy of rhetoric an organization employs, it is continually confronted with rhetorical problems that demand comment. Issues occur when situations force choices of judgment or behavior. Each situation provides motives for a particular response because, as Burke (1945/1969a) concluded, "there is implicit in the quality of a scene the quality of the action that is to take place within it" (pp. 6–7). A rhetorical response may be required by circumstances such as a disaster, a crisis, introduction of a new product or service, unfavorable public opinion, or lack of differentiation in regard to the image of an organization or its products or services.

Opinions differ among public relations practitioners about whether it is best to comment on tough issues or to remain silent. Some companies, for instance, prefer the low profile whereby they say as little as possible on the assumption that comments keep an issue alive. Others believe that openness, candor, and continued communication solve rhetorical problems. Some think that it is best to intervene on issues before they become well defined and are deeply believed. But others doubt that early intervention is feasible because of the array of issues, most of which never mature, and because it is unethical to blunt issues that deserve to receive public discussion.

What one entity does and says can create a rhetoric problem for other entities. Again, the Alaskan oil spill serves as an example. For days after the spill occurred, Alaskan officials, environmentalists, and reporters played up the damage the spill caused to Alaska's pristine environment. This rhetoric was designed to pressure Exxon and to foster the self-interests of those making the statements. Did this claim of disaster have so much impact that tourists—a major part of the Alaskan economy—were discouraged from vacationing there? Media attention to the spill slowed tourism, creating a rhetorical problem for the Alaskan tourist bureau and chamber of commerce. To counter this problem, television ads featured scenic beauty of Alaska, its vast territory, and limitless recreation possibilities. Tagged on these ads was the disclaimer that the oil spill had damaged only a fraction of the state. What some rhetors played up, others played down. In doing so, each attempted to handle the rhetorical problem it was responsible for solving.

Insurance companies have been confronted by the problem of rising premiums. At what point will the public aggressively try to restrain insurance rates? One answer to this rhetorical problem, according to an ad sponsored by State Farm Insurance, is to stop the rising cost of repair. Thirty-three million accidents occur each year. The cost of repairing damaged vehicles has increased 93% over the past 10 years, whereas cost of replacement parts soared 126% in that period. The solution? State Farm works "face to face with automakers to help them design stronger, safer, easier-to-repair cars." And State Farm trains body shop people on the latest repair techniques. To the problem, State Farm answers that it is doing all it can to keep policies affordable.

Rhetorical problems can arise from the kinds of identifications people and organizations have with one another. Statements that polarize interests increase differences, whereas identification appeals are capable of lessening divisions and increasing a sense of community. Organizations may use mild divisions to show how they are different from one another—how their products or services are worth noting and how their image sets them apart from others in their industry. They also like to increase identification by showing how other people and organizations hold the beliefs they do. Such division and merger is a universal human trait, and for that reason, Burke (1950/1969b) concluded, identification is the essence of rhetorical appeal.

Identification is a rhetorical means by which people realize that they share opinions on matters of self-interest. Identification occurs when people agree on some value, action, or policy. Rhetorical identification says to audiences, because of who you are and what you believe, you share interests with one another and with the sponsor of the public relations effort. Because audiences aspire to follow the same ideas, they tend to identify and act as one. Identification can range from joining in a publicity stunt, supporting a community event, preferring a product or service, or agreeing on a public policy stance.

Another rhetorical problem can be an organization's persona. A rhetor is expected, because of its persona, to take a position in response to comments by others. For instance, timber companies and oil companies are expected to respond to challenges by environmentalists. As Burke (1966) said, "A character cannot 'be himself' unless many others among the dramatic personae contribute to this end, so that the very essence of a character's nature is in a large measure defined, or determined, by the other characters who variously assist or oppose him" (p. 84). Some personae attempt to speak in conjunction with those with whom they have formed a coalition. Merger results when a rhetor shows harmony of interests on an issue. Division is created or heightened by a rhetor who compares the stance he or she is advocating to that presented by other voices. In each case, a public relations practitioner may attempt to position his or her statement to be on the side of the audience. This tactic may require being against parties disfavored by the audience, an option that has strained public relations' efforts to defend its ethics. If practitioners try to be all things to all people, they risk losing their identity and rhetorical perspective.

Rhetorical problems, in part, define the kinds of messages that are appropriate and needed under the circumstances. Messages can define an issue, take a stand for or against it, or attempt to clarify and increase understanding of it. Messages include what is said, how it is said, and who says it. The meaning of messages depends on idiosyncratic interpretations by its various audiences. Recent trends in rhetorical theory have discredited the assumption that a message sent by the rhetor is necessarily the same as the message received. A message is more than the text. It is a set of symbols presented in a context by a source and interpreted by receivers.

What is the meaning of the message? One answer has been to point to what participants think the message means. Another explanation can be achieved by taking the poststructuralist stance that a message is the composite of the dominant metaphors in a text. What goes on in any text is the product of the structure of its metaphors (Derrida, 1974). By looking at the metaphors embedded in a public relations message, a critic can sense the interpretations of what is appropriate and meaningful. Throughout this effort runs the incentive to see statements as part of the social effort of creating powerful metaphors that become shared as a view of reality. This critical approach treats message as part of a complex effort people make to derive a useful shared meaning by which to know who they are and what they believe. This stance views meaning as perspectives—ways of viewing and being. An hegemony of thought is one that people do not challenge because they have accepted it as true.

The rhetorical situation can create strains in relationships and thereby generate a rhetorical problem. Addressing the relationship between sender and receiver, Brockreide (1968) suggested that three variables are especially important: liking, power, and distance. Public relations practitioners may work to foster liking between their organizations and their audiences. Power is important because organizations are expected to achieve the ends for which they were designed. Companies must exude power and may try to empower (or disempower) the audience. For instance, products are presented to "empower" the audience to be a better housewife, member of the community, investor, shopper, or environmentalist. Psychological distance, the third variable in this model, can be increased; mystery is tantalizing. It empowers the source. But distance between source and receiver can be narrowed, a friendly approach to public relations based on the concept of identification.

Awareness of the dimensions of the rhetorical situation and its accompanying problems offers a critical starting point from which to ascertain the motives that appear to inspire the sponsor of a message. Part of the interpretation of the persona's message originates with an attempt to determine, as Kenneth Burke (1945/1969a) argued, what act is appropriate to each particular scene. This scene is best interpreted in terms of the rhetorical problem the source is attempting to solve. In the context of a scene, "a prime function of rhetoric is to interpret and make meaningful what is in the process of happening" (Andrews, 1983, p. 9).

In these ways, the situation and its attendant rhetorical problems are crucial focal points of critics' analyses. Rhetoric is situational and responsive to expectations associated with events and opinions. It is a matter of relationships—adjusting parties' interests to one another. Understanding the situation and the rhetorical problems it generates serves as an important focal point for rhetorical critics.

STANDARDS OF TRUTH AND KNOWLEDGE

Public relations is expected to be truthful, honest, and candid. This expectation is legitimate for at least two reasons. First, each statement by someone practicing public relations is made in terms of its sponsor's self-interest; presence of apparent self-interest arouses suspicion about the source's credibility. Second, if rhetoric advises and induces action, its worth is only as good as its candor and truthfulness. Claims based on shaded half-truths do not serve the interest of audiences who expect to use them to form judgments and choose behaviors to strengthen the sense of community (Kruckeberg & Starck, 1988).

A traditional requirement facing rhetors is to use argument and evidence to demonstrate the accuracy of their claims. This requirement assumes that good arguments and evidence help audiences accurately and wisely understand issues. One challenge of rhetorical criticism is to determine whether a rhetor's conclusions fairly and reasonably interpret each issue. In response to the relativism that frustrates judgment, Grunig (chapter 4) calls for an attitude of meliorism to be achieved by presenting information so audiences can decide which position on an issue is best.

In this way, rhetorical demonstration can be thought of as a means of observation, a way of viewing reality. Each rhetor provides information and analysis to justify the veracity of some observation. Standards of truth and knowledge assume that prior to making rhetorical statements rhetors must study the issues and analyze the relevant information and arguments. This effort should produce honest and candid interpretation of details and values related to the situation at hand.

This standard is difficult for public relations practitioners to achieve when they are not technically expert on the subject they are discussing. They may not be privy to management decisions and operating philosophies which they are called on to explain and justify. No one in a company can fully understand the technical aspects of all of its operations or processes. Nevertheless, public relations statements often involve matters of operations, safety, engineering, design, or environmental responsibility. To make matters more difficult, these issues may involve contestable procedures that are debated by persons who disagree even though they have the technical understanding to judge the issues.

An example of contestable procedures was made public after the Exxon Valdez oil spill. Critics claimed the spill would not have occurred if the tanker had a double-hull, a kind of second skin to protect against such accidents. At first blush, this issue seems quite simple; however, industry experts are divided over the issue. Double-hull construction is best if a tanker runs aground, but does nothing if it collides with another boat. In the latter instance, a more probable kind of accident, the "segregated ballast tank" construction is superior. Unwise use of facts can lead to miscalculations of many kinds. Improper tanker design can allow environmental damage, but unwise regulation can add unnecessary cost to products and services—while doing nothing to solve other problems. What are the facts? Life is rarely simple enough for even the most competent and honest public relations practitioner to know with certainty. And reporters want the "facts" *now* because of "deadlines." Truth is often not reducible to 15-second soundbites or two-sentence quotations.

Public relations practitioners are being challenged to explain technical processes and issues to publics who may be disinterested, uninformed, misinformed, or hostile. Such situations require careful analysis and judgment in regard to what is said and how. A critical question to use in estimating the quality of the explanation of technical issues is this: If the audience believed the statements, would it be misinformed on the issue?

Practitioners not only are expected to prove their case, but may also be held to a higher standard of proof than is the case for journalists who are on the attack. A case in point: In 1989, a public advocacy group on "60 Minutes" alleged that harmful effects were associated with a chemical called Alar that is used on fruit. Panic broke out. People believed they—and their children— were unsafe, and the media played up the fear associated with the story. But the allegations had not been proven. Showing how irresponsibly biased the media could be, Hodding Carter III (1989) observed, "The only problem was, and is, that a solid scientific case has yet to be made against Alar. Even if one had been made, the vast majority of all apples and apple derivatives have never been touched by Alar" (p. A17). His charge was that the media can falsely report information and draw irresponsible conclusions with impunity. This leaves public relations practitioners having to find and report the truth to a public that is suspicious of the reports because of apparent self-interest. Journalists under this kind of circumstance can merely go on to the next story without so much as a blush or apology. But the public relations practitioner is left having to explain the truth in a hostile atmosphere.

Rhetorical substance and arguments needed to create knowledge consist of statements of *fact, value,* and *policy.* Standards for analyzing fact center on the extent to which a fact or a proposition of fact corresponds to reality. However, facts often do not "reveal" themselves but must be interpreted and may be contestable. For this reason, analysis of fact may not only consider whether something is fact, but what the fact means in the context of some analysis. Fact: Pesticides can be harmful to organisms other than those which they are used to kill. Fact: Without pesticides, thousands of people and other animals worldwide would die each year and millions of dollars of needed agricultural crops would be destroyed. Fact: Pesticides can be safely manufactured, stored, used, and disposed of. What interpretations are to be made of these facts?

One view of arguments holds that they consist of three primary components: facts or data, a warrant, and conclusion or claim. The warrant is a premise that allows the conclusion to be drawn in light of the data. The conclusion is the claim that is justified given the data and the warrant relevant to the argument (Toulmin, Rieke, & Janik, 1979). Fact: Pesticides can be safely manufactured, stored, used, and disposed of. Warrant: That which can be done safely and which is useful enjoys the protection of public policy. Conclusion: Therefore, the safe manufacture, storage, use, and disposal of pesticides should be allowed.

This view of an argument offers a viable starting point for criticizing the substance of rhetoric. The system of reasoning from warrants is useful because it allows critics to estimate whether sufficient facts exist, in light of the warrant, to justify the conclusion. Or by observing the warrant, an estimate can be made regarding whether the audience for which the argument is intended believes the warrant or whether it must be proved by the rhetor.

According to Toulmin (1969), there are two major kinds of arguments: Those that establish warrants and those that use established warrants. Some statements produce evidence and reasoning that can lead audiences to accept warrants as true. Once they become established in the thoughts of the audience, they can be used to bolster other arguments. For instance, most people accept the notion that some regulated monopolies should exist: such as gas and electric utility companies and telephone companies. But as Olasky (1987) observed, much of the acceptance of this notion came about through the public relations efforts of AT&T president Theodore Vail in the early decades of this century. Through arguments, a warrant was established that said that regulated monopolies provide better service at the most reasonable prices to consumers. Once established as a warrant, this kind of premise supported the telephone industry for years until the principle was successfully challenged by MCI that argued that although some regulated monopolies are wise, the phone company is not serving the public in the best way. Eventually, the warrant eroded, at least insofar as it was applied to AT&T. Now dozens of companies compete for long-distance telephone service, even though key local telephone companies remain as regulated monopolies.

Analysis of this kind can shed insight into the decision processes of corporate managements (Mason & Mitroff, 1981). If public relations experts identify which decision-making premises are used by managements they can be compared against those of key stakeholders to determine whether there is disagreement and disharmony. Such analysis provides insights into the reasons behind the choices and actions companies make and advocate.

RHETORIC OF GOOD REASONS

In addition to facts, the substance of rhetoric consists of good reasons, values that justify choices and actions (Wallace, 1963). Through the good reasons they share, people become identified and have mutual interests (Burke,

1950/1969b). Capturing the essence of the rhetoric of good reasons, Wallace (1963) concluded, "when we justify, we praise or blame; we use terms like right and wrong, good and bad; in general we *appraise*" (p. 243).

Thinking in these terms is an additional means to counter the indictment that public relations is immoral, both in regard to its tactics and the substance of its statements. The challenge is to know and employ the *rhetoric of good reasons*.

Searching for critical perspectives on the substance of rhetoric, Wallace (1963) chastized writers on rhetoric and criticism whose theories merely contain "statements about methods, principles, techniques, and styles of discourse." And although "they talk of the forms and the handling of ideas," Wallace continued, they "are mostly silent about the substance of utterance" (p. 239). How *do* rhetors adjust ideas to people and people to ideas (Bryant, 1953)? Wallace (1963) answered "that speakers and audiences stand on common ground only through commonalities of meaning and partial identities of experience" (p. 239).

What values do people share as the basis of defining reality and knowing which actions are better than others? Wallace (1963) contended that "the basic materials of discourse are (1) ethical and moral values and (2) information relevant to these" (p. 240). He believed that "the underlying materials of speeches, and indeed of most human talk and discussion, are assertions and statements that concern human behavior and conduct. They are prompted by situations and contexts that present us with choices and that require us to respond with appropriate decisions and actions" (p. 241). The proper substance of rhetoric is judgments or appraisals that "reflect human interests and values" (p. 241). Wallace reasoned "that the foundation materials of speeches are statements that are evoked by the need to make choices in order that we may act or get ready to act or to appraise our acts after their doing" (p. 241). In any rhetorical situation, rhetors advise audiences to make certain choices; the substance of those recommendations should be good reasons.

One of the most important calls to make values central to rhetoric came from Richard Weaver (1965) who believed that "the good rhetorician leads those who listen in the direction of what is good" (p. 18). He acknowledged the importance of facts in making judgments, but even more important, he believed, is the way any message relates to values, which for him are not all of equal importance. For this reason, he challenged rhetors to employ the most important values as the substance of rhetoric. He observed, "All of the terms in a rhetorical vocabulary are like links in a chain stretching up to one master link which transmits its influence down through the linkages" (p. 23). By appealing to the highest values, rhetors ask people to seek perfection. This the rhetor does "by showing them better versions of themselves, links in that chain extending up toward the ideal, which only the intellect can apprehend and only the soul have affection for" (p. 25). With no ultimate values in mind, the rhetor lacks force and fails to assist people and society to become better.

Words are "sermonic" (Weaver, 1970, p. 224). They advocate. Values are embedded in key words that constitute propositions for action. For instance, "honesty" is a proposition that corresponds to actions such as openness, truthfulness, or fair dealing. In this way, "worker" is a proposition calling on people to do their jobs. "Environmentally responsible" calls for the highest standards of performance to protect the world in which we live, as "affirmative action" calls for positive hiring, training, and promotion personnel practices. Likewise, "corporate citizen" is a command for companies to be community stewards that cannot ethically mask irresponsible behavior. These propositions can either be god-terms, that demand positive action, or devil-terms, which call for avoidance (Burke, 1941/1973; Weaver, 1965).

Reflective thought, according to Weaver (1970), is required to discover which values are highest and therefore are to be used to guide judgment. Once these values are discovered, they are to be proclaimed by a rhetor. Thus, Weaver reasoned,

> Rhetoric is advisory; it has the office of advising men with reference to an independent order of goods and with reference to their particular situation as it relates to these. The honest rhetorician has two things in mind: a vision of how matters should go ideally and ethically and a consideration of the special circumstances of his auditors. Toward both of these he has a responsibility. (p. 211)

Assessment of value appeals, Fisher (1987) argued, "leads to a determination of whether or not a given instance of discourse provides a reliable, trustworthy, and desirable guide to thought and action *in the world*" (p. 90). For this reason, Fisher (1984) concluded, "Public *moral* argument is moral in the sense that it is founded on ultimate questions—of life and death, of how persons should be defined and treated, of preferred patterns of living" (p. 12). Fisher's analysis of rhetoric focuses on the relationship between the persona of the person giving the message and its content, as he concluded: "With knowledge of agents, we can hope to find that which is *reliable or trustworthy;* with knowledge of objects, we can hope to discover that which has the quality of *veracity.* The world requires both kinds of knowledge" (p. 18). Fisher (1987) believed "that individuated forms of discourse should be considered as 'good reasons'—values or value-laden warrants for believing or acting in certain ways" (p. xi).

Whether public relations intends to or not, its messages contribute to the substance by which society defines itself and implements values. Essential to the choices society makes, values supply the rationale for the "oughts" that lead to motives and choices. With values, people define their circumstances and behavior. The substance of values, such as honesty in business practices, or a world of beauty regarding environmental themes, translates into policies that determine what actions companies are allowed to do by law, regulation, or norm.

Public relations practitioners either attempt to change the values key publics employ or they use the opinions of those publics to support the arguments being made. In either sense, practitioners confirm or disconfirm the values of society, and add to the substance of the discussion about what values mean, which ones are important, and what ones should be applied to discuss particular issues.

Statements by public relations practitioners contain good reasons and are therefore advisory, because they recommend products, admirable qualities for organizations, and responsible actions. The advice takes this form: Given these facts, in light of good reasons (values), then these actions. Such actions extend to public policy considerations even though the vast majority of what is said, visually depicted, and written by public relations practitioners has nothing directly to do with matters of public policy. Nevertheless, advice is predicated on values and choice which translates into the rules promulgated by governmental bodies (Buchholz, 1988). If we include the "oughts" and "shoulds" that public relations typically prescribes, we see how extensive its role is in policy decisions.

This discussion of rhetorical substance becomes even more meaningful when it is viewed in terms of stakeholder analysis (Freeman, 1984; Mitroff, 1983). This analysis assumes that each organization must be sensitive to those parties, stakeholders, who have a self-interest in its actions and who can give or withhold the stakes wanted or needed by the organization. A stake might be willingness to buy products or to give support or withhold opposition on some public policy issue such as air quality standards or personnel procedures. Each stake becomes the basis for the message content used to discuss the issues at hand. For instance, customers want to receive information and advice relevant to products and services provided by companies; customers hold the stakes of buying products from one company rather than its competitors. Investors want information that can help them assess the financial stake they might (or do) have in the organization; depending on the quality of the information they receive, investors may buy stock in one company rather than others. Neighbors are stakeholders who want self-interested information in regard to actions of the organization, particularly on issues of public or personnel safety or environmental aesthetics; neighbors hold the stakes of protest and regulation if they do not approve of the actions of organizations.

The list of stakeholders for any organization is extensive. Stakes help define the substance that is necessary to affect understanding and judgment on the part of those who are interested receivers of public relations messages. For this reason, arguments and claims made by public relations practitioners are expected to help stakeholders obtain the understanding that fosters wise decisions. This standard prevails in regard to the substance of public relations statements; it allows stakeholders to make proper evaluations and reduce the uncertainty that is a natural part of doing business with organizations (Heath, 1990).

PERSPECTIVIST CRITICISM

Advocates seek to lead audiences to accept the perspectives contained in their statements. Statements made by opponents on an issue contain conflicting perspectives—different opinions. For instance, automobile manufacturers attempt to focus responsibility for car accidents on drunk drivers, road design, and recklessness. In contrast, insurance companies reason that automobile accidents could be reduced if cars were made safer—even drunk proof. A copper processing company seeking water quality, waste management, and air quality permits may argue from the perspective that a "little" environmental harm is okay if it results in jobs and a tax base for a community. A conflicting perspective might be that a "little" harm by one company adds to that of all companies and is multiplied by the years that the harm occurs. One perspective minimizes harm, whereas the other magnifies it.

Perspectives are not only embedded in claims that advocates make, but also in the key terms (especially god terms and devil terms) that are current at any moment in a society. For this reason, perspectivism is useful for understanding rhetoric and making critical judgments. If all statements are perspectives, how can any one be better than others? This question focuses on the relativism that plagues perspectivism, but it also illuminates a critical point. Each statement, by its very nature, has meaning and importance because it expresses a point of view in regard to other points of view. Therefore, perspectivism is a powerful critical tool because it operates out of discovering perspectives and making them explicit so that persons observing the criticism can make informed judgments.

If all statements contain perspectives, then one means for conducting criticism is to compare perspectives. Perspectivist criticism assumes that useful insights can be gained by disclosing the perspective advocated by each rhetor. This mode of criticism does not require the critic to advocate that one perspective is superior to the other, but sets perspectives against one another for comparison. Often a critic will imply one perspective is superior to the other, or the preferences held by those reading the criticism will favor one perspective more than others. In this vein, several perspectives—especially a Black perspective, environmentalism, and feminism—have been popular in recent years.

Underpinning for perspectivism is found in Kenneth Burke's (1966) discussion of terministic screens. To explain his point, he recalled how he had once seen several photographs of the same subject matter. The difference was that each photograph had been taken with a different colored lens. For that reason, each picture was slightly different. This illustrates his contention that people see the world differently, depending on the ideology embedded in the key symbols of their idioms. The notion is that people see the world through the terms they use to discuss that world. To accept an argument is to adopt the perspective embedded in the terms used to express it.

The perspectives of environmentalists may not be the same as those of oil companies that wish to open dedicated wilderness areas to oil exploration. Anti-smoking advocates are likely to have different perspectives of cigarettes than do persons who manufacture and sell them, who raise tobacco, and who depend on cigarette advertising for a livelihood. Automobile safety is viewed through different perspectives by automobile manufacturers and insurance companies.

Perspectives are terministic screens that have rhetorical potency when they are widely believed by a group of people whose opinions are important to the fate of some organization that uses public relations to reinforce or counter those perspectives. How do perspectives become widely held? Through interaction, members of a group build perspectives by recalling what has happened or by envisioning events that could occur (Bormann, 1972). These perspectives are "the creative and imaginative interpretation of events that fulfill a psychological or rhetorical need" (p. 434). Individual perspectives become group perspectives in part from repetition, but also out of pragmatics. Perspectives are held because they foster similarity in thoughts and actions of members of groups.

Public relations practitioners participate in this dialogue, helping to develop perspectives. Practitioners also utilize existing perspectives as the source of values, assumptions, and themes to support their conclusions. This kind of rhetorical tactic is potent because statements that grow out of widely held perspectives confirm what audiences believe. When the ideas voiced by public relations practitioners differ from established perspectives or those of key groups, they are at odds with the opinions and judgments of an audience regardless of the veracity of the practitioners' statements.

Perspectives, embedded in language—particularly idioms, are terministic screens that shape perception, evaluation, and behavior. Inside organizations, "power in organizations is seen as a symbolic process, through which individuals and groups control the interpretations and worldviews of others" (Eisenberg, 1986, p. 94). This outcome can be achieved through stories, myths, and dominant metaphors. Such devices are used by internal public relations to persuade employees to accept perspectives preferred by management (Mumby, 1987).

The same can be said for public relations targeted externally. Control of the meaning of terms—the rhetoric of definition—is a powerful means by which perspectives are achieved, maintained, and translated into the actions as well as the judgments of society. Terms become perspectives and imply propositions. "Seat belt" is not only a thing; it is also a proposition—"buckle up"—and a part of the war of regulation between the automobile industry, insurance companies, and safety activists. Other examples of terms that are highly important to the changing perspectives of our time are "animal fat," "biodegradable," "ozone layer," "acid rain," "cancer causing," "technological advance," and "military defense."

Demonstrating how perspectives are embedded in what people say, Meadow (1981) argued that nonproduct advertising is political advertising because it discusses issues such as those regarding the environment, energy, and capitalism. By extension, any comment that favors corporations is political. This argument highlights the position that the discourse of a society contains perspectives that express its value priorities.

If what people think—their perspectives—govern what they do, then critical attention is needed to recognize perspectives and to help understand the components of messages that shape them and make them terministic screens. To demonstrate this point from a feminist perspective, Foss (1989) compared key pairs of terms: bachelor/spinster, grandfatherly advice/old wives tales, and wizard/witch. By comparing key terms—those vital to any terministic screen—a perspectivist critic can disclose how the meaning of terms needs to be altered before the perspective will change. This critical methodology compares the cluster of key terms of two or more perspectives to gain insights into the arguments. In Foss' analysis, the terms associated with the male counterpart are more positive (or less negative) than the female.

In chapter 6, Pearson offers an excellent example of cluster analysis. He isolates the cluster of terms unique to different perspectives on the public relations career of Ivy Lee. The cluster analysis features these terms:

Fiction, lies	vs.	Truth
Secrecy	vs.	Openness
Partisan	vs.	Neutral
Persuasion	vs.	Understanding
Image	vs.	Reality
Propaganda	vs.	Education
Publicity	vs.	Public Relations
Muckraker	vs.	Gentleman of the Press

This example looks at the attitude of one of the major public relations practitioners toward the profession. The terms favoring the profession (god terms) are on the right.

Brief examination of a terministic cluster used by the U. S. Council for Energy Awareness is informative. The Council is sponsored by electric utility companies that use nuclear fuel, labor unions, and companies that supply such fuel as well as build and maintain generating facilities. The Council has repeated this terministic cluster:

Pro-nuclear	Anti-nuclear
Energy independence from foreign sources of oil	Energy dependence on foreign sources
Safe to operate	Unsafe to operate
Less expensive to operate	More expensive to operate

The pro-nuclear perspective asserts that dependence on foreign crude oil supplies used to generate electricity is risky. This nation can be held hostage by foreign countries that have no interest in its security or well-being.

Because of the potency of perspectives, public relations people appropriate key terms from a popular point of view and associate them with positions being advocated. For instance, products are claimed to be "safe for the environment." Public relations practitioners attempt to dissociate their product and service from negative terms (such as cancer) and associate them with positive terms (such as freedom of choice), tactics employed by advocates of the tobacco industry. Cigarettes have been presented as symbols of "freedom" and "torches of liberty" (Pollay, 1990).

Socially constructed reality means that values and interpretations of facts are unique to each subculture and to those who share its idiom. Is a product good because it has additives? In the United States, manufacturers and producers of products can put in anything that is not shown to be hazardous. The burden of proving harm rests with those who challenge the persons producing the product. But that standard does not exist in every country. In some, the burden rests with the person who wants to put an additive into a product. Customs and laws require that the additive be proven to be beneficial (as well as not harmful) or it cannot be used. That is quite a different standard than prevails in the United States and one that establishes a unique rhetorical problem. Should producers of cigarettes be required to prove that they do no harm, or does the responsibility rest with persons who would prove that they are harmful?

One way to examine competing perspectives that confront public relations is to consider the different interests held by the stakeholders of an organization (Freeman, 1984). Each stakeholder is likely to operate from a different perspective, in large part reflecting his or her interests. The position of an advocate and a stakeholder can be compared on crucial issues to determine where there is agreement or difference of opinion. The substance of arguments made to stakeholders can be isolated by looking at the interest of the stakeholder—an investor or a neighbor, for instance. A company needs to tell investors what they want to know about its financial strength. But if the company proudly proclaims that its financial strength is based on a manufacturing process that could be harmful to neighbors, then one party—investors—may be satisfied, but the other is not (see Conrad's discussion of the corporate illusion of efficacy in chapter 9). Will financial appeals assuage the neighbor who is interested in protecting his or her family and property values? In this situation, companies have tried appeals such as this: "If we do not manufacture in this way, we will be unable to get the financial backing needed to stay open. Closing will hurt the economy of the community."

The substance of that statement is oriented toward the stake of the investor in purely economic terms, but not the community. Will that appeal keep the investor interested? Can it signal the beginning of community agitation that can affect the orderly conduct of business? Does it violate the investor's sense of social responsibility? If the company appeals to the community by indicating that massive corrections will be made in operations to end pollution, will the investor shift his or her money to other companies that are not faced with such outlays of capital? Will the community fear that these cost outlays are the first step toward the company being less competitive and going out of business? The interest of the stakeholders is an excellent place to look for the substance of rhetoric, and it suggests the foundation for discovering each rhetorical problem.

Because rhetoric is used to create understanding of issues by framing them as perspectives, perspectives can be used to assess the rhetoric being used. Statements made by a rhetor constitute perspectives; they are perspectives on the perspectives advocated by others. A critical tactic is to set the perspectives of the rhetor against other perspectives to determine what unique definitions and evaluations can be achieved. Several chapters feature this critical methodology: Dionisopoulos and Goldzwig in chapter 10, Condit and Condit in chapter 12, Trujillo in chapter 13, and Porter in chapter 14.

PUBLIC RELATIONS AS NARRATIVE

One reason that perspectives become widely believed is because they are embedded into stories that are told over and over through interpersonal conversation and mass media. Much of the discourse used by public relations relies on narrative—the story. Mention of stories in this context is appropriate, but problematic. Some critics of public relations believe that it does nothing but tell "stories." In that sense, stories are falsehoods, a type of narrative, but narrative need not be false. People tell many true stories, because they provide the context for interpreting facts, as well as knowing which values to apply, and what norms or policies are applicable.

Recent studies (e.g., Fisher, 1987; Lucaites & Condit, 1985; Rowland, 1989) have advanced the use of narrative as a rationale for rhetorical discourse. Narrative form is one way to characterize and analyze the quality of discourse. And stories are potent rhetorical substance because they portray characters, opinions, and actions that foster rhetorical identification (Burke, 1950/1969b; Fisher, 1987). Such themes and characters offer form and substance for the rhetoric of public relations.

Demonstrating the potency of narrative, Fisher (1984, 1987) argued that it is the fundamental communication paradigm because each story is set in the context of larger, more encompassing stories. Narrative is powerful because it is simple and commonplace, and connects with other stories to present points of view that are coherent and orderly. Narrative goes beyond the rational world paradigm that assumes that people are logical and analytical and that these cognitive powers can put together puzzles of fact, one piece at a time, to discover the nature of the social and physical realms. Rather than relying totally on facts, narrative paradigm presupposes that people are storytellers who use "good reasons" for interpreting situations and recommending actions.

Events can be portrayed in narrative sequence, an excellent device for companies to present continuity starting from the moment of their creation and moving to the present and into the future. Running throughout each narrative is one or more principles, a story line of "good reasons" that constitutes a point of view. The image of a corporation can be portrayed in narrative form that emphasizes what the company has achieved since it began "once upon a time" and how it is moving toward the future, "to live happily ever after." Employee publications tell stories about the company, the industry, and employees who serve as role models. The same form works for presenting products and services or even achieving publicity or press agentry. Each step in narrative advances, or reflects, a principle that unifies it. "The plot is unnoticeably ultimate, as the reader need not 'choose between' different phases of its unfolding, but by going through each becomes prepared for the next" (Burke, 1950/1969b, p. 197).

Public relations exhibits a narrative quality when it recounts facts and puts them into context. A press release may dramatize facts and highlight a series of events. To explain an oil spill or development of a new technology, a story may be used. The story not only gives perspective to the facts, but also provides values that allow receivers of the message to judge those facts and draw conclusions. The format of a press release lends itself to narrative form. For instance, "On Friday of last week, engineers at the XYZ Corporation made an important breakthrough in the application of superconductivity to computer design." Consider this example: "For the seventh year, the Big O Company had record sales. This company went from annual sales of $3 million to $10 billion in seven years. No other company in the history of the New York Stock Exchange has surpassed this feat." Think about an example unrelated to a company: "The Helpful Environmentalist continues to buy and set land aside for wildlife preserves." This last example highlights activist groups' efforts to seek rhetorical advantage by dramatizing events, such as the efforts to clean up some environmental disaster or by describing life cycles of endangered animals or migratory patterns that might be interrupted, for instance by the pipeline in Alaska.

Entertainment programming uses narratives that have public relations consequences. On television, "The Simpsons" portrays the operations of a nuclear power generating station. To correct the image presented there, the U. S. Council on Energy Awareness succeeded in convincing the television production company to portray operations in such facilities more accurately. This is one instance of how entertainment programming presents business men and women as "crooks, conmen, and clowns," so says The Media Institute (Theberge, 1981). Narrative is potent because it dramatizes events and employs characters, whether heroic or villainous.

The prevalence of narrative in these statements suggests why public relations relies on that form. This kind of recognition, Lucaites and Condit (1985) concluded, acknowledges "the growing belief that narrative represents a universal medium of human existence" (p. 90). This is true even if the narrative is only one of several paradigms useful to understand rhetorical discourse (Rowland, 1989).

To be effective, narratives are expected to "display brevity, avoid contradictions, demonstrate unities or direction and purpose, and integrate the credibility of narrators, authors, and speakers" (Lucaites & Condit, 1985, pp. 103–104). These standards are consonant with the requirements for effective public relations. Each event in a public relations campaign is like an episode in a drama. Each is likely to be brief because of the limits of audience attention. Within each episode, and across all episodes, one would expect the avoidance of contradictions that would harm the coherence and credibility of the campaign. Likewise, unity of direction gives a sense of development to the story leading people to expect subsequent segments—installments— whereby the persona of the organization will continue the story of its success, its effort to provide good products or services, to serve the community, or to fight the environmental battle. Finally, coherence in the narration is increased if the persona of the narrator and audience fit into a coherent drama.

How many times have public relations people been given the advice, "Tell your story"? Several of the chapters that follow employ narrative analysis. Berg and Robb (chapter 5) discuss crisis communication which is inherently narrative. Conrad (chapter 9) demonstrates the drama of how companies take credit for good performance while blaming negative performance on external circumstances. Dionisopoulos and Goldzwig (chapter 10) show how nuclear generating advocates portrayed women to pose choices to them. Corporate takeovers are inherently narrative, as Trujillo points out (chapter 13).

REFERENCES

Andrews, J. R. (1983). *The practice of rhetorical criticism*. New York: Macmillan.

Black, E. (1970). The second persona. *Quarterly Journal of Speech, 56*, 109–119.

Bormann, E. G. (1972). Fantasy and rhetorical vision: The rhetorical criticism of social reality. *Quarterly Journal of Speech, 59*, 143–159.

Brockreide, W. E. (1968). Dimensions of the concept of rhetoric. *Quarterly Journal of Speech, 54*, 1–12.

Bryant, D. C. (1953). Rhetoric: Its function and its scope. *Quarterly Journal of Speech, 39*, 401–424.

Buchholz, R. A. (1988). Adjusting corporations to the realities of public interests and policy. In R. L. Heath (Ed.), *Strategic issues management: How organizations influence and respond to public interests and policies* (pp. 50–729). San Francisco: Jossey-Bass.

Burke, K. (1966). *Language as symbolic action*. Berkeley: University of California Press.

Burke, K. (1969a). *A grammar of motives*. Berkeley: University of California Press. (Original work published 1945)

Burke, K. (1969b). *A rhetoric of motives*. Berkeley: University of California Press (Original work published 1950)

Burke, K. (1973). *The philosophy of literary form* (3rd ed.). Berkeley: University of California Press. (Original work published 1941)

Campbell, K. K. (1982). *The rhetorical act*. Belmont, CA: Wadsworth.

Carter, H. III. (1989, April 20). Alar scare: Case study in media's skewed reality. *The Wall Street Journal*, p. A17.

Crable, R. E., & Vibbert, S. L. (1983). "Mobil's epideictic advocacy: "Observations" of Prometheus-Bound." *Communication Monographs, 50*, 38–394.

Crable, R. E., & Vibbert, S. L. (1985). Managing issues and influencing public policy. *Public Relations Review, 11*(2), 3–16.

Derrida, J. (1974). *Of grammatology* (G. C. Spivak, Trans.). Baltimore, MD: Johns Hopkins Press.

Eisenberg, E. M. (1986). Meaning and interpretation in organizations. *Quarterly Journal of Speech, 72*, 88–113.

Fisher, W. R. (1984). Narration as a human communication paradigm: The case of public moral argument. *Communication Monographs, 51*, 1–22.

Fisher, W. R. (1987). *Human communication as narration: Toward a philosophy of reason, value, and action*. Columbia, SC: University of South Carolina Press.

Foss, S. K. (1989). *Rhetorical criticism: Exploration & practice*. Prospect Heights, IL: Waveland Press.

Freeman, R. E. (1984). *Strategic management: A stakeholder approach*. Boston: Pitman.

Heath, R. L. (1988). The rhetoric of issue advertising: A rationale, a case study, a critical perspective—and more. *Central States Speech Journal, 39*, 99–109.

Heath, R. L. (1990). Corporate issues management: Theoretical underpinnings and research foundations. In L. Grunig & J. E. Grunig (Eds.), *Public relations research annual* (Vol. 2, pp. 29–65). Hillsdale, NJ: Lawrence Erlbaum Associates.

Kruckeberg, D., & Starck, K. (1988). *Public relations and community: A reconstructed theory.* New York: Praeger.

Lucaites, J. L., & Condit, C. M. (1985). Re-constructing narrative theory: A functional perspective. *Journal of Communication, 35*(4), 90–108.

Mason, R. O., & Mitroff, I. I. (1981). *Challenging strategic planning assumptions: Theory, cases, and techniques.* New York: Wiley.

McKerrow, R. E. (1989). Critical rhetoric: Theory and praxis. *Communication Monographs, 56,* 91–111.

Meadow, R. G. (1981). The political dimensions of nonproduct advertising. *Journal of Communication, 31*(3), 69–82.

Mitroff, I. I. (1983). *Stakeholders of the organizational mind: Toward a new view of organizational policy making.* San Francisco: Jossey-Bass.

Mumby, D. K. (1987). The political function of narrative in organizations. *Communication Monographs, 54,* 113–127.

Nichols, M. H. (1965). The criticism of rhetoric. In M. H. Nichols (Ed.), *A history and criticism of American public address* (Vol. 3, pp. 1–23). New York: Russell & Russell.

Olasky, M. N. (1987). *Corporate public relations: A new historical perspective.* Hillsdale, NJ: Lawrence Erlbaum Associates.

Pollay, R. W. (1990). Propaganda, puffing and the public interest. *Public Relations Review, 16*(3), 39–54.

Rowland, R. C. (1989). On limiting the narrative paradigm: Three case studies. *Communication Monographs, 56,* 39–54.

Simons, H. W. (1983). Mobil's system-oriented conflict rhetoric: A generic analysis. *Southern Speech Communication Journal, 48,* 243–254.

Theberge, L. J. (Ed.). (1981). *Crooks, conmen, and clowns: Businessmen in TV entertainment.* Washington, DC: The Media Institute.

Toulmin, S. (1969). *The uses of argument* (2nd ed.). Cambridge: Cambridge University Press.

Toulmin, S., Rieke, R., & Janik, A. (1979). *An introduction to reasoning.* New York: Macmillan.

Wallace, K. R. (1963). The substance of rhetoric: Good reasons. *Quarterly Journal of Speech, 49,* 239–249.

Weaver, R. M. (1965). *The ethics of rhetoric.* Chicago: Henry Regnery.

Weaver, R. M. (1970). *Language is sermonic.* (R. L. Johannesen, R. Strickland, & R. T. Eubanks, Eds.). Baton Rouge, LA: Louisiana State University.

II

Toward a Critical Method for Assessing Public Relations

Toward the Philosophy
of Public Relations

LARISSA A. GRUNIG
University of Maryland

Most people in business, whether they are CEOs or public relations practitioners, are moral. Their reputation as a group, however, may be unsavory. The reason, according to John Budd, vice chairman of one of the country's oldest and largest public relations firms, is that CEOs lack "philosophical antennae," or a philosophical base from which to make qualitative decisions ("Opportunity & critical area," 1989). His example of takeovers is illustrative of the typical CEO who may be comfortable with quantitative decisions (based, for example, on maximizing shareholder value) but cannot cope with such abstractions as whether the takeover bid is ethical or moral. This chapter offers an important step toward that much needed philosophical base.

Inclusion of this chapter on philosophy is appropriate for a book on critical and rhetorical approaches to public relations, given the field's roots in rhetoric (J. Grunig & Hunt, 1984, p. 15) and its ethical emphasis. The timing, too, is not coincidental. Barely a year has passed since initial publication of the codified body of knowledge in public relations (see the Spring 1988 issue of *Public Relations Review*). Even more recently and for the first time, public relations has been adopted as a general field for doctoral study in public communication at the University of Maryland—on a par with the more established disciplines of, for example, cross-cultural or political communication. And like Norbert Wiener (1948, p. 8) working with cybernetics, I feel the excitement of laboring in the fruitful niche of scholarship that heretofore has been neglected among these more institutionalized fields. Thus, we see that although public relations still cannot be considered so advanced as many other fields, it has reached a stage of maturity wherein we should become introspective and look closely at our presuppositions, our goals, and our methods.

Now for a few words about the title, "Toward the Philosophy of Public Relations." The first is "presumptuous." Perhaps referring to "the," rather than "a," philosophy of public relations is audacious. However, this chapter represents one of precious few contemporary attempts at a comprehensive look at the epistemology and metaphysics of public relations.[1]

Earlier in the decade, Merrill and Odell (1983) published a philosophy of journalism. As useful as their philosophical insights into journalism and mass communication are, public relations cannot be considered a subdiscipline of those fields. As a result, their emphases on, for example, journalistic rights and responsibilities and on censorship are not central here. The cases and examples that illustrate their principles are drawn largely from newspaper reporting, making them largely inappropriate as illustrations of philosophical reasoning in public relations. Thus, the relationship between journalism and public relations might better be seen as business associates than as parent and child.

Even the relatively new *Journal of Mass Media Ethics*, which carries an occasional article on public relations,[2] fails to address the ethical and philosophical concerns relevant to our field. In its promotional flyer, the publisher Lawrence Erlbaum Associates alludes to a discussion of "whether the public relations field has been able to overcome its journalistic origins and subsequent guilt feelings at switching basic roles, to allow it to base ethical and moral judgement on a role emphasizing persuasion rather than the objectivity of its journalistic concerns." I would argue that the role of public relations is not persuasion and that any philosophy of the field should be based on the responsible and responsive exchange of information.

So by contrast, this chapter emphasizes what a philosophy unique to public relations should encompass—to an even greater degree than it will describe that philosophy. Analyzing each concern relevant to the underlying causes and principles of reality in public relations would require a book-length treatise.

Thus, the "toward" in the title suggests that the work presented here should be considered emergent, in all senses of that word. The nascency of a philosophy of public relations has been alluded to earlier. In addition to "newly formed," emergent also means "arising as a natural or logical conse-

---

[1]Pearson's (1989) retrospective reminded us of the seminal but largely uncited work of Sullivan (1965) on the foundations and ethics of public relations.

[2]One significant exception is the Vol. 4, No. 1, 1989, issue of the journal, which is devoted to public relations.

quence," which I would argue has happened in the aftermath of the published body of knowledge in our field and a heightened awareness of ethical concerns on the part of our major professional associations. The dictionary tells us that "emergent" calls for prompt action. Although that may seem optimistic, I would like to think that both teaching and practice would be influenced in immediate and visible ways by the ideas suggested here.

But why is it necessary to belabor the general principles of philosophy? Why not "cut to the chase," in essence, beginning with "the" applied philosophy of public relations? The value in a starting-on-the-ground-floor approach, as I see it, lies in an argument perhaps first articulated by Martin (1988). She explained the scant attention given to ethics in journalism education by the fact that most professors in our field lack degrees in philosophy. Philosophers, according to Martin, agree that those who write the textbooks and who teach the courses outside of philosophy tend to simplify philosophic theory and thus mislead their students. Martin concluded that students need to understand philosophical principles if they are to be ethical in making the decisions that are bound to face them in the turbulent environment of the late 20th century.

Bivins (1989) explained that most authors of textbooks in public relations have failed to write about what he termed "any philosophical underpinnings" that could lead to an understanding of how the PRSA code of professional standards, for instance, was developed. He went on to cite other theorists who echo Martin's argument for a grounding in basic ethical theory, both classical and modern. One example that seems particularly relevant here comes from the work of DeGeorge (1982), whose book on business ethics begins with an explanation of general ethical theory and proceeds to the basics of moral reasoning before attempting to deal with the specifics of issues relevant to business.

From his review of the literature on teaching philosophical concepts, Bivins concluded that "a study of applied ethics. . .is not enough if it is not structured and guided by an understanding of relevant ethical thought" (p. 41). His challenge that "there is no accepted conceptual framework from which to study public relations ethics" led in no small part to the development of this chapter. The decision to begin describing a conceptual as well as an applied approach to the philosophy of public relations also was spurred by Pratt and Rentner's (1989) contention that the public relations curriculum should provide a theoretical framework from which to discuss ethics in "a meaningful, fruitful, and practical way" (p. 63).

QUALIFICATIONS OF A PHILOSOPHER

The arguments I present here derive both from the postulates of philosophy and from my experience in researching, teaching, and practicing public relations. I also am influenced by my feminist perspective. That is, my experiences as a woman, as a teacher of mainly female students, and as a scholar of the new research by and about women have led me to work toward a philosophy and a way of practicing public relations that will help empower women and minorities. I consider myself an expert in public relations; I claim less authority in philosophy. Still, I hope Bertrand Russell (1952) could write of me as he did Poincare, whose philosophical musings he characterized as "not those of a professional philosopher: they are the untrammeled reflections of a broad and cultivated mind upon the procedure and postulates of scientific discovery" (p. 5).

Mark Twain observed that because the only requirements for practicing medicine were ignorance and confidence, nearly anyone could do it. I would not make the same claim of philosophy. I do not consider myself a self-styled expert, hawking a world view with promise for enhanced teaching, research, and practice in public relations.

However, Phenix (1958) alluded to three grades of philosophers. The "greats" have made major contributions to philosophy. An economist cited in a recent issue of *pr reporter* ("Stumped by an ethics problem?", 1989, p. 3) reminded public relations practitioners of the three philosophers[3] who, in his view, offered the greatest promise for relieving the ethical tensions inherent in management. Lavelle recommended a reacquaintance with the works of Immanuel Kant, with his categorical imperative ("if I don't want the act that I'm contemplating to become universal law, then I shouldn't do it"); John Rawls, the American moralist with the "do unto others" theme; and British utilitarian Jeremy Bentham, who determined what is right by balancing costs and benefits.

Phenix's second class of philosophers includes professionals who have mastered the field. They usually write and teach about philosophy. Third— and here I see myself—are intelligent and curious scholars concerned with the goals and problems of their own field. As Brennan (1953) said of this third type, we are not to be dismissed but to be lauded because we reflect on the basic presuppositions or first principles of our disciplines.

In fact, we are to be valued, according to Russell (1952). He characterized the philosophy of any special field developed by professional philosophers as having "too often the deadness of merely external description" rather than "the freshness of actual experience of vivid, intimate contact with what he is describing" (p. 5). After all, philosophy is considered the most general science

---

[3]Interestingly, Aristotle is absent from Lavelle's list. The great philosopher and rhetorician, often considered the first public relations practitioner, regarded women as "naturally" unsuited to what he deemed the intrinsically masculine pursuits of politics and leadership. As a result, feminists such as Jones and Jonasdottir (1988), Harding and Hintikka (1983), and Lange (1983) also rejected Aristotelian philosophy. Parsons (1973) believed that all traditional philosophical methods are flawed by antifeminist bias.

(Runes, no date, p. 235). Thus, I consider it more appropriate for a public relations scholar to attempt to develop the philosophy of public relations than for a philosopher to write about public relations.

R.K. Mautz and H.A. Sharaf (1982) would agree. They urged auditors not to shy away from philosophizing about auditing. They explained, "It is better that auditors turn to philosophy in attempting to work out the fundamental theory of auditing than that philosophers turn to auditing" (p. 7). The same could be said of public relations scholars and philosophers. Pearson (1989) agreed that many public relations practitioners and researchers are capable of philosophical thought (arguing, at the same time, that too few build on any basic philosophy to analyze public relations).

A philosopher can be many things—a student of philosophy, one with the academic degree "doctor of," one who seeks wisdom or enlightenment, or the expounder of a theory in his or her area of expertise. I have been all three, but this chapter is written in the voice of the latter. Further, the voice or mode of expression is indicative, rather than imperative. That is, consistent with the Judeo-Christian tradition, my philosophy is suggestive rather than compulsory (the "shalts" and "shalt nots" of the Bible seem less memorable than expressions such as "God is love" or "The Lord is my shepherd").

WHAT QUALIFIES AS A PHILOSOPHY?

This philosophy of public relations, then, is a vision of the field and its purpose—a vision encompassing the field's core values and its realities that comes from a speculative rather than observational basis. At its broadest, it represents a synthesis of learning that integrates the field's motivating beliefs, concepts, and principles. It is a "world outlook," in the terms of Bottomore, Harris, Kiernan, and Milibrand (1983, p. 120). In a definition with special relevance to the boundary-spanning nature of public relations, White (1959) called philosophy an important means of social integration, "the peculiarly connective tissue of human society" (p. 264). Its functions are both critical and constructive.

My aims, consistent with other feminist philosophers, are both political and intellectual. Although some philosophers may be appalled by such an acknowledgment of political purpose (Sherwin, 1988), I believe that all other philosophers (and public relations practitioners, educators, and researchers) do what they do with personal and professional biases. As Code, Mullett, and Overall (1988) said, feminist philosophy recognizes that "the alleged truths by which philosophers have been living and conducting their enquiries have the form they do at least in part because of the circumstances of their articulation" (p. 6). And like Reinharz (1985), I believe that interest-free knowledge is logically impossible and I accept her argument that "we should feel free to substitute explicit interests for implicit ones" (p. 163). What is most important is that we examine critically the grounds for our fundamental tenets as we analyze the basic concepts of public relations.

My philosopher's stone, consistent with the beliefs we have embraced since the 14th century, should hold the power of transmuting not baser metals into gold but idiosyncratic practices into a systematic understanding of our primary activities and concepts. Here, I follow the contemporary philosophical approach consisting of four parts: comprehension, perspective, insight, and vision (Phenix, 1958).

Comprehension refers to understanding the range of human experience that leads any field to an integrated body of knowledge. In public relations, this means a coherent and comprehensive body of knowledge based on interpreting what we do as a socially useful discipline rather than merely a set of rules about how best to conduct an employee communication program, for example, or to deal with stockholders. *Perspective* calls for an outlook broad enough to grasp the full significance of that endeavor. Public relations practitioners, as boundary spanners, must be particularly careful to transcend private concerns or the vested interests of their employers. Combining the notions of totality and perspective dictates that practitioners consider each relevant issue in light of its aggregate importance and long-term ramifications from both the organizational and the publics' point of view.

Insight deals with the depth of the proposed inquiry or whether practitioners are willing to seek, uncover, and articulate their basic assumptions about their work. These presuppositions, according to Phenix, often are hidden but real progress toward a philosophy is hampered until their nature and their weaknesses are exposed. We are beginning to understand the far-reaching consequences of public relations to society, yet few of our presuppositions have been scrutinized and evaluated. Instead, we have accepted our beliefs rather casually, basing them on implicit rather than explicit premises. Finally, *vision* takes us beyond our immediate concerns with, say, licensing or inclusion in the dominant coalition and on to the wider possibilities of our endeavors. Of the four components of philosophical thought, this last one has greatest implications for establishing the goals and visualizing the prospects of any growing discipline such as public relations.

It is customary, of course, to thank those who contributed their own ideas and suggestions to a manuscript such as this. In this case I feel compelled to take full responsibility, as I have labored in isolation on this project that has become so all-encompassing.[4]

---

[4]In my zeal to develop the philosophy, I hope I have not imposed the patterns of ethical behavior I sought—when in actuality the complex and often contradictory behaviors of public relations practitioners may defy such generalization or categorization. I have tried, instead, to

However, the philosophy itself did not emerge from a vacuum. The pool may have been shallow in terms of numbers but not quality. Significant earlier contributions to a philosophy of the field include James E. Grunig's (1987) paper on the presuppositions of public relations, Dean Kruckeberg and Kenneth Starck's (1988) book that deconstructs the historical roots and promotes the community responsibility of the field, Ronald Pearson's dissertation on ethics, and my own work on organizational responses to pressure from activist groups. This chapter also has built on Morris L. Bigge's (1971) refinement of John Dewey's philosophy of education and on a relatively obscure monograph that describes the philosophy of auditing.

I am indebted to the authors of the latter, in particular, for their cogent explanation of why a philosophy in any technical field is appropriate and even necessary. To some, philosophy represents all learning exclusive of technical precepts and practical arts (*Webster's Ninth New Collegiate Dictionary*, 1983, p. 883). However, as early as 1793 the German philosopher Kant debunked what he called the "old saw" that "that may be right in theory, but it won't work in practice." Kant (1974) did not believe that philosophy is a theoretical activity solely for the purpose of understanding reality. Instead, he contended that the need to understand is rooted in the need to act. The relevance of philosophy, in his opinion, is in providing a basis for making life's decisions—especially those decisions where will plays a determining role. Similarly, theory—in his view—is a guide to action "if the rules are conceived as principles of a certain generality and are abstracted from a multitude of conditions which necessarily influence their application" (p. 41).

Bayles (1971) agreed. He contended that to think of philosophy as anything other than broad, basic theory is to lose for it any legitimate claim to significance in education. He further argued that "the only genuinely practical subject-matter content a teacher can teach is basic, tested theory" (p. vii).

Mautz and Sharaf (1982) advanced the argument that understanding the theory of auditing can lead its practitioners to reasonable solutions for some of the field's most vexing problems. They explained that although many may regard auditing as completely practical—"a series of practices and procedures, methods and techniques, a way of doing with little need for the explanations, descriptions, reconciliations, and arguments so frequently lumped together as 'theory' " (p. 1)—basic assumptions and a body of integrated ideas do exist.[5] The paradox that led to their emergent philosophy is

---

be sensitive to the tensions inherent in juggling my need to give pattern or form to the real, lived experience of practitioners with the expedience that would come in relying on the fictions that have given meaning or value to what they are. Throughout this process, I ask myself whether I am "inventing" the philosophy or am successfully describing what exists.

[5]I like this explanation, particularly because it calls to mind an opposite viewpoint espoused by a favorite author of my childhood. In contrast with Mautz and Sharaf, Louisa May Alcott

that the status of their profession resulted primarily from its practice rather than from any perceptible body of theory to support that practice.

The parallels between auditing and public relations seem obvious. The procedures and forms of our field, too, grew out of custom—and with little conformity and few standards. Both practices developed from different fields of knowledge, borrowing ideas and methods widely. Although we may continue to borrow these tools, we both need to understand our own problems and functions more fully—apart from the more established fields from whence we came. And like our colleagues in auditing, we scholars in public relations continue to rail against the practitioners who devalue the potential contributions of our theoretical research—practitioners who even may reject the notion that public relations can (or should) be taught.

Since the days of P.T. Barnum, however, practitioners of both public relations and auditing have begun to emphasize their reasons for doing what they do. This discussion of the "why" as well as the "how," according to Mautz and Sharaf (1982, p. 3), is the beginning of both theory and philosophy. More specifically, it involves the differentiation of techniques (print news release vs. VNR?), the recognition of standards (accreditation, ranking of educational programs, Silver Anvils), and the classification of procedures and principles (models of public relations).

However, even as we progress from case studies to generalizations and from the teaching of techniques to the teaching of theory, we—like the auditors—remain plagued with unsolved problems. Mautz and Sharaf identified a number of the unsettled areas in their field—questions remarkably similar to the perplexing issues of public relations.

We begin with *advocacy.* To paraphrase Mautz and Sharaf (1982, p. 3), how far in giving advice to clients can a consultant in public relations go without weakening his or her independence? And what clients deserve representation in public relations? Should clients be supported regardless of the potential consequences of their actions? As Frede, the newly retired vice president for public affairs at Baylor College of Medicine, said: "We must retain our integrity, a sense of what's good for the public. In counseling the tobacco industry, for example, there is no place for compromise" (quoted in "PR opportunities," 1989 p. 1).

Responsibility is a second issue. To what extent is the public relations counselor responsible for the client's claims or actions? or responsible for the outcome of programs he or she has advocated? A third question involves *disclosure.* Must the practitioner divulge organizational wrongdoing? What about revealing managerial inefficiencies or faulty judgments? Even the *purpose* of doing public relations is debatable. Are we in the business of

---

(cited in Cheney, 1989) considered a philosopher one who sails in a balloon while friends and family hold the ropes that confine him or her to earth.

persuasion? of information? of negotiation? of cooptation? of cooperation? As Frede said, it is apparent that communicating is not enough. He emphasized the counseling or managerial role of public relations when he talked about contemporary practitioners' concern with their organization's performance: "We want them to *be*, not *seem* to be. So we must counsel with management to put the house in order. Performance must be part of the pr process" (cited in "PR opportunities," 1989, p. 2).

Imposing as even this partial list may seem, neither public relations nor auditing is the only field facing such quandaries. Unlike Simone Weil (1970), however, I do not consider these ponderables insoluble. This French philosopher, journalist, and scholar defined the proper method of philosophy as "clearly conceiving the insoluble problems in all their insolubility and then in simply contemplating them, fixedly and tirelessly, year after year, without any hope, patiently waiting."

Still, the concern for the existence of fundamental questions in a pre-paradigmatic field such as ours is well founded. One might argue that our field has been busy getting itself established and now busies itself trying to become legitimized or even accepted. However, this rationale for avoiding the resolution of central concerns becomes less valid as the field becomes more mature. Do we have no accepted principles that might guide us to their answers? As Mautz and Sharaf (1982) said of accounting, "If we are to have a profession worthy of the name we must work to eliminate them" (p. 4). Their learned profession, and ours, must develop basic laws that govern its activities—an organized body of knowledge that encompasses interrelationships and rapport or consistency with other fields of knowledge. But do we lack practitioners and scholars with the curiosity and the professionalism that would lead them to solve those questions?

We have some. For example, J. Grunig's (1987) analysis of presuppositions suggests that what he called a "symmetric worldview" is not only the most effective approach to public relations practice but the most moral and ethical as well (p. 38). He cited two studies in support of that contention: my own (L. Grunig, 1986) analysis of how organizations attempt to dominate the activist groups that pressure them and Turk's (1986) finding that state agencies in Louisiana fail to win public support for their policies and programs when they rely on similar, asymmetrical means of communication.

However, as Rakow (1989) pointed out, practitioners and scholars cannot even agree on a definition of the field. Most troubling are the reasons for the disagreement. As she explained, top management and practitioners may be at odds on what public relations should accomplish: making the organization palatable to outsiders or reconciling different interests for the good of all. She concluded that scholars have failed to define public relations because "they have failed to account for the **who** is doing the defining and for the fact that definitions may conflict even within the same organization" (p. 11).

Despite the difficulty of defining the field, developing the philosophy of public relations is somewhat dependent on doing so—primarily for pedagogical reasons but also because of the implications for practice.

BUILDING A PHILOSOPHY

Just as boundaries need to be defined for the field of public relations, so too does the task of building a philosophy require ground rules and confines. The philosophers have shown us the rules of their game. We know that creating a philosophy requires more than subjective opinions about public relations or an expressed "philosophy of life."

Thus, a "philosophy of public relations" is not the same as the sum of one's individual ideas or convictions—although such attitudes undoubtedly do help guide one's quest for the "truth" of the field. I believe that everyone who writes has two philosophies: a more or less conscious credo and his or her unconscious vision of life and value system. The philosophy espoused in this chapter, of course, is more the former.

Familiar examples of the latter type of philosophy come to us from sports. In reporting on a recent faculty senate meeting at North Dakota State University, alumni newsletter Editor Jerry Richardson (1989) recounted the retitling of a new course from something like "philosophy of coaching" to something like "theories of coaching." The objection to the initial title was that physical education does not have any conscious credo or philosophy as such. Richardson argued somewhat tongue in cheek, however, that there is an impressive body of sports philosophy. He cited examples that would rival Santayana coming from Satchel Paige ("Don't look back. Somethin' may be gainin' onya!"), Yogi Berra ("It ain't over 'til it's over"), and Duffy Daugherty (that to be a successful coach, one has to be "smart enough to win and dumb enough to think it's important").

Public relations educators and practitioners often make similar philosophical statements, of course, and they may refer to these dictums as their "philosophy." Cummins Diesel, an industry leader respected for its honesty and concern for the public, proclaims as one of its major ethical precepts: "If you're asked to do something that you wouldn't want printed in your hometown newspaper tomorrow, don't do it" ("Stumped by an ethics problem?", 1989, p. 3). In a recent letter-to-the-editor of the *Public Relations Journal*, the director of corporate communications for a Denver bank explained that "my philosophy is, 'If we don't believe in quality and work to make sure everything we produce or have a hand in is of the highest quality, why should anyone else care?' " (McKechnie, 1989, p. 5). Noble sentiments, these two, but not of the grounded sort to be espoused in this chapter.

KEY DIMENSIONS OF THE PHILOSOPHY
OF PUBLIC RELATIONS

Instead, to withstand the scrutiny of experts (whether in philosophy or in public relations), a philosophy must recognize the specific nature of public relations while encompassing the following key dimensions:

- Foundations of the field.
- Its development.
- Ethical issues.
- The nature of practitioners' moral reasoning.
- Public and social responsibility.
- Ideology and values.

Finally, no discourse on philosophy would be complete without a sensitivity to any aspects of oppression that may characterize the field. Like other feminists, I interpret Jurgen Habermas as saying that human knowledge always is connected to and driven by some set of interests of an emancipatory nature (Jones & Jonasdottir, 1988). In fact, feminism is often called a "philosophy of liberation" (Ferguson, 1988). Thus, this chapter suggests ways to apply the tools of philosophy to examine the status of women and minorities who are affected by the oppressive structures detailed, for example, in the Fall 1988 issue of the *Public Relations Review* ("*Women in Public Relations,*" ed. L. Grunig). There, students, educators, theorists, and practitioners—male and female, majority and minority alike—critiqued the monolithic White male perspective that has characterized the public relations classroom, department, and firm to date. Marilyn Kern-Foxworth (1989) gave similar attention strictly to the status of minority practitioners in a recent cover story of the *Public Relations Journal*.

This feminist perspective on the philosophy of public relations is just that—a perspective that still allows for a concentration on the discipline rather than shifting the context from public relations to issues of race or sex as they happen to apply to public relations. In other words, the philosophy will be constructed as if minorities, women, and gender-based interests matter.

By introducing historicity and values often considered feminist, this philosophy will have the potential for introducing a new paradigm. Marcil-Lacoste (1983) argued that taken together, feminist and philosophical thought represent a forceful challenge to the meta-discourse of any field. Code et al. (1988) explained the importance of exposing the "alleged truths" by which philosophers in any field have shaped their inquiries. They contended that one's own circumstances are largely responsible for the way one articulates broader, substantive issues. Likewise, Reinharz (1985) argued that value-free knowledge is logically impossible. She urged the substitution of explicit for implicit values and interests.

What this philosophy should contribute to the feminist critique of public relations is a determination of the role of female and minority practitioners, students, and researchers. More specifically, it will ask whether women and minorities in public relations typically are active agents or objects of oppression. It should show not only how the "isms" of sexism, racism, ageism, and class bias may have oppressed but how those different groups that have been the targets of the "isms" have advanced the field.

Origins of the Field

Although the roots of public relations may be as old as history itself, contemporary practice can be dated only from the end of the previous century. One major contribution of J. Grunig's (1984) delineation of four models of public relations is an understanding of the historical progression these models may represent. *Press agentry* or publicity, the earliest of the models, can be characterized as "promotional wizardry." Its leading historical figure, the promotional wizard himself, is P.T. Barnum. The purpose of this model, dating from about 1850, is propaganda. The organization's goal is control or domination of the environment. Public relations contributes to this goal through advocacy or product promotion.

J. Grunig credited Ivy Lee, an early 20th-century practitioner, with initiating the second stage of public relations practice in this country. Lee conducted public relations as a "journalist in residence," responsible for disseminating truthful information (Hiebert, 1966). In fact, the purpose of the *public information* model is the dissemination of information. It helps the organization achieve its goal of adaptation to or cooperation with the larger environment through this one-way flow of accurate information—an approach to public relations that was developed largely through Lee's impetus during the first two decades of this century.

J. Grunig described the two two-way models of public relations, *asymmetrical* and *symmetrical*, as dating from 1920 and 1960, respectively. The historical figures credited with their development include Edward L. Bernays and a host of public relations educators and researchers. Scientific persuasion is the purpose of the imbalanced model. The organizational goal is environmental control or domination, and public relations contributes through advocacy of the organization's position. The final stage in the evolution of public relations practice, symmetrical, is more balanced than its asymmetrical counterpart. Although it, too, builds on the work of Bernays and other leaders of the profession, it values mutual understanding to a greater degree. Public relations practitioners embracing this model serve more as mediators than as advocates.

Despite the historical progression inherent in these models, all continue to exist in actual practice—either as discrete approaches to doing public relations, as mindsets of practitioners, as values held by the organization's dominant coalition, or in mixed forms that may be more situational than static.

After his initial depiction of the four models, J. Grunig (1987) decided that the two-way symmetrical represents the most ethical (and efficacious) model. I came to a similar conclusion in my own work on activism. In a series of studies that looked at how organizations typically respond to special interest groups pressuring them from outside, I found that although two-way, balanced communication rarely was tried it offers the most promise for mutually beneficial, harmonious relationships in a fractious (and litigious) society (see, e.g., L. Grunig, 1986, 1987, 1989).

Not all practitioners condemn press agentry. Although 1988's Outstanding TPRA Practitioner agreed that the role of press agents was to create the news, take the mundane and make it dynamic, he also contended that "when done with honesty & integrity, it's an art worthy of respect" (Frede, cited in "PR opportunities," 1989, p. 2). Frede acknowledged, however, that contemporary public relations requires more than press agentry or even public information: "We realized the importance of honest and accurate communication. Sending out the message was no longer the only function, but also measuring impact, changing attitudes, creating mutually acceptable goals, obtaining feedback" (p. 2).

Public relations practitioners who fail to understand their origins cannot understand their most important role in society. That, according to Kruckeberg and Starck (1988), is the attempt to restore and maintain a sense of community in urbanized America. This critical role serves both the client or the organization and society as a whole.

Kruckeberg and Starck offered a compelling argument for the loss of community or what sociologists in the Chicago School of Social Thought called the "atomization of individuals" as the impetus for the development of modern public relations. Before the shift from rural to urban America, public relations could be practiced as press agentry. Subsequently, putting people back in touch with each other in a dynamic environment required more of communication facilitators. Thus, in the authors' view, the contemporary practitioner is responsible primarily for relationships between and among groups. They call this model of public relations "communal" or "communitarian." The suggestion that this model actually predates the P.T. Barnum school is just one aspect of Kruckeberg and Starck's text that begs further research.

Historical Development

So, public relations needs its own history. Although many researchers and educators would argue against case studies, developing an adequate philosophy of this fledgling field seems to demand at least case histories. Taught from broad principles or generalizations, these case histories will have what Bayles (1971) called "high retrieval value; they represent the kind of knowledge that makes transfer readily possible and enables a possessor to find it useful" (p. vii).

Caspari (1985) argued that the journalistic perspective that has dominated our field accounts for practitioners even regarding themselves as unethical. She questioned "why public relations has yet to assert an ethical perspective of its own" (Abstract). She concluded that practitioners will remain "outcasts" from what she called the "paternalistic and hostile" culture of journalism until further research is conducted into the history and ethics of public relations as a separate domain.

Writing our own history is critically important. When the "official" history develops from outside any field, it tends to maintain the established authorities or "natural inevitability of existing power arrangements" (Kolodny, 1988, p. 463). Women in public relations may stand to gain the most from a heightened awareness of the need for a revisionist chronicle of the field. One obvious gap in any historical discussion of the four models of the field, for example, is the impact female and minority practitioners have had. So we see that public relations, like the physical and biological sciences, suffers from the same ahistorical and patriarchal generalizations that prompted development of the Society for Women in Philosophy.

To understand why, consider the historical research of philosopher and activist Angela Davis (1972). She portrayed female Black slaves as rebels who managed to undermine significantly the authority of their oppressive masters. The implications of her work are that women and minorities in roles that would seem to make them inarguably victims can resist repression and subjugation. Historical research in the field of public relations might expose similar, albeit less dramatic, instances of female activity eclipsing objectification.

Indeed, feminist historians across the disciplines are replacing any single-sex view of development of their fields with the understanding that women not only have been present but have been active at each stage of the past (DuBois, Kelly, Kennedy, Korsmeyer, & Robinson, 1985, p. 50). Including the story of women's contributions to the development of public relations undoubtedly would change the historical view of the field significantly. Thus, this philosophy of public relations would be enhanced by more investigations along the lines of Henry's (1988) biography of Doris Fleischman, the wife of Edward L. Bernays and a credible practitioner in her own right.

"Contribution theory," however, has its limitations. Feminists have argued that fitting women into existing histories may devalue the role of women and minority practitioners less notable than, say, a Doris Fleischman. Lerner (1975), for example, urged historians and philosophers to develop new conceptual frameworks that may depart from the traditional categories and value systems of the male-derived experience. As Ferguson (1988) said, "Drawing upon the lived structure of women's experiences rather than some essential trait of the female, this view is more historical and more open to recognizing diversity among women and men" (p. 69). Along with Gilligan (1982) and Hartsock (1983), she argued for interpreting women's experience as revealing positive virtues rather than "unrelenting victimization."

To arrive at more than a partial or distorted understanding of the body of knowledge in public relations, then, we need to understand the roles of the women as well as the men who have contributed to the field. As Harding and Hintikka (1983) said, "We must root out sexist distortions and perversions in epistemology, metaphysics, methodology and philosophy . . ." (p. ix). Unfortunately, determining the role of female and minority practitioners—agent or object?—is difficult. As Thornton Dill (1989), founding director of the Center for Research on Race and Gender at Memphis State University, said: "In our philosophical study of race and gender, we've moved from the fundamental concept of victimization to one of resistance. Who knows where we'll go next?" Perhaps the much-needed research in the history of the field will answer the question in much the same way that Cott's (1977) work on women in 18th- and 19th-century New England did. She concluded that women were not solely victims nor active agents but some of both.

Ethics

Kant (1974) defined *ethics* as "a science that teaches, not how we are to achieve happiness, but how we are to become worthy of happiness" (p. 45). Although scholars of public relations agree that ethics should be a priority when teaching or practicing, the literature of our field (as evidenced, largely, in the body of knowledge) reflects little familiarity with ethical theory (Pratt & Rentner, 1988). Thus, Pratt and Renter advocated more research on what philosophical insight could contribute to solving the ethical dilemmas that face our field.

One such dilemma, according to Brain (1988), is openness. He argued that candor with the press and with the public may not always be good ethics, or even common sense. He explained that because most public relations professionals pride themselves on not being deceitful, top management may be reluctant to include them in the organization's power elite—where competitive strategies are discussed and developed. He contended that "in any process involving negotiating, buying and selling, persuading voters or donors, changing minds or influencing decisions, openness will have limitations" (p. 40). He also called "the urge to make malefactors confess" the dark side of the coin of disclosure. For these reasons, according to Brain, an ethical dilemma is just that—a murky situation in which no clear-cut solution making one "worthy of happiness" is apparent. Quantitative evidence may not support the notion, but at least one corporate practitioner believes that the feminization of the field will result in a higher ethical performance (cited in Joseph, 1985, p. 22).

The very question of hiring and promotion practices is of moral and ethical concern to feminists and to philosophers (Pierce, 1975) and, I would hope, to public relations researchers, teachers, and practitioners. The issue of hiring alone may provide an interesting illustration of the complexities of any ethical question.

Pierce (1975) argued that much of the discussion on preferential hiring has centered on whether the moral considerations for hiring women should supercede professional ones. Martin (1973–1974) shifted the focus to suggest that being female may be a professional qualification. In so doing, he rejected Thompson's (1973) argument that being a role model is insufficient as a professional qualification. Martin countered that because the university (for one example) provides many role models for male students, it is obliged to treat female students in the same way in this regard. Further complicating the "preferential treatment" controversy is the question of whether such a remedy is for the future (to bring about a more just society) or for the past (to compensate for historical injustices).

Ethical and moral issues in addition to equal opportunity and preferential treatment that concern feminists and philosophers and that are relevant to a philosophy of public relations include political ideology, sexism in research methodology and assumptions, sexist language, equal pay for equal work, the division of labor (most problematic within the public relations department in terms of the schism between technician and managerial roles), and metaphysical issues such as whether gender is an accidental or essential characteristic.

However, Pearson (1988) argued that ethics in public relations is not a matter of whether it is right or wrong to, say, constrain women in the technical role, to accept bribes, or to engage in insider trading. More fundamentally, in his view, ethics is "a question of implementing and maintaining inter-organizational communication systems which question, discuss and validate these and other substantive claims" (p. 25). He suggested communication systems that are symmetrical: balanced, two-way, dialogic, and interactive. Such communicative structures, in my view, are consistent with both J. Grunig's (1984) two-way symmetrical model of public relations and Kruckeberg and Starck's (1988) communitarian approach.

Moral Reasoning

Little empirical investigation into the moral[6] reasoning of public relations practitioners has been published. Ryan and Martinson (1984) explained that although a handful of scholars in public relations has tried to establish "moral anchors," widespread agreement on these standards for ethical decision making is lacking. Disappointingly, they contended that "if public relations has adopted any underlying principle, it is possibly the subjectivism (or individual relativism) theory that each individual must establish his or her own moral base lines" (p. 27).

However, studies in both psychology and management suggest that the related areas of moral judgment, negotiation, and conflict resolution may contribute to this aspect of the philosophy of public relations. For example, psychological research suggests that gender may play a role in how one makes moral judgments. Gilligan (1982) argued that women's moral reasoning is based on responsibility, whereas men tend to reason on the basis of rights. Bem (1977) found that androgyny, in particular, correlates with greater maturity in moral reasoning.

The literature of business management also suggests that gender may play a role in how one thinks about moral problems. Loden (1986), for example, described a feminist model of management that values intuition as well as rational thinking, that focuses on long-term goals that are good for the whole as opposed to short-term goals that benefit a few, and that prefers a win–win approach to conflict resolution over the more traditional zero-sum game. She tied in these qualities with bottom-line organizational effectiveness.

The literature of negotiation and conflict management shows that, once again, gender plays a role. Greenhalgh and Gilkey (1986) found that mediators with a feminine sex-role orientation tend to approach negotiation as part of a long-term relationship between parties locked in moral disputes, whereas those with a masculine orientation have an episodic, short-term, win–lose approach. Feminine negotiators, they contended, seek outcomes involving mutual gains; masculine negotiators tend to be rigid and uncompromising in their bid to conquer. Yelsma and Brown (1985) also found that in situations of conflict management, women use more "accommodative

---

[6]Morality, according to Kupperman (1978), is a subspecies of ethics. He explained: "Ethics, which includes all of our judgments of what people conclusively should do in their lives, is broader than morality. . . ." (p. 21). The boundaries of morality, in his view, are more irregular and more fluid—more an outgrowth of the ethical traditions that set and reset them.

strategies," they take on a "peacekeeper" role, they express more support and solidarity, and they use more facilitative behaviors. Yelsma and Brown characterized women as compromising during confrontations, whereas in their view, men are more competitive and both verbally and physically aggressive.

Thus, I argue that any philosophy of public relations should take into account the sex-role socialization of its practitioners as one initial step in predicting how moral dilemmas might be solved in the field. This is not to argue that women exhibit greater moral virtues than do their male colleagues.[7] Generalizing about men's and women's styles of management always is risky; meta-analyses of the literature consistently show greater similarities between sexes than within a sex. However, masculinity and femininity or the gendered socialization inherent in our culture seems to be an important determinant of how one would approach moral issues— regardless of one's biological sex.

Public and Social Responsibility

Public relations practitioners concerned with their public and social responsibility would do well to return to the work of the sociologists in the Chicago School. Based on the writings of scholars such as George Herbert Mead, Thorstein Veblen, and Robert E. Park, Kruckeberg and Starck (1988) have redefined the role of public relations—one that denies the prevailing notions of advocacy, persuasion, and manipulation. Instead, they defined *public relations* as interactive, cooperative, complex communication that has the potential for helping create a sense of community.

Kruckeberg and Starck also argued that activities couched in terms of "social responsibility" actually tend to be manipulative, persuasive forms of communication that are self-serving for the organization. They exposed the lip service typically paid to community relations. They proposed, instead, a relational model of public relations that puts people back in touch with each other.

The following implications of this model, which grew out of the case of a Standard Oil (now Amoco) refinery in Missouri, pose a tall order for any public relations practitioner:

1. help both the community and the organization he or she represents become aware of mutual interests;

---

[7]As Gloria Steinem (1971) said, "We [women] are not more moral, we are only less corrupted by power" (p. A15).

2. help individuals in the community overcome alienation or the "atomization" that results from urbanization;
3. help organizations create a sense of community;
4. encourage leisure-time activities as a way for citizens to enhance their sense of community;
5. enjoy consummatory communication for its own sake, as an immediate enhancement of life;
6. help citizens find security and protection through associating with others; and
7. address community welfare, social order, and progress.

Environmentalism, whether in the community or on a global scope, represents one of the most critical areas in which today's practitioners of public relations must operate from a philosophical standpoint. Because of our skill in spreading knowledge, we are called on to establish "a new cultural ethos" of what the chair of the UN's World Commission on Environment and Development called "intergenerational responsibility." Brundtland, cited in a recent *pr reporter* ("Toxic trauma unites," 1989), urged practitioners to acquaint the public with the ecological rights of their children and grandchildren. Frede, remarking on the trends that will impact the careers of future practitioners of public relations, echoed this emphasis on society's concern for a healthy, life-saving environment (cited in "PR opportunities," 1989).

The twin concepts of responsibility and nurturing reflected in the previous discussion speak to the feminization of the field. More than a decade ago, Gorney (1975) was predicting that increased attention to what she considered the humanistic aspects of business (including social and environmental responsibility, consumerism, safety, and minority issues) would broaden career opportunities for women in corporate public relations.

Ideology and Values

A recent lead article in *pr reporter* ("Religion in the workplace," 1989) asserted that today's workers are "hungry for values" (p. 1). Effective organizations have reacted against a materialistic, impersonal era in their search for what the article termed "humanizing balance." The article also articulated good values in public relations as caring for employees and the community.

As with the earlier discussion of ethics, however, any generalizations about what makes for "good values" are risky. As a counselor at Brain Technologies explained, "Certain belief structures have their place and can be very useful, but when applied in the extreme they're detrimental" (Lynch, cited in "Religion in the workplace," 1989, p. 1). He cited fundamentalist beliefs, in particular, as creating a collision of value systems and divisiveness in the typical organization.

The same article decried the new-age philosophies that espouse a "go with the flow," quick-fix approach to organizational training and management. As the personnel director of a rental car company explained: "Corporations shouldn't attempt to change basic belief systems of employees, or promote techniques that accelerate such change. Spiritual growth is important, but they shouldn't prescribe the method" (Watring, cited in "Religion in the workplace," 1989, p. 2).

Watring believed such psycotechnologies may result in lawsuits based on religious discrimination or in psychological damage to participants in training programs. For just one example, consider the Public Utilities Commission's investigation of Pacific Bell, which spent $40 million on the Krone technique of training employees. According to Pennington (cited in "Religion in the workplace," 1989, p. 3), employees objected to the company's effort to "make us think differently, talk differently."

Thus, the philosophy of public relations should preclude an emphasis on new-age or religious values, in particular, that might alienate or even injure practitioners who would otherwise subscribe to it. Although the values of belief systems such as Zen, est, Neuro-Linguistic Programming, Dianetics, Scientology, and mysticism may be positive, too often they are used in a manipulative sense—as a way of controlling others' behavior.

THE EMERGENT SYNTHESIS

Earlier in this chapter, I talked about the importance of resolving the definitional problem of public relations: What is it that we do, or that we should be doing? Related questions include our relationship to other fields of knowledge and, more specifically, to the other disciplines from which we have developed. Although history tells us that public relations has borrowed a great deal from journalism, for example, our field does have an independent identity. Understanding that identity requires a knowledge of public relations' own problems as well as the nature of the borrowed tools.

The philosophical method appropriate for answering these questions is remarkably different from other typical ways of settling problems. Larrabee (1928) pointed out that neither fighting, nor voting, nor compromising compels us to *understand* the questions. Instead, by developing the key questions that beg further study and ultimately comprehension, we should arrive at long last at a resolution that endures. As Larrabee said, "Philosophizing about a thing implies an unusually stubborn attempt to understand it as thoroughly as possible, so as to give it the most thoughtful treatment of which we are capable" (p. 61). In fact, we may not move beyond the questioning stage, and we certainly cannot within the constraints of this one short chapter.

However, I take heart from MacLead (1959), who reminded us that philosophers see questions where others see facts. As a unique field (evidenced in the recently codified body of knowledge), public relations embodies a rational structure of presuppositions, concepts, and techniques that demands rigorous intellectual effort for understanding even the questions.

Still, public relations demands more than analysis. As an applied discipline and as a profession, it has important implications for society. So, any philosophy of the field must provide its students with information they can use to act. In fact, it should both stimulate and inspire. Primarily, however, in my opinion the philosophy must define the goals toward which practitioners work. Further, those goals must be understood in the context of broad, basic, abstract theory. The day-to-day, pragmatic concerns of the field must not supersede the more fundamental. As Mautz and Sharaf (1982) warned of auditing: "Whatever works well is adopted and strongly advocated; what has not yet been found applicable has little appeal. To some extent this is a natural tendency, yet we must keep it in bounds. We must continually test our practices and procedures, not only in actual practice, but against the theory which underlies auditing" (p. 17).

That theory, again, developed from a number of related disciplines. And just as engineering is more than applied mathematics,[8] so too is public relations more than applied communication. In the same way that engineering requires a synthesis of math with concepts and methods drawn also from physics, chemistry, and mechanics, understanding public relations requires synthesizing the concepts and methods of journalism, communication, rhetoric, political science, cognitive psychology, business management, and sociology (some of them "pure" and some of them also applied fields).

Synthesis, here, refers to Dewey's (1938) concept of the basic writing technique: developing one idea, a thesis, then an opposing idea, or antithesis, and finally an emergent synthesis that transcends both but *is not an eclectic compromise between the two*. It is not an intermediate position but a new position that is internally consistent and, in Bigge's (1971) view, more adequate than its precursors. The emergent synthesis, then, reflects the interplay of conflicting ideas and arrives at a new philosophical base.

Bigge illustrated this concept by developing a philosophy he called "positive relativism," synthesized primarily from the thesis/antithesis of logical empiricism and subjective idealism. Unlike the logical empiricists, positive relativists neither assert nor deny an absolute existence. Unlike the idealists, they deal with a reality defined as that which we make of what we experi-

---

[8]I am indebted to Mautz and Sharaf (1982, p. 15) for this analogy.

ence. As Bigge said, "For a positive relativist reality is psychological and thereby different from any objective existence; it is what people gain through use of their five-plus senses" (p. 4).

Thus, we see that this philosophy focuses on experiential situations—making it especially appropriate for public relations, although it was developed as an American educational philosophy. It offers both a method and an outlook for practitioners and scholars in the field. For example, the central theme of *relativism,* according to Bigge, is that objects derive their qualities from the total situation rather than apart from their context. This notion of nothing existing apart from a larger totality is consistent with the systems theory endemic to our theoretical literature. The notion of perceived relationships with other things, events, or ideas is consistent with the relational nature of public relations itself. (This is not to be confused with "ethical relativism," or the notion that no person's [or organization's] view of what is morally right is better than anyone else's because ethical standards either are nonexistent or subjective and unknowable; Pearson, 1988.)

Meliorism is another key tenet of positive relativism. Meliorism contrasts the absolutist positions of pessimism and optimism. In the case of public relations, we would argue that practice is not entirely press agentry and flackery nor totally communitarian, two-way, and balanced. At the same time, we would argue that we have little basis for assuming the field inevitably is getting better or worse. However, because as Bigge contended in his philosophy of education, education can improve conditions, we constantly should try to make them better.[9]

Thus, we see that this same philosophy, adapted and applied to public relations, is affirmative. Growth and learning are key components that govern our ideals, thoughts, and actions. However, positive relativism assumes that people do the best they know how for what they conceive themselves to be. As a result, we should be concerned with the psychological makeup of practitioners as well as their orientation toward the key public relations roles of technician and manager or the roles implied by today's "Mommy track" reasoning.

Positive relativism also has important implications for understanding our publics. Its basic assumption about the nature of people and their relationship with the environment is interactive, rather than active (idealism) or passive (reactive empiricism). Bigge (1971, p. 12) characterized the interactive position, which comes from cognitive-field psychology, as basically neutral. Substituting "publics" for "individuals" would lead us to see our internal and external constituencies not as totally active, self-determined, autonomous bodies nor as reactive, passive recipients of messages or beliefs whose behavior is governed by prior causes. Instead, the interactive nature

---

[9]*Melior* is the Latin word for "better."

of people (applied here to groups) suggests that their behavior depends more on what Bigge called "situational choice," or behavior that may be scientifically predicted although it arises from purposive decisions. Bigge described this paradox as follows: "One may be objective in studying human behavior by being, to some degree, subjective. A teacher [substitute public relations practitioner] may conjecture, What would I be thinking if I were a student [customer, employee, reporter] and were acting that way?" (p. 19). One additional link between the interactive nature of positive relativism and public relations is Pearson's (1989) ethical theory outlined in terms of interactive communication structures.

Positive relativists consider the effects of the past (which I interpret to include experience, socialization, and attitudes) to be indirect—"trace" residue that affects but does not determine or program a person's behavior (Bigge, 1971, pp. 20–21). Through the interactive process, each person (and by implication, each public) acquires and reshapes language, conceptual thinking, and moral and social predispositions. Herein lies the opportunity for public relations practitioners, who can affect and be affected by such interaction.

CONCLUSIONS

The philosophy to be derived from the emergent synthesis described here, of course, is merely suggested. So far, we know it only to be interactive, affirming, and relational in nature. We know, too, that for the last three decades (since the most recent women's liberation movement), philosophers have devoted increasing attention to the nature and history of and the solution for minorities' and women's oppression in a number of fields. So, issues of sex-role and gender discrimination are central to this philosophy of public relations. The comprehensive philosophy also will include a description of the growth of the codified body of knowledge; the structure, purposes, and limits of prevailing models and theories (including the logical relations among those suppositions about public relations); and interpretations and implications of the methods of public relations. It will feature illustrative case studies, taken primarily from this century.

However, even short of presenting the philosophy itself, this chapter has value. By including the earlier delineation of the characteristics of any valid philosophy—and in a professional field such as public relations in particular—the chapter should be useful to rhetorical scholars interested in evaluating other philosophical treatises. It also should serve as an impetus for scholars to begin developing their own philosophical perspective, whether it be an elaboration of the framework presented here or their idiosyncratic epistemological and metaphysical stance. As an introductory work, then, it can point the direction for others in our circle whose thinking has been piqued but whose work has not given sufficient attention to this rich and important project.

And even when the philosophy is no longer "emergent" but established, the issues facing public relations practitioners will need to be identified and re-identified. One way to do so might be to imagine and then to identify and highlight the experiences of the philosophical practitioner. Ayn Rand (1971) said that if playwrights could convert philosophical ideas into flesh-and-blood people in an attempt to create the walking embodiment of modern philosophy, the result would be the Berkeley rebels. To paraphrase as a question, if this scholar had the power to convert philosophical precepts into a flesh-and-blood practitioner, who would be the walking embodiment of modern philosophy in public relations?

Even without identifying such quintessential professionals in our field, I expect we will continue to study the means for solving the ethical dilemmas that we face, both politically and morally. And, rather than searching for the "correct" representation of the ethical and moral practitioner, perhaps we should muse about the effects of any *mis*representation of our field. In this self-conscious way, we will expose what our own stakes are and the stakes of those who created that worldview in the first place. We know that power and reality are deeply connected, so even asking the correct *questions* about why public relations has come to be perceived and to be practiced as it has is critical.

My hope is that even at this point, though, readers will be able to identify and to clarify their own positions on the philosophical concerns voiced here—considering the justifications for or the pitfalls of those stances. To make that happen, I hope too that my words have resonated with the richness that comes from a solid mass lying beneath the veneer reflected in this chapter.

REFERENCES

Bayles, E.E. (1971). Editor's foreword. In M.L. Bigge *Positive relativism: An emergent educational philosophy* (pp. vi–vii). New York: Harper & Row.

Bem, S.L. (1977). On the utility of alternative procedures for assessing psychological androgyny. *Journal of Consulting and Clinical Psychology, 45*(2), 196–205.

Bigge, M.L. (1971). *Positive relativism: An emergent educational philosophy.* New York: Harper & Row.

Bivins, T.H. (1989). Are public relations texts covering ethics adequately? *Journal of Mass Media Ethics, 4*(1), 39–52.

Bottomore, T., Harris, L., Kiernan, G., & Milibrand, R. (Eds.). (1983). *A dictionary of Marxist thought.* Oxford: Blackwell.

Brain, J. (1988, December). Openness—Or irrationality? *Public Relations Journal,* 40–39.

Brennan, J.G. (1953). *The meaning of philosophy.* New York: Harper & Brothers.

Caspari, G.G. (1985, August). *Ethical thought in public relations history: Seeking a relevant perspective.* Paper presented to the Public Relations Division, Association for Education in Journalism, Norman, OK.

Cheney, E.D. (1989). *Louisa May Alcott: Her life, letters, and journals.* Boston: Roberts Brothers.

Code, L., Mullett, S., & Overall, C. (1988). Introduction. In L. Code, S. Mullett, & C. Overall (Eds.), *Feminist perspectives: Philosophical essays on method and morals* (pp. 3–10). Toronto: University of Toronto Press.

Cott, N. (1977). *The bonds of womanhood: "Women's sphere" in New England, 1780–1835.* New Haven: Yale University Press.

Davis, A. (1972). Reflections on the black woman's role in the community of slaves. Reprinted from *The black scholar* in the *Massachusetts Review, 13,* 81–100.

DeGeorge, R.T. (1982). *Business ethics.* New York: Macmillan.

Dewey, J. (1938). *Experience and education.* New York: Macmillan.

DuBois, E.C., Kelly, G.P., Kennedy, E.L., Korsmeyer, C.W., & Robinson, L.S. (1985). New visions in the disciplines. In E.C. DuBois, G.P. Kelly, E.L. Kennedy, C.W. Korsmeyer, & L.S. Robinson (Eds.), *Feminist scholarship: Kindling in the groves of academe.* Urbana: University of Illinois Press.

Ferguson, K.E. (1988). Subject-centeredness in feminist discourse. In K.B. Jones & A.G. Jonasdottir (Eds.), *The political interests of gender* (pp. 66–78). London: Sage.

Gilligan, C. (1982). *In a different voice.* Cambridge, MA: Harvard University Press.

Gorney, S.K. (1975, May). Status of women in public relations. *Public Relations Journal,* 10–13.

Greenhalgh, L., & Gilkey, R.W. (1986). Our game, your rules: Developing effective negotiating approaches. In L.L. Moore (Ed.), *Not as far as you think* (pp. 135–148). Lexington, MA: Heath.

Grunig, J.E. (1984). Organizations, environments, and models of public relations. *Public Relations Research and Education, 1,* 6–29.

Grunig, J.E. (1987, May). *Symmetrical presuppositions as a framework for public relations theory.* Paper presented to the Conference on Applications of Communication to Public Relations, Illinois State University, Normal.

Grunig, J.E., & Hunt, T. (1984). *Managing public relations.* New York: Holt, Rinehart & Winston.

Grunig, L.A. (1986, August). *Activism and organizational response: Contemporary cases of collective behavior.* Paper presented to the Association for Education in Journalism and Mass Communication, Norman, OK.

Grunig, L.A. (1987). The role of public relations during industrial crises. *Industrial Crisis Quarterly, 1*(2), 10–18.

Grunig, L.A. (Ed.). (1988). Women in public relations [Special issue]. *Public Relations Review, 14*(3).

Grunig, L.A. (1989, January). Activism in the Northwest: Surveying the effects of public relations on conflict resolution. In L.A. Grunig (Ed.), *Environmental activism revisited: The changing nature of communication through organizational public relations, special interest groups and the mass media.* North American Assn. for Environmental Education, *5,* Monographs in Environmental Education and Environmental Studies, pp. 83–124.

Harding, S., & Hintikka, M.B. (1983). Introduction. In S. Harding & M.B. Hintikka (Eds.), *Discovering reality: Feminist perspectives on epistemology, metaphysics, methodology and philosophy of science* (pp. ix–xix). Dordrecht, Holland: D. Reidel.

Hartsock, N.C.M. (1983). *Money, sex and power.* New York: Longman.

Henry, S. (1988, July). *In her own name?: Public relations pioneer Doris Fleischman Bernays.* Paper presented to the Public Relations Division, Association for Education in Journalism and Mass Communication, Portland, OR.

Hiebert, R.E. (1966) *Courtier to the crowd.* Ames, IA: Iowa State University Press.

Jones, K.B., & Jonasdottir, A.G. (1988). Introduction: Gender as an analytic category in political theory. In K.B. Jones & A.G. Jonasdottir (Eds.), *The political interests of gender* (pp. 1–10). London: Sage.

Joseph, T. (1985, Winter). The women are coming, the women are coming: Results of a survey. *Public Relations Quarterly*, 21–22.

Kant, I. (1974). *On the old saw: That may be right in theory but it won't work in practice* (E.B. Ashton, Trans.). Philadelphia: University of Pennsylvania Press.

Kern-Foxworth, M. (1989, August). Minorities 2000: The shape of things to come. *Public Relations Journal*, 14–22.

Kolodny, A. (1988, Fall). Dancing between the left and right: Feminism and the academic minefield in the 1980s. *Feminist Studies*, 14(3), 453–466.

Kruckeberg, D., & Starck, K. (1988). *Public relations and community: A reconstructed theory*. New York: Praeger.

Kupperman, J.J. (1978). *Philosophy: The fundamental problems*. New York: St. Martin's.

Lange, L. (1983). Woman is not a rational animal: On Aristotle's biology of reproduction. In S. Harding & M.B. Hintikka (Eds.), *Discovering reality: Feminist perspectives on epistemology, metaphysics, methodology, and philosophy of science* (pp. 1–16). Dordrecht, Holland: D. Reidel.

Larrabee, H.A. (1928). *What philosophy is*. New York: Macy-Masius. The Vanguard Press.

Lerner, G. (1975). Placing women in history: Definitions and challenges. *Feminist Studies*, 3, 5–14.

Loden, M. (1986). Feminine leadership: It can make your business more profitable. *Vital Speeches of the Day*, 52(15), 472–475.

MacLead, W.J. (1959). *Contagious ideas and dynamic events*. Berea, OH: Baldwin-Wallace College.

Marcil-Lacoste, L. (1983). The trivialization of the notion of equality. In S. Harding & M.B. Hintikka (Eds.), *Discovering reality: Feminist perspectives on epistemology, metaphysics, methodology, and philosophy of science* (pp. 121–138). Dordrecht, Holland: D. Reidel.

Martin, C.J. (1988). The case of the lost ethic: Making moral decisions. *Journalism Educator*, 44, 11–14.

Martin, M. (1973–1974). Preferential hiring and tenuring of women teachers in the university. *Philosophical Forum*, 5(1–2), 325–33.

Mautz, R.K., & Sharaf, H.A. (1982). *The philosophy of auditing*. American Accounting Assn. Monograph 6.

McKechnie, P. (1989, August). Caring about quality. *Public Relations Journal*, p. 5.

Merrill, J.C., & Odell, S.J. (1983). *Philosophy and journalism*. New York: Longman.

Opportunity & critical area for public relations guidance. (1989, May 15). *pr reporter*, pp. 1–2.

Parsons, K.P. (1973). Nietzsche and moral change. In R. Solomon (Ed.), *Nietzsche: A collection of critical essays*. New York: Doubleday Anchor.

Pearson, R. (1988, May). *Beyond ethical relativism in public relations: Coorientation, rules and the idea of communication symmetry*. Paper presented to the Public Relations Interest Group, International Communication Association, New Orleans, LA.

Pearson, R. (1989). Albert J. Sullivan's theory of public relations ethics. *Public Relations Review*, 15(2), 52–62.

Phenix, P.H. (1958). *Philosophy of education*. New York: Henry Holt.

Pierce, C. (1975, Winter). Philosophy. *Signs: Journal of Women in Culture and Society*, 1(2), 487–503.

Pratt, C.A., & Rentner, T.L. (1988, October). *Public relations ethics as a measure of excellence: The limitations of selected educational offerings for students, educators, and practitioners*. Paper presented to the Public Relations Society of America, Cincinnati, OH.

Pratt, C.A., & Rentner, T.L. (1989, Spring). What's really being taught about ethical behavior? *Public Relations Review*, 15(1), 53–66.

PR opportunities of the future will involve ability to help management. (1989, Sept. 18). *pr reporter*, pp. 1–2.

Rakow, L.F. (1989, May). *From the feminization of public relations to the promise of feminism*. Paper presented to the Public Relations Interest Group, International Communication Association, San Francisco, CA.

Rand, A. (1971). *The new left: The anti-industrial revolution*. New York: New American Library.

Reinharz, S. (1985). Feminist distrust: Problems of context and content in sociological work. In D. Berg & K. Smith (Eds.), *Exploring clinical methods for social research* (pp. 63–84). New York: Wiley.

Religion in the workplace may be a dangerous hidden agenda. (1989, Feb. 20). *pr reporter*, pp. 1–3.

Richardson, J. (1989, August). Off the wall. *Bison Briefs 2, 29*(2), 28.

Runes, D.D. (Ed.). (n.d.). *Dictionary of philosophy*. New York: Philosophical Library.

Russell, B. (1952). Preface. In H. Poincare, *Science and method* (pp. 5–6). New York: Charles Scribner's Sons.

Ryan, M., & Martinson, D.L. (1984). Ethical values, the flow of journalistic information and public relations persons. *Journalism Quarterly, 61*, 27–34.

Sherwin, S. (1988). Philosophical methodology and feminist methodology: Are they incompatible? In L. Code, S. Mullett, & C. Overall (Eds.), *Feminist perspectives: Philosophical essays on method and morals* (pp. 13–28). Toronto: University of Toronto Press.

Steinem, G. (1971, August 26). A new egalitarian life style. *New York Times*, p. A15.

Stumped by an ethics problem? (1989, April 3). *pr reporter*, pp. 3–4.

Sullivan, A.J. (1965). Toward a philosophy of public relations: Images. In O. Lerbinger & A. Sullivan (Eds.), *Information, influence and communication: A reader in public relations* (pp. 240–249). New York: Basic.

Thompson, J. (1973). Preferential hiring. *Philosophy and Public Affairs, 2*(4), 364–384.

Thornton Dill, B. (1989, September 20). *Gender and race*. Speech presented to the Faculty Study Group Polyseminar Series, University of Maryland, College Park, MD.

Toxic trauma unites public opinion in push for new ethic. (1989, April 17). *pr reporter*, pp. 1–3.

Turk, J.V. (1986). Information subsidies and media content: A study of public relations influence on the news. *Journalism Monographs* No. 100.

Webster's Ninth New Collegiate Dictionary. (1983). Springfield, MA: Merriam-Webster.

Weil, S. (1970). London notebook. (R. Rees Trans. Ed.). *First and last notebooks*. London: Oxford University Press.

White, L.A. (1959). *The evolution of culture*. New York: McGraw-Hill.

Wiener, N. (1948). *Cybernetics*. New York: Wiley.

Yelsma, P., & Brown, C.T. (1985). Gender roles, biological sex, and predisposition to conflict management. *Sex Roles, 12*(7–88), 731–747.

Crisis Management and the "Paradigm Case"

DAVID M. BERG
STEPHEN ROBB
Purdue University

As organizational crises go, it did not seem to amount to much. No one died; no one was injured; the environment wasn't threatened; there wasn't even a scandal. But Judge Kenneth Gills of the Illinois Circuit Court ruled that an estimated 20,000 people were entitled to seek relief in a class-action lawsuit against Kraft USA.

The problem originated from what was to have been the routine test marketing of a promotional contest called "Ready to Roll." On Sunday, June 12, 1989, fliers announcing the contest were distributed with 13 newspapers in the Chicago and Houston markets. The idea was that participants could win prizes by matching game pieces printed in the fliers with those enclosed in specially marked packages of Kraft cheese slices. The promotion was planned to produce winners of one grand prize—a $17,000, 1990 Dodge Caravan van; 100 Roadmaster bicycles; 500 Leapfrog skateboards; and 8,000 packages of Kraft cheese.

On Monday morning, the day following the contest's announcement, the switchboard at Kraft corporate headquarters in Glenview, Illinois, was swamped with calls from people claiming to have won the van. The company responded by immediately cancelling the contest and ordering that the specially marked packages of cheese be removed from store shelves. Corporate spokesperson, Kathy Knuth, in announcing the decision, added that the contest had been invalidated by a printing error that was not Kraft's fault. Winners were told that the company, nevertheless, wanted to be fair and that matching game pieces should be mailed to H. Olson and Company, the firm's contest administrator, at a post office box in Libertyville, Illinois.

The printing error that so radically altered the contest's odds was, apparently, the responsibility of Product Movers, Inc., a division of News America Publishing Company. The consequences, just in the few hours the contest ran before being cancelled, was that about 20,000 game pieces matched, rather than the 8,600 that had originally been planned. Furthermore, over 10,000 people laid claim to the Dodge van.

On Thursday, June 15, four days after voiding the contest, Kraft presented its proposal for compensating those participants who had mailed in their matching game pieces. To begin with, everyone would receive some money, but the amount would vary, depending on which of the prizes their game pieces identified. Thus, a van match was worth $250, bicycles brought $50, skateboards went for $25, and cheese was good for $5. In addition, Kraft would conduct a drawing from among each prize pool to determine who won the various premiums, which had now been quadrupled—4 vans, 400 bicycles, 1,000 skateboards, and 32,000 packages of cheese.

A routine test market promotion, originally budgeted at under $100,000, was now going to cost Kraft about $3 million. But that was before Judge Gills' ruling that contest "winners" were entitled to press their grievances in a class-action lawsuit. From Kraft's perspective, a worst-case scenario would be a court decision that all contest winners are entitled to their prizes, regardless of the fact that the promotion was flawed by a printing error in the contest fliers. If, as reported, the number of van winners totaled about 10,000, the cost to Kraft could exceed $170 million.

LESSONS FROM THE KRAFT CASE

By almost any standard, $170 million is a lot of money. It is certainly enough to ensure Kraft's vigorous resistance to the class-action law suits filed against it. Even the escalation in costs from the $100,000 budgeted to the $3 million of the appeasement package must have come as a nasty shock to Kraft management. Still, whether or not the situation deserves to be called a "corporate crisis" remains problematic. Regardless of the final resolution, the cost is likely to be relatively insignificant when compared with Kraft General Foods 1989 expenditure of $760 million on promotions and $940 million on advertising (Gannett News Service, January 21, 1990). Whatever one calls it, however, the failed Kraft cheese promotion clearly is not in the same category, for example, as the leak of methyl isocyanate gas, on December 3, 1984, from Union Carbide's plant in Bhopal, India, which killed over 2,000 people and injured tens of thousands more. Kraft's problems also pale when compared to those faced by Exxon when its tanker Valdez ran aground, on March 24, 1989, and polluted nearly 1,000 miles of pristine Alaskan coastline. Within the range of corporate crises, therefore, it is probably fair to conclude that Kraft's cheese-promotion-gone-wrong was a pretty trivial affair.

The Advantages of Triviality

As a starting point for an inquiry into the nature of crisis management, however, the relative triviality of the Kraft case is a decided asset. Although Burton Weinstain, attorney for those suing Kraft, charged the company with "taking advantage of that great American obsession with gambling to sell cheese" ("Judge allows suit," 1989, p. D1), it strikes us that those of normal social sensitivity will find the Kraft case virtually devoid of moral or ethical implications. Relieved, therefore, of the need in this instance to factor in larger issues of corporate social responsibility, the student of crisis management should be able to focus, without reservation, on a key question: What should Kraft have done in this case to best serve its own corporate interests?

What the Experts Said

Although the question could be approached in a number of ways, *Chicago Tribune* reporter Shawn Pogatchink has provided us with a ready-made point of entry. On Friday, June 16, the day after Kraft unveiled its plan for compensating contest participants, Pogatchink contacted public relations practitioners in the Chicago area for their reactions to Kraft's handling of the situation. Their evaluations were detailed in the June 18 edition of the *Tribune* (Pogatchink, 1989, pp. 7–1 & 6).

The five crisis management experts cited by Pogatchink were unanimous in their disapproval of Kraft's performance. In their judgment, Kraft did not talk early enough, did not say enough when it did talk, and used the wrong people to do the talking. According to Ted Pincus, Chairman of the Financial Relations Board, "a delay is going to hurt the company, not help it. If you stand still until they collect all the facts, it's too late. It's a matter of showing you can stand up, be honest and open, and take the heat" (Pogatchink, 1989, p. 7–6). Pat Jackson, editor of *pr reporter*, a trade industry newsletter, agreed with Pincus: "When Kraft ducks under the covers, it immediately sends the message, 'they are lying.' . . . Facts have nothing to do with getting people on your side. It's all a matter of perception" (Pogatchink, 1989, p. 7–1).

What Kraft should have done immediately upon having discovered a problem, according to the PR experts, was to "hold a press conference, set up and promote a special bank of telephones to answer consumers' questions and designate key executives to make public statements" (Pogatchink, 1989,

p. 7–1). In contrast, Kraft relied on a single spokesperson, Kathy Knuth, from its public relations department. On Monday, when a problem with the contest became apparent, Knuth issued a statement to the press that included four basic elements: The contest was cancelled because of an error in the printing of the newspaper fliers; the printing error was outside of the company's immediate area of responsibility; Kraft, in spite of the fact it was not at fault, would try to be fair to contest participants; participants should mail their game pieces to the contest's coordinator. Apparently, there was no further public statement from Kraft until Thursday, when the compensation plan was announced.

The brevity of the Monday statement, combined with the lack of comment on Tuesday and Wednesday, was construed by the crisis management specialists as "stonewalling." Even though the problem was not complex and the relatively few relevant facts had seemingly been conveyed to the public in a timely fashion, the specialists felt that Kraft did not communicate an image of truthfulness. As Walter Mulhall, co-director of the Mulhall-Kemplin Company, put it, "the way to handle things right is to offer a lot of explanation and candor, and they're certainly not being candid" (p. 7–1). Pat Jackson concurred, saying that "Kraft should have gone majorly public. If they had carried it off with humility, they could have gotten the public on their side" (p. 7–1).

In the opinion of the *Tribune's* panel of experts, in order to have successfully diffused the situation, Kraft would not only have had to communicate immediately, fully, and contritely, but the message would have had to come from the very top of the company. In the words of Ted Pincus:

> candor by the top executive often is the key element in defusing a crisis. . . . A CEO himself has to have the guts to come out and exert some authority, not hide behind the statements of his PR director. . . . Kraft should have had a press conference the first day involving Chairman and Chief Operating Officer John M. Richman. (p. 7–6)

USING PARADIGM CASES

Kraft's responses to its problems with the promotional contest, and the PR expert's criticism of Kraft's handling of those problems, combine to suggest a number of possibilities for further inquiry. Among them, and perhaps the most significant, is an issue suggested by reporter Pogatchink's observation that "in discussing 'crisis PR,' experts usually trot out as examples Exxon Corp. and the Valdez, Alaska, oil spill; Johnson & Johnson and the cyanide-lacing of some Tylenol capsules; and Chrysler Corp. and the disconnected car odometers" (p. 7–6). Although, at the time this chapter was being written, the final consequences of the oil spill (March 24, 1989) for the Exxon

Corporation were not even close to being realized, the case had become, in the minds of the experts, a paradigm for how not to handle a corporate crisis. Thus, "Pincus noted, Exxon executives laid low after the spill, the same mistake Kraft is making." In contrast, "he cited Lee Iacocca's media-savvy reaction to a Chrysler Corp. crisis in 1987 . . . as 'a classic case of how to defuse a crisis' " (p. 7–6). The PR panel conferred similar exemplar status on the Tylenol situation. " 'How Johnson & Johnson handled Tylenol was superb,' " Mulhall said. 'Its really a case study in the right kind of PR.' The mythic qualities which the Tylenol case has assumed for public relations practitioners was further reinforced by *Time* magazine which, in its decade-ending review of American business during the eighties, called it the "Most Applauded Corporate Response to a Disaster." The company's "frank, decisive responses," according to *Time*, "won back customer loyalty, and is now a textbook case in public relations" ("Most applauded corporate response," 1990, p. 81).

Although we would be among the last to challenge the value of historical lessons, we do suggest that those interested in crisis management should concern themselves both with the accuracy of the evidence from which these lessons are drawn and with the appropriateness of applying them in any given case. With these objectives in mind, therefore, we now turn to an examination of the two most frequently cited examples of how effective crisis management should be conducted: Johnson & Johnson's handling of the Tylenol poisonings and Chryler's approach to problems related to its odometer disconnections.

THE TYLENOL CASE

Johnson & Johnson is the corporate parent of McNeil Consumer Products, the company that manufactures Tylenol. Its problems became public Friday, October 1, 1982, when Chicago area newspapers reported in front-page stories that within the past 2 days, three deaths in suburban Cook County, plus two deaths and one critical illness in adjacent DuPage County, had very likely been caused by "cyanide-filled capsules of Extra-Strength Tylenol" (Houston & Griffin, 1982, p. 1–1). On Saturday, with the death of the critically ill victim and the discovery of another body, the *Chicago Tribune's* headline proclaimed "Stewardess is 7th capsule poison victim."

It took only 1 day for the story to become national news. By October 2, deaths of suspicious origin were being reported throughout the country and poison centers were deluged with calls, but no further links to Tylenol were established. Then, 4 days later, on October 6, a man in Oroville, California, was poisoned with strychnine-contaminated Tylenol capsules. The next day (Thursday), police in Philadelphia established poisoned Tylenol as the cause of a death that had occurred in April. Saturday, reports from Sheridan,

Wyoming, also indicated a possible connection between Tylenol and the earlier cyanide poisoning death of a young man. The *New York Times* observed: "Ramifications of the poisonings and the fear they have caused in many people continues nationwide. Rumors in various cities linked many mysterious deaths to cyanide from Tylenol capsules, at least until tests prove negative" ("Cyanide is discovered," 1982, p. B–12).

Johnson & Johnson, to all appearances, was in deep trouble. On October 8, the *New York Times* ran a long story assessing the damage: "It is a challenge that marketing people hope they never have to face—restoring the image of a product linked in the public mind with death. But that is the sizable—and some say hopeless—task that now confronts the marketing team for Tylenol" (Kleinfeld, 1982 p. D–1). Later, the article cited ad agency chairman Jerry Della Femina's opinion that "you will not see the name Tylenol in any form within a year. . . . I don't think they can ever sell another product under that name" (Kleinfeld, 1982, p. Q–1).

A tainted product image, however, was not the only problem facing Johnson & Johnson. Between September 28 and October 6, the company's stock fell from 47 ⅛ to 38 points, and the *Wall Street Journal* reported that "analysts were growing increasingly pessimistic about Johnson & Johnson's ability to recover from the unfolding events" ("Tylenol containing strychine," 1982, p. 28). Additionally, after published reports linked Tylenol to poisoning deaths in places other than Chicago, the company announced that it was recalling all capsule forms of the product. The estimated 22 million bottles, with a retail value of $79 million, would be destroyed (Waldhole & Kneale, 1982, p. 1). Total costs to Johnson & Johnson, not counting any judgments from wrongful death lawsuits, could reach $600 million, according to *Newsweek* magazine (Beck, Monroe, Sandza, & Shapiro, 1982, p. 41). But there were lawsuits, too. By October 6, three had already been filed. The widow of Adam James, one of the first victims, sought $15 million, while the fathers of Stanley Jones and his wife, Theresa, asked for $10 million. A third suit sought damages for all those required to surrender or dispose of their Tylenol products because of the deaths.

Led by its chairman, James E. Burke, Johnson & Johnson responded quickly to events related to the poisonings. Within an hour after learning of the first deaths on Thursday morning, a team comprised of medical, public relations, and security experts began to assemble at the Fort Washington, Pennsylvania, headquarters of Tylenol's manufacturer, McNeil Consumer Products. Heading the group was McNeil chairman, David E. Collins. Before the end of the day on Thursday, the company had (a) withdrawn 4.7 million capsules of Extra-Strength Tylenol from the lot number associated with the first deaths; (b) notified the U.S. Food and Drug Administration; (c) sent almost a half million mailgrams to doctors, hospitals, and distributors; (d) dispatched scientific, security, and public relations personnel to Chicago by corporate jet to work with authorities and establish a laboratory (staffed by thirty toxologists) to test suspect capsules; and (e) placed 500 salespersons from other divisions of the company on alert to assist in the removal of recalled capsules.

At about the same time, according to *Newsweek*, chairman Burke began "around-the-clock strategy sessions with top aides to control the damage" (Beck et al., 1982, p. 41). Toward that end, he had recruited 25 public relations specialists from other Johnson & Johnson Companies to work with the regular corporate headquarter's staff of 15. The group's first decision, according to vice president for communication Lawrence G. Foster, was "to answer every single press inquiry." To make sure it happened, Foster "stayed at headquarters all night Thursday responding to reporters from as far away as Anchorage, Alaska" (Waldhole, 1982, p. 16). By Friday evening, the company had "halted all commercials for Tylenol and production in one of its two plants. It also posted," the *Wall Street Journal* reported, "a $100,000 reward for information leading to the arrest of whoever was responsible" (Waldhole, 1982 p. 16). In addition, Johnson & Johnson promised to reimburse any merchant or customer for Tylenol returned to the company. When Burke met with reporters on Sunday, he said that his group's focus had been on " 'ending the deaths, finding the perpetrator and solving the problem.' Though he conceded there was concern about damage being done to the Tylenol name, he adamantly maintained, 'we've had no time to even think about reestablishing the brand' " (Waldhole, 1981, p. 16).

By Thursday, October 7, Johnson & Johnson acknowledged that the original damage control group at corporate headquarters had evolved into three task forces working on an "image rescue project." One of the task forces, concentrating on employee morale, had already produced an hour-long videotape from news reports and the comments of company officials. Chairman Burke, in his taped message, informed his employees that "people just don't blame us. They feel we are being victimized just like everyone else." The tape was shown on October 7 on the company's worldwide employees' TV network.

In addition to addressing the problem of employee morale, the task force also proposed, on Thursday, October 7, a three-part program for restoring the Tylenol image. First, it would shift from capsules to tablets. Capsules had something of a medical mystique about them, but tablets were far more tamper resistant. A program whereby consumers could exchange full or partially used bottles of capsules for new bottles of tablets was announced that very day. Second, the company would adopt some appropriate form of tamper-proof packaging. Because the technology for several options was already available, implementation would take little time. Third, J & J would resume advertising with redesigned ads. Questioned by a reporter for the *Wall Street Journal* as to the appropriate time for Tylenol to resume advertising, Arthur Rosen of the medically oriented advertising agency of Sadlar & Hennessey, offered his advice: "You hold back until you've created a new package, and then you advertise your product and package together. You wait until the issue has been resolved satisfactorily in everyone's eyes. Even then the ads should totally ignore the cyanide tragedy" (Waldhole & Kneale, 1982, p. 17).

Because Tylenol rather quickly regained its pre-crisis, 37% share of the American pain-reliever market, Johnson & Johnson's approach to crisis management, including the just described image rescue project, was quickly judged by most commentators as an unqualified success. The *Wall Street Journal* pronounced something of a benediction on the whole affair as early as October 18 when it editorialized: "Johnson & Johnson, the parent of the company that makes Tylenol, set the pattern of industry response" ("The tylenol trouble," 1982, p. 34).

The canonization of Johnson & Johnson's crisis management efforts during the cyanide poisonings seems to rest on two assumptions: first, that the problems involved were virtually insurmountable; second, that the company was able to prevail against such overwhelming odds because of its total candor and its willingness to subordinate company interests to those of the general public. Both assumptions, we think, warrant careful examination.

As a product, Tylenol had nothing to do with anyone's death. This fact immediately distinguishes it from other highly publicized cases of product liability such as Thalidomide, a sedative that during the early 1960s was found responsible for birth defects; Oraflex, Eli Lilly's arthritis remedy that was permanently withdrawn from the market after being linked to several deaths; Bon Vivant, which went out of business after its canned vichyssoise was found to contain botulism; and Rely tampons, which Proctor and Gamble stopped manufacturing after toxic shock deaths were attributed to it.

Perhaps even more important than Tylenol's blamelessness in the poisonings was the fact that it was never even suggested that the product might be at fault. A publicized charge of liability, even if unfounded, can impose on a company a substantial burden of proof—one that it, ordinarily, cannot afford to ignore. Johnson & Johnson faced no such problem. From the very outset, the deaths were repeatedly referred to as the work of a madman. Quoted on the front page of the *Chicago Tribune*, Police Sergeant John Millner said, "We're investigating it as a homicide simply because someone had to be crazy enough to do that"; the Winfield Chief of Police called it the work of "a very sophisticated, very malicious person"; the Cook County Medical Examiner confirmed that "the capsules were tampered with after leaving the manufacturer's plant" (Houston & Griffin, 1982).

Not only was Johnson & Johnson not required to defend itself and its product concerning responsibility for the poisoning deaths, the company became, for many, an object of sympathy. Corporate Chairman, James E. Burke was absolutely correct, therefore, when he reported to his employees that the public perceived Johnson & Johnson as one of the victims of the tragedy.

The conventional wisdom of public relations dictates that a company and its product should, insofar as possible, be disassociated from bad news. After an airline crash, for example, company logos still visible on the wreckage should be obscured, flight numbers should be changed, and advertising should be discontinued. The same conventional wisdom, applied conversely, leads to the conclusion that when a product *is* widely associated with bad news, the product will, inevitably, suffer. It was just such logic that led N.R. Kleinfeld, writing in the *New York Times* on October 8, 1982, to conclude concerning Tylenol:

> But now, of course, the drug's image has been devastated by the tracing of seven deaths to cyanide-laced Extra-Strength Tylenol capsules. . . .
> A brand name that was systematically built up as a pain reliever at a cost of many millions of dollars has taken on an entirely new—and deadly—meaning in the language. . . . Marketing experts concur that, at best, it will take months to alter the new perception. And some feel that the new perception can never be changed. (p. D1)

There is, of course, no question that the story was both widely publicized and that the Tylenol name was conspicuously present. The editors of the *Wall Street Journal,* in fact, noted that one television network gave the incident more coverage than any story since the Vietnam War and that, as a result of such coverage, 85% of the American public became aware of the event.

Contrary to conventional wisdom, however, in this case high levels of publicity actually worked to Tylenol's advantage. First, it helped to eliminate any sense of vagueness or uncertainty the public might have had about a causal relationship between the product and the deaths. News content, whether focused on the manhunt for a deranged perpetrator or on Johnson & Johnson's activities, consistently reinforced the conclusion that Tylenol did not cause the deaths. It certainly was not to the company's advantage that its product was tampered with, but once the event became newsworthy it was to Johnson & Johnson's advantage that public perception of its product's role be clear rather than vague. Heavy coverage of the event, therefore, worked to reduce ambiguity and, in so doing, helped to disassociate Tylenol from the poisonings.

Heavy publicity also worked to Johnson & Johnson's advantage by diverting attention from the one area where the company was potentially vulnerable—its failure to utilize more tamper-resistant packaging. Whether widespread news coverage contributed to the problem by stimulating "copy-cat" responses, or simply exposed the problem by increasing public aware-ness, a variety of product tampering cases began to be reported throughout the country. Within a week of the first deaths, a Chicago market research firm, Leo Shapiro & Associates, concluded from a national survey it had conducted that "people are expressing suspicion of all food and drug prod-ucts; shoppers are exercising more discretion in buying; they think if it happened to one product it could happen to another" ("Tylenol containing strychine," 1982, p. 2). On October 8, two days after publishing the Shapiro report, the *Journal* concluded, "many people are concerned more about what the poisonings mean for society as a whole than about assigning blame to any special product or company" (Waldhole & Kneale, 1982, p. 1).

Given the rapidly growing public anxiety over product vulnerability to tampering, it was predictable that both government and the pharmaceutical industry would be quick to respond. Although Chicago Mayor, Jane Byrne, was the first to act when she announced, on Saturday, October 2, her intention to introduce legislation requiring seals on all medicines sold in the city, just 2 days later the Proprietary Association, a trade organization of drug manufacturers, and the U. S. Food and Drug Administration made public the formation of a Joint Committee on Product Safety. On the same day as the announcement, FDA Commissioner Hayes appeared on ABC-TV "Good Morning America" to talk about more secure packaging, while his Deputy Commissioner discussed the issue on NBC-TV "Today."

On October 15, only 10 days following the announcement of its formation, the Joint Committee on Product Safety presented its completed proposal to the FDA. Johnson & Johnson's vulnerability to charges of neglect already minimized by industry and government acceptance of responsibility, the company's hand was further strengthened by the Joint Committee's identi-fication of 11 packaging options from which manufacturers could choose. Technology for the implementation of most, if not all, of these options was both readily available and affordable. To the extent that the need for better packaging methods posed an obstacle to Tylenol's comeback, therefore, the solution was at hand. There need be no delay while waiting for research and development to devise a better way.

What happened to Tylenol was, without question, highly undesirable for Johnson & Johnson. Upon close examination, however, it is equally evident that the situation, contrary to popular belief, did not constitute a formidable public relations problem. First, the company neither had to defend its product nor accept responsibility for any wrong doing. Quite the opposite, it became the object of some public sympathy. Second, the issue of tamper-resistant packaging—where Johnson & Johnson was potentially vulner-able—was diffused by circumstances that led to a generalized public concern for product safety. As a consequence, government and industry were prompted to assume joint responsibility. Finally, the ready availability of alternative packaging technologies allowed the company to quickly adopt a means for circumventing future problems. This, in turn, became the obvious basis for new marketing strategies.

A second aspect of the myth that has come to surround Johnson & Johnson's handling of the Tylenol poisonings is that the company's actions constituted a public relations *tour de force.* Allowing for the fact that it may be difficult to display great skill in the face of a modest challenge, a detailed analysis of events reveals that there was little extraordinary about Johnson & Johnson's public relations efforts in the Tylenol case.

Those perpetuating the myth often point to the company's decisive and selfless action in removing Tylenol from retail outlets after the tampering was discovered. This, for example, was precisely the focus of the *Wall Street Journal's* editorial commendation of Johnson & Johnson:

> Without being asked, it quickly withdraw Extra-Strength Tylenol from the market at a very considerable expense. Given the circumstances that now appear to be emerging from police investigations, all suggesting that the tampering was on a very small scale—this may not have been necessary. But the company choose to take a large loss rather than expose anyone to further risk. ("The tylenol trouble," 1982, p. 34)

An examination of the evidence indicates, contrary to the *Journals* assertion, that Johnson & Johnson had very little choice in the matter of withdrawing Tylenol from the market. Furthermore, to the limited extent that it was able to exercise its own discretion, it lagged behind others who were in a position to remove the product from store shelves. Although it is impossible to determine the precise order of events on Thursday, September 30, the day when the link between Tylenol and the cyanide poisonings was definitely established, it is clear that Johnson & Johnson's response was as limited as the circumstances would allow. While the FDA issued a national warning against taking any form of Tylenol, while the Jewel Company suspended sales of all Tylenol products from its approximately 200 stores, and while Walgreen withdrew all 50-capsule bottles of Extra-Strength Tylenol from all of its 1,875 stores, Johnson & Johnson withdrew only those Extra-Strength Tylenol capsules from the lot number implicated in the three deaths from Cook County. When asked about a second lot number that had been associated with two other deaths, a spokesman for McNeil said that the company "wouldn't make a decision on extending the voluntary withdrawal of its product to additional lot numbers until there is 'more definitive information' about the capsules consumed by the DuPage woman" ("Houston & Griffin," 1982, p. 2–2).

The following day, Friday, Johnson & Johnson expanded its recall to include the second lot number, but by then many stores throughout the country were, on their own initiative, removing Tylenol products from their shelves, sometimes including liquid and tablet versions along with the capsules. Saturday night, shortly after midnight, Chicago Mayor Jane Byrne called a press conference to announce that she had ordered police and health officers to remove all Tylenol products from all city stores. By 6 p.m. Sunday, all Tylenol had been removed from over 2,000 stores in the city. McNeil Consumer Industries, however, objected to extending the recall beyond Extra-Strength capsules, the only type found contaminated. McNeil's attorney, Paul Noland, further responded to the city's action by limiting his company's previous offer of help with the investigation to the testing of Extra-Strength capsules, and then only at McNeil's own laboratory (Waldhole, 1982, p. 3).

On Monday, October 4, a spokesman for Johnson & Johnson announced that the company had stopped the manufacturer and shipment of Tylenol capsules nationwide. By Tuesday the company said that, "as one of many alternatives," it was considering recalling all capsules to repackage them. Wednesday, after learning of the California strychnine contamination incident, the company asked retailers nationwide to discontinue the sale of all Tylenol capsules. Finally, on Thursday, Johnson & Johnson said that it would destroy the capsules from its nationwide recall.

Johnson & Johnson's incremental approach to the recall, in addition to suggesting a somewhat grudging attitude, also reflected confusion concerning the image management of its product. Reacting to the company's early decision to remove some Tylenol from store shelves, market researcher Leo Shapiro commented that

> such actions help minimize reputational damage. The thing is to stop the consumer from seeing it on the shelf and having to make a decision whether to buy it. . . . If people have a great deal of time to worry about whether they should buy the product on the shelf, the damage will be long term ("Johnson and Johnson pulls tylenol," 1982, p. 2)

It is not clear whether Johnson & Johnson did not subscribe to Shapiro's theory, discounted the threat to reputational damage, or simply was unable at the time to organize a coherent response. What is clear, however, is that by extending the withdrawal of its product over several days, it gave consumers the opportunity to make a considered judgment against buying Tylenol. Under the circumstances, there is some irony in J & J's later decision to exclude the company name from its offer to exchange full or partially used containers of Tylenol capsules for a comparable number of tablets. On October 12, at a cost of $1.5 million, Johnson & Johnson announced details of the exchange program in full-page newspaper advertisements run in 300 markets. The ads, however, "never refer to Johnson & Johnson, choosing instead to refer only to 'the makers of Tylenol.' Marketing experts watching the case had warned of possible adverse affect on other Johnson & Johnson products as more people became aware that Johnson & Johnson makes Tylenol" (Kneale, 1982, p. 56).

By all accounts, Johnson & Johnson, in 1982, was a very successful and very well-managed company. Its performance during the cyanide poisonings displayed a level of general competence one would expect from an organization of its stature. Despite uncertainties concerning the cause and scope of the poisonings, however, the case did not pose nearly the public relations challenge that it is generally assumed to have. Furthermore, given the initiative taken by government and various retail organizations, the company very often did not have a great deal of latitude in its decision making. Finally, the decisions that were made by the company do not reflect the levels of wisdom, candor, and selflessness which have often been attributed to them. The case is certainly one that those interested in crisis management should study. It is not one, however, that establishes a standard of excellence by which all other crisis management efforts can be evaluated.

THE CHRYSLER CASE

In vivid contrast to the crisis facing Johnson & Johnson in 1982, the cause and scope of Chrysler's problems in 1987 were apparent from the outset. Even more important, whereas J & J was the innocent victim of a crime, Chrysler was charged with committing one. On Wednesday, June 24, 1987, a federal grand jury in St. Louis formally charged the Chrysler Motor Corporation and two of its top executives with 16 counts of conspiracy to commit fraud. According to the U. S. Department of Justice, Chrysler had for many years disconnected the odometers of vehicles while executives test drove them distances ranging up to 400 miles. These cars were later sold as new. Furthermore, when vehicles were damaged during the testing period, they were repaired—sometimes only cosmetically—and also sold as new.

Unlike the Tylenol case, which received immediate and massive news coverage, both nationally and internationally, Chrysler's problems received virtually no coverage of any kind until formal criminal indictments were actually handed down by the grand jury. Even then, with just a few exceptions, it was not considered headline news. The *New York Times*, for example, reported the story on page 42, three days after the indictments were made public.

In terms of a public response, nothing was heard from Chrysler until after the company and its two executives were indicted on June 24, 1987. Then, in a prepared statement, company spokesperson Baron Bates denied that Chrysler or any of its employees had done anything either illegal or improper, and contended that the maximum $120 million fine was "an outrage, bore no relationship to the alleged problem, and would be vigorously contested" (Pasztor &. Naj, 1987, p. 3). Bates conceded that Chrysler had disconnected odometers during testing, but he argued that "the aim was to avoid reducing the warranty protection of customers" ("Dear Chrysler," 1987, p. 21).

It wasn't until July 1, nearly 9 months after learning of the investigation and 1 full week following the indictments against his company, that Chrysler Chairman Lee Iacocca himself finally spoke out. Although a casual observer might conclude that Iacocca, during his press conference, repudiated the company's earlier claims that it had done nothing either illegal or improper, the fact is he did not. Some of his argument was implicit, but it was always clear: the customer had not been harmed; the testing program was good; of the many cars tested, only "a tiny fraction were driven more than 40 miles"; only "a tiny fraction were damaged."

By the time he finished redefining the issues, what Iacocca actually confessed to was a lapse in judgment. It wasn't criminal, it wasn't improper, it wasn't intentional. Its significance lay only in the fact that it allowed the public to draw an unwarranted conclusion about the company. To the extent that anyone suffered, it was the company itself. He offered a very large apology for a very small indiscretion. Furthermore, in his assumption of responsibility, as was made clear both before and during the press conference, he was taking the blame for something he did not know about. Once he had been informed, he said, the practice of disconnecting odometers was discontinued. Iacocca's rhetorical strategy, therefore, allowed him to accept responsibility for corporate mistakes, however benign, without assuming personal guilt.

Whether or not it was causal, stories about the odometer incident virtually disappeared from the media 2 days after the press conference. Labor conflict, plant closings, and OSHA violations, however, provided Chrysler more than ample opportunity to deal with bad publicity on a continuing basis. Meanwhile, without press attention, negotiations continued in relationship to both the criminal charges and the dozen or so civil suits that resulted from the testing program. Finally, during mid-December, in brief, inside stories, newspapers noted that a settlement had been reached. In addition to its original offer, Chrysler would pay at least $500 to current owners of every vehicle that could be identified. Approximately 39,500 vehicles were involved and the cost was expected to exceed $20 million. As part of a package that included the dropping of charges against its two executives, Chrysler also agreed to a plea of "no contest" to the criminal indictments, thereby incurring a fine that could reach as much as $120 million.

Although space limitations have precluded a detailed account of the Chrysler case, the foregoing overview does capture its essential character. In their important, substantive aspects, it would be difficult to find two instances of corporate crisis in greater contrast than those of Chrysler and Tylenol. Yet, in the degree to which their mythic qualities diverge from reality, the two cases are much alike. Whereas Johnson & Johnson has been idealized as overcoming nearly insurmountable difficulties through decisive, public-spirited, and selfless action, Chrysler has come to epitomize the value of the open acceptance of blame by a company's CEO as a means of overcoming public hostility.

Disregarding the fact that Chrysler's problems were precipitated by its own actions, its response to those problems provides no exemplar for corporate crisis management from either the perspective of propriety or effectiveness. First, the company was slow to act. The almost 9 months during which it was under investigation by the Justice Department constituted a conspicuous opportunity for Chrysler to take preemptive action. The company could easily have contacted the 39,500 individuals involved—an inconsequential number when compared to the size of most product recalls, construed the situation to its own best advantage, and offered some relatively inexpensive corrective. In so doing, it may also have been able to negotiate a settlement with the government that would have avoided a criminal indictment. Second, when it finally did act, Chrysler exacerbated rather than ameliorated the problem. As Len Keesler, president of LMK Communications, put it, "the incident should have been a 'one-day story,' but . . . Chrysler officials may have helped to make it into a bigger issue by denying they did anything wrong" (Pasztor & Naj, 1987, p. 21).

Third, Lee Iacocca's famous press conference was, very likely, unnecessary. In spite of Chrysler's inept handling of the situation, the case had generated relatively little news coverage before the press conference, and subsequent newspaper ad, created a new wave of publicity. Finally, Iacocca's performance was anything but a candid acceptance of responsibility for misdeeds. Exploiting the guise of candor, he denied any illegality while accepting corporate blame only for allowing the appearance of impropriety (even while maintaining his personal innocence). Iacocca's performance may have been a model of sophistry; it was not a model of contrition.

CONCLUSIONS

Neither the Tylenol nor the Chrysler case bore any significant similarity to the problems confronting Kraft in its promotional contest. There was, therefore, no justification for evaluating the quality of Kraft's crisis management on the basis of either of those situations. Based on an analysis of its own particular circumstances, a persuasive case can be made that, rather than not go far enough, Kraft went too far in its attempt to appease a relatively small group of opportunists who would not be satisfied by any action short of total capitulation.

More important than any conclusions about Kraft's situation, however, are the lessons that the Tylenol and Chrysler crises have to offer with regard to the general use of paradigm cases in either the development or the evaluation of crisis management strategies. The variables in any particular crisis situation are so numerous that no historic case is likely to be comparable to the point of providing an optimal response. Any paradigmatic approach to crisis management is, therefore, suspect. Furthermore, to the extent that the paradigm is constructed of incomplete or false information, as so often seems to be the case, the approach has no value at all. Worse than valueless, in fact, the idealized case creates an illusion of knowledge that may obscure the need for further inquiry.

Ideally, case histories of crisis management will be be approached from a generic perspective. "The genericist," as persuasion theorist Herbert W. Simons (1986) has pointed out, "looks at naturally occurring instances of persuasive discourse with a view toward formulating rules for discourse of that type" (p. 36). The approach requires both the detailed study of large numbers of cases and the accurate identification of the relevant variables of each case, "for the more finely turned one's comparison . . . the more likely one is to generalize reliably about which communication patterns are appropriate for these situations and which are not" (p. 37). The objective, of course, is to discover the most appropriate, not the most convenient, approaches to the management of organizational crises.

REFERENCES

Authorities say cyanide-laced Tylenol likely planted at individual stores. (1982, October 4). *Wall Street Journal*, p. 3.

Beck, M., Monroe, S., Sandza, R., & Shapiro, H. (1982, October 18). A superheadache. *Newsweek*, p. 41.

Cyanide is discovered in Tylenol in an April death in Philadelphia. (1982, October 7). *The New York Times*, pp. AI, B12.

Dear Chrysler: Outsiders' advice on handling the odometer change. (1987, June 26). *Wall Street Journal*, p. 21.

Gannett News Service. (1990, January 21). Adventures look for far-out venues to reach consumers. *Journal and Courier* (Lafayette, IN), p. 88.

Houston, J., & Griffin, J.L. (1982, October 1). 5 deaths tied to pills. *Chicago Tribune*, pp. 1–1, 2–2.

Johnson and Johnson pulls Tylenol lot from market in wake of 5 cyanide deaths. (1982, October 1). *Wall Street Journal*, p. 2.

Judge allows suit in Kraft contest. (1989, July 12). *Journal and Courier* (Lafayette, IN), p. D1.

Kleinfeld, N.R. (1982, October 8). Long, uphill odds for Tylenol. *The New York Times*, p. D1.

Kneale, D. (1982, October 13). Tylenol orders fall 25% but competitors lack enough products to fill market gap. *Wall Street Journal*, p. 56.

Pasztor, A., & Naj, A.K. (1987, June 25). U.S. charges Chrysler altered mileage on cars. *Wall Street Journal*, p. 3.

Pogatchink, S. (1989, June 18). Experts offer Kraft lesson in "crisis pr." *Chicago Tribune*, pp. 7–1, 6.

Simons, H.W. (1986). *Persuasion: Understanding, practice and analysis* (2nd ed.) New York: Random House.

Tylenol containing strychine is found in California as consumer fears mount. (1982, October 6). *Wall Street Journal*, pp. 2, 28.

The Tylenol trouble. (1982, October 18). *Wall Street Journal*, p. 34.

Waldhole, M. (1982, October 4). Johnson and Johnson officials take steps to end more killings linked to Tylenol. *Wall Street Journal*, p. 16.

Waldhole, M., & Kneale, D. (1982, October 8). Tylenol's maker tries to regain good image in wake of tragedy. *Wall Street Journal*, pp. 1, 17.

Perspectives on Public Relations History*

RON PEARSON
Mount Saint Vincent University

If all writing about the past is partly an effort to understand the present, a confusing and contradictory present would seem to call more insistently for historical analysis and explanation. This is particularly true for the profession and academic discipline of public relations. In spite of a consensus about the role of public relations in contemporary organizations—a consensus evident in the many definitions of public relations that stress its role as a management function—a long list of difficult questions about the profession remains. To what bodies of theory can public relations legitimately lay claim? Is there, or can there be, something called public relations theory? Is public relations a profession? Should the practice of public relations be regulated, licensed? What kind of education is required for the practice of public relations? Does the public relations curriculum belong in journalism departments, schools of business, schools of public affairs, or in a department all its own? To what set of values should public relations adhere? What makes the practice of public relations legitimate? In whose interest should public relations be practiced? What constitutes ethical public relations practice?

None of these questions is superficial. The fact that they have provoked discussion for most of public relations' history in the 20th century is part of the context within which any practitioner or scholar of public relations interrogates that history. The need to find answers is an important part of the historian's motivation. Burke (1957) suggested that all writers, including

---

*A version of this chapter appeared in Pearson (1990).

those who write history, write to work through personal problems. And Wise (1980) argued that a text of historical scholarship needs to be understood as a personal response on the part of its author to contemporary situational exigencies, just as the primary recorded texts of historical actors need to be understood as situationally conditioned. Similarly, Berkhofer (1969) emphasized that the situationally conditioned viewpoints of historical actors and historical scholars must be rigorously distinguished. Both the writer of history and the reader of historical texts must be careful to make this distinction.

When historical explanations differ, it is not merely because historians have access to different facts. There are no brute historical facts, only historians' interpretations of them. Indeed the so-called brute facts of history are often the interpretations of others, including historical actors themselves. No single, obviously correct public relations history exists; rather, there are a plurality of public relations histories. Indeed, this doctrine can be seen as a main conclusion following from the themes of postmodern rhetorical theory.

The principal themes of rhetorical theory are intimately related to the themes of philosophy. Taking a postmodern view, Baynes, Bohman, and McCarthy (1987) summarized these themes as (a) a concern with the concept of reason, (b) a scepticism about the concept of the human subject, (c) a scepticism about epistemology, and (d) a fascination with language. All of these are intertwined, and if they can be related to one, single, overriding concern, it is a wariness of the idea of foundationalism, the view that there is one, single reality "out there" that human minds, with varying degrees of accuracy, are able to picture, and that is the final arbiter of truth. One of the most vigorous attacks on this view is by Rorty (1979), who challenges the notion that the mind mirrors nature because it supposes that there are invariant, ahistorical rules—the methods of historical scholarship, for instance—for making in the mind an accurate and complete representation of reality. Rorty denies that these invariant rules exist.

Postmodern philosophy is sceptical about conceptualizing reason in a strong sense as that powerful searchlight, which is the same for all peoples in all times, used by the mind to illuminate reality, historical or otherwise, and see it for what it really is or was. Instead, reason is seen as much more contingent and conventional and bound up always with particular, historical views of what counts as rational. At the same time, these philosophers are not satisfied with the cartesian (modern) concept of man as atomistic and autonomous, standing against the world and peering into it. Instead, relying on insights from phenomenology, many contemporary philosophers are more apt to eschew a subject/object dualism in favor of a view that stresses the mutual dependence of both, such that each plays a role in constituting the other. On this view, human consciousness is seen as having an intrinsically social character and, because the mind cannot be distinguished radically from the body, rationality must take into account feelings and desires.

The historian can no more escape that bit of him or herself that is always in things than he or she can experience a pure interiority empty of the things of which he or she is conscious. It is seen as more realistic to view knowledge as interpretation rather than representation. Once interpretation replaces representation as the dominant metaphor for how we know, then the data of experience are less well described as an experience of things as they are than as an experience of meaning. For one cannot properly be said to interpret a thing; rather one interprets what the thing means. As a result, language, symbols, and rhetoric should move to the forefront of our epistemologies.

Thus, studying public relations historians and their histories can reveal much more about their attitudes and philosophical perspectives than it does about precisely what happened in the past. These historians come to historical texts with different philosophies of history, different social, political, and moral philosophies, and even different assumptions about epistemology and ontology. Wise (1980) used the term *explanation form* to denote the framework of ideas and philosophical assumptions a historian brings to his or her work and he suggested that often one dominates as the master form. Outlining these perspectives and identifying these explanation forms is one valuable way of mapping the terrain within which arguments about public relations occur and of uncovering the sometimes unarticulated philosophies of public relations that are extant in management and public relations literature.

By identifying a range of perspectives that historians take toward public relations' history, this chapter argues the claim that there is no single, privileged interpretation of public relations' past. The historical texts discussed are selected purposefully to represent this range of perspectives. Studying these historians reveals much about contemporary discourse on public relations and suggests that this discourse is complex and many-sided. The chapter begins with Hiebert's (1966) biography of Ivy Lee, a practitioner who is often called the father of public relations. Hiebert's approach to public relations history reveals one important perspective. To set it in relation to others, this section reviews explanations of public relations' evolution by the British historian Pimlott (1951), the American business historian Tedlow (1979), the Marxist communication theorist Smythe (1981) and Olasky (1987), the conservative American historian of public relations. After treating each historian singly, a final section draws conclusions about historical scholarship in public relations and suggests a model for interpreting it.

PR AND THE FLOWERING OF DEMOCRACY: HIEBERT

Following a suggestion of Wise, it is possible to identify in Hiebert's book on Lee a number of paired concepts that together give a sense of the central explanatory framework of the book. These pairs can also be understood as examples of what Barthes (1957/1972) calls symbolic codes, sets of paired signs which produce and organize meaning in a text. These pairs as they are found in Hiebert's book are listed as follows:

fiction, lies	vs.	truth
secrecy	vs.	openness
partisan	vs.	neutral
persuasion	vs.	understanding
image	vs.	reality
propaganda	vs	education
publicity	vs.	public relations
muckraker	vs.	gentleman of the press

Hiebert acknowledged that categories like these are sometimes difficult to separate in real life but he suggested that Ivy Lee had at least made the distinctions in thought and in public statements, even if he sometimes failed to meet his own rigorous standards. Hiebert found in Lee the articulation of a set of ideal public relations values that are captured by oppositions like lies–truth. These values also represent for both Lee and Hiebert what is basic in the idea of democracy.

In 1921, according to Hiebert, Lee told a gathering at the Columbia University School of Journalism: "We live in a great democracy, and the safety of a democracy will in the long run depend upon whether the judgements of the people are sound. If the judgements are to be sound, they will be so because they have the largest amount of information on which to base those judgements" (p. 317). It was the task of public relations to assist in supplying that information. Hiebert's own introductory commentary unequivocally asserts: "Without public relations, democracy could not succeed in a mass society" (p. 7), and later, in a concluding paragraph: "Ivy Lee and public relations played a significant role in preserving the pluralism of American society by opening channels of communication and allowing opposing groups to understand each other" (p. 318).

Lee hoped at one time to become a lawyer and studied for a semester at Harvard Law School. But he was forced to give up these studies when his money run out. As the story is told—Hiebert cited Goldman (1948) but Goldman gave no source for this story—Lee arrived in New York City with only $5.25 after leaving Harvard and, after securing food and lodging, spent his last nickel on a subway ride to the offices of the *New York Journal.* As luck would have it, editor Charles Edward Russell gave him a job.

As a reporter, Lee apparently lacked the cynicism of many of his fellow journalists. He identified with the powerful businessmen he wrote about and generally thought they were good people, although misunderstood. Lee would probably have agreed with the 1908 statement of AT&T president Theodore Vail that if questions about investments, returns, and distribution are clearly and satisfactorily answered, "there can be no basis for conflict between the company and the public" (p. 87), a view that remains as the basis for much current public relations thinking and practice. Gaudino, Frisch, and Haynes (1989), for instance, suggested there remains a strong belief among practitioners—even among those who claim to practice two-way forms of communication—in the myth that "If you knew what I knew, you'd make the same decision" (p. 299).

Hiebert suggested that Lee's move to journalism from law is partly explained by the fact that the two professions have something in common. "Lee saw . . . an opportunity to combine his literary and legal interests; he could use his pen to account for and defend ideas and actions [of business] before the court of public opinion, that great new audience of American readers" (p. 39). But it is impossible to tell from the text whether Lee actually saw this relationship between journalism and law, or whether it is an explanatory construct of his biographer. Hiebert's interpretation suggests that if Lee could not serve justice and democracy as a lawyer, he would have to find another way. Indeed, he would have to invent one.

Hiebert, as much as Lee, is keenly interested in truth, justice, and democracy as ideals that inform the idea of public relations. Hiebert reported that, during his (Lee's) work for the Pennsylvania Railroad, Lee circulated to the press a "Declaration of Principles" to which he planned to adhere as a publicist for the railroad. Hiebert began a passage by quoting part of Lee's declaration:

> This is not a secret press bureau. All our work is done in the open. This is not an advertising agency; . . . Our matter is accurate. Further details on any subject treated will be supplied promptly, and any editor will be assisted most cheerfully in verifying directly any statement of fact. Upon inquiry, full information will be given to any editor concerning those on whose behalf an article is sent out. In brief, our plan is, frankly and openly, on behalf of the business concerns and public institutions, to supply to the press and the public of the United States prompt and accurate information concerning subjects which it is of value and interest to the public to know about. (p. 48)

There is little doubt that more current public relations could be practiced with the rectitude evidenced in Lee's declaration and that the declaration is laudable. But Hiebert wants this declaration to do a great deal; for, in the paragraph immediately following, he interpreted its significance in this way:

> The statement brought about a revolution in relations between business and the public. Where formerly business pursued a policy of "the public be damned," from now on business increasingly followed a policy of "the public be informed."

> A few other companies saw the efficacy of Lee's advice. . . . (p. 48)

Within this second passage a contradiction appears. On the one hand, Hiebert took Lee's declaration as revolutionary; on the other he allowed that only "a few" other companies followed Lee's advice. In fact, it is still a legitimate empirical question whether the revolution as Hiebert understands it has ever taken place. Certainly the modern corporation wants to be attuned to the values, attitudes, and behaviors of its various publics and often tries to influence those behaviors and to adjust its own policies to what it believes are public expectations. But it is an open question whether this activity is quintessentially democratic. Yet for Hiebert, the essence of the public relations revolution is a flowering of democratic values. In the foregoing excerpts, Hiebert's allegiance to this view of public relations seems to make it difficult for the biographer to separate his own view of what the fledgling profession should be from what it is reasonable to believe about the way public relations actually evolved. In other places in his book, it is plain that Hiebert *did* appreciate that, "too much public relations is Machiavellian, concerned with maintaining power regardless of ethical considerations" (p. 317). But if Hiebert understood this, why did he write about a public relations revolution?

A similar tension exists in another of Hiebert's interpretations of Lee. This one is particularly illuminating because it shows how the same set of facts might be given radically different interpretations. Hiebert described Lee's early journalistic exploits:

> Lee's first big scoop of his career came from Grover Cleveland. The president had recently retired from the White House to his home in Princeton. In typical nineteenth century fashion he refused to make any public statements. . . . One evening young Lee organized a group of his fellow students to go to the Cleveland home and serenade the ex-president with college songs and cheers. Cleveland was moved by the gesture and at length came out onto the front porch where he made a little speech to the students. Lee was in the front row, pencil and pad in hand, and took down every word. (p. 28)

As Hiebert reported the president "was moved," should a reader take this as an instance of Lee's sincerity, of his sincere desire to move others? For on the next page Hiebert said, "[Lee] . . . may not have been humble, but he was sincere . . . He was the original 'really sincere guy' " (p. 30). Or is it an example of Lee's cunning orchestration of an event—the pseudo-event about which Boorstin (1961) has written—which both Cleveland, and Lee's biographer, took at face value? It is important for Hiebert to support claims about Lee's sincerity and the transparency of his intentions, because Hiebert wants readers to accept that Lee believed that "the truth was the most effective way to flatter the people in a democratic society. . . . a policy of honesty was the most direct means to public approval" (p. 31). Yet it is not obvious that Lee was honest about his intentions with President Cleveland, for he may well have made use of a staged event to encourage the president to give a public statement.

Hiebert seems more interested in the idea he believes Lee articulated and stood for than he is in the man himself. It is Lee's idea, taken at face value as Lee articulated it on many occasions, with which Hiebert is concerned, for the idea, unlike the man, can be rendered purely, simply and powerfully. But the important question for an understanding of public relations historiography is not how wide a gap exists between Lee the man and the idea Hiebert finds in Lee's writing. Rather, it is more important to draw a conclusion about the nature of the explanatory categories Hiebert used to explain the evolution of public relations and to understand why he used them.

As noted at the beginning of this section, a host of questions surrounds the public relations profession. Most of them have to do with its legitimacy. Hiebert would certainly have been aware of them; he not only taught public relations but practiced it as well. Were he at all concerned about the profession's legitimacy at the outset of his research on Lee, his discovery of the core idea of public relations in the language of democracy would assure him that no profession was more worthy. Moreover, he can show that the view of public relations as democracy in action is not his own construct, but an idea that is part and parcel of public relations' history. Indeed, public relations can be seen as the obvious and predictable response to a set of historical conditions that threatened democratic ideals. On this view, its evolution is natural and explainable as the inevitable evolution of ever-adaptable democratic principles.

Wise (1980) suggested it is important to ask what an historian's explanatory ideas do for him or her, how they act as tools, as a strategic response to a problematic environment. The foregoing analysis suggests, that in the case of Hiebert, his depiction of the history of public relations provided a powerful tool in the debate that was then current, and continues to be current, as to the status of the profession. Moreover, this observation about Hiebert's purpose is not a new one. One reviewer of Hiebert's book (Garraty, 1966) noted:

Hiebert has been so impressed by the novelty of Lee's techniques and his enormous success, and has himself been so captivated by the public-relations mistique, that he fails to come to grips with the moral questions involved in the business or with the fact that his hero, after all, was essentially a lackey. He advances the startling . . . thesis that the public relations business is a bulwark of democracy. . . . That Lee believed this is understandable; that his biographer believes it is an indication of the extent to which he has absorbed his subject's values. . . . In short, he has produced a public relations man's biography of Ivy Lee. (p. 42)

PIMLOTT'S SPECIALIZATION THEORY

One explanation of the evolution of public relations, as has been noted in the foregoing section, sees the profession as an element of maturing democratic ideals. Other explanations, some incorporating the democracy idea and some repudiating it, have been suggested. This and following sections examine some of these explanations to generate a broader perspective on the writing of public relations history against which Hiebert's work can be seen.

Pimlott (1951) introduced a discussion of public relations' evolution by denying that public relations can be explained as a "natural response" to the growth of the mass media; usually such explanations beg the question of why the response is "natural," he said. In making this point, Pimlott made an interesting critical point that any claim about the apparent "naturalness" of a state of affairs is at heart the statement of an ideological position and not the neutral description of "the way things are" that it appears to be. Indeed, Pimlott's position in a way presages the postmodern views described earlier. The attack on foundationalism is also an attack on any effort to privilege one point of view over another based on the claim that the privileged perspective reflects they ways things really are.

Pimlott argued that the quasi-professionalization of the public relations function in the early 1990s—a function that is recognizable in all stages in history in various nonprofessional forms—is an aspect of increasing differentiation of social functions generally. "This in turn was due to increasing wealth, expanding markets, population growth, technological progress—indeed, to all the circumstances which produced the Industrial Revolution . . ." (p. 233). Finally, he made this disarmingly modest statement that suggests he sees nothing revolutionary about the growth of public relations: "There is nothing dramatic about this reason for the evolution of the public relations specialist. Because it is not dramatic it tends to be overshadowed by more colorful theories" (p. 234).

Part of Pimlott's point is that people, leaders of any kind especially, have always been concerned with image. He noted New England businessmen of the mid-1800s attended to their own public relations just as they attended to their own accounting and other aspects of management. For Pimlott, a fundamental reason for the differentiation of public relations as a unique management function is increased complexity in society and increased specialization to deal with it. Here it is worth remarking that an important aspect of Hiebert's explanation is that business had come to be indifferent to its image and thus needed public relations. It is noted later that Tedlow, even more forcefully than Pimlott, questioned this basic assumption about business' lack of concern for its public image.

Having linked public relations' evolution to a general increase in specialization, Pimlott developed a number of related explanatory propositions:

1. Because of increased complexity and "bigness," it became more difficult for an organization to communicate with the public. Moreover, the "public" came to be understood as differentiated into a number of sub-publics—employees, customers, shareholders, etc. "As the organizations increased in size and the 'publics' along with them, they also became remote, more impersonal, more incomprehensible" (p. 235).

2. It became increasingly necessary to bridge this widening communication gap. As Pimlott put it: "It proved to be more efficient to be open than to be secretive. Employers worked better; dealers were more loyal; stockholders were more contented" (p. 236). He also noted new ideas about business' responsibilities resulted in a need by business to justify itself to society. But Pimlott did not cast this observation in the language of democratic rights and obligations; rather he suggested public relations, evolution can be partly understood as a sound business strategy to increase efficiency and productivity.

3. Pimlott acknowledged the mass media as a major contributing factor in the evolution of public relations, but he avoided the suggestion of technological determinism. Because of the structural changes described here, more demands were made of mass media channels. As media themselves became more complex, it became necessary for organizations to employ experts familiar with them.

4. Finally, it must be noted that for Pimlott, public relations is related to democracy, as the title of his book suggests, but the idea of democracy does not play the kind of fundamental explanatory role that it does for Hiebert. Instead he pointed as well to a wide variety of causes of change—economic, technological, social—and suggested that public relations is a rational, and highly functional, management response to the demands of a changing environment. With public relations, organizations and hence society generally, will

function more smoothly. Pimlott concluded that public relations' significance for society is twofold—it is highly functional for the smooth functioning of society and supportive of American democratic ideals.

> They [public relations specialists] are experts in popularizing information. They play an essential part in "group dynamics" . . . The better the job of popularization, the more smoothly will society function, but also the greater the understanding which the plain citizen will have of his own place in relation to the big and seemingly inhuman groups whose interplay is important for the 'dynamics of group behavior'. The more that is understood about group dynamics and the working of the mass media the clearer will be the role of the public relations group. . . . And the easier will be the problem—though it will never be easy—of adapting the mass media to the needs of American democracy and of curbing the excesses of propaganda. (p. 257)

Before leaving Pimlott, it is worth characterizing in general terms the kind of historical explanation he advanced. Pimlott developed the outline of a seemingly neutral, functional explanation for public relations that, on the face of it, does not express an ideological position. Organizations must survive by adapting or adjusting to their environments, and specialized public relations roles allow them to do this. As noted later, Tedlow offered a similar functional explanation as well as debunking one of public relations' most cherished myths.

THE MYTH OF THE BOERISH BUSINESSMAN: TEDLOW

Tedlow (1979), a business historian at the Harvard School of Business Administration, attacked one of the most revered beliefs of public relations—the belief that business, prior to the coming of public relations, was secretive and insensitive, indeed contemptuous, of public opinion. Relying on a number of examples for his evidence, Tedlow supports two claims: (a) American businessmen since colonial times have been notoriously solicitous of public approval, and (b) only politicians have rivalled them in the use of publicity to further their enterprises.

Tedlow also reviewed and reinterpreted some of the classic evidence for the opposite view, namely, the 1882 statement by William Vanderbilt which appeared on the front page of *The New York Times* in which he was reported to have said "the public be damned," a phrase that is reported in most public relations textbooks and interpreted there much as Hiebert interpreted it.

Tedlow returned to the primary document to see what the phrase looked like in context. Vanderbilt apparently made his statement in response to a reporter's question. Wondering why Vanderbilt ran one of his railroads at a loss, the reporter suggested that perhaps it was for the public benefit. In part, Vanderbilt is supposed to have replied: "The public be damned. What does the public care about the railroads except to get as much out of them for as small a consideration as possible . . . Of course we like to do everything possible for the benefit of humanity in general, but when we do we first see that we are benefitting ourselves" (p. 5). When taken in context, according to Tedlow, the statement expresses a sentiment still much accepted today—that the primary responsibility of an executive is to a company's shareholders. He argued the statement bears none of the venomous overtones so many public relations historians have read into it. Additionally, he claimed, Vanderbilt denied using the language attributed to him, further evidence of even Vanderbilt's concern for maintaining a decorous public image. Referring to the so-called robber barons generally, Tedlow concluded:

> It would be wonderfully tidy to show how these economically proficient but socially insensitive moguls were gradually forced to defend themselves in the public forum by making use of the developing profession of public relations counseling. This is the 'scenario' constructed by numerous public relations men who have explored their field's past. Such a sequence is not with some validity, but history is rarely so one-dimensional and it certainly is not in this case. (p. 3)

Two generally accepted explanations for the evolution of public relations, according to Tedlow, are (a) the appearance of PR follows a changed attitude on the part of business to its social responsibilities; and (b) it arose as a defense against anti-business sentiment. Tedlow accepted that these claims exhibit some degree of truth, but in the case of both he suggested the story of public relations is much more complex and ambiguous. He agreed that corporate liberalism and public relations sometimes appeared together, but noted also that many exponents of public relations were quite conservative and would not likely have accepted social responsibility arguments. He also allowed that there is a temporal coincidence between the beginnings of PR and the hey-day of the muckrakers. But he asked: "Why has not public relations diminished in importance with the decline of anti-business sentiment? . . . why did nonbusiness institutions which were not particularly scrutinized by the muckrakers, such as universities, churches, charities, and the armed services, follow the lead of business and experiment with press bureaus at the time?" (p. 16).

Essentially, Tedlow repudiated what he called the views associated with the Progressive period that saw a conflict between "the people" and "the interests." He said this picture ignores developments within the business world itself. Key among these developments are unprecedented rates of growth among corporations, increased rationalization and centralization of management, and the need for larger markets. These changes brought with them new management problems to which some of the responses included Taylor's scientific management, the birth of industrial psychology, welfare capitalism, advertising and, of course, public relations.

In his view, causal explanation in this context is more complex than many explanations of public relations' past suggest. Tedlow viewed public relations as one element of management's response to rapid change along a number of dimensions—economic, technological, and social. He interpreted public relations' history in terms of organizations learning how to function more efficiently and effectively in new environments with little recourse to the more ideologically-loaded language of democracy.

PR, THE CONSCIOUSNESS INDUSTRY, AND CAPITALISM: SMYTHE

Of the writers considered in this chapter, Smythe (1981) is the only one who has not written a book with "public relations" in the title, yet much of his writing deals implicitly with related issues. He is also one of the few writers who consider public relations from a Marxist perspective, a perspective that is rarely acknowledged in histories and texts that mention "public relations" in their titles. Smythe located the evolution of public relations in the same time frame and within the same set of economic and social changes as do the other authors. Yet his account of the ways in which the evolution of public relations is explained by these factors is radically different.

Smythe developed an explanation of public relations' evolution within what he called a materialist–realist theory of mass communication. Among the key propositions of this theory is the claim that in the core capitalist countries (Western Europe, United States, and Canada) the mass media are not preeminently in the business of producing newspapers, magazines, or television shows. Rather, they (a) produce audiences as commodities that are marketed to business organizations that want to advertise consumer goods, and (b) establish a daily agenda of news, entertainment, and information that defines *reality* for the people. Another way of describing these two mutually reinforcing purposes is to claim that the commercial media (a) mass market the consumer goods and services produced by monopoly capitalism, and (b) mass market the legitimacy of the capitalist system itself. Smythe distinguished mass media content as advertising, on the one hand, and the "free lunch" on the other. The free lunch is the news, entertainment, and information. Advertising is related to meeting the first objective listed here, the free lunch to meeting the second. The profession of public relations is an element of business' effort to influence the content of the free lunch.

Smythe situated the growth of public relations in the latter quarter of the 19th century and the early part of the 20th century in the United States—the same time period within which media began to address the twin objectives described earlier. What is of interest in this context is his explanation for these responses on the part of business. According to Smythe, business faced two major problems at the turn of the century. One was a population becoming increasingly hostile toward the practices of big business. Hiebert also described this period of crisis for capitalism, but where he (following Lee) ascribed it to a lack of mutual understanding among business and the public, Smythe said the public understood perfectly—that was the problem. Second was a need that was part and parcel of the "bigness" problem. The larger, "rationalized" business organizations with centralized managements needed larger, rationalized markets. Smythe wrote:

> The principal contradiction faced by capitalism in the last quarter of the nineteenth century was that between the enormous potential for expanding production of consumer goods and the overt political hostility of the workers and a fair proportion of the middle class. . . . In the resolution of the principal contradiction, two problems were identified and solved: 1) The need for an unquestionable conquest by the business system of control of the state and its ideological apparatus. . . . 2) The task of winning the automatic acquiescence of the population to a 'rationalized' system of monopoly capitalism . . . (p. 57)

It is the second problem in which public relations can be seen as playing a role, for Smythe also asserted:

> The second level was the long-range problem confronting the emerging monopoly-capitalist system. . . . that of establishing institutional relations which would win the acquiescence of the population. . . . this problem was one of establishing the hegemony of the business system over people as 'consumers'. . . . It was a problem of establishing domination of consciousness through culture and communication. (p. 57)

Smythe's explanation of the evolution of public relations goes well beyond the core claims of classical Marxism because of the emphasis he placed on the role of consciousness in the maintenance of the capitalist system. At least in the core capitalist countries, capitalism ultimately came to be relatively successful in providing for the material wants of the proletariat, thus reducing the likelihood of the kind of revolution Marx predicted. The "crisis" that would precipitate a new order is not, therefore, an economic or material one, but a crisis of legitimation, or of consciousness. To the extent this is true, public relations can be explained as an element of capital's response. In earlier ages, the response to potential economic crises was the reallocation of material resources—a greater sharing of economic benefits. In current times, the appropriate response takes place in the realm of ideas. Galbraith (1983) has also argued that although capital's power was once related to the control and allocation of material wealth, it is now related to the control and distribution of ideas or in capital's ability to persuade.

PR AND THE SPECTER OF SOCIALISM: OLASKY

Olasky's (1987) recent analysis of public relations' history is most provocative and is especially interesting when it is contrasted with Smythe's. Both Olasky and Smythe agree that public relations is a strategy that big business uses to control markets and to increase profitability. But whereas Smythe made his analysis from a leftist perspective, Olasky approached public relations' history as a free-market conservative.

Echoing Tedlow, Olasky argued that a wrong-headed progressive interpretation dominates the writing of public relations history. For Olasky, this view includes the ideas that public relations has improved steadily since its press agentry beginnings (the idea of progress) and that public relations practitioners are motivated by a sense of serving the public interest. He suggested that an honest reading of public relations' history, however, reveals no evidence that public relations practitioners are becoming more ethical and professional or that corporations have been operating to achieve anything but self-interest.

The thrust of his historical analysis is that corporate public relations activities have been designed to circumvent free market forces in favor of what he called collaborationism—alliances of large corporations with each other and with government. He described the creation of the Interstate Commerce Commission in 1887 and the ultimate public acceptance in the early 20th century of the idea of "regulated monopolies" for telephone and electrical utilities as public relations triumphs that benefited the regulated industries more than they served the public interest. Olasky sees in the public relations campaigns that railroads and utilities waged in favor of regulation a pitched battle between defenders of free enterprise and market forces and those who favored planning and the use of non-market driven policies to control and regulate. He wrote:

> For over a century, many major corporate public relations leaders have worked diligently to kill free enterprise by promoting big government-big business collaboration. Over and over again, many corporate public relations executives have supported economic regulation with the goal of eliminating smaller competitors and insuring their own profits. (p. 2)

Olasky interpreted public relations history in the context of his reading of the United States Constitution. He pointed out that the framers of that constitution wrote a document to safeguard the private rights of individuals. In the constitution, Olasky found a philosophy of freedom and individualism that he believes is threatened by the specter of what he calls collaborationism. Moreover, he reinterpreted the contribution of Lee and Bernays, the premier figures in public relations history, to show how their philosophies were supportive of this collaborationism and showed little sympathy with philosophies of individualism.

Olasky's Lee is quite different from Hiebert's Lee. Whereas Lee in Hiebert's biography is portrayed as a champion of democratic ideals, in Olasky he is just the opposite, a master controller and propagandist who was firmly in the collaborationist camp and whose actions served only to reduce individual freedom and choice.

Olasky suggested that Lee's belief in collaborationism explains what had hitherto been difficult to understand, especially when Lee is seen as the champion of democracy in America, namely, Lee's sympathies for Stalin and the communist experiment in the Soviet Union. Olasky suggested that Lee saw "the United States moving closer to the Soviet Union in social perspective. 'The United States started with complete individualism, every man for himself,' and the Soviets have the opposite position, Lee wrote, but 'we have found it necessary to restrict the power of the individual' " (p. 51) Olasky also suggested that Lee saw movement toward a new cooperative social order as natural, inevitable, and progressive.

Lee also had unflattering views of the multitude, said Olasky, views that would have supported his belief that the public needed to be managed and administered for its own good. For Lee believed that rational discourse was lost on the masses and that the cause of collaborationism was better served by communication that played on the imagination and emotions of the public. In this application of Freudian psychology, with its emphasis on the role of the irrational and the hidden as motivators of human action, Lee would presage the views and practice of Bernays, the nephew of Sigmund Freud, and the man credited with first using the phrase "public relations."

In reinterpreting Bernays, and as a result of his own interview with him in 1984, Olasky discovered a philosophy of public relations that holds that, (a) because among the masses emotion is more powerful than reason, and (b) because there is no God watching over the world, (c) therefore, manipulation of these masses through public relations techniques is essential to prevent chaos and ensure public order. Olasky argued that this "rationale for public relations manipulation based on his lack of confidence in either God or man . . . was his [Bernays'] most significant contribution to 20th century public relations" (p. 83). As in Lee, the focus in Bernays is in protecting the whole from the parts, or the state from the people. Moreover, Olasky pointed out the obvious contradiction in this philosophy:

> Because a democratic society is considered to be one in which 'the people' in general do rule, and an authoritarian society is often considered one in which a small group of people rule, Bernays was trying to square the circle by arguing, in effect, that we must kill democracy to save it. (p. 84)

Olasky also identified another similarity between Bernays and Lee—the affinity of their ideals with socialism. Whereas Lee's collaborationism led him to sympathize with Soviet ideals, Bernays too was a champion of increased economic centralization along with more economic planning and social control.

HISTORICAL PERSPECTIVES ON PR: A SYNTHESIS

The preceding discussion has compared and contrasted different approaches to the history of public relations and different explanations for the evolution of the new profession. What is initially most interesting about these approaches, however, is not their differences, but what they have in common. For all the historians discussed agree on a number of basic facts. Professionalized public relations is a practice that begins in the last decades of the 19th century and first two decades of the 20th century and arises in the context of significant economic, technological, and social changes associated with that time period. These include:

- a crisis of competition in business that led to monopoly capitalism,
- increased social organization and specialization in society generally,
- increased communication problems among groups,
- the advance of scientific approaches to marketing, management, and administration,
- advances in technology generally, especially in the techniques of mass communication,
- an increase in the general level of education, and
- changes in values, the rise of egalitarianism.

Where the historians differ, of course, is in the way they interpret these and related facts and the way they explain the causal relations among them.

- Hiebert, himself a public relations practitioner, emphasized the democratizing influence of public relations. The ideals driving his analysis are the democratic ideals of an informed and active citizenry. In Lee he saw a larger-than-life champion of these ideals. For Hiebert, public relations is part of the natural evolution of these ideals; the growth of the profession is explained partly by the evolution of democracy and partly by the historical role played by Lee, who saw the need for public relations as a bulwark against nondemocratic forces.

• Pimlott too acknowledged a relationship between public relations and democratic institutions, but he emphasized increased specialization of roles in society as a key rationale for the growth of public relations. For Pimlott, there is little that is dramatic or revolutionary in the evolution of public relations. Rather, public relations is a useful social role and helps society function more smoothly.

• Tedlow, whose study of public relations was initially part of a doctoral dissertation in American history at Columbia University (his adviser was the same John A. Garraty whose comments on Hiebert were quoted earlier), focused on business efforts to manage change as a key explanatory factor. He discarded some of the basic explanatory myths of public relations' history and develops a functional explanation for the growth of the profession. Public relations evolves as a specialized organizational role because without it institutions would not easily adjust or adapt to environments that became increasingly dynamic and complex.

• Smythe explained public relations as business' response to a situation in which it needed to control the minds as well as the bodies of its publics in order to promote and secure organizational goals—growth and profit. In Smythe, there is no talk of social responsibility or of democracy. The self-interest of profit-seeking organizations in capitalist economies beset by a crises of legitimacy is the key reason for public relations.

• Olasky focused on the way in which public relations activity threatens what he believes are basic American values—competition and the rights of individuals—values that are often associated with capitalism. With Smythe he saw public relations as a technique of organizations for promoting economic self-interest through the control of markets. But while the Marxist explanation of this phenomenon is that it is a logical and irreversible *outcome* of an ideology of individualism, for Olasky a return to these classic individualist values is the only cure. Smythe saw in public relations the scourge of capitalism, Olasky the spectre of socialism.

By way of effecting some kind of final synthesis or framework within which to view these varied approaches to public relations history, it is worth returning to some of Wise's (1980) considerations on the writing of history. Wise described what can be loosely called the three major paradigms or explanation forms within which American historical research has been carried out, although to his list a fourth category is added to accommodate Olasky. Making use of these paradigms provides one strategy for mapping the different philosophies of history that public relations historians bring to their work.

Progressive historians, who controlled the historical stage from about 1910 to 1950, according to Wise, saw life in America as relatively straightforward and unproblematic. For the progressive historians, said Wise, "Life in America could be made free and open and just if only people willed it so and labored hard to implement their wills. Progressives obligated themselves to lead the way toward a juster, more enlightened society (p. 83). . . . Progress was their Master Form, the single key which explains most everything they thought and did" (p. 87).

When Hiebert published his book on Ivy Lee in the mid-1960s, he was about 35 years old. He had grown up and been educated during a time when little seemed to stand in the way of progress in America; his book came out before the crises and disillusionment that marked the late 1960s. Thus, in spite of the fact Hiebert wrote *Courtier to the Crowd* after the period Wise identified with progressive history, his book seems to fit into the mold Wise claimed motivated most progressive historians. Public relations, for Hiebert, is an instrument of progress that, if only people would come to appreciate it, could play a role in making America "free and open and just."

Counter-progressives, on the other hand, tended to be suspicious of the idea of progress and viewed historical reality as much more complex and ambiguous than did the progressives. Wise situated counter-progressive historians after 1950. Pimlott, possibly, and Tedlow would seem to fit into this category. Tedlow especially attacked some of the truisms and assumptions of the "progress" view of public relations and paints a much more complicated and conservative picture of the evolution of public relations than does Hiebert. Olasky, it might be argued, fits this category because of his questioning of the progress view of public relations. Yet his writing is marked by a fervor that makes it appear more ideologically motivated than the work of Pimlott or Tedlow so that it seems helpful to provide a separate category for Olasky.

New Left historians, according to Wise, began writing in America after 1960. "In their picture, America has not been so much an idea as a structure of power. And that power is anything but innocent. The nation has not been misguided in its acts of oppression; it's been cold, and ruthlessly calculating, and has done what it's done to protect and extend itself. To the New Left, America has not been a blunderer, it's been a predator" (p. 94). Clearly, Smythe fits into this category. It could also be argued that the recent analyses of Gandy (1982) are motivated by a similar view of history.

New Right historians is a category Wise does not mention, but one like it seems necessary to classify Olasky's history of public relations. Olasky's neo-conservatism is not captured by any of the other categories. It might be argued that the analysis of Tedlow is a conservative one in that it does not probe the legitimacy of those organizational goals for which the new public relations role was seen to be functional. But Olasky's conservatism is different, for it is marked by a much stronger and more clearly articulated ideology.

These four historical categories are helpful for bringing some order to the various public relations histories discussed above. But it is also useful to employ categories that (a) emphasize logical distinctions instead of historical ones, and (b) suggest the basis for a model that may help ordering some of the assumptions working behind contemporary discourse about public relations. Thus one can identify what might be called a broad *management paradigm* that favors structural-functional explanation and which occupies a middle or central position. The core idea here is that public relations develops as a specialized role (i.e. as a structural innovation in organizations) because it is functional for organizational survival. This paradigm is an important and perhaps dominant one (Trujillo & Toth, 1987) within current public relations theory and one that stresses public relations' contribution to organizational management. The historical analyses of Pimlott and Tedlow especially seem to be made from within this perspective and are supportive of it.

It can also be argued that Hiebert's explanation fits within this dominant management paradigm in that it provides a rhetoric of legitimation for what otherwise is clearly an explanation positing organizational needs, that is, organizational self-interests, as the driving force in the genesis of public relations. Although the historical explanations of Hiebert, on the one hand, and Tedlow and Pimlott on the other, have differences, they serve each other well. But this is not because explanations that emphasize the functional value of public relations are without ideologies; indeed they are not without ideologies, for the needs of these organizations, in the achievement of which public relations plays an important, functional role, are, by and large, the needs of profit-making organizations in a post-industrial capitalist economy. Rather, it is because this latter ideology is made more palatable when reworked in the language of democracy and social responsibility.

Finally, if it is accepted that Tedlow, Pimlott and Hiebert together represent different aspects of a dominant perspective on public relations, it follows that the historical analyses of Smythe and Olasky articulate assumptions that are critiques of this dominant perspective. Smythe, of course, presents a critique from the left, and Olasky one from the right. For the leftist critique, the rhetoric of democracy and social responsibility falsely legitimate those organizational interests served by public relations because they do not take into account the real needs of individuals (for community, for instance) but rather emphasize false needs of individuals for unfettered freedom as consumers. From the right, the legitimating rhetoric is seen as hollow because it fails to recognize the rights of individuals and subsumes them under the rights and needs of institutions. From the left, public relations is seen as serving the private interests of individuals, from the right public relations is seen as threatening these interests.

REFERENCES

Barthes, R. (1972). *Mythologies.* (A. Lavers, Trans.). New York: Hill & Wang. (Original work published 1957)

Baynes, K., Bohman, J., & McCarthy, T. (Eds.). (1987). *After philosophy: End of transformation?* Cambridge, MA: MIT Press.

Berkhofer, R.F. (1969). *A behavioral approach to historical analysis.* New York: Collier-MacMillan Limited.

Boorstin, D.J. (1961). *The image: A guide to pseudo-events in America.* New York: Harper Colophon Paperbacks.

Burke, K. (1957). *The philosophy of literary form.* New York: Vintage Books.

Galbraith, J.K. (1983). *The anatomy of power.* Boston: Houghton Mifflin.

Gandy, O. (1982). *Beyond agenda setting: Information subsidies and public policy.* Norwood, NJ: Ablex.

Garraty, J.A. (1966). Up from puffery. [Review of *Courtier to the crowd: The story of Ivy Lee and the development of public relations]* *Columbia Journalism Review, 5,* 41–42.

Gaudino, J.L., Frisch, J., & Haynes, B. (1989). "If you knew what I knew, you'd make the same decision:" A common misconception underlying public relations campaigns. In C.H. Botan & V. Hazelton, Jr. (Eds.), *Public relations theory* (pp. 299–308). Hillsdale, NJ: Lawrence Erlbaum Associates.

Goldman, E.F. (1948). *Two-way street: The emergence of public relations counsel.* Boston: Bellman.

Hiebert, R.E. (1966). *Courtier to the crowd: The story of Ivy Lee and the development of public relations.* Ames, IA: Iowa State University Press.

Olasky, M.N. (1987). *Corporate public relations and American private enterprise: A new historical perspective.* Hillsdale, NJ: Lawrence Erlbaum Associates.

Pearson, R. (1990). Perspectives on public relations history. *Public Relations Review, 16*(3), 27–38.

Pimlott, J.A. (1951). *Public relations and American democracy.* Princeton, NJ: Princeton University Press.

Rorty, R. (1979). *Philosophy and the mirror of nature.* Princeton, NJ: Princeton University Press.

Smythe, D. (1981). *Communications, capitalism, consciousness and Canada.* Norwood: Ablex.

Tedlow, R.S. (1979). *Keeping the corporate image: Public relations and business. 1900–1950.* Greenwich, CT: JAI.

Trujillo, N., & Toth, E.L. (1987, August). Organizational perspectives for public relations research and practice. *Management Communication Quarterly, 1*(2), 199–231.

Wise, G. (1980). *American historical explanations: A strategy for grounded inquiry.* Minneapolis: University of Minnesota.

Public Relations and Public Policy: The Structuration of Dominance in the Information Age

OSCAR H. GANDY, JR.
University of Pennsylvania

This chapter develops, through the perspective of political economy, a critique of the role of public relations in the formation and implementation of public policy. A general model of influence production through domination of individual and collective understandings of problems and prospects is introduced, and then expanded through discussion of policies related to the development and use of information technologies. The relations between technology, market relations, and social consciousness are seen to be structured in dominance by large corporate actors through their use of coordinated public relations campaigns. The discussion identifies numerous policy arenas where public relations efforts dominate the policy debate.

Political Economy and the Analysis of Power

Referring to a body of work as *political economy* may cover or uncover a multitude of sins. As identified with its historic origins in practical philosophy, the label has slipped into disuse. In its present form, political economy is easily distinguished from the dominant neo-classical paradigm in economics by its recognition of the existence and importance of power. Within the scope of modern political economy (Staniland, 1985; Whynes, 1984) there are marxist, institutionalist, Austrian, and public choice schools of analysis. There are on its fringes, behavioral, psychological, and even moral/ethical variants (Earl, 1983; Etzioni, 1988). All are concerned with describing

131

the complex relations between technology, social relations, and the institutions and ideological constructs that organize those relations. Radical political economists have traditionally been concerned with bringing critical attention to bear on those institutions, structures, and relations within society that are seen to reinforce inequality and despair, especially with regard to matters of race and gender (Blaug, 1983).

Efforts to develop a political economy of communication and information are of fairly recent vintage (Garnham, 1979; Mosco & Wasko, 1988), although efforts to characterize the U.S. media environment from the perspective of political economy have been published since the late 1960s (Guback, 1969; Schiller, 1969).

Instrumentalist, Institutionalist, and Structuralist Perspectives

Graham Murdock (1982) provided a fairly accessible introduction to the dominant perspectives on power in the realm of mass media. Instrumental perspectives are contrasted with structuralist views in terms of the location of the power to determine the outcomes of decisions or choices. Instrumentalist views focus on the individual acting to exercise control over media organizations through the application of legitimate power vested in ownership, superior resources, authority, or position. Within the traditions of critical political economy, the emphasis is on ownership and allocative control. Control is seen to be motivated by the specific interests of the individual, as well as the generalized interests of the capitalist class. The hypothesis, explicit or implied, is that owners of media systems restrict content to that which is not only sure to produce profits for the organization, but also is supportive of capitalism as a system of social relations (Garnham, 1979).

The structuralist perspective de-emphasizes the power of the individual actor, and focuses instead on the complexity of forces that constrain and shape the flow of images and ideas (Sholle, 1988). With regard to the mass media, structuralist analyses attempt to take into account the influence of the dynamics of the media industry, the nature of competition, the influence of technology, the pressure of professionalism, and to a lesser degree, the interests of audiences and consumers. The regulatory environment itself is included in structuralist views as providing limitations on the instrumental actions of owners. Parsons (1989) offered an attempt to apply Giddens' (1984) theory of structuration to the evolution of regulatory impressions of cable television as a public medium.

Herman and Chomsky (1988) presented what they called a "propaganda model," which seeks to reveal, from a more institutionalist vantage point, how a number of "filters" operate to ensure that elite perspectives come to dominate public discourse. The first filter is primarily the domain of political economy. They suggest that it is the size, ownership, and profit orientation of the mass media that advantage a particular representation of social reality. Bagdikian (1987) echoed their concern with the degree of concentration and conglomerization of the mass media in the United States and globally. Dependence on advertising represents the second "filter" that ensures a hegemonic view. Both these filters have also been described by Mander (1978) as part of the "colonization of experience."

Reliance on official sources from government and industry represents another factor contributing to the uniformity of perspectives in American media. And, when that is not sufficient, Herman and Chomsky (1988) suggested that the media may be brought under periodic assault for creating dangerous threats to the well-being of the system. The raised eyebrow then becomes the full court press of a massive campaign against an irresponsible press corps. In the long run, they suggested that:

> These elements interact with and reinforce one another. The raw material of news must pass through successive filters, leaving only the cleansed residue fit to print. They fix the premises of discourse and interpretation, and the definition of what is newsworthy in the first place, and they explain the basis and operations of what amount to propaganda campaigns. (p. 2)

Public Relations as an Instrument of Power

The focus on public relations in this chapter is offered primarily from an instrumentalist perspective. This perspective emphasizes intentional action meant to produce influence ultimately on the behavior of others. This influence is frequently achieved indirectly through the management of public understanding of issues, options, and the climate of relevant opinion. Although there are a great many definitions of public relations, including those offered by scholars who have a desire to transform the profession so that it might realize more laudible social goals (Grunig, 1989), the dominant view of public relations practice (Kruckeberg & Stark, 1988) is one of persuasive communication actions performed on behalf of clients. Steinberg (1975) described the public relations function succinctly as the "creation, or 'engineering' of consent. . . . a favorable and positive climate of opinion toward the individual, product, institution or idea which is represented" (p. 15). Adding a research or surveillance function to the management responsibilities met by public relations departments does not change its primary role in maintaining the well-being of the organization through efforts to control the environment in which it operates. Surveillance may occasionally lead to the conclusion that the organization must adapt or change to survive in new markets or political environments, but the primary role of public relations is one of purposeful, self-interested communication. Although modern public relations may involve more efforts to "understand" a variety of publics, this apparent concern may be seen as instrumental in that greater knowledge of publics facilitates the more efficient segmentation of those publics for the delivery of targeted communications to them.

Public relations is seen as an instrumental resource that is regularly called into play by actors seeking to influence the outcome of a policy debate. Toth (1986) suggested that definitions of the public affairs function should add the explicit policy dimension of issues management, in which she includes: (a) *government affairs* that include "enhancing and protecting the organization's legitimate interests affected by public issues that will be decided by formal judicial process," and (b) *strategic communications*, or "coordinating all images and messages reflecting basic organizational policy or strategy" (p. 29).

Issues management functions have grown increasingly important to U.S. corporations following the growth of the consumer movement in the 1970s (Heath & Nelson, 1986). By 1982, 91% of the "Fortune 500" companies were said to have established issues management programs (p. 21). A recent survey by the Conference Board (Lusterman, 1988) of firms with sales in excess of $100 million revealed that more than half had established government affairs offices in Washington. Levitan and Cooper (1984) described the emergence of corporate lobbies and their effort to influence national policy as being derived from the lessons they learned in product marketing. American business is described as having developed political sophistication along the way and increasingly, individual firms join coalitions, action committees, or strategy groups to approach Congress or state legislatures with a common voice (Victor, 1988). Lusterman (1988) indicated that many of these "single-issue coalitions" serve the needs of firms that find that their trade associations are incapable of representing their interests on a particular issue.

As corporate resources focused on government policy systems increase, the public relations resources that are brought to bear in support of the incumbant administration's view have also grown (Steinberg, 1980). Government public information officers are a major source of the content of each day's news hole. And, as Levitan and Cooper (1984) argued, the cooperative relations between the Reagan administration and American business produced numerous joint campaigns to influence legislation. They noted that "during this first year in the White House, President Reagan came through with the biggest federal reduction in history. . . . with the help of a massive lobbying effort by business interests, the administration was able to twist enough legislative arms to get the tax cuts through Congress" (pp. 55–56). Helm (1981) described strategic use of the news media by government public affairs officers not in the militaristic terms of targets and attacks, but in terms of an orchestra, where a variety of finely tuned instruments may be called in at will, to blend in and "produce the harmony, strength, and beauty that truly reach an audience" (p. 119).

Although all policy actors may engage in public relations, not all actors have the resources with which to ensure the success of their efforts. Public policy may be considered a game where the outcome is far from certain (Ettema et al., 1989; Laumann & Knoke, 1987), but one is at less risk in wagering on the outcome when the combatants differ greatly in their resource endowments. Although public relations resources may occasionally be brought to bear in a debate on behalf of the interests of the citizen/consumer (Pertschuk, 1986), corporate and government bureaucracies are the primary clients and beneficiaries.

THE PRODUCTION OF INFLUENCE

Control is never absolute. Beniger (1986) suggested that the concept should encompass the broad range of influence or determinations through which one actor can be said to cause modification or maintenance in the behavior of others. Some critical scholars, influenced by the structuralism of Althusser (Resnick & Wolff, 1987), offer a concept of "overdetermination" to express the complexity of influences that come to bear on individuals and systems. In rejecting the notion of any essential cause, or ultimate determinant, Resnick and Wolff nevertheless suggested that analysts must choose an "entry point" from which to begin describing this complex web of influence. Although a great many forces can be seen to influence the formation of public policy, we have chosen to focus on the role of communication and information in structuring the qualities of options that serve as the basis for decisions by policy actors. More specifically, we are concerned with the role of public relations and public relations practitioners in structuring the information environment in ways that privilege certain resolutions of policy debates.

The Policy Environment

Traditionally, analysts have considered the public policy arena to be solely within the confines of governmental organizations. The legislatures, executive agencies, and the courts of our state, local, and federal governments are all vital centers of policy action. Yet, the corporate and foundation board rooms are also important policy centers. As a by-product of their existence and their pursuit of profit, major corporations have introduced disturbances in the environment that affect the health and safety of their workers and the surrounding communities. Clearly the environmental practices of American corporations have the potential to affect the quality of life for all within reach. Policies that affect the lives of various publics, against which individuals have only limited means of recourse, must be considered public policies. The primary difference between policies of government and those of private organizations is the extent to which any constituencies with the right of recall exist outside the formal organization. The policies of private organizations tend to be more isolated from social influence than those of government. At the same time, private organizations are able to exercise substantial influence on the formation and implementation of government policy.

The Public Policy Process

Public policy formation may be seen as a form of collective decision making, constrained by the same factors that limit rational decision making by individuals (Gandy, 1982). The policy process involves the negotiation of agreements among policy actors with standing and resources about the nature of the problem to be addressed by the organization. This identification phase is followed by efforts to formulate alternative solutions that are modified and presented for ratification or adoption by actors with formal authority. Implementation may involve negotiations about the appropriate level of support, or the nature of the resources that should be made available, as well as the specification of the procedures to be followed that ensure that the intent of the policymakers is reflected in its administration. All actors involved in the policy process, at all phases in this process, are governed by their understanding of the costs and consequences of their actions. All policy actors who understand their interests to be affected by those policies have an incentive to influence how all other policy actors understand these issues. Policy actors may be seen to dominate the policy process in particular issue domains as a function of their ability to mobilize information resources in their own behalf.

Stages and Levels of Analysis

Considerable effort within political science has been focused on the formation of public policy at the national level. Laumann and Knoke (1987) explored the nature of organizational influence in the formation of national policy in the domains of energy and health. In addition to energy and health, Gandy (1982) explored policy development in education, and the broad social policy known as "Reaganomics." Mosco (1988), Noll (1986), and Aronson and Cowhey (1988) provided insights into the nature of influence in the formation of telecommunications policy. Browne (1988) examined the struggle of competing interests in the formation of national policies affecting American agriculture. Each of these policy analysts recognized that there were critical stages in the policy process in which the mobilization of information resources, including those of public relations, would come to play an important role, and would help to explain the outcome of the various policy debates.

Laumann and Knoke (1987) are particularly critical of policy analyses that ignore the influence of those critical events which provide context for understanding the roles of specific actors.

> Even the most methodologically sophisticated discussions of structural or contextual effects have dealt exclusively with the composition of actors and their surroundings, ignoring the sequencing and structuring aspects of events in which they engage. . . . To understand how national policy unfolds, one must take into account how organizations perceive and respond to an opportunity structure for affecting policy outcomes that is created by the temporal sequence of policy-relevant events. (pp. 29–31)

Past experience influences how present and future circumstances are understood by policy actors, and thus must be included in any attempt to describe how power is realized in the policy environment. Case studies that focus on the present, without an effort to include the relevant history of the issue and the policy actors involved, are likely to misunderstand the debate as it unfolds.

Although public attention tends be focused on public issues primarily during the legislative debate, or during public hearings, this most visible aspect of the process is by no means the most important. Indeed, many critical observers suggest that by the time the public is informed that an issue is under consideration by the legislature, the more important questions have already been resolved by the policy elites. The early stages of the policy process involve the specification of the problem and the selection of possible solutions. Defining the problem of a trade imbalance in the electronics industry as a problem of unfair competition from Japan leads to policies very different from an analysis that focuses on a tax policy that rewards short-rather than long-term investment, or the creation of new product lines through acquisition, rather than through research and development (Johnson, 1984).

Policy is also made at the level of implementation. Education policy takes on a life of its own as it is operationally defined by the day-by-day practice of teachers and school administrators. State and local boards of education act independently to interpret the regulations as they are received from the administrative agencies. At each level, organized interests have an incentive to influence how policy actors understand the legislative mandate.

THE ROLE OF INFORMATION

At any stage in the policy process advantage may be gained and influence produced by changes in the availability of information. Public policy is the implementation of decisions that involve the selection of those options that emerge as preferred in comparison with others. Information is central to the selection of policy options. Decision makers in organizations rely on information about the environment, its present and future states, and the likely consequences for the organization if one or more of those possible states come to be. Options are evaluated in terms of their potential to eliminate or reduce the negative consequences, or maximize the gains the organization may realize in these uncertain futures. Information provides the basis for the evaluation of any choice. As we have suggested, public relations specialists are frequently the sources for the information that all decision makers utilize to arrive at their policy decisions. We should note, however, information is not limited to that which we might call the objective facts of the case. Projections of the future are theory-based rather than fact-based. Similarly, assertions about the ethical consequences are dependent on more than the facts.

Structuring the Problem

Kahneman and Tversky (1986) suggested that the way in which a problem is framed can have a substantial influence on the decisions many people will reach, even though the objective facts available to them may not have changed. Facts are interpreted in the context of moral, social, ethical, and ideological meaning structures (Etzioni, 1988). Thus, there are dramatic differences in how we might respond to an environmental or health policy issue if it is presented in terms of "lives lost" versus "lives saved." The differences in the framing may also interact with personal, psychological differences in risk aversion and risk seeking. Kahneman and Tversky (1986) noted that "formulation effects can occur fortuitously, without anyone being aware of the impact of the frame on the ultimate decision. They can also be exploited deliberately to manipulate the relative attractiveness of options" (p. 163). Discounts become surcharges, depending on which price in the market can be established as normal. Losses are not treated in the same way as legitimate costs, even though the dollar amounts may be equivalent. People are more willing to pay what they come to see as legitimate or necessary costs, but resist suffering losses that can be attributed to the illegitimate behavior or demands of others.

There are critical differences in the identification of a problem as having systemic or institutional causes, rather than having a basis in individual action, inaction, or competence. The current debate about the crisis of the urban ghetto (Jaynes & Williams, 1989; Wilson, 1989) illustrates the tension between identifying the persistent economic poverty experienced by many African-Americans as a problem of racial and class exclusion in the context of a challenged domestic economy, or as a problem of inappropriate personal values, an absence of initiative, or the lack of a desire to succeed. The *facts* of Black poverty are generally not open to dispute. But whether the costs of programs to eradicate that poverty are seen as necessary, just, and appropriate expenditures, similar to "bail-outs" of the savings and loan industry, or as a charitable contribution to an undeserving mass is influenced primarily by how those facts are structured as a problem. Golding and Middleton (1982) provided a review of the background and contemporary history of public perceptions of welfare claimants as the result of complex interactions between the state and the press in Britain. The complexity of the process of framing is indicated in their identification of welfare ideology as a "message with no messenger" (p. 213). However, even the Labour party can be seen as having utilized public relations at times to influence the transformation of public perceptions.

Identifying the Options

Decision theorists suggest that we can describe all decisions, no matter how complex, as a choice between two options, X and not X. The decision to choose one or the other is thought to be the result of a rational process, which may differ between individuals, but essentially involves a calculation of the expected benefits to be derived from one option in comparison with those likely to be derived from the other. The computation of expected benefits is uncertain at best in that they involve estimates of future states of the environment in which policies will be implemented. Investments in an uncertain future are always risky, but they are even more so when we recognize that the information that we use to estimate the probability of some future event may be the purposive construction of a public relations campaign. Similarly, efforts to estimate the benefits to be derived from a particular option are speculative at best. Policy actors have an incentive to underestimate the costs and to overestimate the benefits to be derived from any option they prefer.

Policy actors may hesitate to be seen to actively support any particular policy option, so as not to risk the loss of their presumed objectivity. Instead, their efforts may be directed toward reducing the perceived value of other alternatives. This approach is common in product advertising, and becoming increasingly so in negative political advertising. Where the primary decision models are presumed to be of the lexicographic form where pairwise comparisons are made on one dimension at a time (Gandy, 1982) strategists focus on those consequences of competing options which would be most meaningful for a target audience.

Marginalizing the Opposition

As Laumann and Knoke (1987) suggested, the reputations of policy actors as knowledgeable informants represent a critical resource that is brought to bear in a policy debate. Identifying other participants as either incompetent, unnecessarily biased, or self-interested reduces their ability to participate effectively in the policy process. Social judgement theory (Keisler, Collins, & Miller, 1969) suggests that individuals are able to make fine distinctions between positions very near their own, and tend to collapse the differences between those with which they disagree. This tendency is used to advantage in a policy era when the label *liberal* has taken on a powerful, negative interpretation. Identifying a proposal or a political candidate as liberal has become an assault akin to slander.

Proposals from opposing camps may be eliminated solely on the basis of the analytical models they utilize. Decision rules vary, and have no necessary basis for dominance in the policy arena (Wright & Barbour, 1976). A conjunctive model may involve pair-wise comparisons of options that fall within pre-established criteria for acceptability, whereas an affect-referral strategy may lead to decisions on the basis of generalized feelings about options, such as a willingness to "trust" bankers to act in their customers' interests. Given the availability of information, one model may be as good as the other, but policy actors can marginalize their opposition by associating them with what may be seen as an inadequate analytical frame. Economic rationalism has replaced moral or ethical argument as a basis for public policy (Etzioni, 1988). Opponents may be cast aside as "philosopher kings" in preference for the scientific allure of mathematical models, even though both arguments may be empty of data or facts, or are weakened by untenable simplifying assumptions.

INFORMATION SUBSIDIES AND PUBLIC RELATIONS

As we have suggested, public policy involves the consideration of alternatives in the context of individual and organizational understandings of the environments in which they exist. Although individuals and organizations may differ in terms of their future orientations, all make policy decisions based on some consideration of the future. To the extent that their own well-being is likely to be affected by policy decisions made by others, individuals and organizations not only have an interest in understanding how others arrive at those decisions, but also have powerful reasons for wanting to influence that process. Public relations represents one means of influencing the decisions of others by structuring the information environment in which those decisions are made.

Through the provision of information subsidies (Gandy, 1982; Turk, 1986; Turk & Franklin, 1987), public relations specialists generally act to reduce the costs faced by decision makers in acquiring relevant information. On occasion, the goal of public relations may be to raise the cost of access to negative information, or information that might lead to the selection of something other than the preferred policy option. As Manheim and Albritton (1983) have suggested, where a nation's image is overwhelmingly negative, image management can be focused on controlling its visibility, as well as its valence (negativity). In the case of the Republic of South Africa, or even Israel, when comments attributed to those sources might increasingly be rejected as "propaganda," the most effective benefits of their public relations contracts would be the reduction of their visibility in the U.S. press.

The Cost of Information

The notion of information subsidies is based on the recognition that access to information represents genuine costs to decision makers. There is still debate and confusion about the appropriate methods for estimating the market value of information (Bates, 1988) because of its unusual qualities. Among these qualities are those that qualify information as a public good. Information is not consumed through use; use by one does not eliminate the possibility of use by another. It is difficult to bar or restrict the use of information by those who have not paid for it. Once generated, information may be reproduced at negligible additional expense, certainly at far lower unit costs than were involved in the production of the first copy. These problems make it difficult to establish market prices for information. However, there is little doubt that there are identifiable costs associated with gathering and processing information into forms suitable for use in decision making.

Because of the cost of information, and the peculiarities of its supply within and outside of formal information markets, there are great disparities in the distribution of information among decision makers. Decision makers are constrained by their budgets. Some people have more time than money. Thus, one person may carefully write down page after page of information from a source in a public library, whereas another may spend $2.50 for a Xerox copy, and yet another may pay $6.50 to download the information to a desktop computer. Rational decision makers try to collect as much relevant information as their budgets of time or money will allow, and it is suggested that the selection of information is governed in part on the basis of its cost.

If information can be considered to be a normal good, where more is preferred to less, an increase in a budget will result in the acquisition of more information. An increase in an information budget can also result from a lowering of the cost of acquiring or processing information, with the same result—increased consumption. If two packages of information are seen as equivalent in terms of value, but one has a lower price or cost, then the rational consumer will choose the lower priced package. Thus, we arrive at the conclusion that policy actors interested in influencing the consumption of information supportive of their preferred policy options have an incentive to lower the cost of that information through the provision of an information subsidy.

Information Subsidies

Information subsidies are quite simply efforts by policy actors to increase the consumption of persuasive messages by reducing their cost, without reducing their perceived value or utility for decision making. This is an important distinction. Just as we assume that price is an index of quality (Lancaster, 1981), there is a tendency to lower our estimation of the value of information based on our assessment of the credibility of the source. Credibility is not only a concern with competence or expertise, but we tend to mistrust a source of information if we believe the source has an interest in the outcome of our decisions. That is, we value information less if we believe it to be self-serving. Because of this tendency to take information from less than credible sources with a grain of salt, there is an additional incentive for sources to hide their identity, or to disguise the nature of their interests.

Issue advertising suffers from the recognition that the source has an interest in the outcome of decisions to which they refer. Yet, Waltzer (1988) reported that its use by corporations and their associations is on the rise. Attempts to lessen the effect of presumed self-interest can be seen in ads that proport to be concerned with the public interest (Olasky, 1987), rather than the interests of the company or the industry that they represent. Advocacy ads are frequently sources of evidence of a government–industry partnership in the formation of public opinion. Waltzer noted that the "W.R. Grace company frequently used the pages of WJR [*Washington Journalism Review*] to argue for implementation of the 'Grace Commission Report' to reduce federal deficit by cutting spending (and not increasing taxes) and invited journalists to call or write for more information" (p. 54).

Highly credible sources are able to provide direct subsidies through reports and testimony. Congressional hearings provide opportunities for representatives of identifiable interests to present a view of the issue as seen from the perspective of their organization. Congressional staffs increasingly serve as the conduits through which such direct subsidies are provided to elected officials (Fox & Hammond, 1977). Lobbyists are seen to be valuable sources of information for Congress because of their special expertise on increasingly complex and technical policies. Associations use their newsletters to inform members of issues that affect the well-being of their industry. Frequently, these stories provide the names and telephone numbers of congressional staff who are gathering comments and suggestions from the field. Letters from constituents, especially those with apparent wealth, influence, and position in their communities, provide valuable evidence of public sentiment on a particular issue. But, it is the indirect subsidy that is the most vital tool of modern public relations.

Indirect Subsidies

The indirect information subsidy still operates to reduce the cost of access to information used by decision makers. However, it increases the effective demand for the preferred information by eliminating the discount that is associated with the perception of self-interest on the part of direct subsidy givers. Policy actors provide indirect subsidies through a variety of means, most of which have to do with using a credible source to deliver a persuasive message. Journalists are blessed with a self-generated cloak of objectivity. Thus, material perceived as news, rather than as opinion, has a higher value to the decision maker. Indirect subsidies are therefore regularly provided through journalists and editors of print and electronic news media.

Public relations specialists have developed an array of techniques used for the management of the press, the purpose of which is to provide indirect subsidies to other participants in the policy process. An important means of providing indirect subsidies is through the use of experts. Scholars and research scientists have a special credibility both within and outside of government. Corporate and government policy actors actively recruit scholars to present the "party line" in conferences, symposia, and professional journals, whereupon the works can be quoted, or submitted into the record. So-called independent research and policy centers are the source for much of this policy relevant scholarship (Alpert & Markusen, 1980). Centers come to be identified with a particular perspective; some even have formal links to the Republican or Democratic party. Some, like the American Enterprise Institute and the Brookings Foundation, occasionally include token scholars from the opposing camps (Dionne, 1989). Because busy legislators are unlikely to read through the dense verbiage of academic scholarship, much of the work from these centers is filtered through the press.

Weiss and Singer (1988) explored the relations between social scientists and the press, noting the importance of the scientists and their information offices in getting notice of their work presented in the nation's press. Institutional sources accounted for 50% of the material that eventually made its way into the media channel. Those sources reached the press primarily through press releases and press conferences organized for the convenience of the press corps. Scientists were seen to have a special advantage over many other sources used by the press.

> Most reporters accepted the expertise of their sources on faith. Several reporters voiced a general scepticism about the social sciences, but when it came to reporting a particular story, they assumed that the research was valid and that quoted experts were basing their comments on social science knowledge. They took for granted that people in these university, research institute, or government positions were qualified by virtue of their positions and their credentials, and did not inquire into the nature of the evidence, the methods used to collect the data, or the cogency of alternative explanations. (p. 38)

This apparent advantage enjoyed by science also seems to apply to the "scientific" trappings of public opinion surveys that are frequently designed more for the public relations impact than for their scientific validity.

The Republican and Democratic parties, as well as the major industry associations concerned with how the grass roots understand policy issues, have invested in the creation of media production facilities to provide high quality subsidies to the electronic press (Armstrong, 1988). These "actualities" are designed so as to be irresistable to the news editor of a local station, at the same time they provide direct access to the citizenry in the context of an objective "news" report.

Indeed grassroots lobbying is a very important means of delivering an indirect subsidy. Whereas the national and capital press are used to deliver subsidies to the legislators in a single hop, the local press is frequently used to deliver a subsidy through a "second hop." News coverage is managed through the provision of a subsidy to the station or newspaper through the wire services, or through satellite distribution. The public is then led to express its opinions to government representatives through the mails. If the news story is not sufficient to generate constituent mail, there are a host of direct mail and telemarketing routines that are readily called into play. Efforts to increase grassroots compliance with the public relations goals include reducing the cost and effort involved in their response, without at the same time giving evidence of manipulation. High-speed laser printers are used to generate versions of constituent mail in hundreds of typefaces, including an approximation of a child's scrawl, at the rate of 6,000 per hour (Armstrong, 1988; Meadow, 1985; Swerdlow, 1988).

There is a growing literature that estimates the varying degrees of success with which public relations offices succeed in having their subsidies delivered through the press (Ettema et al., 1989; Turk, 1986; Turk & Franklin, 1987; Turow, in press). This literature is troubled by the problems of demonstrating effects or estimating the extent of influence. These are problems not unlike those faced by scholars who seek a definitive answer about whether advertising works, or whether it makes sense to advertise (Jones, 1989). The answer is as obvious as its proof is elusive. Anecdotal evidence and case studies abound, yet journalists are driven to deny susceptibility (Hess, 1984, 1986) at the same time that government and corporate officials must deny their own efforts to influence public opinion through management of the watchdog press.

THE IDEOLOGY OF THE INFORMATION AGE

Several authors (Mitchell, 1989; Olasky, 1987) who have examined the history of public relations have noted the importance of changing social and economic conditions that brought industry and government under pressure from the citizenry. These changes have been met historically with a dramatic modification and expansion of the public relations enterprise. Mitchell (1989) argued that the changes in corporate social policy were the result of a crisis of legitimacy. "The ideological resolution to the problem of legitimizing the power of the modern corporation is to shift from denying power to actively justifying it by denying selfishness" (p. 56). Public relations efforts became necessary to make this denial credible. Many authors suggest that we are presently entering a new age that represents yet another change in the fortunes of business, and the relations between corporations and the state (Hall & Preston, 1988; Robins & Webster, 1988). The information age is also an age of global markets and economic interdependence. The giant corporations that were the dominant social concerns at the turn of the century have become transnationals (TNCs) with an uncertain loyalty to the populations in their primary national base. It is this question of loyalty that raises problems of legitimation for the TNCs in search of privilege and security in the marketplace.

Jerry Salvaggio (1987) made an important contribution to our understanding of the role of public relations in structuring dominant views about this future society. He argued that the information industry serves its collective interests by "fostering a technological ideology" (p. 146). This ideology must necessarily overcome the general anxiety with which individuals approach the unknown, and the more specific concerns associated with representations in popular mass culture of an Orwellian dystopia (Meehan, 1988). Salvaggio identified several ways in which the industry, in cooperation with the government, might provide direct and indirect information subsidies to facilitate construction of more idyllic representations of an information society.

His review of advertisements by firms in the information sector identified an emphasis on the ubiquity of the technology and its necessity for the readers of business periodicals. These ads introduced new terms and concepts such as *networking* and *telemarketing* that have since moved into the everyday speech of corporate decision makers. Salvaggio described the route through which the indirect subsidies of information firms make their way into the stream of grassroots consciousness. Hyperbolic press releases are seen to achieve credibility as they make their way into popular nonfiction, such as those published by futurist Alvin Toffler (1980), and the techno-pop features of general and specialized periodicals.

INDUSTRIAL POLICY

Despite the efforts of the information industry to paint a picture of a rosy future, the best available data suggest that the U.S. economy is in a competitive decline. The U.S. balance of trade is overwhelmingly negative, and each day finds another sector where the United States once had dominance, under attack from the Newly Industrialized Countries (NICs) of Asia and Latin America, or from the as yet unrealized "fortress Europe" of 1992. Business and labor interests in the United States are in conflict over the causes and solutions to this critical problem (Johnson, 1984; Steinbruner, 1989). The failure of U.S. goods to succeed in foreign markets is seen to be a problem of protectionism, where other nations, Japan in particular, establish non-tarrif trade barriers that make it difficult for American goods to enter those markets. Other arguments, also directed toward Japan, claim that foreign goods have advantages in the U.S. market because they have benefited from government subsidies during their period of development. Analysis suggests that U.S. business has turned its back on the consumer electronics industry, despite the fact that the leading bets are that the next wave of innovations that bring industrial economies out of their decline will be in applications for this market (Hall & Preston, 1988).

The solutions to the dual problem of competitiveness is protection for U.S. industry through restrictive tarrifs, and through increases in U.S. support for research and development in vital information industries. Both solutions are in conflict with the ideology of deregulation and privitization. This fact leads some observers (Mosco, 1989) to suggest that the ideological arguments of the Reagan administration were a smoke screen for a redistribution, rather than a reduction, of government involvement in the economy.

HDTV and the Last Chance Polka

The debate over the development of High Definition Television (HDTV) contains both these elements of a national industrial policy ("Super television," 1989). The policy regarding HDTV standards is linked to a non-tarrif barrier to foreign technologies that would be incompatible with the U.S. NTSC standard. Deliberations in the United States over HDTV standards will not be limited to the arguments presented by American firms. European firms have organized a consortium to promote their own system and standard, "Eureka 95" ("High definition," 1989). Establishing the European option as the worldwide standard involves considerable lobbying as "many U.S. hearts and minds in the federal government and sectors of the TV broadcasting and production industries will have to be won" (p. 48). Thoughts were that this strategy would best be accomplished by attempting to establish a Euro-American front against Japan.

Ampex Corporation, a manufacturer of professional videotape recorders, presented a series of full-page ads in the *Wall Street Journal* for the purpose of "clearing the air about high-definition television" (Ampex Corporation, 1989). One ad begins with a counterattack against those elements in the U.S. industry that sought to guarantee a federal subsidy by describing the U.S. television industry as being in decline: "many people would have you believe that the U.S. TV industry is gasping for breath. Even that America is 'fighting for its hightech life'" (p. A9B). Their ad and the brochure and letter that followed a request for more information emphasize the standards issue, and reject the troubled industry argument for subsidy or precipitous action.

U.S. firms represented by the American Electronics Association (AEA) present the HDTV issue as a critical moment in the history of the U.S. electronics industry. Failure to re-establish U.S. dominance in this industry is argued to be the linchpin that if lost, would unravel the U.S. position in microprocessors, memories, and other advanced chips ("Super television," 1989). Even the U.S. lead in the market for personal computers was presented as threatened by loss of the HDTV war. The HDTV debate may be a Trojan Horse in the same way that the Race to the Moon, the War on Poverty, and even the Star Wars initiative can be seen as prominent campaigns that sought the support of public opinion and provided a hidden entrance for more basic changes in the domestic policy system. The excitement over HDTV has led to broad acceptance of arguments for changes in anti-trust policy. These changes would allow American firms to cooperate in consortia, joint manufacturing agreements, and other ways that were barred by statute and tradition in the past. Seventeen U.S. firms, among the giants of American industry, indicated a willingness to form an alliance to develop HDTV, with the U.S. taxpayers putting up 49% of the bill ("Super television," 1989).

Ignored in all the debates over standards and quality is the fact that the technology is far more expensive than the average consumer is likely to pay. Thus, we have yet another case of an industry seeking government support to develop a technology for which the demand is nonexistent at the present, and even questionable in the future. The industry has no basis whatsoever for its predictions that the HDTV industry will become a "$20 billion domestic and a $40 billion international market by the year 2007" (Kriz, 1989, p. 470).

Deregulation and Privitization

The transformation of the relationship between state and private firms increasingly involves the dual strategies of deregulation and privitization. It is the role of public relations to make such changes appear normal and rational—simple good common sense. Deregulation involves the elimination of those government restrictions on the pursuit of profit. Whereas regulation requires firms to take responsibility for the negative externalities or spill-over effects associated with their lines of business, deregulation treats them as the costs of progress and global competitiveness. Privitization involves the removal of the state from the provision of services that were previously ignored by business because they were unprofitable. Where the government had previously been involved in the provision of what we have come to describe as public goods, services like education, telecommunications, defense, public works, and even military and police protection services are being provided by private firms. Massive public relations campaigns have been used by states in crisis to effect the transformation of local public utilities into private global competitors.

Newman's (1986) study of the selling of British Telecom describes the historic success of a marketing campaign that not only accomplished the transfer of a public resource into private hands, but at least temporarily, brought thousands of British citizens into the stock market for the first time. The campaign was a classic in social marketing that included direct and indirect subsidies of the press. The audiences were segmented and targeted by specially tailored messages delivered through different sections of selected media outlets. Media planners organized press briefings, personal interviews, and group orientation sessions.

> The effect of such news management was notable for the extent of coverage and perhaps the best example of press relations can be seen in the four feature articles which appeared in the *Financial Times* in October, tailor-made for the city. . . . But to capture the financial journalist and business journalist was not enough. It was essential to spread media coverage of the issue from city pages and business programmes into more generalized areas of family finance pages, documentaries and news programmes. (pp. 138–139)

The British government has been a major user of commercial advertising firms to deliver its social messages. In 1988, the British government was third, behind Unilever and Proctor & Gamble, in paid advertising. It seems that "policies, like soap or candy bars must be sold in the marketplace." In the present era "advertising has become the medium for transmitting the self-help message of Thatcherism" (Lohr, 1989, p. D1). Although much of the budget is allocated for health and anti-drug messages, "the largest Government campaigns have been for the sale of state-owned corporations to private investors" (p. D28).

Economics Over Values

The rationales that are emerging as dominant in policy deliberations, as well as in public discourse, are the result of public relations efforts. Just as corporate public relations accomplished the transformation of the public ideology of American business from profit to public responsibility (Mitchell, 1989), public relations in the corporate interest provided through private foundations has transformed the models of policy analysis. Domhoff (1979) identified a key role for foundations in the policy formation process that includes the funding of research centers and policy planning groups. Duncan Brown (1988) credited the Markle Foundation with the movement to create programs and institutes that would advance the application of economic analysis to problems of communications policy. Seybold (1987) offered an analysis of the transformation of political science through the influence of the Ford Foundation. Ford accomplished the elevation of behavioral methods to a superior position in political science, and social science in general, through a coordinated program that involved "support for individual scholars, the establishment and support of research institutes, the reorientation of professional journals, the recruitment of intermediary organizations, and the training of young scholars in the methodology of behavioralism" (p. 191).

As a behavioral rather than a philosophical or historical method, neoclassical economics was swept along in this movement to enlist the social sciences "in an effort to preserve the stability of the American institutional order" (Seybold, 1987, p. 196). The campaign to introduce economics education begun by the Joint Council on Economic Education, and funded by the Committee for Economic Development in 1949 (Domhoff, 1979), has produced impressive results. Questions of economic efficiency have displaced concern with justice, equality, and fairness not only in congressional and legislative debates, but in the opinions offered by judges in the appellate courts. This ideology of the information age, that of deregulation and privitization, justified on the basis of unproven assumptions about the efficiency of the marketplace, stands as the most important accomplishment of elite public relations.

INFORMATION TECHNOLOGY

The priority of efficiency over values, including the value of human dignity, is also to be revealed in the structuring of policy debates about the use of new technologies in the information age. Deregulation and privitization are joined by commoditization as process labels that point to critical changes in the social fabric of American society. In order to avoid the periodic crises that are common to capitalist economies, it is continually necessary to create and introduce new products into the marketplace (Schiller, 1988). *Commoditization* refers to the process through which resources that were once developed collectively, within families or communities, and were exchanged outside of formal markets, have become transformed into marketable goods and services, and exchanged only for a fee. This process of commoditization brings social production under the control and logic of capitalism. The logic of capitalism ensures that only those commodities that can be sold at a profit will be produced, and only those who can pay can have access. Mosco (1989) referred to this as the "pay-per society" with reference to the increased ability of computer-based systems to charge for information services in convenient units such as a program, an abstract, or a minute of time. This increasingly automated control over mass consumption (Beniger, 1986) is seen by some as a natural extension of the process of rationalizing production and distribution systems with the use of computers (Wilson, 1988).

Computers

The importance of the computer in the information age is not well understood (Rule & Attewell, 1989). The computer is not mainly, or even primarily, a device for computation. It is the core of a control technology that involves the processing of information at high speed. Its place in manufacturing is assured by its ability to control machine processes, to work reliably and continuously. But the place of the computer in the control of distribution, consumption, and system governance is assured by its ability to store, access, compare, and share information.

Public relations campaigns have been necessary historically to cushion the introduction of computers into the factory and the office. The followers of Ned Ludd (Webster & Robins, 1986) were neither the first nor the last to recognize the threats represented by the application of scientific management to the workplace. The debate over whether automation creates more jobs than it eliminates is unquestionably an arena where public relations on behalf of American industry has been influential (Cyert & Mowery, 1989; Miller, 1983; Shaiken, 1984). It is in the interest of American industry as a whole to create an ideological wedge to break through any resistance to computerization that may exist at different levels of the corporate structure. It is similarly in the interest of the government to attempt to guide this movement in directions that minimize the political costs associated with rising unemployment.

The development and introduction of information technologies into the mainstream of social experience is a complex process, never fully planned and controlled, although planning efforts abound. A multifaceted campaign of information subsidies was developed in a partially successful effort to introduce instructional technologies into American classrooms (Gandy, 1976). The campaign that began in 1958 with the passage of the National Defense Education Act (NDEA) involved a high degree of cooperation and coordination between defense-electronics firms, the Washington-based associations of educators, audiovisual specialists, and the federal education bureaucracy. Similar patterns of mutually reinforcing research and dissemination accompany our movement into the electronic age.

The U.S. Office of Technology Assessment (USOTA) joins the National Science Foundation as the site for legislative review of implications for various "stakeholders" of the spread of computer-based information systems. Advisory panels with corporate and academic representation meet regularly to review consultant reports and early drafts of massive studies claiming to present the best thinking available on a problem like "Federal Information Dissemination in an Electronic Age" (USOTA, 1988). It is virtually impossible to engage in a kind of reverse engineering to identify the origins in public relations for the conclusions and recommendations to be found in this or any other OTA report. But it is clear that the message is always forward, ever forward.

Telecommunications Networks

Whereas the speed, power, and capacity of computers continue to grow at exponential rates, a more significant development in the information age is the ability to provide rapid, reliable, and low-cost interconnections between these systems. Telecommunications networks make possible the interconnection and coordination of businesses with hundreds of subsidiaries, such as the giant retail outlets like Sears and Montgomery Ward. They also facilitate coordination of modern manufacturing that depends on the receipt of components from hundreds of independent suppliers spread around the country and the globe. These networks are the essential life blood of the global financial system facilitating the transfer of funds between banks and other financial institutions. Increasingly, telecommunications networks facilitate the remote processing of the credit transactions of the millions of credit and store card customers who seek authorization of their purchases through point-of-purchase terminals in restaurants, gas stations, and even fast food counters (Rubin, 1988). Telecommunications links between remote computers create the reality of centralized control with the illusion of decentralization and independence (Clement, 1988).

Important policy debates in the information age have to do with who will pay for the development, installation, and maintenance of these networks (Aufderheide, 1987). Debates about deregulation in telecommunications are not only about questions of the inefficiencies of monopoly supply, through a state monopoly as in Europe, or a corporate monopoly, as with AT&T in the United States. They have also to do with the extent to which residential consumers should be required to pay (and be convinced of the justice in such demands) for "bells and whistles" in the telecommunications network that they do not need, and are unlikely to use. It is not only residential consumers who are unsure why they might need to be part of an Integrated Services Digital Network (ISDN). Chief executives of middle-level corporations, including those with fairly large telecommunications bills, are unsure of what, beyond high costs, ISDN means for them. Reports of uncertain demand appear regularly in the industry weekly *Communications Week*, to be balanced occasionally by a glowing report by a supplier who has found "surprising interest" in ISDN services (Foley & Nelson-Rowe, 1988).

Despite the uncertainty of demand, and in the absence of any consumer pressure for the elimination of the AT&T monopoly, we find that a coalition of network service providers, in cooperation with the major users of telecommunications for high-speed data transfer, have succeeded in achieving a transformation of the telecommunications industry, an upheaval in its regulatory and pricing structure, and the formation of a domestic position to be pursued in negotiations with foreign partners in trade (Aronson & Cowhey, 1988; Schiller, 1982).

Intellectual Technology

The technology of the information age is not limited to wires, microchips, lasers, and digital displays. Although the machines provide the potential for work, it is an intellectual technology that suggests how this effort should be applied. It is the software, the applications programs that determine how information is to be processed and displayed. It is the development of ways of thinking about information or data in order to generate intelligence as guides to action that have influenced our movement toward the consolidation of bureaucratic power over individual lives (Gandy, 1989).

From the popular spreadsheet programs that allow decision makers to ask a variety of "what if" questions, to the graphics programs that display the answers in animated three-dimensional displays, the range of programs that are available to "make sense" of the complexity of our environment grows at an incredible rate. Three classes of programs or procedures have a particular importance for an analysis of power in the information age. Matching, profiling, and segmentation represent three related components of the same technology of social control. An analytical challenge rests in tracking the ways in which these procedures become accepted as normal, almost casual aspects of the daily routines of individuals (Giddens, 1984).

Matching involves the comparison of names of individuals, images in a database, pictures in a file with similar sets of data. Matching routines are useful for identification, where a match of characteristics of a signature argue for the authenticity of a check. Matching routines are useful for verification of claims or assertions based on a logic that says if X is true, then Y must also be true. Failure to find a matching Y leads the program and analyst to question the initial assertion. Matching routines form the basis for pattern recognition programs that point out similarities and differences in images, movements, and cell structure. Parallel-processing computers allow matching programs to search through mountains of data in an instant. The easier and less expensive it becomes, the greater the incentive to apply the technology for new and more creative matches. A match is a search. Reductions in the cost of search will tend to increase the number of searches, and expand the realms into which searches are made. All that is required is that the data exist in a file, or can be readily transformed into machine readable form.

Profiling involves another kind of matching. Here similarities in attributes and behaviors are associated statistically. Clusters of characteristics are related analytically with other clusters of behavior. Profiles are predictive models that are used to classify individuals as members of groups that have an estimated probability of acting or responding in particular way to a stimulus, a challenge, or an opportunity. In essence, profiles make predictions about the likely behavior of a particular individual on the basis of information about the behavior of others. Profiles are used to select candidates for office, to identify potential criminals, even to provide recommendations for imprisonment or parole. Profiles may be used to identify individuals at risk for particular diseases, or likely to file for bankruptcy.

As with matching in general, increases in the capacity of computers to store, process, and display data, combined with the facilitation that network interconnection provides for access to more data, ensure that developers of profiles will include more and more data in the construction of their predictive models. In advance of personal knowledge we have always used stereotypes to make decisions about persons we come into contact with. In the information age, this stereotyping is automatic and remote, and based on a model developed with limited input from its users. Public relations will be called on to make such uses of stereotypes socially acceptable.

Segmentation refers to the differential treatment that is afforded to individuals once their profile assigns them to a particular category of opportunity or risk. Segmentation allows the delivery of specially designed, targeted messages, thought to be more efficient because the symbols, images, and representations that they present resonate on a similar cultural frequency to those of their targets.

These technologies of matching, profiling, and segmentation are data dependent. Restrictions on access to information about individual attitudes, opinions, and behavior in their roles of citizen, consumer, and employee limit their utility as instruments of guidance and control. Thus, attitudes and formal policies that restrict access to information about individuals represent a serious threat to government and private bureaucracies. A major public relations effort has therefore begun to diffuse this threat.

Surveillance and the Hegemonic Challenge

Critical theorists of social control in the information age (Gandy, 1989; Marx, 1988; Robins & Webster, 1988) call our attention to the role of surveillance in the maintenance of discipline without brute force (Foucault, 1977). Jeremy Bentham's panopticon, a design for a prison where the inmates would always be under surveillance, serves as a powerful metaphor for contemporary surveillance of individuals in their roles as workers, consumers, and citizens. Just as modern prisons are supposed to provide for rehabilitation, the disciplinary, rather than punitive, nature of modern surveillance is designed to provide the continuous monitoring that allows the prevention of wrongful acts. Modern surveillance allows discipline to be anticipatory. The information systems that make possible the collection, processing, and sharing of information about individuals allow organizations to restrict, reward, invite, ignore, prod, and probe almost at will. The primary limitations on this disciplinary technology are individual expectations of privacy. Reasonable expectations of privacy serve as the basis for legal redress for presumed abuse of disciplinary power. Organizations that depend on free access to personal information have every incentive to try and normalize public expectations of surveillance. By stripping the cloak of reasonableness from privacy concerns, the hegemonic web is made complete.

The debate about privacy that is emerging in the courts, congressional hearings, government studies (USOTA, 1986), and the popular and academic press (Linowes, 1989; Rubin, 1988) has become a critical site for ideological struggle. Government and corporate public relations resources have been mobilized to strike a balance between the demands of capital and the values of human dignity and autonomy. Insurance companies have provided the financial backing for the largest surveys of public opinion about privacy (Louis Harris, 1983; Westin & Harris, 1979), and these studies have found broad discussion in Congress. Currently, the protections for individual privacy in the United States pale in comparison to those available in Europe and Canada. Regan (1981) attributed this to a primary incapacity of liberal democracies to recognize the existence of bureaucratic power, combined with an unwillingness to trust the state to take action toward its control. In the face of growing deregulation and privitization, the distinctions between state and corporate bureaucracies in terms of their impact on our expectations of privacy are bound to disappear.

Government Surveillance

In exchange for a largely illusory gain in the struggle with mounting federal deficits, an all out campaign to eliminate "waste, fraud, and abuse" in the delivery of government services has provided the ideological basis for a multifaceted assault on privacy. Stimulated by the recommendations of the Grace Commission (President's Private Sector Survey on Cost Control), federal agencies accelerated their efforts to utilize the techniques of computer matching and profiling to identify potential sources of fraud or indebtedness. Consistent with the mood and philosophy of the Grace Commission, The Office of Management and Budget developed guidelines that would require each of the states to perform a series of matches to determine eligibility before federal funds could be allocated in the state's social service programs. This "front-end verification" procedure is seen (USOTA, 1986) to have created a "de facto national database," despite the long history of public resistance to permitting such a capacity to fall into government hands.

Privacy in the Workplace

The drive for efficiency in business limits our reasonable expectations of privacy with each passing day. The claim that drug use represents a serious threat to the competitiveness of American firms is being used to support widespread, random drug testing throughout the United States. As part of the "Partnership for a Drug-Free America," ads have appeared in the nation's leading newspapers offering suggestions to managers of ways to identify employees with a drug problem. One striking ad presents an attractive, professionally dressed young woman at her desk. The copy suggests that when you interview her, she will tell you about her MBA and her other valuable qualities, but will not tell you about her drug use. "For that you will have to dig a little deeper." The ad provides a telephone number to call to receive a manager's kit of information resources to aid in the struggle.

A cover story in *Business Week* ("Privacy," 1988) provides a basis for understanding the struggle between industry and labor about the definition of the boundary between the individual and corporate bureaucracy. Industry estimates of the rationale for the assault on privacy are given clear voice. In their view:

> It's not that most companies are idly snooping into their employees' lives. Behind the erosion of privacy lie pressing corporate problems. Drug use costs American industry nearly $50 billion a year in absenteeism and turnover. When employer groups opposed the lie detector bills, they cited employee theft, which is estimated at up to $10 billion annually. (p. 61)

In addition to screening and testing for drugs, American corporations feel driven by cost concerns to inquire about the extent of an employee's risk for AIDS. A variety of tests, most of questionable validity, are being developed or are in use to evaluate workers' honesty, devotion to the job, and their reliability as members of the corporate team. Even genetic screening is seen to be within the realm of reason as corporations face rising health insurance costs. Genetic screening would allow personnel departments to avoid hiring persons whose genetic profile suggests susceptibility to particular illnesses.

The *Business Week* article frames worker concerns about privacy as "a turning point in the cycle of management-labor relations" ("Privacy," 1988, pp. 62–63). Although legislative debates and court challenges unfold as workers resist this and other insults to their dignity that flow from the assumption of guilt, rather than innocence (Smith, 1983), it is public relations that will be brought to bear on our understanding of just what is at stake.

Privacy and Direct Marketing

The direct marketing industry, which rivals mass marketing advertising as the dominant form of promotion for products, services, and ideas, is concerned that public resistance to business practices may result in the elimination of their primary marketing tool, the enhanced database of names derived from the computerized matching of files. The threat moved toward a critical stage when the press reported that the Internal Revenue Service (IRS) was using files available from commercial vendors to compare incomes reported in tax returns to estimates of income that the list builders generated with their modeling programs. The Direct Marketing Association has responded to the threat of privacy legislation by establishing a specialized task force begun with an initial $50,000 grant from American Express. Such a task force will allow the direct marketing industry to follow and respond to threats to its survival in any of the courts in the United States. The purpose of the task force is described as part of a "comprehensive legislative and public relations strategy 'to provide a continuing, unified, consistent approach to the handling of privacy issues based on new developments and the direct marketing field's attempts to remain free from burdensome regulations' " ("Privacy task force," 1989).

Efforts to develop a cohesive industry position on privacy issues include debates and discussions in national and regional meetings, publication of articles and editorials in the trade magazine, *Direct Marketing,* and announcements of new developments in the weekly newsletter, *Friday Report.* Part of the struggle to develop a common voice involves efforts to discipline firms on the periphery of the industry that engage in practices likely to raise the ire of consumers. TRW is frequently cited for practices that threaten the future of the direct marketing industry. These citations reflect an ideological tension in between perspectives at the core of an emergent industry posture regarding privacy. American Express, more highly visible because of its cards and traveler's checks, has taken the posture of a model corporate citizen, concerned with the values underlying public concerns with privacy (Papone, 1980). TRW and Equifax, both involved in consumer credit reports to commercial clients, argue that their behavior is well within the limits established by law.

Privacy Versus Commercial Free Speech

Part of the strategy of the industry involves an assessment of the potential for associating its business practices with bedrock values. Although there is a general sense that business is on relatively weak ground when arguing that its practices do not invade individual privacy, many believe that there is a more powerful argument to be made in terms of the First Amendment guarantees of speech. According to Rubin (1988), "in those instances where these two rights have been found to be in conflict, the right to commercial free speech has been accorded a higher priority than has the right of personal privacy" (p. 129). A bill that would give the public the right to determine the source of the list from which they were selected to receive unwanted sexually explicit material was seen to be "part of the slippery slope that leads to restrictive laws that ultimately abridge everyone's First Amendment Rights" ("Sexually explicit," 1989, p. 1). The legislative sponsor of the bill, Representative Wayne Owens (D–UT) argued that he was acting in the public interest because he thought the bill "will help force magazine publishers to use greater discretion in selling or renting their lists. If a postal patron is easily able to determine that the publisher of his or her favorite magazine sold their list to a pornographer, perhaps reputable publishers will not sell their lists so indiscriminately" ("Sexually explicit," 1989, p. 1).

The "Bork" Bill and Transaction Records

The direct marketing industry was able to mobilize its forces with some success in the recent deliberations over the Video Privacy Protection Act of 1988. The Direct Marketing Association (DMA) moved quickly to testify against the bill in congress that would have restricted use of customer transaction information. It seems that during hearings on the confirmation of Robert Bork's nomination to the Supreme Court, a local video store released a list of Bork's rentals, and they were published in a local paper. The legislation as originally drafted would have dealt a fatal blow to the database marketing industry. It would have required the customer to provide specific approval for information about his or her rentals or purchases to be sold or exchanged.

The DMA moved quickly and effectively to express its view to congress that if video lists are made illegal, magazine lists would not be far behind. Although the full details of the industry's assault on this legislation are not known, the results are clear. The DMA won a stunning victory, and it did not hesitate to shout about it. Rather than requiring the vendor to acquire positive approval from customers before it shares personal information, the final Bill introduced a negative option, where the consumer must indicate a desire to prohibit disclosure. In the view of Robert Posh, a columnist for *Direct Marketing*, "assuming we avoid complacency, we have built a Congressional endorsement and trade-off which carry us into the next century" ("Video privacy," 1988, p. 1).

CONCLUSIONS AND RECOMMENDATIONS

The Information Age is a time of great change in the United States, and around the globe. It is characterized by dramatic changes in the nature of work, where increasingly larger shares of the workforce are engaged in the production of information goods and services. It is also a time of change and conflict in social values. The conservative policies that characterized the Reagan and Thatcher administrations represent a stepping back from the social role assigned to the states at the turn of the century. Because of the heightened interdependence of nations in the emerging global economy, we can expect that social policies, and the ideological positions that justify them, will become increasingly similar. Currently, the United States is playing a leading role in spreading the gospel of deregulation and privatization to our trading partners, and to those who would like to join in. This period of great instability and change provides a unique opportunity to observe the role of public relations in achieving this transformation.

The transnational corporations in the information sector, such as AT&T, IBM, and American Express, will play a central role in structuring the debates on a great many issues in policy fora around the globe. Their participation in advisory boards and policy committees will represent only a fraction of the resources they will commit toward structuring the policy debates in their own interests. Information subsidies will abound, but tracking them down will become increasingly difficult. The movement toward cooperative research and development and marketing, not only domestically, but internationally, will make it difficult to identify a particular corporate source for material that reflects the interests of a global industrial combine. Increased dependence on associations, Washington consultants, and single issue coalitions further blurs the lines between public relations campaigns and their authors. But there is a more serious problem still.

Because of the movement toward greater segmentation and targeting of promotional messages, utilizing cable, videotext, direct mail, and telemarketing (Armstrong, 1988), the trail will become harder to find. The same technology that allows a source to send out thousands of different forms of direct mail makes it virtually impossible for a researcher to monitor them without the cooperation of the source. Where it was possible to do content analysis of the mass media, even tracking down duplicates of unsigned editorials from a syndicate that appear in newspapers across the country, this will no longer be the case in the demassified media world (Wilson & Gutierrez, 1985). Indexing services do not track electronic mail. And, what most of us will see in the political advertisement, or hear on the network news, may bear only the most casual relationship to what high priority targets might receive.

Students of public relations must become sensitive to the implications of these trends in the structuring of policy debates. Public relations, issues management, and the engineering of consent are practices that are here to stay. The technology of segmentation and targeting, guided by near total surveillance, advantages the major players still further. The challenge before us is to describe these practices in ways that help citizen/consumers to understand the ways in which their power is being diminished.

REFERENCES

Alpert, I., & Markusen, A. (1980). Think tanks and capitalist policy. In G. Domhoff (Ed.), *Power structure research* (pp. 173–197). Newbury Park, CA: Sage.

Ampex Corporation. (1989, June 23). Clearing the air about high-definition television. No. 2. *Wall Street Journal*, p. A9B.

Armstrong, R. (1988). *The next hurrah: The communications revolution in American politics.* New York: William Morrow.

Aronson, J., & Cowhey, P. (1988). *When countries talk: International trade in telecommunications services.* Cambridge, MA: Ballinger.

Aufderheide, P. (1987). Universal service: Telephone policy in the public interest. *Journal of Communication, 37*(1), 81–96.

Bagdikian, B. (1987). *The media monopoly* (2nd ed.). Boston: Beacon Press.

Bates, B. (1988). Information as an economic good: Sources of individual and social value. In V. Mosco & J. Wasko (Eds.), *The political economy of information* (pp. 76–94). Madison, WI: University of Wisconsin Press.

Beniger, J. (1986). *The control revolution. Technological and economic origins of the information society.* Cambridge, MA: Harvard University Press.

Blaug, M. (1983). A methodological appraisal of radical economics. In T. Hutchinson & A. Coats (Eds.), *Methodological controversy in economics* (pp. 211–245). Greenwich, CT: JAI Press.

Brown, D. (1988, July). *Reshaping the debate over broadcast regulation in the United States.* Paper presented to the Working Group on Communication Policy at the 16th Conference and General Assembly of the International Association for Mass Communication Research. Barcelona.

Browne, W. (1988). *Private interests, public policy, and American agriculture.* Lawrence, KS: University Press of Kansas.

Clement, A. (1988). Office automation and the technical control of information workers. In V. Mosco & J. Wasko (Eds.), *The political economy of information* (pp. 217–246). Madison, WI: University of Wisconsin Press.

Cyert, R., & Mowery, D. (1989). Technology, employment and U.S. competitiveness. *Scientific American, 260*(5), 54–62.

Dionne, E. (1989, June 28). The new think tank on the block. *New York Times.* p. A20.

Domhoff, G. (1979). *The powers that be: Processes of ruling class domination in America.* New York: Vintage Books.

Earl, P. (1983). *The economic imagination. Towards a behavioral analysis of choice.* Armonk, NY: M. E. Sharpe.

Ettema, J., Protess, D., Leff, D., Miller, P., Doppelt, J., & Cook, F. (1989, August). *Agenda-setting as politics: A case study of the press-public-policy connection at the post-modern moment.* Paper presented at the meeting of the Association for Education in Journalism and Mass Communication, Washington, DC.

Etzioni, A. (1988). *The moral dimension: Toward a new economics.* New York: The Free Press.

Foley J., & Nelson-Rowe, L. (1988, December 5). Users spur AT&T's ISDN campaign. *Communications Week,* pp. 1, 47.

Foucault, M. (1977). *Discipline and punish* (A. Sheridan, Trans.). New York: Random House.

Fox, H., & Hammond, S. (1977). *Congressional staffs. The invisible force in American lawmaking.* New York: The Free Press.

Gandy, O. (1976). *Instructional technology: The selling of the Pentagon. The investigation of a subsidy for the capitalization of education.* Unpublished doctoral dissertation, Stanford University, Stanford, CA.

Gandy, O. (1982). *Beyond agenda setting. Information subsidies and public policy.* Norwood, NJ: Ablex.

Gandy, O. (1989). The surveillance society: Information technology and bureaucratic social control. *Journal of Communication, 39*(3), 61–76.

Garnham, N. (1979). Contribution to a political economy of mass-communication. *Media, Culture and Society, 1,* 123–146.

Giddens, A. (1984). *The constitution of society: Outline of a theory of structuration.* Cambridge, MA: Polity Press.

Golding, P., & Middleton, S. (1982). *Images of welfare: Press and public attitudes to poverty.* Oxford: Martin Robertson.

Grunig, J. L. (1989). *Symmetrical presuppositions as a framework for public relations theory.* In C. H. Botan & V. Hazelton, Jr. (Eds.), *Public relations theory.* Hillsdale, NJ: Lawrence Erlbaum Associates.

Guback, T. (1969). *The international film industry.* Bloomington: Indiana University Press.

Hall, P., & Preston, P. (1988). *The carrier wave. New information technology and the geography of innovation, 1846–2003.* London: Unwin Hyman.

Heath, R., & Nelson, R. A. (1986). *Issues management. Corporate public policymaking in an information society.* Newbury Park, CA: Sage.

Helm, L. (1981). *Informing the people.* New York: Longman.

Herman, E., & Chomsky, N. (1988). *Manufacturing consent. The political economy of the mass media.* New York: Pantheon.

Hess, S. (1984). *The government/press connection.* Washington, DC: The Brookings Foundation.

Hess, S. (1986). *The ultimate insiders.* Washington, DC: The Brookings Foundation.

High definition dominates Montreaux. (1989, June 26). *Broadcasting,* pp. 47–51.

Jaynes, G., & Williams, R. (Eds.). (1989). *A common destiny: Blacks and American society.* Washington, DC: National Academy Press.

Johnson, C. (Ed.). (1984). *The industrial policy debate.* San Francisco: Institute for Contemporary Studies.

Jones, J. (1989). *Does it pay to advertise?* Lexington, MA: Lexington Books.

Kahneman, D., & Tversky, A. (1986). Choices, values and frames. In N. Smelser & D. Gerstein (Eds.), *Behavioral and social science: Fifty years of discovery* (pp. 153–172). Washington, DC: National Academy Press.

Kiesler, C., Collins, B., & Miller, N. (1969). *Attitude change.* New York: Wiley.

Kriz, M. (1989, February 25). Turning on the new tv. *National Journal,* pp. 470–473.

Kruckeberg, D., & Stark, K. (1988). *Public relations and community.* New York: Praeger.

Lancaster, K. (1981). Information and product differentiation. In M. Galatin & R. Leiter (Eds.), *Economics of information* (pp. 17–35). Hingham, MA: M. Nijhoff.

Laumann, E., & Knoke, D. (1987). *The organizational state: Social choice in national policy domains.* Madison, WI: The University of Wisconsin Press.

Levitan, S., & Cooper, M. (1984). *Business lobbies. The public good and the bottom line.* Baltimore, MD: John Hopkins University Press.

Linowes, D. (1989). *Privacy in America.* Urbana, IL: University of Illinois Press.

Lohr, S. (1989, May 23). Major British advertiser: Government. *New York Times,* p. D1.

Louis Harris & Associates, Inc. (1983, December). *The road after 1984: A nationwide survey of the public and its leaders on the new technology and its consequences for American life* (Conducted for New England Telephone for presentation at the Eighth International Smithsonian Symposium).

Lusterman, S. (1988). *Managing federal government relations* (Research Rep. No. 905). New York: The Conference Board.

Mander, J. (1978). *Four arguments for the elimination of television.* New York: Quill.

Manheim, J., & Albritton, R. (1983, November). *Changing national images: International public relations and media agenda-setting* (mimeograph). Washington, DC: George Washington University.

Marx, G. (1988). *Undercover: Police surveillance in America.* Berkeley, CA: University of California Press.

Meadow, R. G. (Ed.). (1985). *New communication technologies in politics.* Washington, DC: The Washington Program of the Annenberg School of Communication.

Meehan, E. (1988). Technical capacity versus corporate imperatives: Toward a political economy of cable television and information diversity. In V. Mosco & J. Wasko (Eds.),

The political economy of information (pp. 167–187). Madison, WI: University of Wisconsin Press.

Miller, J. (Ed.). (1983, November). Robotics: Future factories, future workers (entire issue). *The Annals of the American Society of Political and Social Sciences, 470.*

Mitchell, N. (1989). *The generous corporation.* New Haven, CT: Yale University Press.

Mosco, V. (1988). Toward a theory of the state and telecommunications policy. *Journal of Communication, 38*(1), 107–124.

Mosco, V. (1989). *The pay-per society.* Norwood, NJ: Ablex.

Mosco, V., & Wasko, J. (Eds.). (1988). *The political economy of information.* Madison: University of Wisconsin Press.

Murdock, G. (1982). Large corporations and the control of communications industries. In M. Gurevitch, T. Bennett, J. Curran, & J. Woollacott (Eds.), *Culture, society and the media* (pp. 118–150). New York: Methuen.

Newman, K. (1986). *The selling of British Telecom.* New York: St Martin's Press.

Noll, R. (1986). The political and institutional context of communications policy. In M. Snow (Ed.), *Marketplace for telecommunications: Regulation and deregulation in industrialized democracies* (pp. 42–66). White Plains, NY: Longman.

Olasky, M. (1987). *Corporate public relations: A new historical perspective.* Hillsdale, NJ: Lawrence Erlbaum Associates.

Papone, A. (1980, April 23). *Statement of Aldo Papone, President Card Division, American Express. U. S. Senate.* Committee on Banking, Housing and Urban Affairs, Subcommittee on Consumer Affairs, Washington, DC.

Parsons, P. (1989). Defining cable television: Structuration and public policy. *Journal of Communication, 39*(2), 10–26.

Pertschuk, M. (1986). *Giant killers.* New York: Norton.

Privacy. (1988, March 28). *Business Week,* pp. 61–66.

Privacy task force being formed by Direct Marketing Association. (1989, January 6). *Friday Report,* p. 1.

Regan, P. (1981). *Public use of private information: A comparison of personal information policies in the United States and Britain.* Unpublished doctoral dissertation, Cornell University, Ithaca, NY.

Resnick, S., & Wolff, R. (1987). *Knowledge and class.* Chicago: University of Chicago Press.

Robins, K., & Webster, F. (1988). Cybernetic capitalism: Information, technology, everyday life. In V. Mosco & J. Wasko, (Eds.), *The political economy of information* (pp. 76–94). Norwood, NJ: Ablex.

Rubin, M. (1988). *Private rights, public wrongs: The computer and personal privacy.* Norwood, NJ: Ablex.

Rule, J., & Attewell, P. (1989). What do computers do? *Social Problems, 36*(3), 225–241.

Salvaggio, J. (1987). Projecting a positive image of the information society. In J. Slack & F. Fejes (Eds.). *The ideology of the information age* (pp. 146–157). Norwood, NJ: Ablex.

Schiller, D. (1982). *Telematics and government.* Norwood, NJ: Ablex.

Schiller, D. (1988). How to think about information. In V. Mosco & J. Wasko (Eds.), *The political economy of information* (pp. 27–43). Madison WI: University of Wisconsin Press.

Schiller, H. (1969). *Mass communication and American empire.* New York: A. M. Kelley.

Scholle, D. (1988). Critical studies: From the theory of ideology to power/knowledge. *Critical Studies in Mass Communication, 5,* 16–41.

Sexually explicit mail. (1989, March 24). *Friday Report,* p. 1.

Seybold, P. (1987). The Ford Foundation and the transformation of political science. In M. Schwartz (Ed.), *The structure of power in America* (pp. 185–198). New York: Holmes & Meier.

Shaiken, H. (1984). *Work transformed: Automation and labor in the computer age.* New York: Holt, Rinehart & Winston.

Smith, R. (1983). *Workrights.* New York: E.P. Dutton.

Staniland, M. (1985). *What is political economy? A study of social theory and underdevelopment.* New Haven: Yale University Press.

Steinberg, C. (1975). *The creation of consent.* New York: Hastings House.

Steinberg, C. (1980). *The information establishment.* New York: Hastings House.

Steinbruner, J. (1989). *Restructuring American foreign policy.* Washington, DC: The Brookings Foundation.

Super television. (1989, January 30). *Business Week,* pp. 56–66.

Swerdlow, J. (Ed.). (1988). *Media technology and the vote. A source book.* Boulder, CO: Westview Press.

Toffler, A. (1980). *The third wave.* New York: Bantam Books.

Toth, E. (1986). Broadening research in public relations. *Public Relations Review, 13*(3), 27–36.

Turk, J. (1986, December). Information subsidies and media content: A study of public relations influence on the news. *Journalism Monographs, No. 100.*

Turk, J., & Franklin, B. (1987). Information subsidies: Agenda-setting traditions. *Public Relations Review, 13*(4), 29–41.

Turow, J. (in press). Public relations and newswork. A neglected relationship. *American Behavioral Scientist.*

U.S. Congress. Office of Technology Assessment. (1986, June). *Federal government technology: Electronic record systems and individual privacy* (OTA-CIT-296). Washington, DC: U.S. Government Printing Office.

U.S. Congress. Office of Technology Assessment. (1988, October). *Informing the nation: Federal information dissemination in an electronic age* (OTA-CIT-396). Washington, DC: U.S. Government Printing Office.

Victor, K. (1988, April 23). Step under my umbrella. *National Journal,* pp. 1063–1067.

Video Privacy Protection Act of 1988. (1988, November 11). *Friday Report,* p. 1.

Waltzer, H. (1988). Corporate advocacy advertising and political influence. *Public Relations Review, 14*(1), 41–55.

Webster, F., & Robins, K. (1986). *Information technology: A Luddite analysis.* Norwood, NJ: Ablex.

Weiss, C., & Singer, E. (1988). *Reporting of social science in the national media.* New York: Russell Sage Foundation.

Westin, A., & Harris, L (1979, April). *The dimensions of privacy.* Stevens Point, WI: Sentury Insurance.

Whynes, D. (Ed.). (1984). *What is political economy? Eight perspectives.* Oxford: Basil Blackwell.

Wilson, C., & Gutierrez, F. (1985). *Minorities and media: Diversity and the end of mass communication.* Newbury Park, CA: Sage.

Wilson, K. (1988). *Technologies of control. The new interactive media for the home.* Madison, WI: University of Wisconsin Press.

Wilson, W. J. (Ed.). (1989). The ghetto underclass: Social science perspectives [Special issue]. *The Annals of the American Academy of Political and Social Science, 501.* Newbury Park, CA: Sage.

Wright, P., & Barbour, F. (1976). The relevance of decision process models in structuring persuasive messages. In M. Ray & S. Ward (Eds.), *Communicating with consumers* (pp. 57–70). Newbury Park, CA: Sage.

The Corporate Person
(Re)Presents Itself

GEORGE CHENEY
University of Colorado

No matter how effusive their rhetoric to the contrary, most Americans cannot bring themselves to trust the unaffiliated individual. They prefer to repose their confidence in institutions—in a brand name, a corporation, or a bank.

—Lapham (1986, p. 85)

Well, the guy that comes aroun' talked as nice as pie. "You got to get off [the land]. It ain't my fault." "Well," I says, "whose fault is it? I'll go an' I'll nut the fella." "It's the Shawnee Lan' an' Cattle Company. I jus' got orders." "Who's the Shawnee Lan' an' Cattle Company?" "It ain't nobody. It's a company." Got a fella crazy. There wasn't nobody you could lay for.

—Steinbeck (1939, p. 42)

In his 1974 book, *Power and the Structure of Society,* James Coleman explained the rise of the corporate, juristic, or legal person: that is, the organization. According to Coleman, the modern organization (and this category includes the literal, legal corporation as well as other types) arose through the creative efforts of *natural* persons struggling to define new centers of power vis-à-vis the Church and the State in the late Middle Ages. The products of these efforts, corporate persons, by design transcended the lives, resources, energies, and powers of the natural persons who created them. At the same time, however, corporate persons were intended to serve and to enhance the powers of their individual makers. Coleman argued convincingly that, although the sum total of power in organized, industrial society has increased over the centuries, the *proportion* of power held by natural persons has correspondingly narrowed. This point is surely debatable. But another, related point that Coleman made is not: We have yet to learn to cope with corporate persons in our theories and in our everyday dealings.

In communication studies, as well as in other fields across the human sciences, we are perplexed by the meaning of such basic elements of a communication/rhetorical situation as speaker, message, and audience when these terms are construed within the context of "corporate" (used broadly here, referring to a body or group of natural persons) communication. For example, when Exxon "speaks," as it did so frequently following the March, 1989 oil spill in Alaska's Prince William Sound, how should those messages be understood? Indeed, the study of communication in the corporate or organizational context makes especially challenging questions about authorship, intent, attribution, responsibility, audience, and degree of "personalness." (It is instructive to note that among the corresponding terms for "Inc." in French and Spanish is "S.A.," standing for *société anonyme* and *sociedad anónima*, respectively. The corporation is then the anonymous society.) For the layperson, a fundamental question arises: How do I converse with a corporate or collective speaker? These questions take on even greater importance as our society becomes more organized, more thoroughly organizational (see Cheney & McMillan, in press).

Viewed in one way, public relations is the study and practice of corporate public rhetoric: the organization speaking to/with various publics (see Cheney & Dionisopoulos, 1989; Cheney & Vibbert, 1987). And, with the expansion of corporate communications into issue management, identity management, and related activities, the role of the corporate rhetor in American society (and for that matter, in the entire industrialized world) is taking on greater visibility and importance. Today we find all sorts of organizations and collectivities *speaking.*

Nevertheless, we know surprisingly little about messages by, from, and for organizations. Put another way, we have difficulty both in coping with and understanding "corporate" messages, even though we are subject to and party to communications from corporate bodies all the time (messages of businesses, governments, religious groups, lobbies, hospitals, universities, unions, social action groups, and so forth).

Neither rhetorical nor communication theory have fully come to terms with the organizational nature of much of communication in our society. This chapter emphasizes the rhetorical tradition and its potential contribution to our understanding of corporate public communications. The chapter argues first that an individualistic bias (taken in a specific sense) has hindered rhetorical criticism in explaining, understanding, and evaluating the rhetoric of organizational life, particularly the external corporate messages in public relations and related activities (i.e., identity/image advertising, issue management, corporate advocacy). Simply put, rhetorical critics (like the lay public) seem unable to grasp the meaning of the "(good) organization speaking (well)" (Cheney, 1991). Thus, the critical assessment of corporate rhetoric is a notable lacuna in contemporary rhetorical criticism. This chapter then proposes that two key insights of contemporary philosophy can be used to enhance rhetorical understanding of corporate public communications. These insights are: (a) the centrality of images (in the sense of visual symbols) in post-industrial culture and (b) the "decentering" of the individual in corporate rhetoric. The essay concludes by explaining how these points can reinvigorate rhetorical criticism while offering both public relations practitioners and "consumers" better ways to comprehend corporate messages and message-making.

LIMITATIONS OF THE RHETORICAL TRADITION

Although the origins of the rhetorical tradition can be traced to Aristotle, Isocrates, and Plato, the emergence of rhetorical study as an organized field of investigation within the modern academy began in 1915 with the inauguration of the *Quarterly Journal of Public Speaking*. The principal practical interest that brought together rhetorical scholars in separation from English departments was a concern with the *effects* of specific public messages. As the name of the journal (now the *Quarterly Journal of Speech*) suggests, the messages of interest were almost exclusively the speeches of recognized and celebrated persons (usually political leaders). In 1915, such an emphasis on public speaking (practice and criticism) was understandable and appropriate: lecture circuits (e.g., the Chautauqua), as a principal form of public communication during the late 19th century, were still active and prominent; theorizing about leadership then emphasized the characteristics of individual "Great Men"; the age of the electronic media was not to begin for another 5 years, with the advent of radio. All of this is to say that oratory, the art of public speaking to please or persuade, retained an important position in early 20th-century America, although its station was diminished somewhat by the prevalence of written communication for mass audiences and by creeping bureaucratization.

From the early 20th-century debates that formed the speech-communication discipline onward, the discipline retained an emphasis on the *individual speaker*. Rhetorical criticism sought progressive refinement of its techniques of description and analysis, first under the (retrospectively applied) rubric of neo-Aristotelianism and later—after the mid-1960s—under various theoretical and methodological labels (see the review by Leff &

Procario, 1985). In most cases, however, rhetorical critics saw as their primary object the public speaker, the individual orator, addressing a well-defined audience with a discrete message.

Of course, the late 1960s brought ferment to rhetorical scholarship, just as it did to so many other activities and institutions. Black's *Rhetorical Criticism* (1965) challenged critics to move beyond neo-Aristotelianism (as it was generally understood and applied) toward less rationalistic approaches to criticism. Tompkins (1969) urged rhetorical critics to examine "non-oratorical forms" such as novels, plays, and films. And Griffin (e.g., 1964) demonstrated the application of both traditional and new rhetorical principles to the social movements of the day. All of these developments contributed to the heterogeneity of rhetorical criticism. The investigation of social movements was particularly important because it marked the first systematic study of the rhetoric of collectivities. Still, such collectivities (i.e., social movements) were usually treated as (a) being of relatively short duration, (b) posturing against the establishment or working outside the "mainstream," and (c) having identifiable leaders/spokespersons (see the review by Simons, Mechling, & Schreier, 1984). Thus, although the study of social movements broke the hegemony of individual–public–speaker analyses, it did not quite enable rhetorical critics to investigate the rhetoric of institutions and society itself.[1] Studies of the anti-war movement, the civil rights movement, and the women's movement by definition and design focused on anti-establishment social forces.

Only in the 1980s, with the growing influences of Marxism, continental philosophy (particularly "poststructuralism"), and the full development of Burkean (sociologically inclined) criticism, have rhetorical critics begun to embrace the possibilities for the analysis of various organizations, institutions, and social structure generally (see, e.g., the review in McKerrow, 1989; see also Whalen & Cheney, in press). A few scholars have treated the modern organization from an explicitly rhetorical perspective, considering the activities of organizations *as* persuasive efforts, seeing the organization as a rhetor (see, e.g., Cheney, 1983; Crable, 1986; McMillan, 1982, 1987; Tompkins, 1987; Tompkins & Cheney, 1985). And, a number of rhetorically based case analyses of organizational life have appeared (see, e.g., Conrad, 1988; Crable & Vibbert, 1983; Jablonski, 1988; McMillan, 1988; Tompkins, Fisher, Infante, & Tompkins, 1975), including studies of business, labor, government, and organized religion. Finally, at least one organizational communi-

---

[1]This point arose in discussions with Jill McMillan, in preparation for a day-long seminar on "Organizational Rhetoric," at the annual meeting of the Speech Communication Association, New Orleans, November 1988. See especially McMillan (1982); see also Cheney (1991); and Cheney and McMillan (in press).

cation textbook assumes a rhetorical perspective in many of its chapters (Conrad, 1985).

This trend is important to the study of public relations, although the full potential for the rhetorical analysis of corporate public communications has only begun to be realized. Several scholars at several different universities in the 1980s applied rhetorical concepts and principles to public relations and related activities. Heath (1980) called for speech communication, particularly its rhetorically inclined scholars, to explore the growing persuasive activities of large corporations. Goldzwig and Cheney (1984) illustrated how the "corporate advocacy" model of public persuasion is applicable even to rhetorical practice outside the private sector (e.g., to religious organizations). Crable and Vibbert (1986), in their public relations textbook, adapted Bryant's (1953) famous formulation of rhetoric's function—"the adjustment of ideas to people and people to ideas"—to read: "the adjustment of organizations to environments and environments to organizations." And, several other recently published articles employ rhetorical concepts to explain the role of the corporate voice in contemporary U.S. society (Cheney & Dionisopoulos, 1989; Cheney & Vibbert, 1987; Crable, 1986; Crable & Vibbert, 1985).

Much more needs to be said, however. Rhetorical theory and criticism have only begun to grapple with discourse produced by organizations, institutions, collectivities.

> For centuries rhetoric has been thought of as created by *someone*. [However,] this is not strictly the case with . . . corporate, collective voices. While all messages in fact originate with individuals, many present themselves otherwise, as the voices of artificial or corporate persons. Therefore, the rhetorical theory that is required in an organizational age therefore cannot be exclusively a theory of the "good *person* speaking (well)." Rhetorical analysis of *organizational* rhetoric requires simultaneous conceptualizations of individually and collectively created discourse. (Cheney, 1991, p. 21)

Rhetorical scholars must come to terms with the corporate rhetor, the corporate message, and the corporate audience. In this way, the activities of contemporary public relations can be better understood for what they *say* about our society and how they may be used to improve our society.

INSIGHTS FROM CONTEMPORARY PHILOSOPHY

Contemporary philosophy is undergoing transformations, following the "linguistic turn" (e.g., Wittgenstein, 1958) and the systematic attack on representationalism, the view of language as a mirror to "reality" (e.g., Rorty, 1979). As a result, epistemology has to a great extent fallen from its privileged position from which it validated knowledge claims across the sciences and the humanities. What this means in practical terms is that the persuasive aspects of all disciplinary knowledge are now recognized and *rhetoric* (explicitly or implicitly) is seen as a useful perspective from which knowledge, information, and communication can be understood. For example, when an economist offers a "curve" to represent an economic trend, that curve itself is but a metaphor for something that the economist posits. But that metaphor is persuasive indeed in its capacity to shape one's view of the economic world, especially if it holds practical, predictive value (see McCloskey, 1985). And that economist's concepts and models, however presented as facts and "pure" information, are to some degree shaped by values, beliefs, and the accepted symbols of the discipline. This predicament is shared by all disciplines, practices, and arenas of activity, although it is acutely relevant to those domains *where symbols are the media and substance of all activity* (such as public relations).

Public relations is in the business of producing symbols of, by, and for organizations. Contemporary public relations is fundamentally concerned with *representing* major organizations and institutions of our society with values, images, identities, issue-positions, and so forth. Thus, it is crucial that we probe the structure and meaning of that process of representation. Here, two insights of contemporary, "postmodern"[2] philosophy are instructive: (a) the image-based nature of contemporary western culture and (b) the "decentering" of the individual in theory and in practice. These two insights are closely related and are explained here with specific application to corporate communications.

The Image

It is a truism that we live in an image-dominated culture. We speak of some persons as being image-conscious. We are daily bombarded with many types of images, with some images designed to distract us from competing ones. Advertising is a central and pervasive activity in American life. As Ewen (1988) explained, "the ability to capture and preserve the disembodied countenance of things"—as in a photographic ad of a model wearing new fashions—has become a primary source of power in contemporary American society (p. 24). Our large organizations invest time, money, and energy

---

[2]*Postmodernism* is a polysemic, diffuse, and slippery term. It has been used to refer to art, architecture, literature, the media, technology, social thought, and social trends. Postmodernism has been identified with the present period by some and treated out of the context of time by others. I thus use the term advisedly and loosely here (see Gitlin, 1989).

in crafting appropriate and compelling images for their various publics, defining identities as well as styles.

Accordingly, at least two commonplace understandings of the term *image* are relevant here: (a) *visual or pictorial symbols*, such as corporate logos; and (b) *an impression* created at a particular time, as in "company Y's positive image." These two senses are of course analytically interrelated, for a central part of an organization's Image$_b$ often involves how it presents itself in terms of Image$_a$. These two senses of image are closely connected in everyday discourse, as when an executive is concerned about projecting a professional image through dress, manner, and word choice. And both types of image figure prominently in contemporary corporate communications.

The growing role of image-based communication, with its reliance on quickly assimilated pictorial and verbal messages, is profound in its implications. One implication is that many of today's public messages appeal more to the "logic" of feelings than to cold reason. Witness, for example Benetton's "United Colors" ad series, which appears on buses and billboards worldwide: the ads "speak" dramatically for themselves in establishing transcendent identifications across nations, races, and ethnic groups. Of course, the charge—that pictorial images and brief verbal ones rely heavily on *pathos* (or predominantly emotional appeals) for their persuasiveness—has been leveled against much of the content of contemporary television (Postman, 1985). The widely criticized U.S. presidential campaign of 1988, in which "sound bite" became a household phrase, is a case in point (see Jamieson, 1988). Consider as more immediately relevant examples the almost ubiquitous advocacy advertising of Mobil, AT&T, and United Technologies. All three corporations offer brief statements with accompanying logos and visuals (usually less than one page) to advocate such positions as unbridled technological advance and sharply limited governmental regulation. For instance, in its ad entitled "The Way Beyond Babel," AT&T asserts the catchy premises: "Telecommunity is our goal. Technology is our means." Along with the adjacent photo of a steam locomotive, these slogans emphasize the seemingly unstoppable march of technology. Another example is the series of "I'm the NRA" ads by the National Rifle Association, where Americans of many walks of life are pictured under the titular caption and with rifle in hand: These ads identify individual with issue and organization. Still another case where visuals dominate is the ad by defense contractor General Dynamics that shows a collection of U.S. political buttons, thereby identifying the corporation with the American political process. Beneath the buttons is the bold-face slogan, "They All Pinned Their Hopes On Peace." And the four brief paragraphs that follow the slogan identify the corporation as well with that goal, although nowhere do the words explain *why* this is so.

Thus, both corporate commentary or advocacy and traditional advertising are likely to be given the forms of brief magazine copy or short spots on television. Images seem to prevail in the competition with extended discourse. Images, of course, are not new, but their predominance in the communicative world of late 20th-century America is striking and important. By condensing, coloring, and pictorializing content for modern mass media, communications from corporations (and other large organizations) displace or suppress details and connections that would be required for carefully reasoned analysis of whatever subject is considered (cf. Sproule, 1988). In this way, corporate communications have taken on and promoted the type of message that our society as a whole has come to embrace: the *image.*

However, there is a more perplexing sense in which the concept of image is important for understanding today's public relations and other activities of corporate communications. This is explained by Baudrillard (1988) through his concept of the *simulacrum.* Baudrillard employed this term to convey the quality of contemporary western society (and the "postmodern condition," as he put it) in which many of our symbols, our images, cease to reference that which is "real"; rather, they exist in uninterrupted relation to one another. In a certain sense, of course, we may say that all symbols can be connected to one another, just as the symbols of language are interrelated such that "good" is understood in dialectical relation with "bad" and the sentences of a paragraph are interconnected in con-*text.*[3] But Baudrillard explored this question on a deeper level; he said essentially that there are different levels to the functioning of images and that postindustrial society manifests a level of image-making that contradicts the very notion of an image *as an appearance, a reflection, or a representation of something else.*

The four levels of images Baudrillard called "successive phases of the image." Here I explain and illustrate each, before showing their relevance to contemporary corporate communications. According to Baudrillard, an image can function as (a) the reflection of a basic reality, (b) a mask or perversion of a basic reality, (c) a mask for the *absence* of a basic reality, or (d) the condition by which the image "bears no relation to any reality whatever: it is its own pure simulacrum" (p. 170). On the first level, the image is seen as a *good* appearance; such is the case when public statues are used to memorialize great persons. On the second level, the image is seen as an *evil* appearance, as when personal credentials are fudged or forged to create an inappropriate impression. (The 1988 presidential candidacy of Senator Joseph Biden ended because of the exposure of this type of image-making when it was discovered that Biden had plagiarized large portions of his speeches.) On the third level, the image "plays at being an appearance," as with sorcery, or magic, or a television character's direct reference to the

---

[3]The notion of and perspectives on "textuality" are discussed extensively in Cheney and Tompkins (1988).

medium: "I'm on TV" (which became common in the 1980s). On the fourth level, the image "is no longer in the order of appearance at all, but of simulation" (Baudrillard, 1988, p. 170). The image becomes its own reality.

The fourth level of the image is the most perplexing and troublesome, according to Baudrillard (1988). He offered Disneyland as a vivid illustration of that level as well as of the other orders of simulation. Baudrillard explained that although Disneyland and other "imaginary stations" are presented as "imaginary in order to make us believe that the rest is real," in fact they take on a new type of reality, a hyper-reality, *in themselves* (p. 172). In a very real sense, Disneyland and other such cultural centers *are* "America," according to Baudrillard. (The ill-fated "Autoworld" in Flint, Michigan, where an indoor theme park was designed to present the city *as it was* before plant closings by General Motors in the late 1980s, provides another, even more powerful example.)

The image thus becomes the reality, the substance of the society, in a very real sense. And, everywhere we can see the celebration of the image *as* experience. New technologies of telecommunication make this fourth order of the image all the more compelling and real. Advanced video and holographic techniques will soon enable us "to be" on a tropical island or on Mount Everest while remaining in the living room. Teleconferencing has advanced to such a state that a conference table can be "extended" visually so that two groups at two locations can experience the sense of being joined in one place (in a "virtual meeting"), thereby recasting face-to-face experience in purely electronic form. Additionally, the images of persons, things, and organizations take on a placeless, omniscient quality that heightens their own "reality" and significance (cf. Meyrowitz, 1985). Images often appear as if from "above," without referencing source or place, as is the case with many satellite communications "beamed" around the world seemingly from no particular, identifiable place.

Our preoccupation with and reliance on images has important implications for the study and practice of corporate communications. The image without any clear or certain relation to "reality" is perhaps becoming the dominant form in both external and internal corporate public communications. Major corporations and other large organizations now invest huge sums in *creating* images and identities for themselves. For example, in the early 1970s several oil companies came under one symbolic umbrella when they spent more that $100 million on the search for "Exxon." That name was selected because (a) it would create a powerful impression and (b) the double "x" does not appear naturally in any language except Maltese. Specifically, "research indicated that ['Exxon'] conveyed the idea of a large, international enterprise and suggested the petroleum and chemical business in a way that was significantly superior to other names" (Enis, 1978, p. 9). United Technologies, AT&T, IBM, Honeywell, RCA, and other corporations consider carefully their "self-presentation." And, many of their messages that are ostensibly designed for external audiences (e.g., advertising, public relations, and marketing communications) serve also as instances of organizations "talking to themselves," asserting their identities to members (Christensen, 1991).

Not surprisingly, there is a new industry, found at the intersection of public relations and advertising, which focuses on the creation of "images" and "identities" for large organizations. In the parlance of this industry, *identities* refer to the specific identifying aspects of an organization, such as names, logos, distinctive slogans and architecture, and so on. *Images* are the broader impressions that are projected by organizations, the perceptions held by various publics. What is most interesting in terms of this discussion is that identity and image consultants seek to—in their terms—"give" identities and images to organizations. As explained to me by Janet Martin, vice-president of Communication Arts in Boulder, her firm wants its creations (copy, visuals and architecture) *to become* the client organizations in the minds of their employees and other publics. Such a strategy invokes to some extent the fourth order of images, as discussed by Baudrillard (1988). Identity and image consultants aim to "remake" organizations in ways that are instantly recognizable, appealing and usable. The well-crafted corporate images are intended to be central and generative in the minds of various audiences.

Today we are literally surrounded by corporate identities and images. For many months Exxon struggled to improve its tarnished image following the Exxon-Valdez disaster through congressional testimony, open letters to the public, traditional press releases, and televised images that associated the name of the corporation with environmental concerns and that minimized the disaster. And in a related magazine ad by the state of Alaska, an analogy was drawn between the oil spill and the insignificance of a blemish on the face of Marilyn Monroe. Such ads are especially interesting because they do not make a systematic "case": They are largely nondiscursive, visual presentations that immediately suggest connections. In so much of today's corporate communications (as with public communications in general) the sheer juxtaposition of images is used as a substitute for reasoned discourse, for argument. Images are appealing. As Langer (1942) explained, presentational or pictorial symbols are often better equipped than discursive symbols for expressing sentiment because the mind is able to read them in a "flash" and preserve them in a disposition or an attitude. This is not to say that images do not make arguments. Certainly, Picasso's haunting "Guernica" is one of the most powerful statements against war that was ever made. And a series of images can form a narrative, as in a child's picturebook. But an uncritical reliance on images, without the clear expression of claims, warrants, and evidence, suppresses needed dialogue about the issues of the day. Many images speak powerfully to our emotional "logic" and function as unassailable arguments in practice. This was seen clearly in the ads used by the 1988 Bush presidential campaign against the Massachusetts prison-furlough program of Democratic candidate Michael Dukakis: The ads featured a revolving door and made implicitly racist appeals. As a society, we both worship and surrender control to the images of our own making.

As Burke (1966) noted, we build up a reality out of symbols (words and others) and convince ourselves that those symbols merely *represent* reality when in fact *our* world is largely symbolic. Words and images are magical in that they often bring something new into being. And the vivid, visual image can be especially powerful in this regard. The State Farm Insurance Companies, for example, see their trademark as a *repository* for the values of stability, quality, competitiveness, and dependability. The corporate logo "is" the organization in the corporate view, and there are strict rules for its use throughout the corporation. Thus, the question of *what represents what* becomes circular and for many organizational actors irrelevant. Much of the power and mystery of contemporary images is derived from their collective, corporate nature. (The controversy in 1989–1990 over the lawfulness of burning the U.S. flag is a case in point.) Many messages that we "receive" are not easily (or not at all) attributable to individual persons. *Who* is Mobil, or AT&T, or TRW? Many corporate messages are decidedly vague about their sources. A good example is much of the advocacy advertising on behalf of nuclear power that regularly appears in our news magazines. Such ads, which offer a variety of strongly worded statements to promote greater use of nuclear energy, typically include as their sole byline, "U.S. Council for Energy Awareness." The Council nowhere acknowledges its composition— the nuclear power producers—or its primary activities, lobbying in Washington, DC and grassroots organizing across the United States. This mystery that surrounds the authors of corporate messages often obscures their workings and their effects. Whom does one contact, for example, to carry on a dialogue with the Council? And, what shape could such a conversation take?

The Decentered Self

Another aspect of corporate messages that complicates their analysis is the way many verbal messages are structured. The grammar of organizational pronouncements frequently is in the form of the "divine passive": "It has been decided that . . ." (see Sennett, 1980). And, when the active voice is used, so is the powerfully ambiguous corporate "we" as in "We at Megacorp believe . . ." (Cheney, 1983). Or, a synecdoche or a personification may be employed: "The White House said today"; "The Pentagon reacted"; "Ma Bell announced," etc. These conventions make the analysis of corporate messages difficult: observers are often left wondering, "Decided by whom?" or "Who are 'we'?" or "Who at the White House?"

To borrow and adapt a term of contemporary philosophy and literary criticism, corporate messages tend to *decenter* the individual (see, e.g., Foucault, 1984; Valdes & Miller, 1985). Just as legal "incorporation" limits and diffuses individual responsibility, so do corporate messages complicate matters of authorship, voice, attribution, and responsibility. When E.F. Hutton speaks, just *who* is doing the talking? When *Time* quotes "a highly placed White House official," how *official* is such a message? When Exxon's chairman apologizes on behalf of "everyone at Exxon," whom should we credit for the apology? These are challenging questions to answer, in theory and in practice. They can be subsumed under the larger and more penetrating question, "What does it mean to speak with a collective or corporate voice?" (see Cheney, 1991). This is a question that must be addressed by both "producers" and "consumers" of corporate communications.

Of course, there is a paradox inherent in the matter of "individuality," for natural persons in the West appropriate large parts of their individual identities through association with and participation in organizations, institutions, and collectivities (Cheney & Tompkins, 1987). Thus, one individual proudly proclaims "I'm a an IBMer," and another smugly declares, "I work for GM." In a society where organizations do much of the socializing of individual persons, the individual defines him or herself in large part through collective labels, such as professional titles and organizational roles. The corporate logos that are commonly displayed on contemporary clothing are a good example. At times, these symbols refer only to *fictitious* collectivities (e.g., the "Status City" Polo Club), thus asserting the importance of the corporate image *qua* image, the symbols of Corporate America. In practice, then the individual or self is to some degree decentered through self-definition and self-diffusion in corporate symbols, images, messages: Corporate symbols become important resources of individual identity for citizen-consumers. Today, when many organizations have adopted comprehensive communications strategies, the full meaning of this decentering must be appreciated. The *corporate* image must be assessed for its persuasiveness as well as its pervasiveness.

To understand fully this power we must understand western individualism as a persuasive force. The western emphasis on individual pursuits—and this reaches its apotheosis in contemporary U.S. society—is not a primordial or irreducible condition, although it is often treated that way. Individualism is an ideology, a set of beliefs that masks its own functioning as a set of beliefs and choices. Individualism arose with widespread literacy, the Renaissance, capitalism, industrialization, and specialization. The stress on "identity" *as uniqueness*, one that Americans easily take for granted, appeared first in the literature of the British romantics in the first part of the

19th century (Mackenzie, 1978). Of course, the cultural significance of American individualism was observed and questioned as early as the 1830s and 1840s, in de Tocqueville's classic commentary on the American experience.

In its extreme form, *individualism* means that "a person's relation to the moral and natural universes is unmediated by the surrounding social community" (Meyer, 1986, p. 210). In other words, each individual person is encouraged and free to develop him or herself as much as possible, to produce and consume as much as possible, and to see society merely as being rationalized around personal ends. U.S. society has been described as "identitarian" for its stress on *self*-indulgence (see discussion by Jay, 1973).

Such a picture, which is frequently offered as descriptive of contemporary America, is not without its ironies. As mentioned earlier, the modern individual is defined significantly through organizational affiliations. Thus, out of "samenesses" individual persons achieve difference. This can be seen readily in Japan, where the corporation has taken on much of the role formerly ascribed to the family as a locus of identity. In the United States, college students often find it comfortable and appealing to "package" themselves in appearance, belief, and attitude, thereby adopting the appropriate image for potential employers that interview on campus, all the while asserting their individuality and their autonomy. For my purposes here, what is most important about individualism is that it conceals its own implications for conformity and for social control.

As Meyer (1986) argued, "much of the effort of modern society goes into constructing appropriate individuals" (p. 212). Socialization occurs on a mass scale; although they are not always well coordinated, the major institutions of contemporary society (government, business, education, religion) produce coherent corporate identities around which individuals can orient themselves. And the technologies of communication make the corporate images omnipresent and vivid. The strategies of Iacocca's Chrysler provide a good example: Chrysler's product advertising, public relations activities, and issue advocacy blend together even as they are addressed to multiple and overlapping audiences. The Chrysler employee, for instance, receives work-related messages during work time, but he or she is also subject to numerous other messages while off the job. Most of these messages personify or embody the organization in the figure of Iacocca, who became a folk hero in the 1980s.

Interestingly, organizations such as Chrysler (during its revitalization) and Exxon (during the oil-spill crisis) relied on personalized faces or *personae* (in the form of the CEO speaking), whereas other organizations (United Technologies is a good example) use impersonal *corporate* images. The effort to personalize the image of an organization—as both Reagan and Carter sought to do for the executive branch of the federal government—is surely in part a reaction against the depersonalization and alienation of our large, "faceless," bureaucratic institutions. What it means in terms of corporate rhetoric is that some corporate messages become identified with individuals and those individual speakers become the embodiment of organizations. Thus, for many of the stakeholders of the Chrysler Corporation, Iacocca *is* Chrysler. This "personal" image, however, functions similarly in practice to the "impersonal" corporate image in that most of us will never have the opportunity to respond to Mr. Iacocca or to his ads.

To understand fully the role of corporate message-making in contemporary American society requires an understanding of the decentered "individual." One must examine how the individual is "located" in society and take a critical perspective on that process. Corporate communication specialists, such as public relations officers, necessarily play an important part in that process. They build corporate images that function rhetorically in the appropriation of identity, both individual and collective. The long-running U.S. Army recruitment campaign, "Be All You Can Be" was at once an appeal to individualism and careerism and a compelling linkage of the individual to the organization.

In summary, the decentering of the individual is a perspective we should apply to the ways both natural and corporate persons come to be defined in today's society. We must understand better how organizations "speak" and how their messages operate in practice. A focus on such decentering (irony intended), as well as on the role of the image, is instructive for rhetorical critics, for students of public relations and related activities, for the practitioners in those fields, and for all of us as members of audiences or publics.

CONCLUSIONS AND IMPLICATIONS

Recently, scholars have begun to appreciate the value of applying rhetorical theory and criticism to public relations and related forms of corporate communications (see the reviews in Cheney & Vibbert, 1987; Putnam & Cheney, 1985; Trujillo & Toth, 1987). However, rhetorical scholars have not yet come to terms with the nature of *corporate* rhetoric. A model that features the individual rhetor must be complemented with one that accounts for the corporate, collective nature of much of contemporary rhetoric, while avoiding the danger of reifying the organization (i.e., separating it analytically from its individual contributors). Because much of persuasion today is organized and organizational in nature, its analysis must treat patterns of messages more than single ones, impersonal sources as much as personal ones, and audiences whose worlds are full of images that cannot be fully appreciated in isolation. Although all messages in some way originate with individuals, many messages today present themselves "on behalf" of organizations or collective bodies. The corporate message, the corporate rhetor, and the corporate audience shape much of our communicative world. Therefore, to comprehend corporate or organizational rhetoric we must engage social structure and process writ large. Individual organizations both reflect and contribute to the society of which they are constitutive parts.

Public relations, along with the related activities of corporate advocacy, issue management, and identity management, provides an important and expanding arena for the investigation and understanding of corporate or organizational rhetoric. For such investigation to be fruitful, however, theorists and critics must recognize the image-based nature of much corporate rhetoric and the decentering of the individual in the same. By incorporating these insights from contemporary philosophy, rhetorical scholars can make better sense of the pattern of corporate messages that is our society.

The appreciation of these two points is vital also to the study and practice of public relations (and related activities). Public relations experts necessarily *re-present* their organizations through symbols of their own creation. Practitioners need to recognize the role they play in the shaping of society, its images, and its characteristic forms of communication. Public relations experts need to appreciate the larger context of their endeavors. Practitioners are routinely responsible ("response-able") to multiple publics: employees, shareholders, top management, consumers, competitors, regulators, etc. (i.e., all those who have a "stake" in or are affected by the organization's activities). Rapidly displayed and assimilated pictorial images, therefore, should not be relied on to the total exclusion of reasoned discourse; otherwise, informed debate is precluded or suppressed. The world of sound bites and flashy visuals must not be made impermeable to direct arguments. Practitioners should make their arguments clearly and directly and not allow images to speak for themselves. In the conversations of the marketplace and of public policy, audiences or publics must be able to "access" corporate messages; they must be able to ascertain *what* is said (the logic) and *who* said it (the source). Attributions must be made to entities—individual or collective—that are capable of demonstrating moral responsibility. To some degree, image makers should be accountable, even in a rapidly changing communications environment with the relative indeterminancy of the meaning for specific messages (see, e.g., Culler, 1982). And, practitioners must be sensitive to how their symbols are used by individuals; many of those symbols by design have the potential for great influence.

Allow me to offer a brief analysis of a case of corporate rhetoric, of public relations, which reveals the difficulty of the problems now facing researchers and practitioners in these areas. Kaiser Aluminum and Chemical Corporation responded to an ABC-TV "20-20" broadcast in 1980 about low safety in aluminum wiring. In full-page ads in 10 major U.S. newspapers, the corporation argued "not only that Kaiser *did* not act unethically, but also that

Kaiser *could not* act in such a way, since such acts were not in keeping with its character as a corporate agent" (Dionisopoulos & Vibbert, 1983, p. 18).

In this case, the image, the identity, of the organization is reified; it is treated as a specific and *understood* point of reference. In other words, *the organization* speaks about itself to itself and to other audiences. The corporate image is defined as powerful, so powerful in fact that it comes to *be* the organization. A particular type of character is ascribed to the organization: "Kaiser *acts* this way." With such an understanding as that advanced by the corporation, the image becomes more that a persona projected by a corporate actor; the organization "acts" as a self-referential agent. Kaiser's image thus is seen *as* the actor in question, and the image is no longer directly tied to the organization and the actions of its members.

This case suggests also that the application of a *consistency* rule to corporate image-making is two-sided in its effects. If we demand that an organization represent itself in the same way over time and to various publics, we run the risk of solidifying or reifying the image, the identity of the organization, as occurred with Kaiser. As Kenneth Boulding (1956) explained: "It is usually essential to the operation of an organization that there should not be the same image of the organization in the minds of the various participants" (p. 57). The role, the perspective of the stakeholder is important here. But on the other hand, how much inconsistency should be accepted in the ways an organization presents itself to various publics? When do we say that an organization is not being "itself" or is misrepresenting its interests? There is a delicate balance to be maintained by the practitioner, in the interest of both audience adaptation and rhetorical integrity.

All of this is to articulate an imperative for rhetorical scholars and students of public relations alike: to come to terms with the corporate rhetor, the corporate message, and the corporate audience. Working from a rhetorical perspective and incorporating the insights of contemporary philosophy, students of public relations can profitably address such important questions as: What is the identity of a particular corporate rhetor? How do an organization's messages reflect its interests? What are the implications of a particular organization's rhetoric for individual audience members? What assumptions are made in the rhetoric of an organization about the organization, its members, other stakeholders, society in general? How are images employed by a corporate rhetor? What do those images *say* about the organization and other groups? Whose interests are represented by corporate messages? Of course, generalizing beyond individual cases is also important here: Students of public relations can explore the developing role of corporate communications in contemporary society, assessing its efficacy and its ethics on a broad scale.

A final word here concerns the audience, that is, "consumers" of corporate public communications. As frequently described, the "postmodern condition" (although admittedly a polysemic term) is characterized in part by a rampant juxtapositioning of signs, of images (Baudrillard, 1988; Jameson 1981; Lyotard, 1984). For Americans, the images of Madison Avenue, Las Vegas, and Hollywood all come together in a huge "text" that celebrates the images that comprise it. "In order to adapt, consumers are pried away from traditions, their selves become 'decentered,' and a well-formed interior life becomes an obsolete encumbrance. Even 'life-styles' become commodities to be marketed" (Gitlin, 1989, p. 55).

Although this charge is sweeping and more than a bit cynical, it does call to our attention a potential danger of an unreflective indulgence in corporate image-making: We can come to elevate style over substance and lose ourselves in the process. As audiences to the images of a global marketplace, we must not abandon our critical faculties but engage them. Audience members should, for example, work to *spell out* the arguments implicit in (or even suppressed by) corporate messages that are image-based. Even more importantly, audience members should examine their organizational memberships, associations and affinities for what they represent, what they "say," what they mean in practice. Through these and related strategies, we can make sense of corporate persons and enhance the power of natural ones.

ACKNOWLEDGMENT

The author thanks the editors and Lars Thøger Christensen for their helpful comments on an earlier draft of this chapter.

REFERENCES

Baudrillard, J. (1988). Simulacra and simulations. In M. Poster (Ed.), *Jean Baudrillard: Selected writings* (pp. 166–184). Stanford, CA: Stanford University Press.
Black, E. (1965). *Rhetorical criticism: A study in method.* New York: Macmillan.
Boulding, K. (1956). *The image.* Ann Arbor: University of Michigan Press.
Bryant, D.C. (1953). Rhetoric: Its functions and its scope. *Quarterly Journal of Speech, 39*, 401–424.
Burke, K. (1966). *Language as symbolic action.* Berkeley: University of California Press.
Cheney, G. (1983). The rhetoric of identification and the study of organizational communication. *Quarterly Journal of Speech, 69*, 143–158.
Cheney, G. (1991). *Rhetoric in an organizational society: Managing multiple identities.* Columbia, SC: University of South Carolina Press.
Cheney, G., & Dionisopoulos, G.N. (1989). Public relations? No, relations with publics: A rhetorical-organizational approach to contemporary corporate communications. In C. Botan & V. Hazleton, Jr. (Eds.), *Public relations theory* (pp. 135–158). Hillsdale, NJ: Lawrence Erlbaum Associates.
Cheney, G., & McMillan, J.J. (in press). Organizational rhetoric and the practice of criticism. *Journal of Applied Communication Research.*

Cheney, G., & Tompkins, P.K. (1987). Coming to terms with organizational identification and commitment. *Central States Speech Journal, 38,* 1–15.

Cheney, G., & Tompkins, P.K. (1988). On the facts of the text as the basis of human communication research. In J.A. Anderson (Ed.), *Communication Yearbook 11* (pp. 455–481). Newbury Park, CA: Sage.

Cheney, G., & Vibbert, S.L. (1987). Corporate discourse: Public relations and issue management. In F.M. Jablin, L.L. Putnam, K.H. Roberts, & L.W. Porter (Eds.), *Handbook of organizational communication: An interdisciplinary perspective* (pp. 165–194). Newbury Park, CA: Sage.

Christensen, L.T. (1991, June). *The marketing culture: The communication of organizational identity in a culture without foundation.* Paper presented at the International Conference on "Organizational Culture," Copenhagen, Denmark.

Coleman, J. (1974). *Power and the structure of society.* New York: Norton.

Conrad, C. (1985). *Strategic organizational communication: Cultures, situations, and adaptation.* New York: Holt, Rinehart & Winston.

Conrad, C. (1988). Identity, structure and communicative action in church decision-making. *Journal for the scientific study of religion, 27,* 345–361.

Crable, R.E. (1986). The organizational 'system' of rhetoric: The influence of megatrends into the twenty-first century. In S.W. Hugenberg (Ed.), *Rhetorical studies honoring James L. Golden* (pp. 57–68). Dubuque, IA: Kendall/Hunt.

Crable, R.E., & Vibbert, S.L. (1983). Mobil's epideictic advocacy: "Observation" of Prometheus-Bound. *Communication Monographs, 50,* 380–394.

Crable, R.E., & Vibbert, S.L. (1985). Managing issues and influencing public policy. *Public Relations Review, 11,* 3–16.

Crable, R.E., & Vibbert, S.L. (1986). *Public relations as communication management.* Edina, MN: Bellweather Press.

Culler, J. (1982). *On deconstruction: Theory and criticism after structuralism.* Ithaca, NY: Cornell University Press.

Dionisopoulos, G.N., & Vibbert, S.L. (1983, November). *Organizational apologia: "Corporate" public discourse and the genre of self-defense.* Paper presented at the annual meeting of the Speech Communication Association, Washington, DC.

Enis, B.M. (1978). Exxon marks the spot. *Journal of Advertising Research, 18,* 7–12.

Ewen, S. (1988). *All consuming images: The politics of style in contemporary culture.* New York: Basic.

Foucault, M. (1984). *The Foucault reader* (P. Rabinow, Ed.). New York: St. Martin's Press.

Gitlin, T. (1989, July/August). Postmodernism defined, at last! *Utne Reader,* pp. 52–61.

Goldzwig, S., & Cheney, G. (1984). The U.S. Catholic bishops on nuclear arms: Corporate advocacy, role redefinition, and rhetorical adaptation. *Central States Speech Journal, 35,* 8–23.

Griffin, L. (1964). The rhetorical structure of the 'New Left' movements: Part I. *Quarterly Journal of Speech, 50,* 113–135.

Heath, R.L. (1980). Corporate advocacy: An application of speech communication perspectives and skills—and more. *Communication Education, 29,* 370–77.

Jablonski, C. (1988). Rhetoric, paradox, and the movement for women's ordination in the Roman Catholic Church. *Quarterly Journal of Speech, 74,* 164–183.

Jameson, F. (1981). *The political unconscious: Narrative as a socially symbolic act.* Ithaca, NY: Cornell University Press.

Jamieson, K.H. (1988). *Eloquence in an electronic age: The transformation of political speechmaking.* New York: Oxford.

Jay, M. (1973). *The dialectical imagination.* Boston: Little, Brown.

Langer, S.K. (1942). *Philosophy in a new key.* Cambridge, MA: Harvard University Press.

Lapham, L. (1986, February) Brand names. *Harpers,* p. 85.

Leff, M., & Procario, M.O. (1985). Rhetorical theory in speech communication. In T.W. Benson

(Ed.), *Speech communication in the twentieth century* (pp. 3–27). Carbondale: Southern Illinois University Press.

Lyotard, J-F. (1984). *The postmodern condition: A report on knowledge* (G. Bennington & B. Massumi, Trans.). Minneapolis: University of Minnesota Press.

Mackenzie, W.J.M. (1978). *Political identity.* New York: St. Martin's Press.

McCloskey, D.N. (1985). *The rhetoric of economics.* Madison: University of Wisconsin Press.

McKerrow, R.E. (1989). Critical rhetoric: Theory and practice. *Quarterly Journal of Speech, 56,* 91–111.

McMillan, J.J. (1982). *The rhetoric of the modern organization.* Unpublished doctoral dissertation, The University of Texas at Austin, Austin, TX.

McMillan, J.J. (1987). In search of the organizational persona: A rationale for studying organizations rhetorically. In L. Thayer (Ed.), *Organization—communication: Emerging perspectives* (Vol. 2, pp. 21–45). Norwood, NJ: Ablex.

McMillan, J.J. (1988). Institutional plausibility alignment as rhetorical exercise: A mainline denomination's struggle with the exigence of sexism. *Journal for the scientific study of religion, 27,* 326–344.

Meyer, J.W. (1986). Myths of socialization and of personality. In T.C. Heller, M. Sosna, & D.E. Wellbery (Eds.), *Reconstructing individualism* (pp. 208–221). Stanford, CA: Stanford University Press.

Meyrowitz, J. (1985). *No sense of place: The impact of electronic media on social behavior.* New York: Oxford University Press.

Postman, N. (1985). *Amusing ourselves to death: Public discourse in the age of show business.* New York: Penguin.

Putnam, L.L., & Cheney, G. (1985). Organizational communication: Historical development and future directions. In T.W. Benson (Ed.), *Speech communication in the twentieth century* (pp. 130–156). Carbondale: Southern Illinois University Press.

Rorty, R. (1979). *Philosophy and the mirror of nature.* Princeton, NJ: Princeton University Press.

Sennett, R. (1980). *Authority.* New York: Random House.

Simons, H., Mechling, E.W., & Schreier, H.N. (1984). The functions of human communication in mobilizing for action from the bottom up: The rhetoric of social movements. In C. Arnold & J.W. Bowers (Eds.), *Handbook of rhetorical and communication theory* (pp. 792–868). Boston: Allyn & Bacon.

Sproule, J.M. (1988). The new managerial rhetoric and the old criticism. *Quarterly Journal of Speech, 74,* 468–486.

Steinbeck, J. (1939). *The grapes of wrath.* New York: Bantam Books.

Tompkins, P.K. (1969). The rhetorical criticism of non-oratorical works. *Quarterly Journal of Speech, 55,* 431–439.

Tompkins, P.K. (1987). Translating organizational theory: Symbolism over substance. In F.M. Jablin, L.L. Putnam, K.H. Roberts, & L.W. Porter (Eds.), *Handbook of organizational communication: An interdisciplinary perspective* (pp. 70–96). Newbury Park, CA: Sage.

Tompkins, P.K., & Cheney, G. (1985). Communication and inobtrusive control in contemporary organizations. In R.D. McPhee & P.K. Tompkins (Eds.), *Organizational communication: Traditional themes and new directions* (pp. 179–210). Newbury Park, CA: Sage.

Tompkins, P.K., Fisher, J.Y., Infante, D.A. & Tompkins, E.L. (1975). Kenneth Burke and the inherent characteristics of formal organizations. *Speech Monographs, 42,* 135–142.

Trujillo, N., & Toth, E.L. (1987). Organizational perspectives for public relations research and practice. *Management Communication Quarterly, 1,* 199–231.

Valdes, M.J., & Miller, O. (Eds.). (1985). *Identity of the literary text.* Toronto: University of Toronto Press.

Whalen, S., & Cheney, G. (in press). Contemporary social theory and its implications for rhetorical and communication theory. *Quarterly Journal of Speech.*

Wittgenstein, L. (1958). *Philosophical investigations* (G.E.M. Anscombe, Trans.). New York: Macmillan.

III

An Explanation of the Practice of Public Relations

Corporate Communication and Control

CHARLES CONRAD
Texas A & M University

Almost a decade ago Jeffrey Pfeffer (1981) called attention to the symbolic dimension of management, arguing that managers not only direct organizational actions and make strategic decisions, but also foster supportive beliefs among various internal and external constituencies. Managers who appear to be effective in guiding their organizations through competitive, chaotic environmental seas tend to energize and direct the activities of employees while reassuring investors about the stability of their capital (Bowman, 1976, 1978). A vehicle for maintaining this "illusion of efficacy," especially with external audiences, is the corporate annual report to stockholders (Bettman & Weitz, 1983; Staw, McKechnie, & Puffer, 1983).

The limited amount of research on annual reports has focused on the symbolic strategies that organizational rhetors use to explain the successes or failures encountered during the year. Important research has demonstrated that annual reports are grounded in "attribution theories" of individual action. In short, attribution theories suggest that persons' explanations of the effects of their actions tend to be self-serving (for reviews see Lau & Russell, 1980; Zuckerman, 1979). Persons tend to attribute favorable outcomes to internal factors (their choices, capacities, and so on) and unfavorable outcomes to factors external to them or their control. The former process tends to *enhance* self-image and self-esteem; the latter serves to *protect* self-esteem. Consistently, annual reports rely on this pattern of attributions (Staw et al., 1983), especially when the overall economic situation is bad (Bettman & Weitz, 1983). The ratio of self-serving to nonself-serving messages ranges from 2:1 to 3:1 (i.e., positive outcomes are attributed to internal factors twice to three times as often as they are attributed to external factors and vice-versa). As important, the motivation for these attributional biases seems to be to enhance the credibility of management:

> The presentational biases [biases in attribution], moreover, could represent either attempts to enhance management's esteem or strategic efforts to present management as being sufficiently in control of the organizational outcomes as to encourage people to participate in the organizational coalition. Our empirical analyses were undertaken to attempt to rule out all but the last of these possibilities, and considering everything, this interpretation stands up well to the evidence. (Salancik & Meindl, 1984, p. 251)

Attributional biases thus seem to serve a rhetorical purpose. Their goal is to create and sustain an "illusion of efficacy," the impression that upper management is capable of either controlling the pressures they face or of responding quickly, efficiently, and decisively to those pressures.

If read as a unit, past research offers provocative insights into the requirements that must be met for successful maintenance of the illusion of efficacy. The core requirement is that annual report rhetors must successfully obscure their attributional biases (Bowman, 1976). This task is particularly difficult because the audience of the reports is relatively stable over time, and a purely self-serving rhetoric eventually would be detected. As important, the textual sections of annual reports are presented in a narrative structure (Bettman & Weitz, 1983). This form imposes a complex set of requirements on the writer (Conrad, 1990), the most important of which involves the active agency of the key characters. Protagonists (management) must have antagonists, and must deal with them actively if the expectations created by the narrative form are to be fulfilled (Burke, 1931/1968).

The credibility of the narrative thus depends on a particular type of relationship among characters. Management's discourse will be credible only if it develops and exploits an appropriate set of character relationships. Unfortunately, existing research provides little insight into the particular rhetorical strategies used to fulfill these requirements.

Between 1975 and 1985 the American automobile industry faced what has become a continuing challenge. Because the three firms faced essentially the same economic situation, addressed the same audience throughout the decade, and experienced fluctuations in organizational performance, they provide an excellent comparative case study of the rhetorical strategies used to maintain an illusion of efficacy. Although the popular press focused its attention on the Chrysler Corporation during this era, both Ford and General Motors reported year-end losses and declines in market share of historic proportions. However, during the era all three firms also reported excellent years that followed major "turnarounds" in corporate performance, and their rhetoric reflected these changing fortunes in different ways.

ILLUSIONS OF EFFICACY IN THE WORST OF TIMES/THE BEST OF TIMES

Two themes dominate the Big Three annual reports published between 1975 and 1985. One theme extols the "capable team" that makes up the organizations—rational managers, cooperative workers, faithful customers, and, late in the era, modern technology. The other describes competition from external "enemies," both foreign firms and government bureaucrats. In the following section I describe the various ways in which these themes are woven together in the rhetoric of annual reports. In the final section I argue that this tapestry is persuasive largely because of its congruence with an American cultural mythology, myths of the "American Dream" and of "managerial rationality."

Rhetoric and the Illusion of Efficacy

An efficient means of introducing the rhetoric of Big Three annual reports is to compare GM's 1977 version (after a good year) with Ford's 1978 issue (after a comparable year). In the 1977 "letter to stockholders" GM and America were one—"1977 was a year of achievement . . . The measures of success were not only the conventional guides of production, sales, employment, payrolls, products, and earnings, but also progress in meeting national goals" (p. 1). GM and its customers, working together, had increased fleet fuel economy by 58%, "surpassing the required 18 mpg Federal standard," resulting in "significant dollar savings for the customer, as well as substantial energy conservation for the nation."

Continued improvement will depend, not on government pressures, but "upon customer acceptance of new, more fuel efficient designs." On a related issue, GM's technological advances "have brought us to the threshold of removing the automobile as a significant factor in air pollution," and progress will continue as long as the GM–customer teamwork continues: "unfortunately these gains in cleaner air and greater fuel economy also carry some cost penalty to the consumer, but we are working to keep this to a minimum" (p. 13).

Because of the GM–customer team, "the 1970s will be recorded as the decade in which the automobile came to terms with its environment—and without significant sacrifice of its capacity to move people and the goods of the world" (p. 3). The team must—and will—continue:

even as we help to meet national goals, General Motors is acting upon its conviction that the satisfaction of the individual customer is the basic building block of our success. . . . we know it [customer satisfaction] remains, as always the essence of successful competition in free enterprise. (p. 3)

With the team intact, "we expect both General Motors and the industry to set new sales records in the United States and elsewhere in the world" (p. 3).

However, an outside force—government agencies—threatens the success of the team. The problem is not that the agencies have evil intentions, but that they are inherently slow to act and constantly buried in their penchant for ambiguity. In contrast to the auto industry's rapid and successful response to the energy crisis—a response that "will exceed even the Apollo space program that carried men to the moon"—was "little [governmental] action to increase the nation's energy supplies. . . . This vital objective lies outside the province of the auto industry, but certainly not outside our concern. A comprehensive national energy policy relying more on the market mechanism, for which we have been calling since before the oil embargo of 1973, is yet to be enacted" (pp. 2–3). Fortunately, the automakers have succeeded in pressuring the government to clarify some of the ambiguities that have "bedeviled" the industry, as in the Clean Air Act Amendments of 1977. Clarification is important because GM is committed to achieving national goals independent of federal pressure. For example, "we plan to act before the mandate for passive restraints" (p. 3). But, because of their lethargic and ambiguous nature, government actions may impede even GM's capacity to meet national goals.

As attribution theory suggests, GM credits its success to "internal" factors. However, its rhetoric only implicitly applauds management for the success. Credit—and presumably responsibility during years with negative outcomes—is shared while management is depicted as the agent that unifies and directs the team. Significantly, GM's rhetoric also defines "insiders" and outsiders and does so in a way that allows the investor-audience to feel that they also are potential actors in the drama. Readers also are voters, and are legally empowered to pressure government to act in ways which allow the GM team to succeed. The narrative establishes clear, cooperative relationships among all the characters. The following year Ford Motor Company had a comparable, moderately profitable year. Although its annual report discussed many of the same topics as GM's 1977 report, the tone was quite different. The dominant theme was simple, the federal government is the enemy of the American way. The federal government's inability to provide a stable economy combined with its regulatory interference in Ford's activities caused Ford's profits to decline:

Despite higher operating efficiencies, the Company's North American profit margin fell from 3.6% in 1977 to 2.7% in 1978, reflecting the inability to keep pace with inflation and high costs required for programs . . . to improve fuel efficiency and reduce exhaust emissions. (p. 16)

Unlike GM who expressed pride that its company–customer team was meeting national goals by exceeding federal fuel efficiency standards, Ford complained that "the law requires corporate average fuel economy to rise to 27.5 mpg in 1985" and

> present[s] risks to the U.S. economy of increased inflation resulting from price increases to recover higher costs, a reduced number of full-line U.S. competitors and reduced industry and supplier employment. There also may be problems stemming from the premature use of unproven technology. . . . [Complying with emission-control standards in 1977] cost about $200 per car. We estimate that the cost to reach the next plateau . . . will be more than double the cost to achieve the initial . . . reduction. (pp. 2–3)

Similar attacks were made on federal safety recall requirements (p. 5).

Involved in litigation with almost everyone throughout the 1975–1981 era, Ford's 1978 annual report expressed a consistent adversarial relationship with a number of different groups. The Securities and Exchange Commission requires companies to describe any legal proceedings that could influence the value of their stock in their annual reports. Consequently, it is the way in which the report describes these actions that is of interest. Ford chose to describe The Federal Trade Commission's investigation of possible monopoly practices by the Big Three as an unnecessary "waste of the government's and the Company's resources" (p. 12); investigations of Ford by the Securities and Exchange Commission, National Highway Traffic Safety Administration, and Environmental Protection Agency were described in similar terms with the notation that success in any of these actions could create "substantial financial exposure" for the company (p. 12). A suit by stockholders "purportedly on behalf of the company" charging financial misconduct by the Board of Directors had been dismissed, although Ford noted, almost grudgingly, that the "plaintiffs may seek to appeal this order or to commence an action in another jurisdiction" (p. 12). Worried about the integrity of its employees, "Ford has [initiated] formal policies directed against illegal or improper payments or other behavior by any of its employees, and a formal system for monitoring adherence" (p. 11).

In a rhetoric highly consistent with the predictions of attribution theory, Ford blamed its problems on external factors and credited its successes to itself. Its reduction in profit resulted from inflation and "continued high costs of achieving government-mandated requirements" (p. 4); its optimism about the future resulted from its commitment to quality (which it admitted "does not always meet Company or customer expectations") and rapid technological advancement. Unlike GM's "people-centered team" message, the theme of Ford's report is that technology had teamed with effective management. The Chairman's report repeatedly claimed that Ford is "on the leading edge of high technology" and views its capital expenditures to retool its factories as a "significant opportunity to improve its products" (p. 3). This focus is somewhat surprising because the issue also provides data that indicate that Ford responded to the 1974 oil embargo by reducing spending in its research and development (R&D) division, and continued those reduced levels until 1977.

Although these two reports differ substantially in tone, the content of their arguments is quite similar. Both (a) express confidence in the economic future, both in general and in terms of their own corporate success; (b) articulate an unrestrained faith in the ability of technological advances and technical reason to solve organizational and societal problems; and (c) call for limiting governmental activities to an appropriate realm and level. Although each of these themes recurs throughout the annual reports, they do not stand alone. Instead, they are presented as dimensions of a broader frame of reference, one that I call *hysterical optimism*.

The Mythology of Hysterical Optimism

It had been a challenging year for the American automobile industry, but one that the annual report says has led the Company to be stronger and better. Its products had, as the subtitle of the report indicated, been named "car of the year on two continents" (pp. 2, 5). It emerged from the year in a stronger and more competitive position:

- It "now has its most innovative and competitive product line, and its broadest market coverage in history;"
- It "now offers subcompact-size cars" for all its dealers;
- The only all-new full line of cars for 1976, including a station wagon unique in its class . . . which . . . took nearly 30 percent of the compact car market in January.
- A personal luxury car . . . with more than 50 percent of its trade-ins coming from owners of competitive models in 1975.
- A strong mid-size line. . . .
- Full-size and luxury cars . . . priced to give top product value.
- A line-up of compact vans and wagons that captured 37.5 percent of their market in 1975, and outsold every foreign and domestic competitor.
- A complete line of light-duty trucks, and compact trucks that now

account for more than 20 percent of all our U.S. vehicle sales. (pp. 5–6)

Of course, this very favorable summary results from a careful selection of available data. The company was Chrysler; the year was 1975. Chrysler had lost $259.5 million (not including a $22.8 million loss that was not included because of a change in the company's accounting system), four times as much red ink as the previous record loss in 1974. In spite of the Board's expectation that "the continued efforts of this management to move the company ahead will bring a significant improvement in Chrysler's results in the months and years ahead" (p. 6), the firm was on the verge of bankruptcy.

However, the selective use of optimistic data is characteristic of all these annual reports. The strategy is constrained somewhat by the audience. Securities and Exchange Commission rules strive to keep reports from being "excessively" misleading. The reports deal with this constraint through a creative manipulation of "time" and "place." Like Ford in loss year 1979, Chrysler concentrated attention on a profitable fourth quarter, although the year as a whole included staggering losses (p. 11). Similarly, it reported that in January (1976) Chrysler's market share rose to 15.8%, "the highest since August, 1975, one of the Company's least profitable 1975 months" (p. 6). And, although Chrysler was having serious problems in its major market (United States and Canada), it saw promising trends in the United Kingdom, France and "world automotive markets" (p. 5). Evidently, in multinational firms things are going well somewhere, at least for a brief period of time, no matter how bleak the overall picture might be. Authors of annual reports find and highlight those places/times, regardless of how minor they might be.

They also depict management as capably and rationally responding to crises and actively planning for future contingencies. In 1975, Chrysler "took action with respect to those operations which showed the prospect of being a continuing financial drain on the corporation," including selling its Airtemp Division at a $55 million loss (p. 4). Consistently, the rational response to crisis involves cutting costs and restructuring for increased efficiency:

> To adjust to these unparalleled economic problems, Chrysler made significant and permanent reductions in its operating costs . . . restructured its operations for greater efficiency and productivity, and accelerated its programs of parts standardization. . . . in order to react more quickly to market changes. (p. 7)

Its new "product plans" have positioned it for the market of the late 1970s and beyond (p. 6), and it is planning further changes that will enable it to expand its market and increase its efficiency.

At Chrysler the key to the success of these plans is technological advancement: "R&D expenditures are essential for the development of innovative products that strengthen a company's position in the marketplace" (p. 8). Curiously, Chrysler reported in the same paragraph that it had reduced its research and development budget in 1975 by approximately 20%, but did so by becoming more efficient, "by greater use of automated test equipment and computer-aided design techniques, by closer co-ordination of North American and overseas R&D efforts, and by stringent cost control programs." Because of its rational decision making and R & D efforts, Chrysler was "moving ahead . . . [toward] increasing its market out ahead" (p. 6).

But, it is neither fair nor accurate to single out Chrysler for its selective use of data, time, and place. In 1980, Ford reported a net loss of $1.5 billion, its largest in history. GM had its first loss ($765 million) since before the Great Depression (1921) (GM, 1980, p. 21). The arguments presented in Ford and GM reports during their red ink years are identical to those offered by Chrysler—reasoned managerial decision making designed to increase market share and reduce operating costs, reliance on technological "fixes," and optimism grounded in carefully selected favorable times and places.

However, there was one major difference. The "government-as-enemy" theme that had become a standard part of Ford's annual reports, became a dominant theme for both of the Big Two during times of decline. Essentially three arguments were developed: (a) the federal government has failed to adequately control the overall economy, its primary area of responsibility; (b) government interference in the activities of automakers must be controlled; and (c) the government must control foreign competition in order to re-create a fair competitive marketplace.

As should be expected from earlier reports, both Ford and GM attributed their problems during 1979–1981 to external factors. Ford was explicit: "recovery from the present depressed level . . . will be difficult . . . It depends on external factors, such as the reduction of inflation without inducing massive unemployment" (Ford, 1980, p. 3). The most important step would involve the federal government getting its own house in order: "Wage and price controls, however, would only mask underlying economic problems. . . . [Ford would] encourage continued efforts to reduce federal deficit spending, to curtail excessive expansion of money supplies, and to reduce unneeded regulation" (1980, p. 4).

Ford was so concerned that it added a "Supplementary Inflation Data" appendix to its 1979 report. Its goal was in part to explain new accounting procedures that had been adopted to cope with double-digit inflation. But it also made a final appeal to place blame for Ford's problems where it belonged:

> Inflation during 1979 exceeded 13%—the highest levels since 1946. Ford's ability to meet the demands of the 1980s will depend importantly on how the U.S. government shapes the environment in which our customers live and we

do business. The high level of inflation is one of our country's most serious domestic problems. Effective and consistent government policies are required that will control inflation, stabilize energy supply, and increase incentives for capital formation—which would improve productivity, lower inflation, and help make U.S. industry more competitive. (p. 35; also see GM, 1980, p. 2)

What government should not do is continue its unnecessary and counter-productive interference in the automakers' business. First of all, government control is unnecessary. This argument is implicit in GM's earlier "customer–company team" theme. It is made explicit in reports of "successes" in meeting national goals of fuel economy and environmental protection, each of which is attributed to company initiative rather than government action. Ford is so satisfied with its progress on fuel economy that it chides the government for its misplaced emphasis: "If the rest of the country would do as well as our industry, it would be a remarkable achievement" (1979, p. 4).

Second, government interference is expensive and counterproductive. In 1979 Ford predicted that regulations would add an average of $1,000 to the price of a 1980–1985 car (p. 4); in 1980 it re-asserted that "we fully support the goals of vehicle safety and a clean environment, but we believe there are opportunities to cut back on unproductive, marginal requirements and halt additional regulations of questionable merit" (p. 3). GM, which normally extols the virtues of a cooperative relationship with government, proclaimed that "we must be free from excessive and costly government regulations. Such is not the case at present" (1980, p. 2). By 1980, GM had noticed another government-imposed burden:

the escalating burden of taxation, both foreign and domestic, imposed on business and industry by government at all levels continues to be a major concern . . . Excessive tax and regulatory burdens represent an unwarranted barrier to private initiative and its counterparts—strong economic growth, high employment and a low inflation rate. (p. 14; also see p. 8)

The federal government's adversarial attitude about American automakers is in marked contrast to the cooperative perspective of many foreign governments:

There are regulations in overseas markets, too, but governments abroad generally show a greater understanding of the time requirements involved in making sweeping changes in an industry as complex as ours. We would welcome in the United States the degree of cooperation shown by European and Japanese governments toward their automobile companies. It would strengthen the domestic manufacturers, maintain jobs in the United States, and improve the balance of trade. (Ford, 1979, pp. 4–5)

The most important fruit of this new cooperation would be appropriate restraints on the negative impact of imported cars. Although the Big Two were meeting this challenge with planning and new technology (Ford, 1979, p. 7; GM, 1980, p. 2), "short-term" limits on imported Japanese cars would allow American manufacturers the time needed to compensate for the economic crisis created by federal policies (Ford, 1979, p 3; GM, 1980, p. 2). With these three simple steps—repairing the economy, eliminating needless interference, and re-creating a fair international trade situation—the federal government can reverse the adverse effects of its hostile attitude and re-create the cooperative atmosphere desired by American automakers.

Bettman and Weitz (1983) noted that attributing negative outcomes to external factors is particularly prevalent when the national economy is depressed. During general declines, they argued, external attributions are most credible and serve to most effectively enhance the credibility of management. The rhetoric of Big Three annual reports supports their conclusion, with two additions. First, external attributions are not new arguments developed in response to bad years. Even during good times, the federal government and its policies are depicted as enemies of the cooperative team. Instead of introducing these arguments during eras of decline, a strategy that could easily be interpreted as self-serving, they are merely accented during those years. Second, the depressed economy is depicted as a cause of the company's difficulties, not merely described as a context within which those difficulties arose. Consequently, not only are external attributions more credible during times of general economic malaise, but the economy is also used to enhance the credibility of the attributions.

Happy Days Are Here Again, Or Tom Peters Goes To Detroit

The year 1983 was the "year of the turnaround" (their phrase) for American automakers. In good attribution theory form, success was attributed to internal factors, including, somewhat surprisingly, the efforts of autoworkers. In previous reports, particularly during down years, employees rarely were mentioned. When they were, it was as an example of "overhead" being rationally reduced by management or as unfortunate victims of failing federal economic policies. With the exception of Chrysler, in 1983 they became competent, contributing partners with management. In 1983, workers joined the "team." Similarly, customers, who previously had been mentioned only as an "external pressure" because of their sudden preference for small cars and their complaints about product quality, became the Big Three's reason for existence. It seems like Peters and Austin's (1985) *A Passion for Excellence* had become the official bible of Detroit.

GM's mood changed markedly, but, as usual, not as exhuberently as Ford's:

> It was the turnaround year we have been waiting for . . . General Motors earned a record income of $3.5 billion . . . [although] earnings of $11.84 per share were not a record. . . . . The improving economy and higher production volumes contributed to this success. Much of the increase, however, is directly attributable to the continuing spirit of cooperation between GM and its employees which produced outstanding improvements in product quality and operation performance. (p. 2; also see p. 12)

For Ford, whose "profit improvement represented the largest one-year turnaround from a loss position in U.S. corporate history,"

> 1983 was a significant turnaround year . . . . Although economic conditions and industry sales improved . . . these factors were not the primary reasons . . . The achievement resulted from a new spirit of teamwork. . . . [and] our driver-centered philosophy. (p. 2)

The company's concern for and cooperative relationship with its employees had been demonstrated during the depths of the Reagan recession:

> General Motors and the United Auto Workers cooperated in two "Care and Share" food donation programs, one in early 1983 and another before Christmas . . . which provided the equivalent of about 20 million cans of food for America's needy. The need for such programs is just one reminder that we all witnessed too much suffering during the past recession. (p. 3)

But a "new spirit" of labor–management harmony blossomed as GM recalled 90,000 U.S. employees to work:

> We believe a real spirit of cooperation between management and labor is taking hold in the auto industry, and we have the opportunity to build and expand on this new spirit in labor negotiations in the months ahead. We have come this far, working together, and we must continue to exert our best efforts, working together. (p. 3)

The spirit was made concrete by a new profit-sharing program that "is a milestone in history. No other company anywhere in the world, at any time in the past, has ever shared such a large amount of profits with its employees" (p. 12). Through its Joint Study Center, an "unprecedented union–management partnership" had been "established upon the principle of complete union and worker involvement in all aspects of manufacturing and assembly plans and processes" (p. 8). In its new Saturn plant "GM people will perform a greater variety of operations and be responsible for a total sub-assembly to increase teamwork, involvement, and quality of work life" (p. 8).

At Ford, the spirit was translated into a new commitment and new programs of worker involvement:

> The continuing development of Ford's human resources . . . lies at the heart of our plans for the future. We are expanding our efforts to involve all employees in work-related problem-solving and decision-making tasks, we are increasing work skills and knowledge through improved training and retraining programs and we are continuing to attract and develop the best people and provide them with stimulating and rewarding work. (1983, p. 4)

> The crux of this effort is Employee Involvement. . . . EI has facilitated new relationships based on mutual trust and open communication and it has generated significant improvement in many areas of performance. . . . EI activities among salaried employees also have contributed to increased efficiency and satisfaction in the workplace (p. 18). . . . In addition to involving employees more directly with their work and workplace, Ford is helping them make the most of their individual capacity for growth. (p. 19)

But at Chrysler, whose employees had taken major cuts in pay and benefits during the three previous years, the new spirit was subdued. At most, its employees were one element of a successful "team:"

> All of Chrysler's constituents made sacrifices to help Chrysler survive and prosper. One such sacrifice came from the United Automobile Workers. . . . The Chrysler turnaround demonstrated . . . that a private corporation, together with its employees, dealers, stockholders, bankers, suppliers, and Federal, State and Canadian Provincial Governments can save jobs and restore a competitive basic industry. (p. 3)

In much of Chrysler's rhetoric, workers still were depicted as one of many "pressures" on the firm's "break even point" (1983, p. 13).

Instead, at Chrysler the key to independence was rational, strategic managerial decision making. Through management's "aggressive action" (p. 14) to reduce costs, improve productivity, and minimize debt load, Chrysler was able to reduce significantly its break-even point to less than half what it had been in 1979. Through creative use of new technology and aggressive efforts to anticipate and respond to changing customer demands, Chrysler management had solved its major problems. Fortunately, management also had successfully negotiated a new "forward-looking" (p. 12) labor agreement with employees "who realize that the best job security comes from making high quality cars that people will buy. The new labor contract means that

Chrysler can count on continued labor cooperation in our drive to improve our products and the way we make them" (p. 8).

In 1983—and in every subsequent annual report—Chrysler employees were one part of a team that contributes to organizational success by accepting the leadership of management (for instance, see 1986, "America's Team"). When workers' contributions are mentioned, it consistently is as adjuncts to new technology (1986, pp. 14–17, "People and Technology Building Excellence").

However, the Big Two also seemed to be ambivilent about labor's role in the cooperative team. At Ford, the new spirit of labor as equal partners was short-lived. Although subsequent reports include brief sections which describe Quality Control programs, the exhuberent affirmation of worker input disappeared after 1983, to be replaced by a focus on "Technology and the Ford Team" (1986, pp. 18–21).

Only at GM does the spirit continue through its 1986 report. But even there, the "spirit" retained a quite traditional kind of manager–worker relationship. Strategic decision making would continue to be in the hands of leaders. Although workers would contribute to organizational effectiveness by providing technical expertise about problems in their areas, it is clear that management would maintain their role as "leaders" while workers were transformed into satisfied, efficient and productive team "members." As Quality of Working Life is envisioned at GM, or the "new spirit" emerged at Ford, worker–manager relations were to be based on Frederick Taylor "four principles" of Scientific Management: strategic decision making through rational processes based on information gathered from carefully selected employees whose realistic concern for individual and organizational economic security and gain would maximize organizational efficiency, minimize costs, and increase job satisfaction (Conrad, 1985, esp. pp. 23–44).

This ambivalence reveals an important tension within the ideology of corporate annual reports. Organizational rhetors must simultaneously present management as the dominant actors in the drama while retaining an important role for the other team members. Without the former characteristic, the narrative form with its effective protagonist cannot be maintained. But, excessively de-emphasizing the other members reduces the potential flexibility and power of the rhetoric. Technology can be used to explain past successes, or to reasonably project successes into the future. Customer attitudes and preferences can easily be used either as evidence of managerial responsiveness, or as challenges to which management is aggressively responding. Worker cooperativeness can be a sign of effective leadership; worker intransigence can be presented as evidence that management's cooperative vision for the future still must be persuasively communicated. The "cooperative team" metaphor can be employed for a wide range of persuasive purposes, as long as the image of the active, responsive manager is the central part, but only one part, of the metaphor.

Big Three annual reports confront this tension by developing an image, a persona of a rational, technology-oriented, flexible manager struggling against an irrational, inflexible, insensitive government bureaucracy. Like all rational actors, Big Three managers had "learned important lessons" during the down years: "valuable lessons were learned and will not be forgotten. Because of progress in all the fundamental areas of our business, Ford is prepared to meet the challenges of the future" (1984, p. 5; also see GM, 1984, p. 3). The loss years were even depicted as a time of heightened management rationality which culminated in an almost-religious zeal for excellence:

> The results highlighted here are the culmination of several years of patiently implemented business strategies. These were designed not merely to achieve short-term profitability but, more importantly, to provide a foundation for continuing prosperity. Their essence is constant and scrupulous attention to the fundamentals of our business—product quality, operating efficiency, technology, marketing and people. Last year we pledged our efforts to continuous improvement in these areas. We renew that pledge. (Ford, pp. 4–5)

Aggressive action based on careful strategic decision making has brought the Big Two through a "time of trial" (GM, pp. 2, 3; Ford, p. 5).

Technology and technical reason will bring the Big Three through in the future. Ford's "ability to conceive and apply new technologies" is fundamental to its future (1984, p. 4). The Big Two's many recent technical breakthroughs (Ford, pp. 6, 12–14; GM, 1984, pp. 6, 18) and success in the technologically competitive field of automobile racing suggest their continuing faith in technical reason and competence in R&D (see especially Ford, 1986, pp. 16–17). By the end of the era, all three car makers included extended "new technology" sections in their annual reports; for Ford and Chrysler these sections encompassed almost one-half of the text.

Consistently, Big Three managers asserted that what seem to be positive government actions actually are unnecessary threats to the team and its constituents. As long as the federal government maintains its new-found cooperative attitude (Ford, p. 15); focuses its attention on control of outside threats—unfair foreign competition and drivers who use alcohol and do not use seat belts (GM, p. 8); and maintains a controlled economy, American automakers and all of their constituents will prosper.

At Chrysler, criticism of government policies began in earnest in 1984 (the year after its early repayment of Federal loan guarantees) and became a crusade by 1986. This most recent report concluded with a full-page indictment of government policy entitled "Toward a Level Playing Field" (Chrysler annual reports have been filled with sports metaphors since Iaccoca became chair). The U.S. trade deficit, Federal budget deficit, lack of a national energy policy and "escalating cost of health care" (in 1986 GM's largest single supplier cost was to Blue Cross/Blue Shield of Michigan), "cripple our competitive strength." In the "macho" voice that has characterized Chrysler's reports during the Iaccocca era, Chrysler claims it

> isn't walking away from a fight [with "foreign producers and governments that are tough, long-term players"] we're eager to get on with it. But we're disadvantaged by federal trade, fiscal and energy policies that simply are not competitive. . . . The uneven international playing field hurts everyone in this country—every business and every citizen. We simply can't continue surrendering our industrial base today without also compromising our economic leadership, our standard of living and our ability to defend ourselves tomorrow. (p. 23)

Not only is the Federal government not helping Chrysler meet national goals, it is less committed to those goals than the Company is:

> Chrysler is doing its part to save energy. We were the only U.S. automaker in 1986 to meet the original 27.5-mile-per-gallon . . . standard . . . Unfortunately, the government chose to weaken those standards rather than enforce them. But with or without federal standards, we will continue to work for optimum fuel economy . . . because it's in the best interest of Chrysler Corporation and the American economy. (1983, p. 23)

In an important way, Chrysler's 1983 report offers a return to the conceptual structure of GM's optimistic 1977 version. Selective use of performance data, faith in managerial rationality and technical reason (which was defined in progressive more "technological" terms as the era progressed), and a concern for achieving an "appropriate" role for government combine to generate a degree of optimism that is maintained independent of the specific characteristics of the firms' economic position. At this level, the Big Three annual reports articulate the assumptions about social and organizational control that seem to characterize their cultures. But at another level they function to normalize and legitimize a particular "optimal control reality." In this reality team members accept and support technical, managerial strategic reason, and maximize their own efficiency and productivity because it is in their own, their company's and their nation's self-interest to do so. Government accepts its responsibility to maintain a "level capitalist playing field" by controlling outside threats to fairness, not controlling American Teams (except in the rare cases when they deviate from fairness), and controlling themselves and their proper realm of responsibility.

CONCLUSION AND INTERPRETATION

Big Three annual reports articulate a fundamental cultural myth: the "American Co-operative Economic Dream." Articulated in its purist form during times of high profit, this mythology is composed of myths of rational managerial decision making and of the cooperative team composed of management, labor, customers, government, and technology. Of course, the dream is never fully realized. But it is always there, as a direction and tendency and as a ready justification for efforts which, in the short term, seem to lead in other directions.

Myths of rational decision making are particularly potent in Western cultures, and especially in Western organizations (March & Olson, 1976). These myths suggest that organizations function and managers manage because they possess superior information and have superior capacities for "technical reasoning" (Perrow, 1979). Thus, they are able to predict future contingencies based on lessons they have learned systematically from past experiences in decision making and/or respond rapidly and correctly to current crises (Benson, 1983). When combined with structural factors which limit outsiders' and lower level employees' access to strategically sensitive information, these myths of rationality serve as potent parameters for controlling the interpretations and actions of internal and external constituents alike. Mumby (1988) concluded:

> the very notion of managers as individuals motivated by rational decision making is in itself a political position, and is intrinsically tied up with issues of power. . . . Managers maintain power by framing everything within a techno-rational context, and systematically excluding other organizational perspectives. (p. 2)

In Big Three annual reports the entire pattern of argument—selectively presenting data, focusing attention on favorable aspects of the organization's operations, and projecting claims of increased efficiency, improved productivity, and enhanced allocation of resources into the future—supports the rationality myth (de Certeau, 1984). The effect of this approach is to place management's claims of efficacy beyond critical analysis (Habermas, 1975). Even the simplest test of management's claims (e.g., using the statistical evidence available in the reports to question the validity of management's interpretations) would involve a denial of culturally sanctioned myths of managerial rationality. Since management, by (cultural) definition, is able to take a broader and more "far-sighted" perspective on data, such challenges can easily be pre-empted or refuted. In fact, the act of challenging managerial interpretations itself provides evidence of the uniqueness (which in this case implies superiority) of managerial vision.

The second myth, offered particularly during times of organizational decline, expresses faith in the "Redemptive Power of The Team." Two themes are woven together in this myth—"a devil is in the house" and "in cooperation lies salvation." The devil typically is an excessively intrusive (because temporarily misguided) federal government. For salvation to come, the devil must be converted. While the devil is being reformed, a return to the things that made America great—cooperative pursuit of efficiency and economic growth through technological progress—can start the company and country on the way back.

The second theme involves the seemingly paradoxical identification of the federal government as both part of the organizational "team" and as the team's greatest enemy. Forester (1982) noted that:

> Power may be understood not as a possession of an actor working mysteriously upon another actor, but rather as a normative relationship binding the two actors together, a relationship which structures one agent's dependence on the other's information, deference to the other's supposed authority, trust in the other's intentions, and consideration of the other's claim to attention. (p. 12)

Casting the government as potential ally has the dual function of legitimizing its attempts to influence the automaker's activities and legitimizing management's right to reject government mandates. However, the legitimation of government is bounded by the considerations of technical reason. When government errs it does so because it lacks adequate information or suffers from an excessively uncooperative attitude about the other members of the team; when it succeeds it is because it accepts the tenets of managerial rationality and acts in accord with them. In short, when government "intrudes" in the automakers' operations it violates the criteria of mutual dependence, deference, trust, and consideration that are the basis of its right to exercise control over the companies.

On the surface this rhetoric legitimizes government involvement in the industry. At a deeper level it legitimizes a mode of decision making that both places management's validity claims beyond attack and supports the myths of rationality that underlie the primacy of technical reason. The myths in turn allow management to legitimately use an image of technical expertise as grounds for claiming credibility in nontechnical areas (trade policy, pollution control, macroeconomic policy, and so on) and using that credibility to critique existing government policy (Habermas, 1975). In short, government acts as part of the team when it accepts managerial rationality; it alienates itself from the other members, including its constituents, when it questions managerial discourse.

The potential impact of annual report rhetoric is substantial. As Deetz and

Mumby (1990) have noted, the history of American organizations during the 20th century has witnessed an increasing isolation of owners from the operations of their firms. Although their discussion focuses primarily on structural features, the analysis that I have presented in this essay suggests that managerial rhetoric addressed to stock owners serves similar control-related functions. As long as owners participate in the cultural myths expressed in annual reports, their "partnership" with the managers who they presumably control will be an unequal one. Corporate rhetoric places management's validity claims beyond possible dispute by those who actually own the company.

REFERENCES

Benson, J. (1983). Paradigm and praxis in organizational analysis. In L. Cummings & B. Staw (Eds.), *Research in Organizational Behavior, 5*, 33–55.

Bettman, J., & Weitz, B. (1983). Attributions in the board room. *Administrative Science Quarterly, 28*, 165–183.

Bowman, E. (1976). Strategy and the weather. *Sloan Management Review, 17*, 49–62.

Bowman, E. (1978). Strategy, annual reports, and alchemy. *California Management Review, 20*, 64–71.

Burke, K. (1968). *Counter-statement.* Berkeley: University of California Press. (Original work published 1931)

Conrad, C. (1985). *Strategic organizational communication.* New York: Holt, Rinehart & Winston.

Conrad, C. (1990). Drama, culture and ethnographic accounts of organizational action. In J. Anderson (Ed.), *Communication yearbook* (Vol. 13, pp. 95–106) Newbury Park, CA: Sage.

de Certeau, M. (1984). *The practice of everyday life.* Berkeley: University of California Press.

Deetz, S., & Mumby, D. (1990). Power, discourse, and the workplace: reclaiming the critical tradition in communication studies in organizations. In J. Anderson (Ed.), *Communication yearbook 13* (pp. 18–47). Newbury Park, CA: Sage.

Forester, J. (1982). Know your organizations. *Plan Canada, 22*, 3–13.

Habermas, J. (1975). *Legitimation crisis.* Boston: Beacon Press.

Lau, R., & Russell, D. (1980). Attributions in the sports pages. *Journal of Personality and Social Psychology, 39*, 29–38.

March, J., & Olson, J. (1976). *Ambiguity and choice in organizations.* Bergen: Universitets-Forlaget

Mumby, D. (1988). *Communication and power in organizations.* Norwood, NJ: Ablex.

Perrow, C. (1979). *Normal accidents.* New York: Random House.

Peters, T., & Austin, N. (1985). *A passion for excellence.* New York: Random House.

Pfeffer, J. (1981). Management as symbolic action. In L.L. Cummings & B. Staw (Eds.), *Research in Organizational Behavior, 3*, 1–52.

Salancik, G., & Meindl, J. (1984). Corporate attributions as strategic illusions of management control. *Administrative Science Quarterly, 29*, 238–254.

Staw, B., McKechnie, P., & Puffer, S. (1983). The justification of organizational performance. *Administrative Science Quarterly, 28*, 582–600.

Zuckerman, M. (1979). Attribution of success and the failure revisited, or: The motivational bias is alive and well in attribution theory. *Journal of Personality, 47*, 245–287.

The Atomic Power Industry and the NEW Woman

GEORGE N. DIONISOPOULOS
San Diego State University

STEVEN R. GOLDZWIG
Marquette University

Since the days of the Eisenhower Administration's "Atoms For Peace" campaign, atomic power had been offered as a "benefit [for] all mankind" (Hilgartner, Bell, & O'Connor, 1982, p. 41). Atomic technology was promoted as being able to provide limitless electricity that would be, in the words of Lewis Strauss, Chair of the Atomic Energy Commission, "too cheap to meter" (Stoler, 1985, p. 141). For some, however, acceptance of nuclear technology has proven to be problematic, and the public relations history of the atomic power industry has been a continuing story of trying to "sell" and "re-sell" the idea of nuclear power.

Underpinning the industry's campaign to create a "pro-energy environment" has been a view of the "public" as a "natural resource full of potential power to be harnessed" to help secure favorable public policy decisions concerning the future viability of nuclear power (Farrell & Goodnight, 1981, p. 298). Previous research has focused on the industry's attempts to help "harness" this "natural resource" via the mass-mediated dissemination of pro-nuclear messages aimed at a general audience (Dionisopoulos, 1986; Dionisopoulos & Crable, 1988; Heath, 1988). However, atomic power industry public relations efforts were not all targeted to an amorphous audience. In fact, for certain identifiable segments of the American public, acceptance of nuclear technology has proven to be especially difficult, and the industry has expended considerable effort to sculpt its pro-nuclear appeals toward these problematic constituencies.

Industry research has consistently indicated that one such problematic group has been women—a plurality of which are seen as particularly anti-nuclear. As summarized by S. Renae Cook (1982), special projects manager for the Atomic Industrial Forum:

> The nuclear industry's interest in working specifically with women as a special constituency was intensified when opinion polls measuring attitudes on nuclear issues revealed that women were more opposed to nuclear energy than their male counterparts. Over the last 6–7 years women have continued to rate the desirability of nuclear [power] at an almost constant 20% below men. (p. 2)

The New York Times observed that a "similar pattern of strong differences by sex [is] rarely if ever found on other issues" (Clymer, 1979, p. A16). In response to this pronounced opposition, a concentration of the atomic power industry's public relations effort has been directed toward American women.

Between 1975 and 1985 the industry's campaign to "sell" atomic power to American women was coordinated by the organization New Energy Women (NEW), self-described as "a national network of women from industry and citizen advocacy groups who promote knowledge and understanding of energy, with an emphasis on facts about electricity from nuclear energy" (NEW, 1983). This chapter examines NEW's 10-year campaign to "promote knowledge and understanding of energy" as a suasory effort to structure and define the atomic power issue for designated audiences.

Hunsaker and Smith (1976) defined an *issue* as a "question occurring in a rhetorical context in actual or potential form, which is relevant and requires resolution. 'Issue' is the articulation of a perceived choice of belief or action, and thus forms the basis for human conflict" (p. 144). Thus, a critical concentration on issues focuses on the efforts of a communicator to manipulate a target audience's perception of the problem (Hunsaker & Smith, 1976). Our exploration of NEW's presentation of the atomic power "issue" examines the "strategies" and "tactics" involved in its ongoing campaign. Bowers and Ochs (1971) maintained that any individual or group involved in public argument "must make choices among the means of persuasion. The more general choices we call strategies: the more specific choices governed by these general choices we call tactics" (p. 16). Although these authors were originally writing about groups agitating for social change, we maintain that a critical concern for the rhetorical strategies employed in NEW's campaign will help illuminate the "issues" as defined by its messages.

We suggest that NEW's campaign is best understood as grounded in a rhetorical strategy of transcendence that sought to structure, for the target audience, discursive "realities" concerning a "nuclear imperative" for this country. Burke (1966) noted that transcendence "is a sheerly symbolic operation" (p. 187). Indeed, the "machinery of language is so made that things are necessarily placed in terms of a range broader than the terms for those things themselves. . . . And I submit that wherever there are traces of that process, there are the makings of transcendence" (p. 200).

Wherever terms stand in dialectical opposition, the critic is advised to "look for a *motive that can serve as ground for both these choices*, a motive that, while not being exactly either one or the other, can ambiguously contain them both. A term serving as ground for both these terms would, by the same token, 'transcend' them" (Burke, 1969b, pp. 10–11).

Rhetors who employ strategies of transcendence adopt a larger, wider, or more subtle perspective in which disputed points are transformed or revalued in an attempt to achieve consensus. These appeals are crafted to identify symbolically "with what is large, good, important, and of the highest order in society" (Stewart, Smith, & Denton, 1984, p. 123), and are, thus, often legitimated by references to size, altruistic mission, or purpose.

In actual process, "the ways of transcendence, in aiming at the discovery of *essential* motives, may often take the historicist form of symbolic *regression*. That is, if one is seeking for the 'essence' of motives, one can only express such a search in the temporal terms. . . as a process of 'going back' " (Burke, 1969a, p. 430). Often the terminological grounding involves, "the addition of moral terms that solve a technical problem" (Burke, 1969a, p. 428). This is also referred to as a *bridging device*: defined as a "symbolic structure whereby one 'transcends' a conflict in one way or another." Bridging devices are literally a "way across" to help one find "many other ingredients" that will help resolve conflict (Burke, 1984, p. 224).

Burke (1969a) argued that the strategy of transcendence involves a new motive "discovered en route." When a transformation of values and/or motives regarding any issue occurs, "the position at the end transcends the position at the start, so that the position at the start can eventually be seen in terms of the new motivation encountered en route" (pp. 421–422). The effectiveness of any transcendent or bridging device is dependent on this outcome.

We suggest that NEW's public relations efforts tried to provide audiences with a "new motive en route"—a motive designed to yield a favorable outcome for the industry. However, to appreciate this effort more fully, some background perspective is necessary.

HISTORY OF NUCLEAR POWER IMAGE CREATION

From its earliest days, the "atomic age" was presented as "the promise of modern science" (Bresler, 1979, p. 5). This promise was accompanied by an early public relations campaign to present "the sunny side of the atom" (Hilgartner et al., 1982, p. 72). The nuclear power industry "boasted of the atom providing cheap, clean and safe energy" (Hertsgaard, 1980, p. 271). As Bresler (1979) observed, it was "difficult to imagine such an imposing technology not bringing immense benefit to mankind. . . . [N]uclear power was symbolic of our potency and was almost synonymous with American supremacy" (p. 5).

In the latter half of the 1950s and through the decade of the 1960s, the public relations efforts of government and industry included the use of "films, brochures, TV, radio, nuclear science fairs, public speakers, traveling exhibits, and classroom demonstrations" (Hilgartner et al., 1982, p. 74). Members of the industry and the Federal Government's Atomic Energy Commission worked together to establish the American Museum of Atomic Energy in Oak Ridge, Tennessee; helped the Boy Scouts create an Atomic Energy Merit Badge; and circulated "clean-atom booster films" such as "The Mighty Atom," "A is for Atom," and "Go Fission."

One of these early booster films was aimed particularly at women. In the mid-1960s the Connecticut Yankee Power company—in an effort to create "enthusiasm among women for the state's first nuclear power plant"—produced a film entitled "The Atom and Eve." This film introduced the audience to "Eve," whose life of "convenience and pleasure is inextricably linked to the unlimited public demand for energy and the unlimited supply necessary to meet that demand" (Nelson, 1983, p. 32).

As Nelson noted, the film presented Eve as a "prototypical American woman—one who possesses a virtually uncontrollable desire for products, appliances, energy, and luxury." This desire is underscored as Eve dances "through a world charged with electricity and filled with marvelous gadgetry. She hurls herself across a self-cleaning stove, caresses a freezer, and fondles a spray iron." According to the film, Eve's lifestyle is only made possible by "The Atom," "seen pulsating centerstage as Eve prances about in a display of flirtatious and servile gratitude" (p. 32). Like many of the booster films of the 1950s and 1960s, "The Atom and Eve" was anything but subtle in its message: Atomic power would "make life easier for all the little Eves of the world by powering toasters, hair dryers, and washing machines" (Hilgartner et al., 1982, p. 74).

At the dawn of the 1970s, the nuclear power industry prepared for a prosperous decade. By 1974 however, cracks began to appear in the industry's public image. A small but vocal group of activists was warning of the dangers associated with nuclear power. This effort was aided greatly when the "defection" of several nuclear engineers to the anti-nuclear movement helped to fuel the atomic power debate in this country.

As a statement from the Atomic Industrial Forum summarized: "Not since the nuclear industry came into being through enactment of the Atomic Energy Act of 1952 has the establishment that guides and regulates the industry been so thoroughly shaken up as it was in 1974" (cited in Stuart,

1975, p. A22). In response, in 1975 the industry intensified and focused its public relations efforts. The Atomic Industrial Forum doubled its public relations budget, and the industry launched "a strong campaign to turn the tide of opposition to atomic power" (Stuart, 1975, p. A21).

This campaign took a drastic turn on March 28, 1979, when a coolant pump failed in Unit Two of Metropolitan Edison's nuclear power generating facility at Three Mile Island. Located near the media centers of New York and Washington, DC, the accident attracted so many reporters that one industry official complained that Three Mile Island "received more media attention than any event since the assassination of President Kennedy" ("They're troublemakers," 1979, p. 4). The accident was a "big bad publicity blast" for the industry ("Atomic plant safety," 1979, p. 33), changing "the public's perception about nuclear risks just as dramatically as a miracle changes the faith of those who witness it" (O'Driscoll, 1989, p. 116).

From the perspective of those in the atomic power industry, their public relations problems had become as hot as the core of the Unit Two reactor. In response, the industry engaged in an intensified "campaign designed to convince Americans that the United States cannot survive as a free and prosperous nation without nuclear power" (Hertsgaard, 1983, p. 6). Thus, although the industry's campaign has been ongoing since the mid-1970s, it acquired a new sense of urgency after Three Mile Island.

The underlying strategy of the atomic power industry's public relations campaign was provided by a 1975 memorandum from Cambridge Reports, Inc., one of the country's major public relations polling firms. This memo suggested: "The nuclear debate should *not* be 'Should we build nuclear power plants?' but rather, 'How do we get the energy/electricity needed for *your* jobs and home?'" (cited in Hilgartner et al., 1982, p. 80). In other words, this memo argued that the atomic power industry's public arguments should be grounded in a strategy of rhetorical transcendence.

From the industry's perspective, this transcendent strategy would provide a very fertile grounding for its public relations campaign. In application, the transcendent strategy dictated that the public argument of the industry would only discuss nuclear power *in the context of the country's total energy need.* In so doing, the issue of the "need" for nuclear power would be established against the higher hierarchical frame of projected energy requirements, thus effectively transforming the debate over the future of atomic energy into a debate concerning the demand for energy in general— with all the concomitant concerns over such cultural values as "progress," "opportunity," and "growth." Thus, the "issue" of nuclear power would become subsumed within a larger issue of energy need.

To disseminate the industry's message, a decision was made to "reach and use people" as "voices" for the industry (Taylor, 1979, p. 20). As specified by one spokesperson, the "top priority" of the industry's public relations effort was "to reach specific groups who have a definite stake in adequate energy" (cited in Hertsgaard, 1983, p. 199). One such approach called for the use of "citizen action" at a "grassroots" level. In a paper entitled "Citizen Action: A Key in the Nuclear Controversy," Dr. Kenneth D. Kearns (1979) of Westinghouse emphasized that citizen participation was the only feasible approach for building a link between the public and policymakers.

The industry's primary public relations organization, the U.S. Committee on Energy Awareness (CEA)—founded immediately after the accident at Three Mile Island "as part of the industry's new effort to combat bad publicity" ("Nuclear industry versus," 1980, p. 573)—maintained that such a link was important in the creation of a "pro-energy climate" (CEA, 1979, chapter 1, p. 2).

In 1979, the newly created CEA circulated a manual entitled *To Those Interested in Supporting Citizen Action*. This manual argued that there was a need to encourage "pro-energy citizens to speak out" (p. 1), and cited the benefits of citizen action to the industry.

> Citizens can provide credible, non-industry spokespersons able to reach decision makers, educate the public and challenge the opposition often more effectively than the industry. They provide a balance to a vocal anti-energy minority. Their pro-energy messages are better received and often their actions can be more attention getting than corporate activities. Citizen activists also broaden and increase support for favorable actions by decision makers. (chapter 2, p. 2)

Additionally, citizen action groups were viewed as helping increase corporate credibility. Kearns (1979) labelled the cultivation of citizen support groups "the primary strategy of nuclear proponents" (p. 5).

However, the use of this tactic presented the industry with recruitment problems: spokespersons had to be identified, encouraged and, often, financially supported. The CEA (1979) manual detailed the type of support that the industry should give to the citizen groups. Among the suggestions listed

— staff support time to aid the citizen group
— information resources
— mailing and secretarial time
— printing or xeroxing
— money for direct contributions (chapter 1, p. 4).

The "return" on this type of investment was viewed as "significant" in terms of developing and maintaining popular support for nuclear power (Burnham, 1979). People within the industry felt that "pro-energy activists" would present "good information" with "enthusiasm [and] credibility" (West, 1979). Toward that goal, industry communications offered further suggestions concerning the mobilization and recruitment of "allies" in the community who would carry the "pro-energy message."

For example, in a paper entitled "Student Oriented Activities," Tom Miller (n.d.), of the Massachussetts Voice of Energy, warned industry members: "the students most likely on your side do not major in sociology, English, psychology, or political science. They do major in engineering, physics, and industrial management." Biology majors should be "approached with caution," but "business majors have potential" (p. 1).

Industry communications also highlighted the perceived importance of women as a target audience and suggested various way to reach them. The CEA (1979) manual observed that women were becoming an

> increasingly important audience to reach on energy matters. While energy has in many ways been a key to women's freedom in recent times, polls show that they are more opposed to domestic development than the general public. They also are a very large voting block representing a majority of the population and having a better than average voting record. (chapter 3, p. 1)

In addition to targeting women as a constituency, the booklet stated the importance of involving women as "pro-energy activists." "Many nonworking women have both time and interest in participating in activities to reach decision makers and the public" (CEA, chapter 3, p. 2). Also, members of the industry were warned not to overlook the people within their own organizations. Kearns (1979) also provided a "partial list" of potential pro-energy advocates, including: "Employees and wives of nuclear suppliers;" and "Employees and wives of large energy users" (p. 11).

In summary then, it is important to realize that the industry's campaign directed toward women was actually part of a bigger public relations effort to establish a "liaison with a variety of special audiences" (Cook, 1982, p. 2). This liaison could then be used to disseminate the industry's message concerning a "nuclear imperative" for this country. That message was grounded in a transcendent rhetorical strategy that emphasized the *need* for energy. We now turn specifically to the industry's persuasive efforts to reach one particular special audience, American women.

THE INDUSTRY'S FOCUS ON WOMEN

NEW, organized in 1975 by 14 women from within the nuclear industry, focused its attention on the "importance of reaching [the] influential audience" of American women (Cook, 1982, p. 3). Originally designated as an Atomic Industrial Forum (AIF) "Task Force on Women," NEW was formed out of the "aware[ness] of a growing need for dialogues with other women about the nation's increasingly complex energy situation and factual information about all forms of energy" (AIF, n.d.a). Within 3 years, NEW boasted a membership of 200. By 1979 it was listed as one of the industry's foremost "pro-energy citizen groups," with a national office in Washington DC, and 15 regional chapters across the country (CEA, chapter 4, p. 3).

NEW's self-proclaimed goal was to "promote knowledge and under-standing of energy, with an emphasis on facts about nuclear energy." Toward completion of that goal, NEW established a number of programs "to meet the educational needs of women" (AIF, n.d.a). As CEA's Wilkins ob-served, some of these programs were "invisible" (cited in Hertsgaard, 1983, p. 199) and focused on trying to influence opinion leaders and women's organizations. For example, part of NEW's plan "called for meeting with female editors of women's magazines and the 'life-style' sections in daily newspapers and impressing upon them the connection between the avail-ability of cheap and plentiful energy, a dynamic growing economy, and women's progress toward equality" (Hertsgaard, 1983, p. 199). In addition, NEW could upon request: arrange for energy speakers from industry, research, government and academia, organize energy workshops, help locate "relevant" sources of information, provide energy education exhibits, arrange tours through a "variety of energy facilities," promote media inter-views with "energy experts," and help with "energy articles for member publication of state and national organizations" (AIF, n.d.a).

As part of the goal to "work cooperatively with women's organizations and share information on nuclear energy" (Cook, 1982, p. 3), NEW

> closely followed the evolution of the policy positions taken by [women's] organizations, and has worked diligently to influence positions. For example, out of the 14 more influential women's groups [eight] have relatively sup-portive positions on nuclear and these [eight] groups represent approximately 1 ½ million women. With considerable effort, NEW has been able to defer, and in some cases completely reverse the passage of anti-nuclear resolution among several of these women's groups. (Cook, 1982, p. 15)

In its effort to "work cooperatively with women's organizations," NEW compiled and updated a directory entitled "Women's Organizations and Energy." Earlier versions of this Directory identified "some groups as decid-edly pro-nuclear, some as vacillating or non committal, and some as war-ranting NEW's attention because of their antinuclear leanings" (Nelson, 1983, p. 34). The 1984 update of this directory listed the executive officers, mailing addresses and phone numbers of 36 "Women's Organizations" (e.g. Church Women United, Girl Scouts of the U.S.A., National Federation of Business and Professional Women's Clubs, League of Women Voters of U.S.A.), and indi-cated those that had "taken a position on energy" (NEW, 1984).

We assume that these efforts were aimed at disseminating the industry's message to American women: that there was a "nuclear imperative" for this country in that America's "need" for energy could only be met by the continued and expanded use of nuclear power. The "behind the scenes" organizational nature of this "invisible" work means that there is little by way of explicit argument available for critical analysis. However, not all of NEW's efforts were "invisible." We turn next to an examination of the industry's rhetoric of transcendence. This strategy was crafted for women and can be made more "visible" by reference to three specific tactics: (a) the use of "psuedo-events" such as open door forums and "energy coffees," (b) a slide show entitled "Women and Energy: The Vital Link," and (c) the use of promotional materials.

Psuedo-Events: NEW's Use of Open Forums and "Energy Coffees"

Historian Daniel Boorstin (1961) used the term *psuedo-event* to refer to a happening that would not have occurred except to gain news coverage. According to Boorstin, a psuedo-event is "not spontaneous, but comes about because someone has planned, planted or incited it." A psuedo-event usually happens "for the immediate purpose of being reported or reproduced. . . . Its success is measured by how widely it is reported" (p. 11). NEW made wide use of psuedo-events in its effort to reach American women with its pronuclear message.

For example, in 1977 NEW "developed and conducted over a dozen national and regional energy workshops for representatives of major women's groups" (AIF, n.d.a). In 1978–1979 NEW conducted or was involved in seminars and workshops entitled "Women Discovering Energy" in Boston, "Sun Day" in Pittsburgh, and the "National Conference on Energy Advocacy" in Washington, DC.

In the aftermath of Three Mile Island the industry undertook a "nationwide public relations campaign" to "[take] on its largest most vocal opponent . . . women" (Jaffe, 1980, p. 28). Poll data following the 1979 accident suggested that Three Mile Island had exacerbated the opposition of American women to the development of nuclear power (Clymer, 1979). After the accident, NEW intensified its efforts with a massive persuasive campaign to stabilize the damage done to the industry's image among women. NEW contracted with the public relations firm of Hill & Knowlton, and charged them with the task of promoting the idea that "nuclear energy will help keep women free" (Jaffe, 1980, p. 28).

During the Fall of 1979, NEW was involved with a series of psuedo-events that were labelled collectively Nuclear Energy Education Day (NEED). This was, "by far . . . one of the most ambitious undertakings NEW ha[d] launched and ha[d] netted continuing paybacks by expanding the base of supporters for nuclear energy" (Cook, 1982, p. 14). Among the objectives Cook listed for the NEED project were to "provide facts about nuclear energy to tens of thousands of people through local coffees and special events" and to "reach millions of more people through the media, by being able to use local and regional outlets covering events in local areas" (p. 15).

During NEED, NEW sponsored "open door" forums in several major cities across the United States. At these forums, energy "experts" from the nuclear industry delivered the industry's message of "pro-nuclear feminism." NEW determined that the most effective spokespersons would be women who had some experience with nuclear power. At the various forums, NEW speakers—virtually all of whom came from within the nuclear industry—delivered the message that, "nuclear energy will help keep women free."

For example, at one forum Jan Carlin, a nuclear engineer for Westinghouse and an advocate for NEW, told a group of women: "We've had abundant energy in this country which has allowed women to enter the workforce—and to leave the washing and the dishes. . . . But without sufficient energy to keep more jobs coming in and the G.N.P. growing, women are just not going to make it" (cited in Jaffe, 1980, p. 28).

In addition to the major forums, NEW also organized small "energy coffees," given in private homes. During these gatherings, groups of women would meet with friends to discuss nuclear power. The coffee, cookies, and an industry "expert" were all provided by NEW. During the Fall of 1979, over 4,000 of these "energy coffees" took place across the country, with over 300 in New York City alone (Jaffe, 1980, p. 30).

At these "coffees," NEW speakers concentrated on communicating the benefits of nuclear power to the target audience. For example, at one such coffee, held in Washington, DC., Dr. Estelle Ramey delivered a talk to the assembled women in which she credited the progress of women's rights in this country to the availability of cheap energy. She added that it was intolerable for the United States to depend on oil from the Middle East, where, "they keep their women in comfortable slavery." At another coffee, Theora "Bunny" Webb, a member of NEW and an employee of the industry's Committee for Energy Awareness, said that she was "promoting the continuing development of nuclear power" because it meant "growth and production and that means jobs" (De Witt, 1979, p. A20).

NEW's program manager, S. Renae Cook (1982) maintained that NEED was an unqualified success. "Without any doubt, all [the] goals were exceeded. An estimated 100,000 citizens were directly involved in NEED, however the significance was not just the impressive numbers, but in the expanded base of supporters identified and in the improved skills that will be key to more effective pro-energy messages in the future" (p. 15). Industry sources have not revealed the price tag for events such as NEED, but the use of psuedo-events underscores the substantial amount of effort that the atomic power industry in general—and NEW in particular—directed toward disseminating the pro-nuclear message to American women. These psuedo-events were tactical devices that attempted—through a strategy of transcendence—to convert fears about nuclear power into wider issues regarding feminism, freedom and equal participation in the workplace.

"Women and Energy: The Vital Link"

NEW's 20-minute slide show entitled "Women and Energy: The Vital Link" was developed in 1979. According to promotional material from NEW and the AIF, this show was designed to "make the general public, and women in particular, more aware of the vital role of energy in their lives" (AIF, n.d.b.). Energy is presented as an "important source of freedom" for American women. The unique freedom of American women to "choose a lifestyle, whether it's homemaker, business woman, politician or professional" is directly tied to the availability of energy—an "important source of our freedom." As the narrator emphasizes: "Energy has proven an essential ingredient for an expanding job market and a developing society—one in which women will be able to know their economic potential and be free to develop their capabilities and interests. Energy is needed to give us that freedom" (AIF, n.d.b).

The audience is told that women will be particularly hard hit by decreased energy production because "energy for labor-saving devices in the home will be the first cutback." As slides show women using outdated laundry machines or doing wash by hand the narration tape warns: "Daily household tasks will become a real inconvenience. . . . Have you ever tried to wash things by slamming them against a flat rock? It's tough enough on clothes, but on dishes, it's murder" (cited in Nelson, 1983, p. 32).

"Women and Energy" observes that "Labor-saving devices have done as much to shape women's destiny as suffragettes or liberationists," and warns that women will be "giving up the most as we cut back on our consumption of energy and return to the simple life. Instead of appliances wearing out we will." But fortunately there is a source of energy production that is comparatively inexpensive and has "a most enviable safety record"—nuclear power (cited in Nelson, 1983, p. 32).

Opposition to nuclear power is acknowledged, but opponents are portrayed as a "small but very vocal minority" that "wishes to use a shortage of energy to make fundamental changes in our society." The audience is cautioned that "One person's version of conservation must never be the cause of another person's deprivation or unemployment. Minority groups and society's poor are counting on expanding economic opportunities."

As Nelson (1983) wrote, NEW's not-so-subtle message in "Women and

Energy" is that in "rejecting nuclear power, women risk discrimination and social disruption. . . . Any diversion from the nuclear path foreshadows a bleak future" (p. 32). This "bleak future" is portrayed in slides showing unemployment lines, school closings, and images of looting and "manacing street youth" (p. 34).

The show ends with acknowledgment of the role of women in social questions such as abolition and women's suffrage, and by urging members of the audience to help "bring the country around to a rational energy plan." "Today's woman has a lot riding on the outcome of our energy dilemma. . . . The future of energy is the future of womankind. Without it, we become nothing. With it, we become whatever we wish to be" (Nelson, 1983, p. 34).

Promotional material from the AIF stated that "Women and Energy: The Vital Link" offered the industry's message in "straightforward terms." The slide show was designed to provide "information about energy resources, and . . . encourage citizen participation in energy decision making—hopefully leading to a national program of rational energy development and a strong energy future for America" (AIF, n.d.b). By connecting purported energy shortages to a "bleak" economic future that falls particularly hard upon women and the poor, this slide show was a "vital link" in NEW's transcendent campaign.

Promotional Material

NEW also made use of promotional materials in the form of pamphlets and booklets, which could be easily distributed as "companion literature" at organizational meetings (in which a NEW "energy expert" would speak on issues ranging from food irradiation to nuclear waste disposal), during NEW-sponsored promotional tours of various nuclear facilities, and at the various pseudo-events in which NEW took part. The information contained in this promotional material was primarily grounded in the transcendent strategy of the industry, focusing on the argument that the economic well-being of the United States is dependent on the use of atomic power. However, as with the other information distributed by NEW, the argument took on the distinct patina of the industry's vision of pro-nuclear feminism.

One of the more elaborate versions of NEW's argument was developed in the pamphlet "Women and Energy: A Decisive Role" (NEW, 1983). It was published in June 1983, following a troubling period for the American economy. The basic message was that the "uncertain state of the economy" dictated that no one could afford to take a job for granted. Energy—defined as nothing more "than the capacity to do work"—played a "decisive role in the economic well-being of America's working families." Because energy was "the driving force underlying mobility and the freedom to choose," America's "100 million women have a special stake" in questions about energy and economic policies. It was now time for women "to reinforce [the] basic bond" between "reliable and affordable energy" and a prosperous economy. This pamphlet observes that the oil crises of 1973 and 1979 had "opened up what was once a debate primarily for energy experts." That energy policy debate had been joined by "thousands of groups from all walks of American life," ranging from "corporations with investments in energy resources" to "citizen activists adept at using energy issues to promote political causes and goals."

However, readers are told, women—and organized women's groups— "have tended to remain in the background," and some had even "taken positions endorsing *limited* energy growth, a *slowdown* of electricity plant construction and an *abandonment* of existing technologies in favor of alternative and largely untested energy sources." However, these positions went "against the grain of progress" because periods of "healthy economic growth and plentiful employment" have always been marked by "a rising level of energy use." On the other hand "energy use fell dramatically, in tandem with jobs and the stock market, during the Great Depression and again during the 1980–82 recession." Women had the most to lose because they were "more likely than men to lose their jobs. . . . [and] less likely to find quality jobs and to advance in their careers."

Fortunately, our country is rich in "energy resources" including coal, uranium, and sunshine. America's "elusive search" for energy self-sufficiency is "not a pipedream" but instead, "an attainable extension of the American Dream we can pass on to future generations." A stable energy supply and "solid economic growth" were only attainable by "supporting proven technologies—coal and nuclear power." "Even in a country of freedom, the challenge ahead allows little choice."

After observing that "energy is critical to progress," the pamphlet defines for the audience the "issues" of the energy policy debate. Concerns about "the technicalities of coal vs. nuclear power, solar vs. synfuels, or even energy vs. the environment" were "subsidiary and divisive to the heart of the debate. . . . The heart of the energy debate today is about people, their hopes and aspirations: What kind of America do we want to live in tomorrow?" On one side was "limited economic growth and strenuous conservation," on the other was "strong economic growth and expanded energy production." American women would "play a decisive role" in making this decision about America's energy future. "Their tradition of active involvement and influence demands it."

The transcendent strategy is also evident in another industry pamphlet, entitled "NEW: Nuclear Energy Women" (AIF, n.d.a). Energy, the pamphlet begins, "portrays a vital part in the freedom enjoyed by all Americans." Women, in particular, have a "tremendous stake in how this country approaches its energy future. Energy—particularly electricity—has played a very important role in the progress of women in our society," as "work saving inventions have offered women the convenience and time to pursue interests outside the home."

Additionally, "energy has provided a great many of the jobs that women now hold." Therefore, it is "natural and necessary that women are taking an active role in determining America's energy future." NEW is a part of this "active role," promoting "knowledge and understanding of energy, with an emphasis on facts about nuclear energy, programs are established to meet the educational needs of women, women's organizations and opinion leaders."

Still another booklet offered examples of women and men who left "dead-end" jobs to work in the nuclear industry. Entitled "Working with the Atom: Careers for You," this manual argued that such work was challenging, offered a sense of responsibility, and was patriotic, for "by not using nuclear energy we're endangering our entire way of life" (cited in Nelson, 1983, p. 34).

A final NEW booklet examined for this chapter was entitled "Viewpoint: Women, Electricity & Nuclear Energy" (NEW, 1985). This booklet contained pictures and comments from 16 women, most of whom were connected with some aspect of the atomic power industry. Former Washington governor, Dixy Lee Ray's introduction set the tone of the messages that would follow. "Electricity and only electricity" has made the technology of our age possible. "Because we rely so heavily on electricity it is imperative that we develop what energy sources we have: coal and nuclear energy." Women have "a lot at stake when it comes to electricity's future and growth" and they "must speak up and promote the wise use of our energy resources." The individual statements within the booklet make clear that the phrase "wise use of energy resources" means nuclear power.

Many of the statements in this booklet evidence a pronounced concern for the environment. For example, E. Marcia Katz—associate professor of Nuclear Engineering at the University of Tennessee—maintained that "nuclear engineering students and professors, like many other people, are concerned about the environment and the quality of life." Bernice Paige—Fellow of American Nuclear Society and retired supervisor of Fuel Reprocessing—observed, "You really appreciate electricity when you travel in underdeveloped countries and hike the trails of the Himalaya where simple sanitation and electric lights are non-existent." Udell Fresk—coordinator of public affairs for the Exxon Nuclear Company—is pictured complete with backpack and walking stick, hiking the Pacific Crest Trail. Her experience as a mechanical engineer on coal, hydroelectric, geothermal and nuclear power systems, has convinced her that "nuclear energy is safer and has less impact on the environment" than other energy resources.

Statements by others featured the argument that nuclear power is needed to maintain the American standard of living. For example, Roberta Bromberg—manager of nuclear information for Northeast Utilities—maintained that "we must accept the fact that we are an energy intensive society, and to fuel our economic growth the only practical options are coal and nuclear energy." Florence Mangan—Nuclear Services Integration Division of Westinghouse Electric—speculated that people will eventually realize "that in the world of limited resources we can't afford not to have nuclear."

But most of the comments in the booklet focus specifically on the industry's message of pro-nuclear feminism. Betty Maskewitz—director, Engineering Physics Information Centers for Oak Ridge National Laboratory—stated: "Without the boundless energy which frees women today from household drudgery, I would never have been able to pursue my personal quests. Nuclear fuels help to make this energy available. . . . I cannot conceive of women rejecting such a positive influence on their lives." Patricia Ross—director of public affairs for Scientists & Engineers for Secure Energy—wrote: "There are significant parallels between the changing roles of women and the expansion of electricity supply and applications in this century. If women are to continue advancing in the workplace, a secure energy supply for homes and industry is an absolute necessity." Carol Thorup—vice president of the Nuclear Assurance Corporation—lamented that we have not taken "full advantage of the developed technologies of coal and nuclear power." She argued that if "our country is to have sufficient energy to provide jobs for the 53–60 percent of all women who will work outside the home by 1995, then we must step forward and take responsibility for our future needs."

These pamphlets stress "progress" through nuclear energy. Energy leads to economic stability. Economic stability leads to equality and full participation in the workplace. Thus, the ultimate transcendant strategy is to link nuclear energy to the American Dream. NEW's version of that dream includes an America of tomorrow where one can rely on nuclear power and still be secure in a safe environment and maintain a high quality of life while protecting the standard of living to which Americans are accustomed. Nuclear energy is promoted as both a haven from "drudgery" and the key to "freedom."

CONCLUSION

We have examined the persuasive efforts of the atomic power industry to "structure" the "issue of atomic power" for American women—a target audience identified by the industry as distinctly anti-nuclear. We examined a campaign coordinated by Nuclear Energy Women between 1975–1985. A

1984 industry memorandum observes that during these 10 years NEW "emerged as a proven mechanism for reaching out to women" (Mangan, 1984).

We agree with Jaffe's (1980) observation that efforts such as NEW's illustrate that the nuclear industry was "taking women's opinions seriously" (p. 31). However, we would add that although we can concur with the application of the term *serious* to describe the amount of effort expended, we find it a bit more difficult to take the arguments employed in this campaign seriously.

NEW's campaign offered engaged audiences discursive "realities" concerning America's "nuclear imperative." These realities were grounded in the industry's transcendent rhetorical strategy that considered questions of atomic power only in conjunction with higher order hierarchical questions of energy need. As such the arguments of the industry did not address the case for nuclear power *qua* nuclear power. Instead, the "issue" of atomic power was developed along the lines of a fairly simple—albeit Manichean—choice dichotomy: nuclear power and progress versus no nuclear power and no progress. On one side of this issue was a small "but vocal minority" that would use concerns about energy to make "fundamental changes in our society." On the other side were responsible citizens who understand the "facts about electricity from nuclear energy." Those who really understood the "facts" about nuclear power realized that any deviation from the nuclear path presented grave dangers to our way of life—the realization of the American Dream. Thus, as presented by NEW, these two alternatives really offered little "choice."

NEW presented this dichotomy with a distinctive slant toward women, in which terms like *energy* and *progress* were linked with *liberation* and *choice*. There was also the threat, explicit and implicit, that women would lose the most if the nuclear future is abandoned—because it "is only in an expanding economy, stimulated and sustained by an abundant supply of reasonably priced energy that those seeking employment find opportunities for the jobs that offer possibilities of upward mobility in both pay and standard of living" (Cook, 1982, p. 4). Thus, the industry's message for American women focused on defining the atomic power "issue" along the theme that "liberation" was dependent on "abundant energy," and "abundant energy" meant atomic power. Here again, *any* deviation from the nuclear power path would risk all that women have achieved. As presented, this dichotomy left engaged audiences with no real latitude for questioning the wisdom of pursuing a nuclear future.

Moreover, words like *progress, equality, participation in the economy,* and *energy for the future* are terms that try to transcend the natural order by directly appealing to abstract motives in the sociopolitical realm. These key terms serve as bridging devices for resolving conflict among the various and diverse orders of existence. The biophysical repercussions of nuclear power—concerns regarding nuclear waste stockpiling or the possibility of a "meltdown"—are "bridged" by terms which underplay the biological threat by focusing on hard-won sociopolitical sources of motivation.

Equally significant is the attempt by NEW to use symbolic "regression" as a means of reinforcing motive "essence" in the nuclear power debate. By projecting negative historical images of women in "slavery"—whether by reference to domestic drudgery or the threatened loss of the "labor-saving devices" that have provided "liberation"—we find a chronological appeal that asks audiences to "go back" to a time before electricity in an attempt to reinforce the industry's key theme of "progress through energy." However, as Burke (1961) wrote, there are "only two ways in which a terminology can transcend itself: either by tautology or *non sequitur*. If the operation is contrived by *non sequitur*, this means the work is inconsistent with itself (p. 128).

We believe that NEW's discourse represents a *non sequitur* form of argumentation. The consistencies or inconsistencies of the arguments can be documented by discovering whether or not they provide the audience with a new motive en route. Here we must state that our reservations clearly stem from the refusal of this discourse to (a) address seriously the reasons associated with public misgivings over nuclear power, and (b) acknowledge adequately the presence of alternative forms of energy.

We find NEW's public arguments troubling. First, the dichotomy constructed in NEW's discourse presented American women with a choice between only two alternatives—nuclear power with progress and liberation or a non-nuclear future of stagnation and social retrenchment. This discourse poses a false dilemma—described by Kahane (1984) as reasoning or argument "on the assumption that there are just two plausible solutions to a problem or issue" (p. 80). Obviously, one could be against atomic power and still support progress and liberation, but NEW's arguments seem to discount even that possibility. This kind of public argument is disturbing—particularly when it is offered under the guise of "promoting knowledge" concerning nuclear power.

This false dilemma is at least partially crafted through NEW's use of the term *energy*. As Pringle and Spigelman (1981) observed, in its struggle to stay viable the atomic power industry "seized on the growing concern over the 'energy crisis'." But "the term 'energy' was a political buzz word, a metaphor that obscured the variety of things for which it was used" (p. 408). Although purporting to offer the "facts about electricity from nuclear energy," much of NEW's public argument tries to establish for engaged audiences a clear link between "energy" and "nuclear power."

Obviously "energy" is needed for any prosperous economy: however, it is not obvious that nuclear technology is the best method of securing that energy. As Hertsgaard (1984) wrote, "A national policy based on conservation and solar energy would produce far more jobs, economic growth and protection against another oil embargo than would an expansion of nuclear energy" (p. A25). Others, as does Charles Komanoff—director of the consulting firm Komanoff Energy Associates, maintain that the real energy questions facing this country go beyond a consideration of which technology should be employed in the construction of new generating facilities. Instead we should focus on whether there is a need to build new plants at all. As Komanoff put it, "Anybody who takes as an article of faith that we'll always be using more electricity is making a serious error" (cited in Marcus, 1984, p. E9).

Our point here is not to engage in the argument over the superiority of one technology over another. It is instead to illustrate that the NEW campaign sought to minimize concerns for any alternative perspectives by getting audiences to identify the general term *energy* with the specific technology of *atomic power*—thus constructing a false dilemma that maintained that the only viable solution to an energy problem would be increased use of atomic power. There were and are alternatives to atomic power that were not addressed in the NEW campaign.

Second, the NEW campaign attempted to co-opt the history of the women's movement in this country. In linking the "issue" of nuclear power with such historical social questions as women's suffrage, and equal pay for equal work, and by suggesting—as NEW's S. Renae Cook (1982) said: "Work saving, energy using inventions have done more to shape women's destiny than suffragettes and liberationists" (p. 4)—the NEW campaign presented a skewed and possibly deceptive picture of the struggle for nuclear power as part of the ongoing sociopolitical history of women's liberation in this country.

The NEW campaign presented a simplistic message grounded in the industry's redefinition of the term *liberation*. In essence, the messages in the 1970s and 1980s had changed little since the early 1960s when Eve danced around a collection of household appliances and paid servile homage to "Atom" for making her life easier. Even people within the industry now realize that such a simplistic "articulation of a perceived choice of belief or action" was probably demeaning to the audience. According to Ann Bisconti (personal communication, June 28, 1989) of the United States Council for Energy Awareness, today women feel more options and the "old argument" about the "need for energy" for a career would "challenge the latitude of acceptability" of most women.

Although Nuclear Energy Women is no longer an active organization, the industry is still very attentive to the opinions of American women. According to Ms. Bisconti, CEA media campaign advertisements are placed in "women's" magazines like *Good Housekeeping* and *Harper's*, and its program of ad testing takes care to check that the persuasive messages are as "meaningful to women" as they are to men. However, it is quite possible that as presented in the simplistic arguments of the NEW campaign, the "issue" of nuclear power probably alienated as many women as it reached.

REFERENCES

Atomic Industrial Forum. (n.d.a.). *NEW: Nuclear Energy Women.* (Available from Atomic Industrial Forum, Public Affairs and Information Program, 7101 Wisconsin Ave., Washington, DC 20014).

Atomic Industrial Forum. (n.d.b.). *NEW: Nuclear Energy Women presents a slide show.* (Available from Atomic Industrial Forum, Public Affairs and Information Program, 7101 Wisconsin Ave., Washington DC 20014).

Atomic plant safety—the big questions. (1979, April 9). *Newsweek,* pp. 33–39.

Boorstin, D. J. (1961). *The image: A guide to psuedo-events in America.* New York: Harper & Row.

Bowers, J. W., & Ochs, D. J. (1971). *The rhetoric of agitation and control.* Reading, MA: Addison-Wesley.

Bresler, R. J. (1979, July) Reflections of Three Mile Island: The invisible wound. *USA Today,* pp. 4–5.

Burke, K. (1961). *The rhetoric of religion: Studies in logology.* Boston: Beacon.

Burke, K. (1966). *Language as symbolic action: Essays on life, literature and method.* Berkeley: University of California Press.

Burke, K. (1969a). *A grammar of motives.* Berkeley: University of California Press.

Burke, K. (1969b). *A rhetoric of motives.* Berkeley: University of California Press.

Burke, K. (1984). *Attitudes toward history* (3rd ed.). Berkeley: University of California Press.

Burnham, D. (1979, December 26). Pronuclear groups seek citizen action. *New York Times,* pp. A1, B11.

Clymer, A. (1979, April 10). Poll shows sharp rise since '77 in opposition to nuclear plants. *New York Times,* pp. A1, A16.

Committee on Energy Awareness. (1979, Summer). *To those interested in supporting citizen action.* Unpublished manuscript.

Cook, R. S. (1982, March 11). *The role of women in energy.* Paper presented to the JAIF, Tokyo.

De Witt, K. (1979, October 19). Women gather to hear nuclear power promoted. *New York Times,* p. A20.

Dionisopoulos, G. (1986). Corporate advocacy advertising as political communication. In L. L. Kaid, D. Nimmo, & K. R. Sanders (Eds.), *New perspectives on political advertising* (pp. 82–106). Carbondale: Southern Illinois University Press.

Dionisopoulos, G., & Crable, R. E. (1988). Definitional hegemony as a public relations strategy: The rhetoric of the nuclear power industry after Three Mile Island. *Central States Speech Journal, 39,* 134–145.

Farrell, T. B., & Goodnight, G. T. (1981). Accidental Rhetoric: The root metaphors of Three Mile Island. *Communication Monographs, 48,* 271–300.

Heath, R. L. (1988). The rhetoric of issue advertising: A rationale, a case study, a critical perspective—and more. *Central States Speech Journal, 39,* 99–109.

Hertsgaard, M. (1980). There's life after T.M.I. *The Nation, 230,* pp. 269–271.

Hertsgaard, M. (1983). *Nuclear inc: The men and money behind nuclear power.* New York: Pantheon Books.

Hertsgaard, M. (1984, April 7). Nuclear reformists vs. hard liners [Editorial]. *New York Times,* p. A25.

Hilgartner, S., Bell, R. C., & O'Connor, R. (1982). *Nukespeak: Nuclear language, visions, and mindset.* San Francisco: Sierra Club Books.

Hunsaker, D., & Smith M. (1976). The nature of issues: A constructive approach to situational rhetoric. *Journal of the Western Speech Communication Association, 40,* 144–156.

Jaffe, S. (1980, June). Organizing: The pro-nuke lobby targets women—wooing support with coffee, cake and crock pots. *Ms.* pp. 28, 30–31.

Kahane, H. (1984). *Logic and contemporary rhetoric: The use of reason in everyday life* (4th ed.). Belmont, CA.: Wadsworth.

Kearns, K. D. (1979). *Citizen action: A key in the nuclear controversy.* Unpublished manuscript.

Mangan, F. (1984, November 29). Unpublished memo from F. Mangan to NEW leadership.

Marcus, S. J. (1984, January 22). Coal's future could rival its past. *New York Times,* p. E9.

Miller, T. (n.d.). *Student oriented activities.* Unpublished manuscript, University of Lowell, MA.

Nelson, L. (1983, July). Atom and Eve: The nuclear industry seeks to win the hearts and minds of women. *Progressive,* pp. 32; 34.

Nuclear Energy Women. (1983). *Women and energy: A decisive Role.* (Available from Nuclear Energy Women, 7101 Wisconsin Ave., Suite 1200, Bethesda, MD 20814).

Nuclear Energy Women. (1984, April). *A directory: Women's organizations and energy.* (Available from Nuclear Energy Women, 7101 Wisconsin Ave., Bethesda, MD 20814).

Nuclear Energy Women. (1985, February). *Viewpoint: Women, Electricity, & Nuclear Energy.* (Available from Nuclear Energy Women, 7101 Wisconsin Ave., Suite 1200, Bethesda, MD 20814).

Nuclear industry versus Amory Lovins. (1980, August 1). *Science,* p. 573.

O'Driscoll, P. (1989, March 21). Industry, foes spar over safety. *USA Today,* p. 5A.

Pringle, P., & Spigelman, J. (1981). *The nuclear barons.* New York: Holt Rinehart & Winston.

Stoler, P. (1985). *Decline and fail: The ailing nuclear power industry.* New York: Dodd, Mead.

Stewart, C., Smith, C., & Denton, R. E. (1984). *Persuasion and social movements.* Prospect Heights, IL: Waveland Press.

Stuart, R. (1975, May 25). Nuclear power campaign is on. *New York Times,* pp. 21–22.

Taylor, M. (1979, June 7). Nuclear industry's plan to woo the public. *San Francisco Chronicle,* pp. 1; 20.

They're troublemakers, exec says of n-foes. (1979, May 24). *New Orleans Times-Picayune,* p. 4.

West, A. L. (1979). *The national conference on energy advocacy: "Our strength is in our diversity."* Paper presented at the meeting of the Atomic Industrial Forum, Kansas City, MO.

Trade Associations: Whose Voice? Whose Vice?

JAMES S. MEASELL
Wayne State University

Within the early chapters of virtually all public relations textbooks, one may find some coverage of the genesis and development of the field of public relations in the United States and elsewhere. Often, this history takes the form of recounting the efforts of key individuals, such as Ivy Lee and Edward L. Bernays (Baskin & Aronoff, 1988), or of isolating important trends and events, such as westward expansion or the era of muckraking journalists and so-called business and industry robber barons (Newsom, Scott, & Turk, 1989). The thrust of many of these historical accounts is, of course, to shed light on the antecedents of modern public relations programs and to underscore the growing professionalism of public relations practitioners in the late 20th century.

Unfortunately, there has been little discussion in treatments of public relations history of some of those institutions, such as trade associations, which are indigenous, if not ubiquitous, to contemporary public relations practice. Perhaps understandably, there are few studies of trade associations and their communication activities that employ a rhetorical perspective, although trade association executives have become acutely aware of the need to craft carefully formulated communication programs, especially in crucial areas such as adaptation to change (Smith & Tucker, 1983).

PURPOSE AND DEFINITION

The trade association is an institution whose contemporary importance is granted by public relations educators and practitioners alike (Wilcox, Ault,

& Agee, 1989). Indeed, the impact of trade associations in the spheres of lobbying and public education is readily acknowledged (Cutlip, Center, & Broom, 1985). This chapter discusses the evolution and development of trade associations in America from the Civil War to the present with a view to isolating those rhetorical aspects of trade association management and practice that are of particular significance to scholars in public relations today.

Trade groups formed in the glass tableware industry are used to illustrate the typical patterns of trade association development in the 19th century. As is seen, the roles of trade associations have changed over time, but the essential activities and programs of trade associations are generally unchanged. Of particular import to an analysis of contemporary trade associations, especially "councils" formed to address particular issues, is careful consideration of ethical issues (Olasky, 1987).

At the outset, trade associations should, by definition, be differentiated from professional and technical societies. The most recent issue of a major trade association directory, the *National Trade and Professional Associations of the United States* (NTPAUS; 1988), endorses the following definition, which was developed and promulgated some years ago by C. Jay Judkins, who was then the head of the Trade Association Division of the U. S. Department of Commerce:

> [a trade association is] a nonprofit, cooperative, voluntarily-joined organization of business competitors designed to assist its members and its industry in dealing with mutual business problems in several of the following areas: accounting practice, business ethics, commercial and industrial research, standardization, statistics, trade promotion, and relations with Government, employees and the general public. (p. 5)

In contrast, professional and scientific/technical societies are those that are generally devoted to the expansion of knowledge for its own sake as well as the development of professional standards (NTPAUS directory, 1988; Gilb, 1966).

Thus, the essential defining characteristic of the trade association is that it brings together those who are otherwise competitors. The purpose of these confederations of competitors is generally economic self-interest rather than intellectual interchange or professional development, although these goals may be served as secondary or tertiary ends of the association. According to the most recent directory of *National Trade and Professional Associations of the United States* (1988), there are at least 3,400 national trade associations of one sort or another at present and over 2,300 professional societies. Cutlip et al. (1985), using data supplied by the American Society of Association Executives (ASAE), reported 8,500 national trade associations and 5,000 professional societies; the NTPAUS directory does not report those groups whose sole function is accreditation, so this may account for the discrepancies in numbers.

TRADE ASSOCIATIONS: ROOTS AND RHETORIC

Just as the rhetorical practices of today's trade associations must be viewed within the context of contemporary times, so must the genesis of trade associations themselves be seen in the backdrop of the historical periods in which they were established and began to flourish. As is shown later, the early trade groups, forming and developing between 1860 and 1900, reflected the particular economic and political pressures of their times.

The predecessors of most of today's trade associations emerged after the Civil War. At this time, in the late 1860s, the United States was a divided nation—in both political and economic terms (Whitten, 1983). The prolonged armed conflict had left both the industrial North and the agrarian South in dire economic straits, and the South was devastated physically as well. Political differences between the North and the South remained, and Reconstruction policies under President Johnson did not always lessen the friction. The beckoning vistas of the West remained largely undeveloped, although westward expansion was to become an important factor in the nation's economy later in the 19th century.

Between the Civil War and 1915, the population of the United States increased greatly, from about 31 million to 96 million, and equally dramatic rises occurred in the number of business firms (Cochran, 1972) and in industrial production (Douglass, 1971). Important analysts (Douglass, 1971; Chandler, 1977; Cochran, 1972) who have studied this period are in general agreement that a number of key social and economic factors and forces emerged: the growth of a national market, especially for manufactured products; advancing urbanization; increasing education and literacy; enhanced communication (both telegraph and newspapers as well as telephone); improved land transportation through steam and electric railways and, later, automotive means; and, finally, skepticism toward business interests themselves, as manifested in the "robber baron" portraits near the turn of the century.

Within the business community itself, marked changes were occurring: the shift from small, individual entrepreneurs serving a nearby populace to larger firms with regional, if not national, distribution networks; the growth of retail mail-order catalogue houses, such as Sears Roebuck (Emmet & Jeuck, 1950) and Montgomery Ward (Latham, 1972) and the rise of the chain stores (Lebhar, 1963); the emergence of the modern corporation and of scientific management (Nelson, 1975; Wiebe, 1967); and the growing wealth of extractive industries—natural gas, oil, and mining (Whitten, 1983).

Historian Albert Chandler, Jr. (1977) has characterized the era as one in which the influence of the invisible hand of natural market forces gave way to the visible hand of managerial decisions. In brief, Chandler argued that the simple pressures of supply and demand no longer were the sole determinants of success or failure in business. A business concern, through managerial decision making, could control much of its own destiny. These business decisions, of course, included raising more capital through sales of stock in order to expand facilities as well as the inception of marketing strategies—advertising and public relations. Trade associations played key roles in these latter spheres, especially as large corporations and other firms sought the advice of publicists such as Ivy Lee to cultivate the favor of newspaper editors.

Although some writers (Bradley, 1965) have noted the existence of trade associations at local, state, regional, and national levels, it would be inaccurate to assume that small, local associations inevitably evolved into larger and larger organizations, eventually becoming national in scope and membership. On the contrary, patterns of regional association were the first to emerge, simply because the establishment of some industries depended on such factors as the availability of fuel sources, labor, and transportation rather than on the political climate of a particular city or state. Among the first such associations were the Writing Paper Manufacturers Association, the United States Brewers Association, the National Association of Wool Manufacturers and the New England Cotton Manufacturers Association, all of which were formed in the 1860s (National Industrial Conference Board, 1925). One of the earliest trade groups, formed in 1855, was a confederation of manufacturers known as the American Iron and Steel Association; this group later became the American Iron and Steel Institute.

During the last half of the 19th century, trade associations took on several forms. The most common was the so-called "horizontal" trade association, in which competitors in a given enterprise banded together for some anticipated mutual benefit, such as a measure of financial stability to be gained from sharing information about the credit standing of wholesale buyers. When a buyer was tardy in making payment or "failed" by declaring bankruptcy, the trade association acted as a collection agency or settlement agent in behalf of its member firms who were creditors. Thus, the exchange of information allowed individual firms to lessen their respective risks, of course, and it also brought to bear the force of pressure when an account became delinquent or a shady buyer attempted to relocate and resume business.

Even the relatively small early trade associations recognized the potential power inherent in their collective organization. For example, the Western Flint and Lime Glass Protective Association (WFLGPA), a Pittsburgh-based trade association, sought favorable treatment (i.e., reduced rates and new classification schedules) from railroad freight agents, and it sometimes lobbied Congress on this important matter by sending its representatives to Washington (Measell, 1983). Often, success was achieved by direct negotiations with the railroads themselves, which were in their own process of development as organizations. The WFLGPA seldom needed to go further, but, when the railroad lines were recalcitrant in meeting the glassmen's wishes, the association sought help directly from Washington, usually by persuading Congressional representatives from Western Pennsylvania to become active in behalf of their constituents, the glass companies of the region.

Among the most clearly demonstrable effects of an early trade association is the establishment of standard time zones across the United States by the railroad industry. These time zones, which exist today from Eastern Standard to Pacific Standard, facilitated scheduling and made cooperation and integration of freight cars possible from road to road, offering economic benefits to the railroad companies that handled increased loads. Chandler (1977) listed more than a dozen separate trade associations that embraced various facets of the railroad industry. Of most importance, of course, are the associations of managerial executives, for these groups brought about the standardization of rail gauge necessary for car handling as well as the combined effort necessary to sustain lobbying efforts for protective legislation.

For the most part, the early trade associations were concerned with matters of economic survival and the need to sustain themselves. They gathered statistics and issued reports, and they provided information about themselves and their membership to an eager press. They lobbied Congress on issues of importance to their constituents, and they supported politicians who expressed sympathy and encouraged their activities.

The influential trade associations formed in the American glass tableware industry during the last half of the 19th century provide representative examples of the nature and development of these organizations during this time period. During the Civil War, glass manufacturers met annually from 1860 to 1863 in a loosely organized national meeting. There is some evidence that local alliances had been formed in glassmaking centers. Glass factory owners in Pittsburgh, for example, both endeavored "to gather the statistics of the trade, domestic and foreign" and to establish and maintain a firm schedule of wholesale selling prices to which all of its members would adhere (Measell, 1985). Similar sentiments were behind the establishment of the earliest national trade associations, such as the Writing Paper Manufacturers Association and the New England Cotton Manufacturers Association, which evolved into the National Association of Cotton Manufacturers early in the 20th century.

Regional trade groups in the glass industry that had been formed in the 1870s eventually consolidated themselves into well-organized, influential national organizations. The Western Flint and Lime Glass Protective Association, which embraced the glass tableware plants west of the Allegheny mountains when it was formed in 1874, soon became an effective regional voice for its membership. The organization collected credit data on members' customers, and it standardized prices charged for wooden shipping containers (called packages) as well as cash discount and credit schedules. A similar confederation of Eastern glass manufacturers operated in the Philadelphia area under the leadership of James Gillinder (Measell, 1983), and this group met once a year in a joint gathering with the WFLGPA to discuss such national concerns as railroad freight rates and Federal import/export regulations, including the tariff.

The Eastern and Western groups merged in 1887 to form the American Association of Flint and Lime Glass Manufacturers; about 60 separate companies, roughly 90% of the glass tableware industry, were involved. The American Association, as it was generally known, existed primarily for the standardization of credit terms and package charges, as well as exerting some force as a collection agency and dealing with the customers of members (American Association of Flint and Lime Glass Manufacturers, 1910). The group functioned until 1934, when it was reorganized (and renamed the American Glassware Association) under the provisions of the National Industrial Recovery Act (Dougherty, 1949).

Some trade associations were formed in the late 1800s as direct responses to the growing strength of organized labor, and the glass tableware industry offers several illustrative examples. The skilled glassworkers' trade union, called the American Flint Glass Workers Union (AFGWU), was established in 1878, and it grew steadily in strength over the next decade. In 1893, the National Association of Manufacturers of Pressed and Blown Glassware (NAMPBG) was established solely for the purpose of negotiating with the AFGWU. An earlier trade group founded in 1888, the Associated Manufacturers of Pressed Glassware, had been dedicated to this same purpose, but its leadership soon deteriorated, eventually becoming concentrated in manufacturers in the Findlay, Ohio, natural gas belt, far from Pittsburgh. The group disbanded in November 1893, but the National Association of Manufacturers of Pressed and Blown Glassware was founded less than a month later.

The NAMPBG met the workers in yearly conferences from 1894 until 1951, and work rules and production guidelines were established through a complex of committees and caucuses. Although the NAMPBG claimed that it engaged in association-wide bargaining, the agreements reached between the NAMPBG and the AFGWU really had nationwide status, for both the unionized and the non-union plants tended to adhere to the conditions and wages which emerged from the annual conferences. A key feature of NAMPBG/AFGWU relations was the so-called Star Island Agreement of 1903, wherein wildcat strikes were outlawed and a system for grievances was set in place.

Despite the power of this trade association, almost all of the NAMPBG's negotiating work was carried out in private. The glass trade journals might speculate upon the possible terms of pending agreements, but the NAMPBG generally shunned publicity, save for such ceremonial occasions as the signing of contracts and the retirements or deaths of important executives among its membership. The yearly meetings of the American Association, on the other hand, were usually held in a New Jersey shore resort town, such as Cape May, and the glassmen freely granted interviews to the trade press, although the business meetings were closed.

It may be interesting to note the lack of direct connection between the trade associations in the glass tableware industry and the trade journals that served that endeavor as well as other closely related glassmaking operations such as window and bottle glass. The first trade publication was *Crockery and Glass Journal*, which began publication in 1874. During the heyday of the industry, 1880–1910, the journal appeared weekly and issued a thick Holiday Number which often contained 200 or more pages, replete with advertising for the firms' new glassware products and glowing accounts of the various company's artistic and financial successes during the previous year. In this trade publication, like most of the others mentioned here, there is a rather clear correlation between the amount of editorial space allocated to descriptions of a firm's products and the size of its advertisements in the journal itself. "News" concerning major advertisers, such as the giant United States Glass Company, filled the columns of *Crockery and Glass Journal* in the mid-1890s, and coverage was almost entirely favorable, especially while the firm maintained a strong anti-union stance and weathered several strikes and general labor unrest.

In 1879, *Pottery and Glassware Reporter* began publication, but this trade journal ceased publication in 1893. The *National Glass Budget*, a technical publication that served all branches of the glass industry, appeared in 1884 and is still published today. *China, Glass and Lamps,* another weekly that is still published today as the monthly *Tableware,* began in 1890. During the late 1890s and the first decade of the 20th century, several short-lived periodicals served the glass tableware industry briefly: *Illustrated Glass and Pottery World, Housefurnisher: China Glass and Pottery Review,* and *Glass.* These were either absorbed by *China, Glass and Lamps* or *Crockery and Glass Journal* or failed and ceased publication.

Although none of the glass trade publications was published by the trade associations themselves, the editorial content of these journals was greatly dependent on the cooperation of both the individual firms and the trade associations. Shortly after its inception, the WFLGPA membership directed its actuary to "write a letter [each] week" to *Crockery and Glass Journal*, "giving items of interest in the Glass Ware business" (Measell, 1983, p. 318). These reports appeared in the *Journal* under headlines such as "Pittsburgh Letter," "The Glass Factories," or "Trade Report" for many years, with never any indication that the information came from a glass industry trade association. Other glass tableware trade publications carried stories bylined to an unnamed "special correspondent" who visited glass factories and reported news of personnel changes, new glass colors or designs, and the positive prospects of the trade.

Until the Sherman AntiTrust Act of 1890 was passed by Congress, it was not illegal for businesses to engage in production controls and/or price-fixing. Often springing from the base of a trade association, many short-lived cartels developed in the 1870s–1880s. Chandler (1977) suggested that competition routinely gave way to cooperation through merger and consolidation, often through trade associations. In the glass tableware industry, the Pittsburgh and Wheeling Goblet Company attempted to control both output and prices by establishing a central committee to oversee the operations of its member plants (Measell, 1988).

In several secretive meetings, members of the WFLGPA discussed "pooling" arrangements in 1884, but major consolidations did not occur until 1891 and 1899, when the United States Glass Company and the National Glass Company, respectively, were incorporated. This development in the glass business parallels that of other industries, including such major ones as steel, oil, and railroads: The independent entrepreneur, acting out of economic self-interest, initiates or becomes part of cooperative arrangements for the mutual benefit of all who joined the arrangement.

As Olasky (1987) has indicated, public relations tactics, often of a questionable nature, were an integral part of pooling and other trust arrangements. In the railroad industry, he reported, such devices as bribes, free travel passes, and subsidy publication were commonplace as the railroad executives sought to influence opinion leaders and secure favorable governmental action, including legislation, to maintain the pools.

Olasky (1987) concluded that railroad public relations soon stretched beyond mere press agentry to encompass the beginnings of modern programs aimed at government and education. He also concluded that the role of government in promoting railways "for the public welfare" (p. 31) was an important outcome of the railroads' concerted public relations efforts through their trade associations. Furthermore, the first governmental body to oversee the railroads, the Interstate Commerce Commission, was initially a tool of the railroads themselves, for they controlled appointments to the board and drafted regulations. Later, when governmental regulations became strict, the railroads used public relations activities to "keep the public happy" rather than improve the nature of rail service (Olasky, 1987, p. 31).

Matters of ethics aside, the rhetorical techniques employed by the railroads were sound enough. In a time of growing literacy, newspapers and magazines were the ideal channels through which to reach an increasingly sophisticated mass audience that was generally negative toward the existence of cartels. The newspaper stories and magazine articles carried an implicit cachet of credibility, and the public was influenced. This was not simple press agentry, and Olasky (1987) credited the railroads and their trade associations with "the forerunners of today's elaborate governmental relations, educational relations, and corporate contributions programs" (p. 31).

Nineteenth century trade associations tended to be governed by constitutions and by-laws approved by the membership. Officers were elected from the ranks of the member firms, and the day-to-day affairs of the association were conducted by a board of directors or executive board rather than by a full-time paid staff. In the WFLGPA, for example, the sole employee was the actuary (Measell, 1983). He was responsible for all financial record keeping, and he also performed the functions of recording and corresponding secretary. The NAMPBG also had a small staff. From 1893 through the 1950s, the staff consisted of an executive secretary, his assistant, and a stenographer-receptionist. Most of their time was taken up by research and routine correspondence on questions posed by member firms as well as preparations for regular monthly meetings and the annual conferences held with the glassworkers' union.

An interesting feature of the 19th-century trade associations is a noted ambivalence toward the press. Although the railroad groups courted the press both openly and covertly, some of the glass trade associations kept a low profile, indeed, providing no flow of information save to the editors of a few trade publications, all of which were somewhat dependent on the glassware manufacturers for advertising revenues. There is a single reason for this ambivalence: the power of the press. When well-courted and in line, the press, in the form of the big daily newspapers, could disseminate the railroads' point of view on a variety of subjects, ranging from carriage rates to the need for extending a particular road to improve the economy of a state or region. This same press had little positive utility for the glass tableware industry, simply because their enterprises had relatively modest economic impact except in the smallest of towns, where the editors of small weeklies could be counted upon to publicize even the smallest bit of news involving the glass factories (Measell, 1986).

Shortly after World War I, several comprehensive examinations of Amer ican trade associations were published (Department of Commerce, 1923; Naylor, 1921; NIBC, 1925) Most of these were concerned with the applicability of anti-trust law to trade association activities and with the regulatory role of the Federal Trade Commission vis à vis trade associations. All three were in agreement that the trade associations of the time were of mutual benefit to the industries, the government, and the consumer. The NIBC report, which indicated the existence of "between 800 and 1,000 trade associations of national or international character" (1925, p. 326), concluded that "voluntary cooperation" through trade associations made possible "the elusive synthesis of freedom and authority in the economic sphere" (p. 316). It is this same question of freedom and authority which must be addressed in considering the activities of trade associations today.

CONTEMPORARY TRADE ASSOCIATIONS

A recently published comparative analysis of American and Japanese trade associations (Lynn & McKeown, 1988) lists nine separate functions of the contemporary trade association:

1. promotion of products or services;
2. labor relations;
3. standardization of products and/or processes;
4. data collection;
5. research and development;
6. economic services to members;
7. educational services;
8. conventions and other meetings; and
9. public relations.

Many of these, of course, were part and parcel of trade associations three quarters of a century ago, but the contemporary articulation of these functions is decidedly more sophisticated and considerably more controversial.

Cutlip, et al. (1985) reported that nearly a half-million persons were employed by trade associations in the 1980s. The typical group has a staff of several dozen, including lobbyists and other public relations persons, and many have multi-million dollar budgets for advertising and other promotions.

Contemporary trade associations are far more involved with lobbying and governmental relations than were their 19th-century precursors. In their recent study of U.S. trade associations in manufacturing, Lynn and McKeown (1988) were particularly interested in the growth of governmental relations functions. Between 1982 and 1985, they noted, increases occurred in legislative response networks and representation in Washington, whereas political action committees (PACs) declined due to fundraising difficulties. The felt need on the part of trade associations for legislative response networks is easily seen when one considers the paramount concern of the manufacturers during the 1980s, namely, product safety (Lynn & McKeown, 1988).

Current public relations textbooks, although mindful of the role of trade associations in disseminating information via the mass media, do not usually call attention to the other roles of trade associations. Cutlip et al. (1985) suggested that trade associations often suffer from divisions within their memberships that preclude real strength except in areas "in which there is an obvious, predetermined unanimity or a substantial majority" (p. 503). In fact, some associations are formed precisely for the focusing of concerted efforts born of unanimity. Several examples are considered here.

Critiques of contemporary trade association activities and of the ethical implications of those activities are not hard to find. Several years ago, Jeff and Marie Blyskal (1985) published a strong indictment of the relationship between news media and public relations in their *PR: How the Public Relations Industry Writes the News*. Their premises are straightforward enough: (a) the media set the agenda for public debate, and (b) PR often sets the agenda for the media. If one accepts these premises, the ethical constraints upon the public relations activities of trade associations become clear.

Many of the Blyskals' examples came from the public relations activities of trade associations. In one instance, the makers of aerosol spray products created a trade association for the specific purpose of delaying government regulation of the industry. The story begins with *The New York Times'* ("Team up to manage," 1974) coverage of Harvard professor Michael McElroy's view of the depletion of the ozone layer by the fluorocarbon propellants in aerosol sprays. Public relations practitioner Kenneth Makovsky, according to the Blyskals, orchestrated the response of the industry, working through such trade associations as the Aerosol Education Bureau and the Council on Atmospheric Sciences, both of which were used to legitimize the industry's views in press releases to a plethora of magazines and newspapers.

When federal legislation regulating aerosol propellants was passed in 1977, fluorocarbons were banned, so one might suppose that Makovsky's public relations campaigns had failed, at least in terms of securing government support. Blyskal and Blyskal (1985) revealed that Makovsky regarded them as a "smashing success," because their purpose was to "buy time for the industry so it could come up with an alternative aerosol propellant" (p. 173). The implications are clear: The rhetoric of the public relations campaigns generated by the trade associations was designed primarily to impede or stall public opinion favorable to legislation, not to provide information relevant to the scientific debate over aerosols.

The rhetorical impact of the trade association names should not go unnoticed here. Buzz words such as "education" and "council" carry the connotations of reasoned debate and scientific inquiry. Just as the introduction of a speaker by a third party can set one's *ethos* before an audience, so also can the name of a trade association do much to cast an image in the public's mind of the credibility of an organization.

The creation of "councils" is not new, and Olasky (1987) discussed the role of public relations pioneer Carl Byoir in the founding of such noble-sounding groups as the National Consumers Tax Commission, the Emergency Consumers Tax Council, and the Business Property Owners, Inc. Each of these groups was opposed to taxes on chain stores, but all were, in fact, founded by Byoir, who also had the head of the Business Property Owners, Inc., on his payroll.

Legally, neither a hastily formed ad-hoc council nor a trade association is under any obligation to disclose its purposes, save for the perfunctory phrases required by state incorporation statutes. The Michigan Coalition for Safety Belt Use, whose budget comes entirely from the automotive industry, is equally candid about its purposes (to encourage the use of safety belts through public programs of information and motivation) and its funding sources. Rhetorically, this forthright stance serves to blunt the possible impact of an expose' article or news report produced by an investigative reporter. Indeed, the disclosure of the Coalition's sources of funds may deter the reporter's efforts before they can begin.

Two recent public relations textbooks (Cutlip et al., 1985; Wilcox et al., 1989) provide some helpful background through which the rhetorical activities of trade associations can be examined. The American Society of Association Executives (ASAE) estimates that there are about 8,500 trade association (Cutlip et al., p. 501). Several associations—the nationwide American Bankers Association (ABA), the California Milk Advisory Board and the Dairy Council of California—are singled out for their lobbying efforts and advocacy advertising. The ABA and the United States League of Savings Institutions (USLSI) were instrumental in repealing federal regulations which required withholding on dividends and interest (Keller, 1983). The ABA and the USLSI mobilized their members in letter-writing campaigns and supported lobbying efforts in Washington, of course, but both targeted the banking patrons through advocacy advertising in newspapers as well as through direct mail pieces which accompanied monthly bank statements.

A former ASAE president, James Low (1978) may have set the tone for trade association activities in the 1980s when he declared that the efforts of consumerist organizations, such as those founded by Ralph Nader, were, in fact, an effective stimulus for enhanced rhetorical activities by trade associations (Jones, 1976). Scholars in rhetorical criticism have long noted the presence of movements and counter-movements in American society, but most have focused their attentions on individual advocates rather than on the collective voice of a group such as a trade association.

VOICE OR VICE?

Trade associations and their rhetorical activities have clearly played a vital role in the shaping of American economic life. As the dynamics of the nation's business and industries evolved after the Civil War, trade groups emerged that shaped changes in the lives of employees and consumers. The voices of trade associations have been loud, and they have been influential in determining public policy. One must ask this question: When does a voice become a vice?

Certainly, the Blyskals' (1985) examples of trade association maneuvering and underhandedness give one pause. It is tempting indeed to point the finger of accusation at those in the most reprehensible positions. But, the activities of the worst practitioners must not become the standard by which all are judged. Nonetheless, those public relations practitioners employed or retained by trade associations are under an obligation to act as the conscience of their organization. Virtually every public relations textbook suggests that practitioners, particularly at the managerial level, must be willing to express views reflecting a broader social conscience than that addressed by a typical profit-motivated marketing plan or a "no news is good news" approach to internal communication. The difference between a voice and a vice may lie in the purposes of the organization, both legitimate and ulterior, as they are known to the public relations practitioner.

On the other hand, Cutlip et al. (1985, p. 506) listed many "associations in action" that have added impetus to some socially responsible causes in contemporary American society. The activities of trade associations in the social arena may further the collective goals of the association itself. But, as Olasky (1987) pointed out, social responsibility quickly becomes a double-edged sword when one confronts thorny questions of public interest and corporate advocacy in an era of rapid technological change. Just as there are times when one may shudder at the legitimate legal activities of a powerful trade association, ancient or contemporary, so also are there times when one must recognize the legitimacy of dissident voices in the marketplace of ideas, even when a particularly strident one is the collective sound of a trade association.

REFERENCES

American Association of Flint and Lime Glass Manufacturers. (1910). *Constitution and by-laws.* Pittsburgh: Author.

Baskin, O. W., & Aronoff, C. E. (1988). *Public relations: The profession and the practice* (2nd ed.). Dubuque, IA: Wm. C. Brown.

Blyskal, J., & Blyskal, M. (1985). *PR: How the public relations industry writes the news.* New York: Morrow.

Bradley, J. F. (1965). *The role of trade associations and professional business societies in America.* University Park, PA: Penn State University Press.

Chandler, A. D. (1977). *The visible hand: The managerial revolution in American business.* Cambridge: Harvard University Press.

Cochran, T. C. (1972). *Business in American life: A history.* New York: McGraw-Hill.

Cutlip, S. M., Center, A. H., & Broom, G. M. (1985). *Effective public relations* (6th ed.). Englewood Cliffs: Prentice-Hall.

Department of Commerce. (1923). *Trade association activities.* Washington DC: U.S. Government Printing Office.

Dougherty, G. (1949, September). 87 Years of glassware history. *Crockery and Glass Journal,* pp. 76–78.

Douglass, E. P. (1971). *The coming of age of American business: Three centuries of enterprise, 1600–1900.* Chapel Hill: University of North Carolina Press.

Emmet, B., & Jeuck, J. E. (1950). *Catalogues and counters: A history of Sears, Roebuck and Company.* Chicago: University of Chicago Press.

Gilb, C. (1966). *Hidden hierarchies: The professions and government.* New York: Harper & Row.

Jones, W. H. (1976, July 4). Trade associations flourish. *Washington Post,* p. F1.

Keller, B. (1983). Lowest common denominator lobbying. *Washington Monthly, 15,* 32–39.

Latham, F. B. (1972). *A century of serving consumers: The story of Montgomery Ward.* Chicago: Montgomery Ward.

Lebhar, G. M. (1963). *Chain stores in America, 1859–1962.* New York: Chain Store Publishing Corporation.

Letwin, W. (1965). *Law and economic policy in America: The evolution of the Sherman Antitrust Act.* Edinburgh: Edinburgh University Press.

Low, J. P. (1978). Associations discover need for expanded communication efforts. *Journal of Organizational Communication, 7,* 19–20.

Lynn, L. L., & McKeown, T. J. (1988). *Organizing business: Trade associations in America and Japan.* Washington, DC: American Enterprise Institute.

Measell, J. S. (1983). The Western Flint and Lime Glass Protective Association, 1874–1887. *Western Pennsylvania Historical Magazine, 66,* 313–334.

Measell, J. S. (1985). Pittsburgh's first glass trade association? *Western Pennsylvania Historical Magazine, 68,* 387–389.

Measell, J. (1986). *Findlay glass: The glass tableware manufacturers, 1886–1902.* Marietta, OH: Antique Publications.

Measell, J. S. (1988). The Pittsburgh and Wheeling Goblet Company. *Western Pennsylvania Historical Magazine, 71,* 191–195.

National Industrial Conference Board. (1925). *Trade associations: Their economic significance and legal status.* New York: NICB, Inc.

National trade and professional associations of the United States. (1988). New York: Columbia Books.

Naylor, E. H. (1921). *Trade associations: Their organization and management.* New York: Harper.

Nelson, D. (1975). *Managers and workers.* Madison: University of Wisconsin Press.

Newsom, D., Scott, A., & Turk, J. V. (1989). *This is pr: The realities of public relations* (3rd ed.). Belmont, CA: Wadsworth.

Olasky, M. N. (1987). *Corporate public relations: A new historical perspective.* Hillsdale, NJ: Lawrence Erlbaum Associates.

Smith, R. F. & Tucker, K. (1983). Team up to manage change. *Association Management, 35,* 131–137.

Tests show aerosol gases may pose threat to Earth. (1974, September 26). *The New York Times,* p. 1.

Whitten, D. O. (1983). *The emergence of giant enterprise, 1860–1914: American commercial enterprise and extractive industries.* Westport, CT: Greenwood.

Wiebe, R. H. (1967). *The search for order: 1877–1920.* New York: Hill & Wang.

Wilcox, D. L., Ault, P. H., & Agee, W. K. (1989) *Public relations: Strategies and tactics* (2nd ed.). New York: Harper & Row.

12

Smoking OR Health: Incremental Erosion as a Public Interest Group Strategy

CELESTE MICHELLE CONDIT
University of Georgia

DEIRDRE MOIRA CONDIT
Rutgers University

Tobacco has been a controversial product since our nation's founding. In 1776, abolitionists and plantation masters battled over the slave labor needed to produce tobacco. Later, the morality of tobacco smoking became the central contested issue. In the 20th century, the conflict has been between health groups and tobacco interests. Modern tobacco farmers reap over $1 billion a year, but their $3,000 dollar an acre profits are dwarfed by $35 billion worth of cigarette sales (Baccardi, 1989; Wilson, 1989). The farmers and cigarette companies are joined in the pro-tobacco coalition by the one third of the population that uses tobacco products, the retail stores who reap profits from tobacco's sale, the advertisers who profit from its promotion, and local, state, and federal governments who net over $10 billion a year by taxing it (Wilson, 1989).

These substantial pro-tobacco forces are opposed by a collection of non-profit and benevolent organizations concerned about the health of Americans, including the American Medical Association, the Surgeon General, the American Heart Association, and citizens' groups such as Action on Smoking & Health (ASH). These tobacco and health forces have been battling each other for several decades, each using rhetorical means to influence public attitudes and law. An exploration of one particular episode of their war—the introduction of the cigarette-like product called PREMIER—reveals some general features of this long-standing rhetorical contest, as well as illustrating the useful strategy of incremental erosion, which is particularly well adapted to public interest groups of all kinds.

241

"CONSORH" AND PUBLIC INTEREST GROUP RHETORIC

One key organization among the anti-smoking forces is the Coalition on Smoking OR Health (ConSORH). It is this organization's goals, strategies, and perspectives upon which we focus here. ConSORH is a federal lobbying organization formed by the alliance of the American Heart Association, the American Lung Association, and the American Cancer Society. The rhetorical goals, strategies, and constraints of ConSORH are similar to those of other citizen activist organizations. These groups seek to protect consumer health and safety, the environment, and product quality from those private companies who devote their attention to the "bottomline" of self-profit, at the expense of other vital social concerns. These public interest groups generally face opponents who are well-organized, better-funded, and motivated by intense self-interest. They also often face well-established laws and habits.

Like many other activist groups, ConSORH is a relatively recent development—a product of the consumer movement of the 1970s. Consumer groups generally evolve only after a long history has allowed their opponents to shape laws, customs, and language in ways that are difficult to surmount. Consequently, the opponents of activist groups tend to be too powerful to allow a sweeping frontal assault. ConSORH, for example, cannot simply get the government to ban smoking; political support for tobacco is too strong for that. ConSORH has, therefore, adopted cost efficient and feasible rhetorical strategies to make whatever progress is possible at the time.

One of the central strategies available in such constrained conditions is that of *incremental erosion*. Working on different target audiences at different times, the activist group attempts to chip away at the various supports underlying its opponent's position. It makes a series of gradual and small moves designed to manuever opponents into a position where they have no more rhetorical options. This is done by establishing rhetorical *exigencies*—needs, conditions, or demands to which the opposition must respond—while simultaneously establishing rhetorical *constraints* that limit the strategies available for response (Bitzer, 1968). The rhetorical exigencies might include the need to produce counter-rhetoric to forestall regulation or to defend challenged actions in public (e.g., by publicizing oil spills or automobile recalls). The rhetorical constraints might include legal or financial limitations on the channels the opponent could use or the language and claims available to be made (e.g., the Federal Trade Commission's regulation of the truth content of advertising).

This tactic of incremental erosion is well-illustrated by the efforts of the anti-smoking lobby, especially with regards to ConSORH's opposition to the introduction of "PREMIER" by the R.J. Reynolds company in 1988. We review how the anti-smoking groups gradually set up the conditions for immobilizing the tobacco industry, and then explore the way in which those conditions eventually caused Reynolds to swallow the billion-dollar promotion of its new product and to withdraw PREMIER in defeat.[1]

THE FIRST BATTLE LINES: SMOKING AND HEALTH

Although tobacco products had been banned on aesthetic, moral, and unsubstantiated health grounds in some states at the turn of the 20th century, by mid-century they were fully legalized throughout the United States for adults (Surgeon General, 1989). In the 1950s, however, scientists gradually began to document the health hazards of smoking. As they did so, the tobacco companies responded by intensive marketing of cigarettes that were supposedly less dangerous. Various cigarette manufacturers had always promoted their cigarettes as being more healthful than those of the competition. In the 1930s and 1940s for example, Old Gold was advertised with the slogan "not a cough in a carload" (from the petition of the ConSORH requesting classification of low tar and nicotine cigarettes as drugs under the Food Drug and Cosmetic Act, 1988, p. 12). The scientific concerns about smoking and health intensified such marketing efforts. Lorillard, for example, launched a product with a "micronite filter," which promised "the greatest health protection in cigarette history." Kent's "micronite" filter was described as made of a material "so safe, so effective it has been selected to help filter the air in hospital operating rooms" (from the 1988 petition, p. 13).

The intensified safety claims of these cigarettes were not necessarily tied to proven safety. Cigarette companies did not have to disclose the contents of their products or subject them to public testing. Much later, however, evidence surfaced suggesting that "micronite" originally contained the dangerous substance asbestos. Moreover, these "safer" filtered cigarettes were accompanied by substantial increases of nicotine and tar contents (from the 1988 petition, p. 23).

The first move in the modern battle between tobacco forces and their opponents was thus the scientific attack on the healthfulness of cigarettes. The cigarette companies, seeking to protect their markets, responded with new products, which they portrayed as safer, although without extensive substantiation of these claims.[2] This pattern would be repeated as formal organizations evolved to unseat the tobacco industry's stronghold in the American marketplace.

---

[1]External estimates of the cost of the program are larger than internal estimates, which run as low as $300 million. It is difficult to estimate the costs because they involved not only a long product development, a marketing effort, and a regulatory battle but were embroiled in a leveraged buy-out and personnel shift, and entailed the development of new manufacturing processes and a new factory. In the end, Reynolds claimed to lay off about 10% of their workforce as a result of Premier's failure, thus producing substantial lay-off and/or retirement costs as well (see Schiffman, 1989).

[2]RJR (James A. Goold, personal communication, July 19, 1989) denies making health claims.

Rhetorical Balance Sheet
PHASE I:

Exigence:
Scientific confirmation that
smoking is unhealthy

Tobacco Industry　　　　　　　　　　　　　　Anti-Smoking Groups

Target Audience: Consumers　　　　　　　Consumers
Strategy: Promote "Safer" Products　　　Scare Consumers into Quitting
Constraints:
　(1) Legal Limits on advertising　　　　　(1) Precedent
　(2) Americans take health seriously　　(2) Limited funds for persuasion
　(3) Opposition's credibility　　　　　　　(3) Congressional reluctance based on
　　　　　　　　　　　　　　　　　　　　　　　　opponent's broad coalition (consumers,
　　　　　　　　　　　　　　　　　　　　　　　　growers, manufacturers, taxers).
　　　　　　　　　　　　　　　　　　　　　　(4) Addicted consumers

Outcome:
Near stalemate with smokers;
tobacco companies lose support of nonsmokers

PHASE II: ORGANIZED TARGETING OF CONSUMERS

These early health offensives against smoking were tentative and poorly organized. The anti-smoking group received its first major official sanction in 1964 when the Surgeon General provided a report confirming that cigarette smoking was harmful to health. The anti-smoking group's major tactic at this stage was to target consumers. A host of organizations set to work to convince individuals not to smoke.

The anti-smoking organizations had one unique advantage in this effort. Organizations like the American Heart Association and various scientific groups had a high level of public credibility because of their perceived altruistic motives. This credibility helped induce many smokers to give an open-minded hearing to the arguments, even when addiction provided strong incentives to resist the message. With fair rapidity, a public consensus

---

Its denial rests on the separation of "health" from claims about tar and nicotine levels. However, since the common perspective is that tar and nicotine levels are related to health (as RJR notes in FDA, 1988, pp. 115–123), the advertisement of lower tar and nicotine levels necessarily makes an implicit health claim. In addition, in the massive research volume on the new cigarette prototype, which R.J.R. produced, the reviewing scholars concluded "Although the studies were only of 90-day duration they did clearly demonstrate the decrease in adverse biological activity from the new cigarette when compared to effects induced by smoke from reference cigarettes," which was one of RJR's listed objectives (see "Chemical and biological," 1988, p. xii, ix). "Decrease in adverse biological activity" seems to translate rather directly in lay terms to "healthier."

arose—a majority of people agreed that smoking was bad for health. Eventually, three quarters of all smokers would report the desire to quit. Moreover, immediately after the Surgeon General's report, there was a 20% decline in cigarette sales (from the 1988 petition, p. 20).

This decline was only temporary, because the anti-smoking groups did not have the rhetorical stage to themselves. The cigarette companies launched a counter-offensive, again by promising tobacco products that might be perceived as more healthful. Between 1968 and 1981 the average tar and nicotine content of cigarettes fell by 39% as companies competed to promote their brand as "lowest" in these presumably harmful components (from the 1988 petition, p. 22). In the late 1970s and early 1980s, eight different cigarettes were advertised as "lowest" in tar or nicotine (from the 1988 petition, p. 33). As the "tar wars" heated up, the advertising messages became stronger. Carlton claimed in one ad that "Ten packs of Carlton have less tar than one pack of. . . ." and listed a variety of other brands (from the 1988 petition, p. 29).

The cigarette companies' counter-offensive worked fairly well. Surrounded daily by advertising images that portrayed healthy and happy people smoking, by ad copy touting the preference for "low tar and nicotine," and by the promotion of both scientific and pseudoscientific information claiming low tar and nicotine cigarettes were reasonably healthful, the fears of smokers were somewhat quieted (from the 1988 petition, pp. 31–33). Polls showed that over one third of cigarette consumers believed that "It has been proven that smoking low tar and low nicotine cigarettes does not significantly increase a person's risk of disease over that of a nonsmoker," and another third declared themselves to be "unsure" (from the 1988 petition, pp. 37–38). Moreover, both smokers and nonsmokers would continually underestimate the *degree* of the health risk associated with smoking (Surgeon General, 1989, p. 23). With health concerns dampened, cigarette consumption rose.

Again, however, the health effects of the cigarette companies' new products were unclear. As the tar and nicotine in cigarettes were decreased, some smokers simply engaged in "compensatory smoking." That is, they tended to smoke more cigarettes and inhale more deeply than they previously had, in order to get the same dose of nicotine (FDA, 1988, p. 118). Also, in order to make these lower tar cigarettes continue to have taste, cigarette companies added flavorings or revised manufacturing methods (FDA, 1988, p. 50), potentially introducing products with co-carcinogenic effects.

The tobacco companies had more-or-less stalemated the anti-smoking arguments directed to individual consumers. The anti-smoking groups began, therefore, to broaden their targets. Although large-scale initiatives targeted at individual consumers continued, anti-smoking groups launched new campaigns targeting government agencies.

THE NEW BATTLEGROUND: GOVERNMENT AGENCIES

Early regulatory skirmishes focused on laws that shaped the persuasive messages reaching the consumer, and both sides experienced incremental victories. The health groups won a virtually uncontested battle in 1970 to ban cigarette advertising from television, and they succeeded in strengthening health warning labels.

When the regulatory contest was shifted from consumer influence to direct federal control, however, the advantage slipped back to the tobacco coalition. The key battle occured in 1977 when the courts upheld the Food and Drug Administration's decision not to assume regulatory authority over cigarettes. The tobacco industry, riding high on the Courts' decision, was further bolstered by the new, anti-regulatory wave that rushed in with the election of Ronald Reagan to the presidency. Corporations all across America were beginning to adopt a major new strategy—direct confrontation that challenged public opposition to business and aggressively supported deregulation (Morris, 1984; Schmertz, 1986). In this spirit, tobacco industry groups such as the Tobacco Institute and the industry giants (Philip Morris and R.J. Reynolds) began to attack the consensus that smoking was unhealthful and to engage in several anti-regulatory campaigns (from the 1988 petition, pp. 38–41; "Before the FTC," 1988). In this milieu of regulatory struggle, the cigarette-like product called Premier was conceived and launched.

PHASE III: THE PREMIER BATTLE

According to R.J. Reynolds, Premier was a new kind of cigarette. According to ConSORH it was simply a "nicotine delivery device"—a new drug. We adopt the label used by the head of the FDA in testimony to Congress and call it a "cigarette-like" device (Young, 1988). Premier looked much like a conventional cigarette, but it consisted of a charcoal source that burned to heat the contents of a "flavor packet" wrapped in tobacco. Because the tobacco never burned, it produced little sidestream smoke (FDA, 1988, p. 4), and hence would be less offensive to nonsmokers in the area. In addition to its advantages in the "secondary smoke" controversy, the process of heating instead of burning the tobacco also potentially reduced the health consequences of the tobacco to smokers themselves. Reynolds could hope that Premier would provide a substitute for conventional cigarettes that would present fewer grounds for regulatory controversy and for consumer concern.

The Rhetorical Exigencies

R.J. Reynolds was driven to develop this product by two rhetorical exigencies—two actions requiring reaction—created by the anti-smoking groups. The first was the "passive smoking" challenge.

Nonsmokers, unencumbered by the influence of nicotine addiction, had never been satisfied by cigarette company reassurances about the healthfulness of newer tobacco products. When some scientific evidence began to suggest that "second-hand smoke" could be harmful to them, nonsmokers acted. Anti-smoking groups persuaded over 320 localities to pass initiatives restricting smoking in public places because of the annoyance and perceived or real health hazards of cigarette smoke to nonsmokers (Ruberry, 1989). This restriction limited social smoking. It also constituted a strong and visible symbolic sanction against smoking that was of major long-term significance for the toleration of smoking in American society, a factor recognized by tobacco company spokespersons (Almond, 1989). If successful, Reynolds's Premier could be expected, in part, to nullify the complaints against second-hand smoke and hence to prevent such sanctions.

R.J. Reynolds, although it refuses to acknowledge this, was also trying to address the health concerns of smokers by what it elsewhere described as "identification of individual constituents of tobacco smoke involved in the smoking-and-health controversy and application of technology to remove them" (FDA, 1988, p. 45).[3] Many smokers had opted for "healthier" low tar and nicotine cigarettes in lieu of quitting, but the number of smokers was gradually declining, threatening the tobacco industry over the long run (FDA, 1988, p. 35; Surgeon General, 1989;). Additionally, most smokers continued to express substantial concern about the healthfulness of their habit. If Premier were to be perceived as mitigating the health consequences of smoking, this might give RJR a market share advantage, deter smokers from quitting, or even attract new smokers. Premier's role in ameliorating the unhealthfulness of smoking, although never explicitly admitted by RJR, was implied by the advertising claim that Premier was "cleaner" and that it "substantially reduces many of the controversial compounds produced by burning tobacco" (R.J. Reynolds, 1988b). It was this health factor that caused a *New York Times* editorial to endorse the product ("Give the smokeless," 1988).

R.J. Reynolds thus generated Premier in response to two rhetorical exigencies impinging upon its market—it tried to provide a product that eliminated the impetus behind passive smoking initiatives and that appeared to

---

[3]This is again evident in the massive and expensive effort R.J.R. undertook to document the health impact of the cigarette (see "Chemical and biological," 1988).

reduce what it called the "yields of 'tar,' nicotine, and other smoke constituents" (FDA, 1988, p. 123). Anti-smoking groups, in opposing the marketing of this cigarette-like device, faced similarly powerful exigencies.

The opposition of health groups to Premier took the company by surprise (Morris & Waldman, 1989). R.J. Reynolds claimed that it had expected health groups to welcome a healthier cigarette, but nonsmoking groups had serious concerns about the product. In the first place, ConSORH was not convinced that the product was really healthier. For example, Richard Cooper, on behalf of R.J. Reynolds, had claimed in testimony before Congress that the "flavor packets" that were heated in these new devices consisted of ordinary food additives, which had been declared safe. ConSORH argued that the prior testing of the safety of these products covered only their consumption as food—not when heated and inhaled as smoke.[4] More seriously, if the claim that these products were "cigarettes" held, the industry would not face scrutiny about future contents, or be required to subject them to safety testing, and company spokespersons suggested that additional additives were planned for the future (Morris & Waldman, 1989).

ConSORH faced, therefore, a critical juncture. If Premier were successfully marketed and defined as a "cigarette," it feared that Premier might serve as a product model that delivered an addictive drug (nicotine) and that the product model could thereafter be variously modified without governmental regulation. ConSORH noted that the patent for Premier even listed tobacco as an "optional" ingredient. (Petition to classify R.J. Reynolds new alternative nicotine delivery product to be subject to the jurisdiction of the FDA, 1989).[5] The unlimited variability of future Premier-like products arose because, if Premier were indeed merely another cigarette, then it was presumptively intended for "smoking pleasure" and therefore exempt from regulation by the Food and Drug Administration (FDA). The FDA mandate allows the FDA to regulate only drugs that are on an official pharmacological list, or those products *"intended"* by the manufacturer to alter the structure or function of the body or *intended* to meet health needs. As long as cigarette manufacturers were able to market their products as being *intended* for "smoking pleasure," the precedent established by prior decisions of the courts mandated that the FDA did not have to claim legal authority to regulate them.

Ironically, the government's reluctance to breach precedent by recog-

---

[4]These objections were expressed by Scott Ballin of ConSORH in interview. He argued that the RJR study, *Chemical*, neglected and thereby downplayed the impact of Premier on important diseases (e.g., those resulting from carbon-monoxide inhalation).

[5]RJR argued that the FDA had only to rule on the "embodiment" of the patent—the specific product Premier, not the entire invention that was patented (and the full range of products it envisioned). They also argued that non-tobacco containing models generated less acceptance by potential consumers (FDA, 1988).

nizing that "smoking pleasure" was in substantial part the pleasure of a nicotine "fix" resulted from the extensive evidence demonstrating that cigarettes were inherently harmful. Because of the level of harm, regulatory oversight might plausibly lead to an outright ban. The political influence of the cigarette coalition was simply too powerful to allow a total ban on tobacco sales and use. The power of this lobby had repeatedly and directly exempted tobacco products from other consumer protection legislation, including the Consumer Product Safety Act, the Fair Labeling and Packaging Act, the Federal Hazardous Substances Act, the Controlled Substances Act, and the Toxic Substances Act.

ConSORH thus faced a situation in which Congress was unwilling to act to restrict tobacco products, and consumer protection agencies had been disempowered to act. The anti-smoking coalition's only possible avenue of resistance was to pressure the FDA into classifying Premier as something other than "a new cigarette." It would thereby be excluded from the protection of old precedents. ConSORH urged the FDA to label Premier a "new drug," in which case the FDA might require testing and safety assurances that ConSORH suspected Premier would not meet.

Both R.J. Reynolds and ConSORH were responding to serious rhetorical exigencies. Reynolds faced long-term decline and ConSORH faced the possibility of an unregulatable product on the market. These counter-poised needs put them in conflict with one another. Their battle ground encompassed two different audiences—the regulatory agencies, and consumers.

The Regulatory Strategies

The regulatory battle focused on the Food and Drug Administration. The agency itself would decide whether or not it would regulate Premier (although its decision was subject to review in court). However, because of the political potency of the issue, a subcommittee of the House of Representatives held hearings on the subject, and the debate spilled over into the press (Subcommittee, 1988). Reynolds' rhetorical strategy was to portray Premier as a "new cigarette," which, as such, would be open to no new regulations. It argued

> R.J. Reynolds's new product, announced last September, is a cigarette, which will be marketed to adult smokers solely for smoking taste and enjoyment. The cigarette contains tobacco, which is essential to its performance . . . Thus, in its essential characteristics—its function and purpose, its use of tobacco, and production of smoke—it is just like any other cigarette. (Cooper, 1988, p. 1)

In the first four pages of his well-crafted testimony before the committee, Richard Cooper, representative for the Reynolds company, managed to label his product a "cigarette" 23 times. In addition, Cooper emphasized that the product would be treated by the company like any other cigarette in all ways. Specifically, he noted that:

> precisely because it is a cigarette, the new cigarette and its advertising will bear the Surgeon General's warnings, mandated by Congress for all cigarettes. In addition, the new cigarette will be labeled, advertised, and marketed in conformity with the legal requirements and restrictions applicable to all cigarettes; and it will be taxed in the same way as all other cigarettes. (Cooper, 1988, p. 4)

Finally, aware of ConSORH's efforts to put low tar and nicotine cigarettes under FDA regulation on the grounds that advertisements for those products claimed health benefits, R.J. Reynolds was careful to choose the word "cleaner" rather than "safer" to use in its advertising. It stressed this usage in the hearings:

> In its advertising and labelling of the new cigarette . . . it also will not make any claim or representation that the new cigarette is "safe", or that it is "safer" than any other cigarette. (Cooper, 1988, p. 4)

Reynolds thus made a substantial argument for treating Premier as just another cigarette, to stave off FDA regulation.[6]

ConSORH's reply was also substantial. ConSORH sought to portray the new product as a "drug." In Scott Ballin's (1988) letter (reprinted here) to the editor of *The New York Times,* he called it a "drug vaporizer."

> To the Editor:
>
> In "Give the Smokeless Cigarette a Chance" (editorial, Sept. 10), you suggest that the Food and Drug Administration allow a new, high-tech nicotine delivery device that the R.J. Reynolds Tobacco Company is now test marketing to be sold to the American public without first examining it for health and safety purposes. While you tacitly concede that the F.D.A. is empowered by law to regulate this new drug vaporizer, which is called Premier, you suggest that the agency should ignore the law.
>
> You assert that Premier is "safer" than genuine cigarettes and should be sold without F.D.A. oversight. In this, you are dead wrong. No one knows if it is safer or perhaps more dangerous than cigarettes. The overriding concern is not whether Premier is safer, but who will make the judgment on its relative

---

[6]RJR's broad rhetorical strategy was to emphasize continuity; they described Premier as simply one more step in the technological evolution of the cigarette (FDA, 1988, pp. 6, 51 ff.), they recounted the similarities in manufacturing procedures ("its manufacturing process, the cigarette [Premier] starts out as a roll of tobacco wrapped in paper," (FDA, p. 3) and they highlighted the similarities in labelling and packaging (FDA, p. 36).

safety for the American consumer. All anyone knows is that Premier's manufacturer is describing the product—which includes a metal "flavoring capsule," a substantial amount of artificially added nicotine, carbon monoxide and numerous other lethal elements—as "cleaner."

Your conclusion that the product is "obviously" designed to appeal to "health-conscious smokers" is the conclusion the F.D.A. should draw. By using the word "cleaner," R.J. Reynolds makes a transparent attempt to cast a veil over the company's real intent, since the primary meanings of "clean" are "free from dirt or pollution" and "free from contamination or disease." And Premier is not only clean, says R.J. Reynolds, but it is even cleaner.

You conclude also that "Millions of addicts have quit, but the millions who can't deserve understanding and the chance to choose a less risky, more socially acceptable alternative." We agree. But if a product is laced with an addictive drug and hundreds of other chemicals, it must first be tested by an appropriate Government agency for safety and effectiveness and sold with specific guidelines for the drug's prescription and use. Why should the tobacco industry's invention be held to a lower standard than products like nicotine chewing gum, which is regulated by the F.D.A.? The consumer will be protected only if the F.D.A. exercises appropriate oversight.

Before another tobacco industry weapon appears on store shelves, the public is entitled to know more about it from an objective third party. F.D.A. regulation of Premier could save countless lives.

Scott D. Ballin
Washington, Oct. 11, 1988

The writer speaks for an antismoking coalition of the American Heart Association, American Cancer Society and American Lung Association. (Letter reprinted by permission of the author from *The New York Times*, October 27, 1988, p. A26)

In the well-written petition before the FDA and in letters to the editor, Premier was called a "nicotine delivery system." Throughout the campaign, ConSORH stressed the nature of the product as a "drug," thereby drawing on the intense negative associations with that term in the 1980's. For example, in the petition ConSORH noted that

Nicotine, when used by itself or as part of any product other than a traditional cigarette, is subject to the Food and Drug Administration's jurisdiction. Nicotine is recognized as a serious and potent drug with substantial pharmacologic effects on the body, including effects on the nervous system. Nicotine also is recognized as a major source of drug dependence (from the 1989 petition, p. 2).

ConSORH further argued that Reynolds's portrayal of the "intended use" of the product for "smoking pleasure" was a ruse. It suggested that instead Premier "is intended to satisfy smokers' nicotine dependence and to be used as a nicotine delivery system by smokers seeking to avoid or mitigate the health risks of smoking" (from the 1989 petition, p. 1). ConSORH also insisted that even though the advertising copy for the product did not include the term *safer*, it implied health benefits, and that in news conferences and other sources, Reynolds had portrayed the product as serving health imperatives. They pointed out that the courts had long accepted implied intent as sufficient, suggesting that the product, because it "has been portrayed implicitly, if not explicitly, as a mechanism for a smoker to avoid and/or mitigate the risk of those diseases caused by traditional tobacco products," fell under FDA jurisdiction to regulate products making health claims (from the 1989 petition, p. 1).

The ConSORH argument was a potent one because of its strong health claims, because of the prevalent "anti-drug" sentiment, and because cigarettes were "the only major consumer goods not regulated for health and safety by any responsible federal agency" (from the 1989 petition, p. 3). Reynolds' competing argument gained force from the history of nonregulation in a legal and regulatory structure based on precedent. It also had strength because the 1980s were the era of "deregulation," and the FDA was seeking to avoid the conflict over regulation of tobacco products.

Who won this rhetorical battle? The contest went undecided because the war between Reynolds and ConSORH was won on another front before the FDA ruled. The regulatory battle influenced the outcome of the consumer contest.

CONSUMERS AND CONSTRAINTS

Conventional marketing wisdom portrays consumers as having a set of more-or-less fixed "demands," which smart and able companies then attempt to fill. In fact, however, the "demands" that consumers have are often largely rhetorical constructions. Women as consumers "demand" high-heeled shoes not for any natural and necessary reason, but because they have been persuaded (by advertising, beauty magazines, and peers) that high-heels are attractive. Similarly, the desire of "macho-type" consumers to purchase a truck with a mock "roll bar" is rhetorically constructed. The ability of manufacturers to provide products that meet such "constructed demands" is, in part, limited by physical and economic factors—the availability of metals that can withstand certain kinds of stresses, or the price of certain materials. However, manufacturing is also frequently limited by rhetorical constraints. Sometimes, because of the particular configuration of material and rhetorical constraints, companies cannot manufacture and market a product that meets public demands. This is the situation in which R.J. Reynolds found itself in the attempt to market Premier.

There is no doubt that substantial demand persists for a "cigarette" that does not have the negative side effects of tobacco-smoking. Polls repeatedly show that a majority of cigarette smokers want to quit smoking for health reasons, but find themselves unable to do so. A "healthy cigarette" would solve their problems. A low-smoke cigarette would also solve the conflict between smokers and nonsmokers, and perhaps between parents who want to smoke and their concerns about the impact of tobacco smoke upon their children.

In spite of the theoretical desireability of such a "healthful cigarette" for a substantial group of consumers, in producing and marketing such a product, R.J. Reynolds faced several problems that eventually led to consumer rejection. As with all "substitute" products, Reynolds faced a certain amount of resistance to change. The Reynolds product was substantially different, and it would therefore have to be clearly better than old products in order to survive in the market place. Premier, however, could not successfully present itself as substantially better because of the rhetorical conditions it faced.

The first problem was that the primary marketing advantage of the new product rested in its appeal to the "health-conscious" smoker, but RJR was constrained from using advertising that directly mentioned health advantages. If it used the term *safer* or *better for your health*, it was walking right into the rhetorical trap laid by ConSORH, which argued that any product that made health claims was "regulatable" by the FDA. Hence, Reynolds could not attract the health-oriented consumers it wanted to target, without risking losing the regulatory battle. Although not successful at reaching its regulatory goals, ConSORH's regulatory rhetoric had successfully undermined the marketing of Reynolds's new product, by influencing the marketing strategies it used.

Second, Reynolds was also trapped by the need to emphasize the "cigaretteness" of its product. To avoid regulation, it had to call the product a "cigarette," and to downplay its differences from other cigarette-like products. However, there were significant differences. Perhaps the largest reason for rejection of Premier by consumers who tried it was that improper lighting of it made it taste bad (Morris & Waldmen, 1989). In order to ensure good taste, Premier needed to be lighted by a clean butane lighter, and it had to be thoroughly lighted. Consumers, assuming it was "just another cigarette," tended to light it with matches, and therefore to be dissatisfied with its taste. R.J. Reynolds could not strongly emphasize these differences in its advertising copy, for fear of undermining its regulatory claim that Premier was "just another cigarette." Again, the constraints established by the regulatory rhetoric led Reynolds into unsuccessful communication with potential consumers.

Additionally, Reynolds may have been strapped by the cross-currents between safety and good flavor. To avoid arousing consumer ire that would support the regulators, Reynolds had to announce the product with components it could claim were safe and that could be portrayed in a rhetorically attractive way—as two normal additives to food products. Although the company has not publically admitted this, the constraint may have led it to avoid more tasty, but more controversial, additives.

There were also, of course, material constraints, but even these were influenced by rhetorical factors. Premier was more expensive than previous cigarettes by 25% (Helyar, 1988). This price increase occurred at precisely the time when anti-smoking rhetoric had reduced the number and proportion of high-income smokers and had made increased taxes on tobacco products more rhetorically attractive. Anti-smoking arguments had scared off much of the high income audience, leaving only a low income target audience—consumers who were less capable of paying for the more expensive product, and thus were less inclined to try Premier. Additionally, the product was more difficult to use, entailing technical ad copy and a four-page instruction manual. This also was particularly problematic for a low-education target audience. As Alvin A. Chenbaum, a New York marketing consultant predicted, it was too complex for people to WANT to understand and he presciently suggested, "it's going to bomb. . . . It sounds like it's too mechanical" (Helyar, 1988, p. 1).

In the end, Reynolds swallowed hundreds of millions of dollars and withdrew Premier from the market. ConSORH, with a staff of four and an annual budget of less than $1 million (spread across 40 different initiatives), had won this rhetorical battle (budgetary figures provided by Scott Ballin, personal communication, 1989). ConSORH had made it impossible for RJR to use marketing rhetoric that might have effectively reached potential customers. ConSORH's had not been the only anti-smoking organization involved, and the battle was not decisive in winning the war—the tobacco industry would soon try again with a different product and a different approach. The incremental approach, however, allowed the anti-smoking coalition to limit the immediate expansion of a line of products it found new and threatening. Given the slowly declining market for conventional cigarettes, the incremental approach helped keep the tobacco industries on the path which ConSORH preferred—that of extinction.

CONCLUSIONS

Public interest groups like ConSORH face formidable obstacles in trying to use persuasion to limit the environmental, health, and other damage that is perhaps the inevitable by-product of private industries whose primary attention is fixed to the "bottom line." Industries usually have more money to

Rhetorical Balance Sheet
PREMIER PHASE

Exigence:
Passive smoking controversy

Tobacco Industry   ConSORH

Target Audience: Consumers   Regulatory agencies
Strategy: New product: FDA Regulation
          A "Cleaner Cigarette"   A "New Drug"
Constraints:
  (1) Can't call it "safer"   (1) Regulatory precedent
  (2) Must call it a cigarette, but (2) Premier's perceived health
      thereby confuse users about   benefits
      differences

Outcome:
Stalemate with FDA, but
regulatory constraints lead to
marketing disaster: Premier
bombs with consumers.

spend on waging public campaigns, lobbying Congress, petitioning agencies, and fighting court suits. In a "free market" system "free speech" is only effective if it is well-financed enough to have substantial presence. In addition, industry is often able to offer products attractive (if not addictive) to consumers, who provide another base of support. Industry is also capable of mobilizing a network of distributors and suppliers of raw products. Finally, public interest organizations tend to arise and act only after a substantial history of problems arouses substantial public opposition. In such cases, industry has time to establish precedents of law and public opinion in its favor.

These substantial advantages do not go completely uncountered. Because of their altruistic nature, public interest groups often carry more credibility than do self-interested industries. Additionally, public interest organizations tend to arise and gain public support only when there are real and substantial problems created by industry—hence they are usually supported by logic and the existence of substantial harms that carry significant argumentative impact. Consequently, if their rhetorical strategies are apt, public interest groups can sometimes succeed in countering industry initiatives.

As the battle over Premier shows, the strategy of incremental erosion, although it is a long term effort, can provide a particularly well-adapted approach to meet the constraints faced by public interest groups. Further, even when such regulatory initiatives are not fully successful, the threat of regulatory initiatives may limit the rhetorical options of industries dependent on successful marketing and so constrain their expansion.

REFERENCES

Almond, S. (1989, February 5). "Cleaner" cigarette controversy smolders. *El Paso Times, 28,* C1.

Baccardi, S. (1989, February 13). "Tobacco firm tries to kindle opposition here." *Democrat and Chronicle, 28,* D3.

Ballin, S.D. (1988, October 27). Let F.D.A. examine smokeless cigarette. *New York Times,* pp. A26.

Before the Federal Trade Commission: Opinion of the commission, (1988). U.S. Docket No. 9206.

Bitzer, L.F. (1968). The rhetorical situation. *Philosophy and Rhetoric,* 165–168.

Cooper, R.M. (1988, July 29). *Testimony presented Before the Subcommittee on Health and the Environment, Committee on Energy and Commerce,* Washington, DC.

FDA. (1988). *Comments of the R.J. Reynolds Tobacco Company* (FDA Docket NOs. 88P-0155/CP and 88P-0155/CP0002). Washington, DC: FDA.

Give the smokeless cigarette a chance. (1988, September 10). *New York Times,* p. 26.

Helyar, J. (1988, August 30). RJR plans to market smokeless cigarette as breakthrough with hefty price tag. *Wall Street Journal,* Section 2, p. 1.

Morris, B.A. (1984). *The unconscious conspiracy: Reagonomics and the rhetorical emergence of the corporate citizen.* Unpublished doctoral dissertation. Indiana University, Bloomington, IN.

Morris, B., & Waldman, P. (1989, March 10). The death of Premier. *Wall Street Journal,* p. B1.

R.J. Reynolds Co. (1988a). *Chemical and biological studies on new cigarette prototypes that heat instead of burn tobacco.* Winston-Salem, NC: Author.

R.J. Reynolds (1988b, October 7). Special Report to Consumers: No 3 (Advertisement). *Arizona Republic,* p. B8.

Ruberry, W. (1989, February 19). Taxes, ads, regulation: New attacks on tobacco may be fiercest yet. *Richmond Times-Dispatch,* pp. C14–D2.

Schiffman, J.R. (1989, March 22). R.J. Reynolds to reduce cigarette staff by about 10%. *The Wall Street Journal,* p. A4.

Schmertz, H. (with Novak, W.). (1986). *Good-bye to the low profile: The art of creative confrontation.* Boston: Little, Brown.

Subcommittee on Health and the Environment, Committee on Energy and Commerce. (1988, July 29). Washington, DC.

Surgeon General. (1989, January 11). *Twenty-five years of progress: Reducing the health consequences of smoking.* Rockville, MD: U.S. Department of Health and Human Services, et al., prepublication version.

Wilson, D.J. (1989, June 1). Quarter century after first report non-smokers still battle industry. *Houston Post, 28,* D1–14.

Young, F.E. (1988, July 29). *The Commissioner, Food and Drug Administration, before the Subcommittee on Health and the Environment, Committee on Energy and Commerce.* Washington, DC: U.S. House of Representatives (release).

White Knights, Poker Games, and the Invasion of the Carpetbaggers: Interpreting the Sale of a Professional Sports Franchise

NICK TRUJILLO

California State University, Sacramento

In recent years, "interpretive" approaches to the study of human behavior have attracted widespread attention from organizational researchers (see Burrell & Morgan, 1979; Frost, Moore, Louis, Lundberg, & Martin, 1985; Jones, Moore, & Snyder, 1988; Louis, 1980; Morgan & Smircich, 1980; Pfeffer, 1981). Scholars in public relations and organizational communication have turned to interpretive approaches with particular interest because these approaches treat communication not merely as a tool for information exchange or media relations but rather as the central process through which the reality of the organization itself is created and managed by internal and external audiences (see Carbaugh, 1988; Cheney, 1983; Conrad & Ryan, 1985; Crable & Vibbert, 1983; Goodall, 1989; Kendall, 1985; Mickey, 1983; Putnam & Pacanowsky, 1983; Trujillo & Toth, 1987). The purpose of this chapter is to illustrate how interpretive approaches can help the research and practice of public relations and the mass media in contemporary American society.

Specifically, this chapter uses an interpretive approach to study how the sale of a company—perhaps the most important event in the life of an organization—is mediated by the press and experienced by members of the organization and public alike. The chapter examines the mediated sale of an unusual—and perhaps the most "public"—type of organization: the professional sports franchise. In particular, it considers the sale of the Texas Rangers Baseball Team, a franchise that was purchased in 1989 by a large group of investors led by George W. Bush (the son of President Bush) after a lengthy and well-publicized process involving several potential owners. However, although this analysis focuses on the case of a professional sports franchise, the ultimate lessons from the case should help us understand how the sale of any company is socially constructed by members of the organization and the mass media.

The chapter begins with a brief overview of some of the defining characteristics of interpretive approaches and their implications for public relations researchers. Second, the chapter notes the relationships between sports organizations and media organizations in American society and points out how this relationship provides an important context for interpreting the sale of a sports franchise. Third, the recent sale of the Texas Rangers Baseball Team is examined in terms of the "facts" of the case and then, more importantly, in terms of the mass-mediated "stories" that reveal how the actions of organization owners and managers are reported and interpreted by members of the mass media. The chapter concludes by suggesting some implications of this study for research in public relations.

CHARACTERISTICS OF INTERPRETIVE APPROACHES

As developed by Burrell and Morgan (1979), the "interpretive" paradigm is an overarching perspective that, in contrast to a "functionalist" paradigm, adopts a more *subjective* than objective view of organizational reality and focuses more attention on the *symbolic* rather than instrumental aspects of organizational life. Although functionalist research studies how instrumentally real entities—such as hierarchies, technologies, and press releases—impact organizational publics, interpretive researchers examine how various publics interpret organizational phenomena as real. With respect to public relations, a functionalist approach emphasizes how organizational reality "determines" public relations whereas an interpretive approach emphasizes how public relations "creates" organizational reality.

Of course, the interpretive and functionalist paradigms are umbrella perspectives that cover a variety of academic traditions, and each tradition adopts an orientation toward organizational reality that can be placed at a position on an objectivist–subjectivist continuum (see Morgan & Smircich, 1980). At the objectivist extreme are behaviorism and social learning theories that view organizational reality as "an externally real concrete structure" and which treat organizational publics as "responding mechanisms" who "respond to events in predictable and determinate ways" (Morgan & Smircich, 1980, p. 495). At the subjectivist extreme are phenomenological traditions that view organizational reality as a "product of human imagination" and that treat publics as "transcendental beings" who "shape the world within the realm of their own immediate experience" (Morgan & Smircich,

1980, p. 494). As Morgan and Smircich concluded, most researchers place themselves between these polar extremes in the actual production of their research:

> The transition from one perspective to another must be seen as a gradual one, and it is often the case that the advocates of any given position may attempt to incorporate insights from others. Consequently, the success of efforts to determine who advocates what may be limited to determining the relative emphasis an advocate gives to one or more adjacent positions. (pp. 492–493)

Advocates of interpretive approaches tend to emphasize at least five characteristics, and each one has implications for public relations and organizational communication. (For an extended discussion of these characteristics, see Trujillo, 1987.) First, interpretive researchers emphasize the *subjectivity* of organizational realities and deemphasize their objectivity. These researchers do not focus on how organizational phenomena like hierarchies, technologies, and press releases impact the behavior of publics but rather focus on how publics interpret these organizational phenomena. Thus, interpretive approaches emphasize the *meanings* of organizational phenomena to various publics.

Second, interpretive researchers emphasize the *dynamism* of organizational realities and deemphasize their stability. As Morgan (1980) (perhaps over) stated:

> the interpretive paradigm directly challenges the preoccupation with certainty that characterizes the functionalist perspective, showing that order in the social world, however real in surface appearance, rests in precarious, socially constructed webs of symbolic relationships that are continuously negotiated, renegotiated, affirmed, or changed. (p. 9)

In other words, interpretive approaches invite us to take seriously the idea that organizational phenomena are constantly (if subtly) in flux, because publics ongoingly engage in actions that shape and reshape their view of the organization.

Third, interpretive researchers emphasize the *relativity* of organizational realities and deemphasize their causality. Indeed, interpretive approaches invite researchers to develop more detailed understandings of particular organizational *contexts*. As Putnam (1983) summarized, interpretive approaches "aim to understand social phenomena by extracting the unique dimensions of situations rather than by deducing generalizable laws that govern social behaviors" (pp. 40–41).

Fourth, interpretive researchers emphasize the *voluntarism* of organizational realities and deemphasize their determinism. Researchers who adopt more deterministic positions assert that the external environment determines organizational behavior. Interpretive researchers, in contrast, assume that organizational publics are active choice-making individuals who do not react to behavioral laws but who conform to organizational rules and social conventions. In so assuming, interpretive researchers understand any given organizational action in the context of the wider range of alternative actions available to organizational members and publics.

Finally, interpretive researchers emphasize the *pluralism* of organizational realities and deemphasize their unity.[1] Although interpretive extremists argue that organizations have as many realities as individuals, most adopt a qualified position that organizations are collections of different individuals, groups, and constituencies who have different (and often competing) interests. Interpretive approaches invite researchers to uncover the multiple (and often conflicting) organizational realities interpreted by various publics.

These five characteristics of interpretive approaches have implications for public relations and organizational communication research in general as well as for this study of the mediated sale of an American company. First, although the sale of a company such as the Texas Rangers "exists" in its objective formalization in legal contracts and balance sheets, an interpretive study focuses on the subjective understanding of the sale by members of the organization, the press, and the public. Second, an interpretive approach invites one to study the company sale as an ongoing negotiation—even after the presumedly terminal contractual consumation—because that sale is ongoingly interpreted and reinterpreted by organizational publics. Third, an interpretive approach to the company sale should include an examination of the broader relational, situational, and historical contexts which influence the meanings of the sale to various publics. Fourth, an interpretive study of a company's sale should examine the alternative actions that could have been adopted by organizational insiders and outsiders. Finally, an interpretive approach invites researchers to uncover the multiple (and often conflicting) interpretations of the company sale by members of the organization, the press, and the public.

The next section of this chapter considers how the relationship between sport organizations and media organizations provides an important context for interpreting the sale of any sports franchise in American society. The chapter then focuses on the particular case of the sale of the Texas Rangers

---

[1]Those more critically inclined emphasize *polysemy* not pluralism. As Stuart Hall (1980) cautioned: "Polysemy must not, however, be confused with pluralism. . . . Any society/culture tends, with varying degrees of closure, to impose its classifications of the social and political world" (p. 135).

Baseball Team, first uncovering the "facts" of the sale and then examining the "stories" of the sale presented in the mass media.

PROFESSIONAL SPORTS, PUBLIC RELATIONS, AND THE MASS MEDIA

The relationship between professional sports, public relations, and the mass media in American society has been subject to much discussion in recent years. On the one hand, many have argued that the relationship is a cooperative and dependent—even symbiotic—one in which sports organizations and media organizations have offered mutual support and have experienced complementary growth. Indeed, professional sports organizations have enjoyed significant growth in fan bases and bottom lines due, in large part, to the mass media. As Reiss (1980) summarized about the early prominence of baseball in American culture:

> Crucial was the ideology developed by cooperative sports writers which made the sport appear directly relevant to the needs and aspirations of middle America. The national pastime was portrayed in such a way that it supplied some of the symbols, myths, and legends needed to bind its members together. (p. 5)

Similarly, the mass media have enjoyed their own successes due, in large part, to professional sports. Indeed, for better and for worse, many readers still subscribe to our daily newspapers in order to read the morning sports section. So, too, sports programming remains a vital key to the market positioning of the big three (not quite four), cable, and local networks. In short, the marriage between professional sports and the mass media has produced substantial dowries for both parties.

On the other hand, some have suggested that this marriage between professional sports and the mass media has become a rocky if somewhat battered one in recent years. Klatell and Marcus (1988), for example, described the "love/hate" relationship among sports organizations, media organizations, and advertisers as one "in which mutual back-scratching occasionally draws blood" (p. 26). Although separation or divorce is not imminent—there is too much money involved—the conflicts between the parties have become more pronounced. To take one example, contemporary sports reporters have adopted more investigative journalistic stances in their stories on drug abuses, salary disputes, gambling allegations, and the general corruptions in sport, unlike the uncritical (although possibly better written) offerings of their sportswriting ancestors. Thus, as Telander (1984) summarized in his examination of player–press relations, "the relationship between sportswriters and the people they write about has never been worse than it is today" (p. 3).

However one interprets the relationship between sports and the mass media, it should be remembered that media coverage of sports is dominated by the same ethics and constraints as media coverage of other events and organizations in society. Like other news stories, for example, sports stories are productions of media organizations and, thus, are subject to the same budget and profit concerns, publication deadlines, distribution structures, market competitors, and emphases on conflict-oriented stories. The bottom line is circulation and readership and sportswriters have the same incentives to scoop their competitors and to print sensationalized stories that sustain that circulation and readership.

The Public Nature of Professional Sports Organizations

Although professional sports franchises are privately owned corporations, they are perhaps the most "public" companies in America. First, a sports franchise is perceived by the public not as another bank or manufacturing firm in the area but as a community institution that engenders a powerful sense of identification, a perception recognized by franchise owners and managers. As the Rangers' managing partner, George W. Bush, put it: "Baseball is a public sport. . . . In politics, you have to care about your voters; in baseball, you have to care about your fans. Fans have to know that you do care about what they think" (Bush, personal communication, September 1989). Indeed, residents consider the team to be "their" team, even though it is usually owned by wealthy capitalists who sometimes exercise rigid and unpopular control (e.g., George Steinbrenner). As one sport sociologist put it, "team loyalties developed over the course of many years provide spectators with a sense of roots, of stability often missing in industrial America" (Duncan, 1983, p. 32). Consequently, representatives of sports organizations regularly pay homage to their publics—their "fans"—in their communication with various (especially external) audiences. Needless to say, the sale of a local franchise, especially to "outsiders," can stimulate much talk from and tension in these fans.

Second, a sports franchise is also "public" in the sense that it has a higher mediated profile than most other companies in America. The franchise is featured *daily* in local (and sometimes national) newspapers and on local (and sometimes national) news broadcasts. Indeed, although a newspaper's business desk will use various reporters to cover various business events and will only assign particular reporters to cover particular companies for relatively short periods of time (e.g., Exxon during its Alaskan crisis), the newspaper's sports desk will give one or two reporters the *sole* assignment to cover the local franchise. For example, the Dallas–Fort Worth area has three major dailies, each of which has one or two reporters whose *only* beat is the Texas Rangers. The Ranger's director of media relations explained the difference between public relations in sports and industry:

> Sports public relations is so entirely different than industry public relations. A lot of industry public relations involves creating an audience and selling a story. Our audience is already here. If we make a trade or have a game, many reporters are going to write about it whether we send a press release or not. (personal communication, November 1987)[2]

Consequently, the media relations tasks of a sports franchise include producing mass quantities of (often statistical) information for media guides and press releases and providing regular access for sports reporters.

This "public" nature of professional sports organizations has implications for how a proposed sale of the franchise is discussed by members of the organization, covered by reporters, and interpreted by fans. Not surprisingly, the sale automatically is defined as news because of the visible nature of the franchise in the city and because of the reportorial resources already invested in covering the franchise. Accordingly, franchise representatives will, if possible, take great care in stressing how a change in ownership will not hurt the fans. Reporters, on the other hand, will explore (and exploit) an element of drama to create conflict-oriented "war stories," even though the sale of a sports franchise is fundamentally a *business* story that involves a negotiated (and ultimately consensual) agreement between two or more parties. In the case of a proposed sale to outside interests, conflict-oriented reporters will also use the threat to community as a central element of their stories. Such was the case with the mediated sale of the Texas Rangers Baseball Team.

The next section of the chapter reviews the *facts* of the recent sale of the Texas Rangers, beginning with the proposed agreements between owner Eddie Chiles and a group of Florida businessmen and between Chiles and minority owner and media magnate Edward Gaylord, and ending with the approved sale to a large group of businessmen led by Bush. The following section then examines how these facts were used by reporters in their *stories* about the sale.

---

[2]One powerful example of the public nature of sports franchises occurred when the struggling Rangers hired new general manager Tom Grieve in 1984. Grieve brought his own secretary from his former office with him and fired the secretary of the former GM. Stories in the sports pages reported the firing and described it as "another example of Ranger mismanagement."

THE SALE OF THE TEXAS RANGERS—THE FACTS

Here are the "facts" of the Ranger sale, as first reported by the *Dallas Morning News*, as subsequently released by the Rangers' Media Relations Department, and as covered by the media for a period of time starting in July 1988 and ending in March 1989.

The *Dallas Morning News* Breaks the Story

On Tuesday, July 26, 1988, a sportswriter for the *Dallas Morning News* reported an "exclusive" story, titled "Tampa Buyers Talking to Rangers," which stated that Ranger owner Eddie Chiles had begun " 'serious' discussions about the purchase of the Texas Rangers." The story reported that anonymous "sources close to major league ownership" revealed that Frank Morsani, a Tampa, Florida auto dealer, and Bill Mack, a New Jersey construction magnate, were trying to complete a deal with Chiles. The *News* also reported that Morsani and Mack were members of two organizations—the "MXM Corporation" and the "Tampa Bay Business Group"—both founded with the sole purpose of bringing major league baseball to Tampa, Florida.

That same night, the sports anchor for the Dallas CBS affiliate Channel 4, mocked the *Morning News* story with the lead, "What's the news here?" After all, the *News* and the other two Dallas–Fort Worth dailies prematurely had reported a pending sale of the Dallas Cowboys football team for several weeks with no sale forthcoming—at least not until the following February 1989 when Arkansas millionaire Jerry Jones took the Cowboys' reins, figuratively and literally—and Ranger owner Eddie Chiles had been trying unsuccessfully to sell the Rangers for several years. In fact, Chiles had tried unsuccessfully to sell his majority interest in the team in 1986 to media magnate Edward Gaylord, then one of the few minority owners, but that sale was rejected by major league owners who complained about Gaylord's ownership of a local independent television station that had the capacity to become another so-called "superstation" similar to WTBS and WGN which broadcast Atlanta Braves and Chicago Cubs games, respectively. Despite the sports news anchor's misguided sarcasm, stations and newspapers in the Dallas–Fort Worth and Tampa–St. Petersburg markets picked up the story about a possible sale and reporters scurried to find leads.

Over the next few days and weeks, the *Dallas Morning News* (DMN), the *Dallas Times Herald* (DTH), and the *Fort Worth Star-Telegram* (FWST) reported the hot (non)story in articles and columns with headlines such as "Chiles: Sale Not Close" (DMN, 7/27/88), "Players Unfazed by Stories of Sale" (DMN, 7/27/88), "Bases Full and Chiles is Up to Bat" (FWST, 7/31/88), and "Chiles Needs Relief From Ownership" (DMN, 7/28/88). Although the agreement to sell the team would not be reached for another month, papers speculated on whether the Rangers would be moving to Tampa, Florida, to a new stadium in their current Arlington, Texas home, or to nearby Dallas. Headlines included such provocative leads as "With Rangers Shopping, Who Will Act?" (DMN, 7/31/88), "Chiles: Arlington Not in Rangers' Future" (DTH, 7/27/88), "Most Rangers Prefer Playing in Heat to Dome" (DTH, 8/26/88), "Tarrant's Team Ain't Leaving" (FWST, 7/28/88), and "Rangers to Go? Good Riddance" (FWST, 7/28/88). Papers also speculated on whether Edward Gaylord would exercise his right of first refusal as minority owner and buy the team, preventing a sale to the Tampa, Florida group.

The Rangers Announce "Agreement in Principle" with Mack and Morsani

A Texas Rangers' news release, dated 6 p.m. (CDT), Friday, August 26, 1988, announced the following: "H.E. Chiles, Chairman of the Board and Chief Executive Officer of the Texas Rangers, announced today that he has signed an 'agreement in principle' to sell the majority interest in the partnership that owns that American League club to the New York-New Jersey based Mack Family and Frank L. Morsani of Tampa, Florida." The release also stated the following regarding Edward Gaylord: "The Gaylord Broadcasting Company, under terms of its contract signed when the Dallas-based broadcasting company purchased one third of the Texas Rangers' stock in February 1985, has the right of first refusal in any agreement of the purchase of the ballclub. Per that agreement, Gaylord Broadcasting has 30 days to match the purchase price of the agreement, to agree to sell its share of the Rangers, or to remain in its current position as minority owner."

Bold headlines announced the sale in the next day's newspapers with "Chiles Agrees to Sell Rangers" (DMN, 8/27/88) and "Chiles OKs Offer for Rangers" (DTH, 8/27/88). The papers reported that Mack and Morsani agreed to purchase Chiles' 53% share of the franchise for $46.4 million, putting an $80 million price tag on the team, Arlington Stadium, and the 119 acres surrounding the stadium. One report, headlined "Chiles' Losses Forced Team to the Block" (DMN, 7/27/88), explained that the sale was due to the estimated $600 million that Chiles' Western Company, an oil field service and drilling company he founded in 1939, had lost in recent hard times. Whatever the case, the Rangers had been sold, pending Gaylord's decision and the approval of the American League owners.

In the next few days and weeks, reporters speculated on two major items related to the sale agreement. First, despite well-publicized front-page assurances by then-Commissioner Peter Ueberroth that "the Texas Rangers are going to stay in Texas" (DMN, 8/30/88), reporters questioned whether the

Tampa businessmen would try to move the Rangers to Florida because Mack and Morsani would not agree to a no-move provision in the agreement. Second, and more importantly, papers speculated about whether Gaylord actually would exercise his right of first refusal and whether he actually would be approved by league owners this time. As one sports columnist asserted bluntly, "Rangers will be gone without Gaylord's gift" (FWST, 8/28/88).

Gaylord Exercises His Right of First Refusal

In a statement issued from his office on September 14, 1988, in Oklahoma City, Edward Gaylord announced that he indeed would exercise his right of first refusal and take a second chance on becoming the majority owner of the Texas Rangers. The next day, *The Daily Oklahoman*, Gaylord's paper, reported that a large factor in Gaylord's decision was his desire to keep the team in Texas. Chiles also was quoted in that report confirming Gaylord's interest in keeping the team local: "Mr. Gaylord has an interest in the [DFW] Metroplex. He's part of the Metroplex, really. It's a home-owned team. I think it's a nice lucky thing."

Unfortunately, league owners would not meet to vote on Gaylord's fate until February 1989, almost 6 months after Gaylord made the agreement in principle with Eddie Chiles. Not surprisingly, however, those 6 months were punctuated in the newspapers with speculations about the merits of Gaylord as majority owner and about the likelihood of his approval, either by a majority vote from league owners or by a unilateral decision by the outgoing Ueberroth with his czar-like authority to do anything that is in "the best interest of baseball."

Virtually all of the published speculation suggested that Gaylord would be approved as owner. Indeed, even before the agreement in principle was announced, one sports columnist asserted that "after checking around the league, there seems every reason to believe the Rangers are close to being sold to Edward Gaylord and that approval will be a mere formality" (DMN, 8/11/88). One month later, another columnist made a qualified prediction that "my best guess is that Commissioner Peter Ueberroth will engineer a narrow approval," even though he suggested that "baseball owners fear Gaylord's financial clout" more than his superstation potential. As the impending decision was to be announced, one beat writer, substituting for a vacationing columnist, boldly stated, "Consider this source: Gaylord will get Rangers" (DTH, 2/11/89).

On March 8, 1989, the American League owners, following the recommendation by the ownership committee, officially rejected Edward Gaylord's bid to become majority owner of the Texas Rangers. Published reports revealed that Gaylord's bid was rejected again because his potential superstation coverage of Ranger games might hurt the local broadcast rights of A.L. teams. Although Ueberroth supported Gaylord's bid, the outgoing commissioner did not exercise his "best interests of baseball" powers; instead, he supported another ownership group.

Chiles Announces Final Sale of the Texas Rangers

In the next few days and weeks, papers reported various possible groups that might purchase the Rangers. The most likely group of buyers was one led by Texas businessmen Bush and Edward "Rusty" Rose. This group was supported by Ueberroth, who had adopted as his personal mission the approved sale of the Rangers before his tenure as commissioner would end in April 1989.

Finally, in a 4:30 p.m. (CST), Saturday, March 18, 1989, news release, the Texas Rangers announced the long-awaited outcome: "Texas Rangers owner Eddie Chiles announced today he has signed an agreement to sell his controlling interest in the baseball team to a Dallas/Fort Worth investor group led by George W. Bush and Edward W. (Rusty) Rose." The release stressed the local ties of the investor group, quoting Bush: "Bush said his group's purchase of Chiles' interest of the club means 'the Rangers will be owned by Texans— serious, baseball-minded individuals with deep Texas roots, individuals committed to putting a team on the field that will make the Dallas-Fort Worth area proud and the rest of the American League sit up and take notice.' "

Although the release predictably stated that "terms of the sale were not announced," the Sunday papers predictably speculated on the details: "A source close to the negotiation's said the deal was for $25 million in cash, payment of a $9 million note owed to Mr. Chiles by the organization, $12.5 million in Arlington Stadium debt and two-thirds of the Rangers' $750,000 line of credit. The new owners also would assume approximately $25 million in long-term debt" (DMN, 3/19/89). More importantly—at least to most readers—the Sunday papers also featured the local ties (and local commitment) of the new owners, quoting Bush: "So long as Rusty and I are managing general partners of the Rangers, the team is not to move from the metroplex, period" (DMN, 3/19/89).

One month after this agreement was announced, league owners unanimously approved the sale of the Rangers. Headlines read "Bush approved without a nay vote" and the lead paragraph in one report put it this way: "Yesterday marked a milestone for the Bush family. 'I finally won an election on my own,' George W. Bush said. 'And it's the first time the Bush family ever won an election by a unanimous vote.' " (FWST, 4/19/89). Thus, the long process to sell the Texas Rangers had reached fruition, at least until the Bush–Rose et al. group decides to sell.

These, then, are the "facts" of the sale of the Texas Rangers Baseball Team. Let us now consider the "stories."

THE SALE OF THE TEXAS RANGERS—THE STORIES

The actual facts of the sale of any company—even a major league baseball team—are not particularly newsworthy to most readers. The economic and legal details of the Ranger sale, for example, were of interest only to the accountants and lawyers who engineered the ledgers and legalities of the contractual agreements. So, too, the agreements between Chiles and the various parties were settled over a period of several weeks and the ultimate rejection of Gaylord and acceptance of Bush–Rose et al. by major league owners took several months. Finally, any possible move of the Rangers to a new stadium (or a new city) would take several years, as estimated by Ranger, government, and league officials. However, these considerations do not make for "good copy," especially in a media market with three major dailies and three major local newscasts. Accordingly, the media transformed these not-so-newsworthy facts into dramatic headlined stories.

This section of the chapter examines how the facts of the Ranger sale were packaged into dramatic conflict-oriented stories. In particular, the chapter focuses on the metaphors used by reporters and columnists in these stories to frame the sale of the Rangers to readers. Metaphors, of course, are language forms that cast one concept (e.g., "world") in terms of another (e.g., "stage"), as in the familiar dramatistic axiom "All the world's a stage." Organizational researchers have argued that metaphors "lead us to see and understand organizations in distinctive yet partial ways" (Morgan, 1986, p. 12) insofar as they reflect, shape, and ultimately create our organizational realities (see Hirsch & Andrews, 1983; Koch & Deetz, 1981; Weick, 1979). Accordingly, mass-mediated metaphors reveal how reporters interpret the realities of the organizations they cover and how readers experience the realities of the organizations they read about.

Invasion of the Carpetbaggers (and Stadium Wars)

The dominant interpretive frame used by the media to characterize the early phase of the Ranger sale was the most conflict-oriented metaphor possible— *war*!! Morsani and Mack and their MXM Corporation—the organization created by the two Florida businessmen to bring major league baseball to Tampa—were cast by the Dallas–Fort Worth media as an "enemy army" whose "secret mission" was to "invade" Texas and take "our" team (DMN, 7/28/88). One columnist issued an open call "for a few good men" to "stand guard at Arlington Stadium" and he suggested that one lookout be posted on the roof of the nearby Sheraton Hotel with a lantern: "One if by land. Two if by sea. Three if by Lear jet" (FWST, 7/27/88). Indeed, the true spirit of Texas lore (a la the Alamo) was invoked in these and other military images to present the proposed sale of the Rangers to these outsiders as a threat to community. As the (melo)dramatic columnist from the Star-Telegram concluded: "We're not giving up on our team without a fight, Mr. C. [Chiles]. Not by a long shot" (FWST, 7/27/88).

A few months later, this same columnist directly enlisted community members into the battle when he wrote: "We can't sit back and do nothing while a fast-talking car salesman steals our baseball team. We have to act." And just what did this sports columnist have in mind? "If you care about the Rangers, say so. Pick up a pencil and a piece of paper and write, 'We want to keep the Rangers in Texas.' . . . We'll forward it to Ueberroth and ask that he make note of our concern to the other owners. Let's bury him in mail"(FWST, 9/3/88).

Two weeks later, the columnist reveled publicly in columns for two consecutive days about the response: ". . . There were 1,275 of you out there, give or take a dozen or so, who were willing to step forward and fight for your Rangers. Two cardboard boxes full of your cards and letters. . . . From 45 different North Texas communities [he listed them all], you wrote of your love for the Texas Rangers, those woebegone losers who have brought us so much disappointment over the years" (FWST, 9/16/88). He noted that there were responses "from all age groups and all walks of life" including "many senior citizens," "many businesses," "artists, police officers, restaurant owners, investment bankers, ministers, and even a manager's wife (thanks, Mary Valentine)" (FWST, 9/16/88). "My favorite," he disclosed, "came from little Kellyn Clark, who sent photos of herself in her seat at Arlington Stadium and with pitcher Bobby Witt. On the back of one photo, Kellyn, who looks to be only 4 or 5, writes, 'Don't take my Rangers away!' " (FWST, 9/15/88).

Not surprisingly, Morsani and Mack were depicted in villainous terms as the enemy. They were "hit men" (DMN, 7/29/88), "Florida sharks" (DMN, 9/15/88), and "carpetbaggers" (FWST, 7/27/88). Morsani, who appeared at an hour-long press conference at Arlington Stadium to meet with some question-slinging reporters, was characterized as a "billion-dollar power hitter who swings a crooked bat" (DTH, 8/31/88), as one who "speaks with forked tongue" (FWST, 8/31/88), and as a "vampire" who would make "garlic necklaces . . . the next hot item at Arlington Stadium concession stands" (FWST, 8/31/88).

This evil characterization of Morsani was, in most respects, unfair. After all, he called a press conference to meet with enraged Texas reporters, most of whom focused on Morsani's assumed intent to move the Rangers to Tampa, a move that he courageously did not confirm or deny. One Fort

Worth writer, noting that Morsani's "only sin is not being Texan," commended Morsani for his honesty, quoting his response to a question about why he did not agree to a no-move clause in the agreement: "I wouldn't give anybody that guarantee. If we had gone in with snake oil, we could have postured ourselves differently. But we didn't want to do that" (FWST, 8/31/88). Another writer at least gave Morsani "credit for being honest enough not to come to town blowing smoke at us" (DTH, 8/31/88). Nevertheless, Morsani ultimately was portrayed as the villain who posed a serious threat to the Texas community.

Eddie Chiles did not fare particularly well in the media either. He was characterized as a "traitor" who "sold us out to a bunch of bandits from the east" (FWST, 8/28/88) and who "sold out fans along with Rangers" (DMN, 8/27/88). Chiles himself invited the additional wrath of sportswriters when he later confessed that he had made a "mistake," that he was "sorry" he sold to "them," and that he would "feel better and sleep better" if Gaylord exercised his right of first refusal to keep the team in the Metroplex (DTH, 9/8/88). Sportswriters countered that he should not have sold to "them" in the first place but that he "listened to his heartless accountant instead of his heart" (DMN, 9/8/88). Thus, sportswriters also cast Chiles as a villain—although not as evil a villain as Morsani—despite the fact that Chiles rescued the Rangers years before and that his Western Company had declared Chapter 11 bankruptcy in 1986, prompting the then 78-year-old businessman to get his finances settled so he could retire gracefully.

Finally, when Edward Gaylord came forth and agreed to buy the team, he was lauded by some as a patriotic hero who had rescued the team. He was cast as a "white knight" (DMN, 9/15/88) and the "Rangers' Sooner savior" (FWST, 9/15/88). "John Wayne never did it better," wrote one Fort Worth columnist in a story titled "It's Gaylord to the Rescue," adding: "Oklahoma sharpshooter Edward L. Gaylord, guns blazing, shot Tampa Bay's would-be bandits out of the saddle yesterday. . . . Bull's-eye. Right between the eyes. Now Frank Morsani and Bill Mack can slither back under the rocks they came from while our baseball team stays where it belongs" (FWST, 9/15/88). Another columnist speculated that Gaylord—"the rather mysterious little billionaire from Oklahoma City"—would turn the Rangers into a "first-class, do-it-right, civic treasure of a pennant winner" (DTH, 9/15/88). Of course, as another columnist pointed out, "today's White Knight might be tomorrow's Darth Vader" (FWST, 9/15/88), offering a fitting (if unintentional) historical irony to the situation—after all, Eddie Chiles had been portrayed by sportswriters in a similarly heroic manner when he purchased the team from former owner Brad Corbett.

Stadium Wars.   The Texas media deployed a second arsenal of military metaphors in stories and speculations about a possible stadium move—not the unlikely move to Florida but the more probable move from their current home in Arlington to Dallas, a move of about 20-30 miles, depending on the potential location of a new stadium. One of the well-publicized problems with Arlington Stadium is that it was built as a minor league ballpark with too many low-priced outfield seats, a situation that will create serious economic problems for the team in the early 1990s as the salaries of the young Ranger players escalate. Not surprisingly, then, one agenda item during the various negotiations for the sale of the Rangers was the possibility of a new stadium. And, not surprisingly, speculations from Ranger officials, city council members, and sportswriters about where such a new stadium might be placed filled the papers.

"Stadium wars rage for teams," one headline put it (FWST, 9/8/88) after Dallas officials speculated publicly about where, not when, a new Dallas stadium for the Rangers would be located. Arlington mayor Richard Greene countered that the move of the Rangers from Arlington "would be like if the whole French Quarter burned down in New Orleans" (FWST, 9/15/88) and he argued that "Arlington is fighting against the power, the wealth, and the influence of Dallas, which includes the most powerful force in our society, which is the press" (*Arlington City Journal*, 9/11/88). One editorial announced a "call to arms" to "resist Dallas' bid for Rangers" (FWST, 9/9/88); the editor of the editorial page called Dallas' bid a "misguided power-grab for Rangers by the soulless city to the east" (FWST, 9/11/88).[3] Although one Dallas paper editorial softened that "baseball shouldn't disrupt regional cooperation" (DMN, 9/24/88), the stadium wars raged on until October 1990, when Ranger officials announced plans to build a new stadium adjacent to the current location of Arlington Stadium.

In summary, sportswriters used military imagery to characterize the impending sale of the Rangers to Tampa businessmen as a foreign invasion that endangered community and to depict Gaylord's response as a patriotic and heroic act that saved community. On the other hand, the use of military imagery to characterize the so-called "stadium wars" was used by the media to reveal a disrupted and fragmented community. The implications of this difference are discussed in the conclusion of this chapter.

Poker Games, Trump Cards, and Games of Money and Power

The second dominant interpretation of the Ranger sale was revealed in the use of the game metaphor. There were, of course, cliché-ridden uses of

---

[3]The battle between Dallas and Tarrant counties—the latter including Fort Worth and Arlington—was brought to outrageous fruition when one Fort Worth wrestling columnist named Betty Ann Stout challenged a Dallas sports columnist (Skip Bayless) to a mud-wrestling or column-writing match. Regrettably, they opted for the column-writing match.

baseball vernacular—as in "Bases Full and Chiles Up to Bat" (FWST, 7/31/88) and "Mayor Pitching Hard to Keep Team" (*Arlington City Journal*, 9/4/88). However, the game metaphor that revealed a deeper interpretation of the Ranger sale was a high stakes financial one, often cast as a poker game but described simply as a "game of power" by one columnist.

One sportswriter revealed the power of the poker game as an explanatory metaphor for the sale in his column titled, "Who's Holding Which Cards on Rangers?" (DTH, 8/27/88). This writer suggested that Chiles' agreement to sell the Rangers to Morsani and Mack was simply the "first hand in a high stakes game" and that "Gaylord must call or fold within the next 30 days." But as he summarized: "We can't see who's holding what. We don't know who's bluffing or if there's a joker in the deck. We don't know if Chiles, who has dealt and dropped out, can read the cards face down."

A few days later, the same writer embellished his high stakes poker imagery as he critiqued the idea that Gaylord was a white knight:

> I'm reluctant to measure Gaylord for white armor until someone explains why Chiles didn't sell directly to Gaylord. . . . My case is purely circumstantial. But it goes like so. . . . Chiles tried to high-ball Gaylord. Gaylord tried to low-ball Chiles. . . . Gaylord might have told him, this is my price. That's it until you show me someone willing to go higher. Chiles said OK, and found a way to call the bluff. . . . My last guess has Gaylord saying to himself, this is great. I stiff Chiles once on buying the Rangers and I'm the White Knight. Do it again, I'll be a hero. (DTH, 8/30/88)

Another writer, speculating on why Gaylord would purchase the Rangers given the fact that league owners had rejected him once before, suggested that Ueberroth was Gaylord's "trump card" with his "best interest of base-ball" power that he could have invoked to approve Gaylord's bid despite his rejection by league owners. Indeed, this writer revealed (inaccurately) that "one source says Ueberroth has given both Gaylord and Chiles assurances he will push the deal through this time, and there's no reason to doubt that" (DTH, 9/11/88).

The use of the poker game metaphor to characterize the Rangers' sale revealed an interpretation of baseball not as a game for ballplayers or for fans but as a game for businessmen. Indeed, this point was stated directly by two columnists during the coverage of the sale, both of whom also objected to Gaylord's mediated knighthood by some of their sports writing colleagues. One columnist put it simply that "good businessmen . . . do not heroes make" and that Gaylord in particular was not "a good guy or a bad guy, merely a practical businessman" (DMN, 9/16/88). Another columnist put it more di-rectly to the fans in his column titled, "Ownership is a Game of Power" when he stated bluntly "never confuse your heart strings with an owner's purse strings," adding: "Owners play in a different league. You play softball. They play hardball. Sports is your fun. It is their business. Never let your fun get in the way of their business. The final score always has been, always will be: Owners, in the millions, You, 0. Be thankful, then, this morning that Mr. Gaylord's business interests and your interests of the heart happen to coincide. This time." He concluded with the chilling lesson that "the true bottom line in this game is that owners of professional sports franchises couldn't care less about you and me" (FWST, 9/15/88).

CONCLUDING REMARKS: "COMMUNITAS" VERSUS "CORPORATAS" AND THE MEDIATED SALE OF AN AMERICAN PASTIME

This chapter has examined how mediated images of one important event in the life of an organization—the sale of the company—emerge in the newspapers after a lengthy process involving members of sports organizations and media organizations. Two dominant interpretations of the sale of the Texas Rangers Baseball Club were revealed by examining the metaphors used in newspaper stories to frame the particular facts of the sale. The first interpretation was revealed in the use of military images that cast the potential outside buyers—Morsani and Mack—as enemy invaders who threatened community and the potential inside buyer—Edward Gaylord—as an heroic "white knight" who saved community. On the other hand, the poker game metaphor suggested that baseball is, at its core, a business that is not designed for fans but for high-stakes political players (a lesson also revealed during the 1990 spring training "lockout" and management–player negotiations). These two images suggest that a powerful sense of "communitas" and "corporatas" may be at the heart of major organizational events such as the sale of a company. This concluding section considers these two notions in more detail and their implications for public relations research and practice.

Anthropologist Victor Turner (1974) developed the notion of *communitas* as a particularly rich sense of community in his study of religious pilgrimages. As Turner explained, communitas is community as "anti-structure" that transcends particular ethnic, religious, gender, and class lines to reveal humanity as a "homogenous, unstructured, and free community" (p. 169). Indeed, pilgrims who visit sacred places such as Mecca, Lourdes, and Jerusalem (and I would add Cooperstown) come from all walks of life and experience a foundational bonding with their fellow pilgrims that cannot be matched in most social settings. "Communitas," Turner (1974) concluded, "is spontaneous, immediate, concrete—it is not shaped by norms, it is not institutionalized, it is not abstract" (p. 274).

In one (perhaps limited) sense, sport—as an important cultural ritual—

does function to create this sense of communitas. Perhaps Michael Novak (1988) said best when he argued that sports "feed a deep human hunger, place humans in touch with certain dimly perceived features of human life within this cosmos, and provide an experience of at least a pagan sense of godliness" (p. 20). Indeed, baseball parks are interpreted as shrines by many Americans and non-Americans alike who make yearly (sacred) pilgrimages to some or all of the 26 major league ballparks each summer (see Wood, 1988). Quite simply, the ritual of sport has the potential to engender this powerful sense of communitas.

However, this chapter examined how sports organizations and media organizations use—and exploit—community as a resource when "our" team is put up for sale. For example, the Texas sports media used community as a resource when they cast the local community as a threatened one in light of the enemy invaders who came to steal "our" team and when they issued calls to arm community members to defend "our" team until it could be rescued by a white-knighted savior. These sportswriters understood the unique identification that fans have with their team and in their calls for action (and in their published responses to those calls) they mediated a limited sense of communitas that transcended ethnic, gender, and class lines. In this way, the mass-mediated threat to community is one interpretive frame through which reporters and editors serve a public relations function by mediating the relationship between organization (e.g., baseball franchise) and publics (e.g., fans) and by revealing the importance of community. Of course, reporters and editors have an incentive to mediate (indeed, to commodify) community in this context to keep the team at home so they can stay and report on the team.

On the other hand, the military imagery used by the media to characterize the "stadium wars" between the cities of Arlington and Dallas served not to create regional community but to fragment community regions. Although this mass-mediated militarism no doubt facilitated newspaper readership and sales, it created a disruptive and derisive context for regional cooperation. As one reader argued fittingly in a published letter to the editor: "Rather than bickering over which community has the greatest moral claim to the Rangers, fans throughout the Metroplex should be interested in what is best for the team. Even Arlington fans should prefer the Texas Rangers in Dallas to the Tampa Rangers" (DTH, 9/19/88). Unfortunately, although not surprisingly, city officials—as well as managers of sports and media organizations—are motivated less by the communitas of the fans base and more by the corporatas of the marketplace.

In addition, sports organizations use community as a public relations commodity when they pay homage to the "fans" in their external communication and when they stress the importance of the local fan base. For example, press releases prepared by the Texas Rangers about the proposed (but rejected) sale to minority owner Edward Gaylord and about the proposed (and approved) sale to current managing partner Bush stressed the *local* ties of these possible owners and reassured that these owners planned to keep the team in the present community. Ironically, however, the first agreement to sell the team to Florida outsiders Mack and Morsani suggested that the threat to community also is used as a resource by owners and managers of sports organizations in levering the best price for a team. Indeed, the threat to leave community has been used by a number of owners (most notably by Al Davis of the Oakland/L.A./Raiders) to increase revenues. In this way, (the threat to) community is a bargaining chip for corporate selling and, thus, it reveals the second dominant image of the Ranger sale as a poker game.

As reporters socially constructed this poker game, the team's majority owner bluffed by agreeing to sell to outside owners, forcing the minority owner to up the ante with his bid; the minority owner, in turn, played his hand because he had a trump card or ace in the hole in the Commissioner's support and unilateral power. Accordingly, the metaphor of the poker game revealed that baseball is, at its core, a business that is designed not for ballplayers or for fans but for wealthy political players who use the team and the community as bargaining chips.

The high-stakes imagery of the poker game suggests a sense of *corporatas* wherein the company and the community are commodities to be exploited by corporate owners or, as noted above, a bargaining chip in a bidding game played by high-stakes gamblers for power and profit. Corporatas, thus, can be understood as a calculated, highly stratified, formalized process for selected capitalists in profound contrast to the spontaneous and informal sense of communitas that cuts across ethinic, gender, and class lines.

In this sense, then, corporatas is anti-communitas not because it seeks to destroy community but rather because it reveals that community is ultimately powerless and clearly irrelevant. For example, the poker game for the Rangers was not cast by the media as a threat to community per se; however, community was revealed as irrelevant and unimportant in the entire matter. To put it another way, although the team may be "ours" in our hearts and souls, it is "theirs" in their boardrooms and on their balance sheets.

In summary, although this chapter has examined the facts and stories of the sale of a particular baseball franchise, the implications revealed can help us understand how corporations and the mass media orchestrate coverage of major events such as a company sale. Every major corporate event in a city or region will involve issues of community and corporation that are used and exploited by company officials and media reporters alike. As organizational boundary spanners who, in principle, serve both companies and publics, public relations professionals must be prepared for the inevitable tensions between community and corporation which result when major corporate events are proposed and executed. As scholarly educators who also, in principle, serve both companies and publics, public relations researchers should study how the oppositional senses of communitas and corporatas that result from such corporate events are interpreted and managed by corporate executives, public relations professionals, and the media.

ACKNOWLEDGMENT

An earlier version of this chapter was presented to the North American Society for the Sociology of Sport, Cincinnati in November, 1988. The author thanks Lawrence Wenner, who was the respondent at the North American Society for the Sociology of Sport panel, for his suggestions.

REFERENCES

Burrell, G., & Morgan, G. (1979). *Sociological paradigms and organizational analysis.* London: Heinmann.

Carbaugh, D. (1988). Cultural terms and tensions in the speech at a television station. *Western Journal of Speech Communication, 52,* 216–237.

Cheney, G. (1983). The rhetoric of identification and the study of organizational communication. *Quarterly Journal of Speech, 69,* 143–158.

Conrad, C., & Ryan, M. (1985). Power, praxis, and self in organizational communication theory. In R.D. McPhee & P.K. Tompkins (Eds.), *Organizational communication: Traditional themes and new directions* (pp. 235–258). Beverly Hills, CA: Sage.

Crable, R.E., & Vibbert, S. L. (1983). Mobil's epideictic advocacy: 'Observations' of Prometheus-Bound. *Communication Monographs, 50,* 380–394.

Duncan, M.C. (1983). The symbolic dimensions of spectator sport. *Quest, 35,* 29–36.

Frost, P.J., Moore, L.F., Louis, M.R., Lundberg, C.C., & Martin, J. (Eds.). (1985). *Organizational culture.* Beverly Hills, CA: Sage.

Goodall, H.L. (1989). *Casing a promised land: The autobiography of an organizational detective as cultural ethnographer.* Carbondale, IL: Southern Illinois University Press.

Hall, S. (1980). Encoding/decoding. In S. Hall, D. Hobson, A. Lowe, & P. Willis (Eds.), *Culture, media, language,* (pp. 130–145). London: Hutchinson.

Hirsch, P.M., & Andrews, J.A. (1983). Ambushes, shootouts, and knights of the round table: The language of corporate takeovers. In L.R. Pondy, P.J. Frost, G. Morgan, & T. Dandridge (Eds.), *Organizational symbolism* (pp. 249–279). Greenwich, CT: JAI Press.

Jones, M.O., Moore, M.D., & Snyder, R.C. (Eds.). (1988). *Inside organizations: Understanding the human dimension.* Newbury Park, CA: Sage.

Kendall, R. (1985). *Public relations as art: A prologue to criticism.* Paper presented to the Association for Education in Journalism and Mass Communication. Memphis, TN.

Klatell, D.A., & Marcus, N. (1988). *Sports for sale: Television, money, and the fans.* New York: Oxford University Press.

Koch, S., & Deetz, S. (1981). Metaphor analysis of social reality in organizations. *Journal of Applied Communication Research, 9,* 1–15.

Louis, M.R. (1980). Surprise and sense making: What newcomers experience in entering unfamiliar organizational settings. *Administrative Science Quarterly, 25,* 226–251.

Mickey, T.J. (1983). *Sociodrama as public relations theory.* Paper presented to the International Association for Business Communication, Atlanta, GA.

Morgan, G. (1980). Paradigms, metaphors, and puzzle solving in organization theory. *Administrative Science Quarterly, 25,* 605–622.

Morgan, G. (1986). *Images of organization.* Newbury Park, CA: Sage.

Morgan, G., & Smircich, L. (1980). The case for qualitative research. *Academy of Management Review, 5,* 491–500.

Novak, M. (1988). *The Joy of Sports.* Lanhem, MD: Hamilton Press.

Pfeffer, J. (1981). Management as symbolic action: The creation and maintenance of organizational paradigms. *Research in Organizational Behavior, 3,* 1–51.

Putnam, L.L. (1983). The interpretive perspective: An alternative to functionalism. In L.L. Putnam & M.E. Pacanowsky (Eds.), *Communication and organizations: An interpretive approach* (pp. 31–54). Beverly Hills, CA: Sage.

Putnam, L.L., & Pacanowsky, M.E. (Eds.). (1983). *Communication and organizations: An interpretive approach.* Beverly Hills, CA: Sage.

Reiss, S.A. (1980). *Touching base: Professional baseball and American culture in the progressive era.* Westport, CT: Greenwood.

Telander, R. (1984). The written word: Player-press relationships in American sports. *Sociology of Sport Journal, 1,* 3–14.

Trujillo, N. (1987). Implications of interpretive approaches for organizational communication research and practice. In L. Thayer (Ed.), *Organization ↔ communication: Emerging perspectives II* (pp. 46–63). Norwood, NJ: Ablex.

Trujillo, N., & Toth, E.L. (1987). Organizational perspectives for public relations research and practice. *Management Communication Quarterly, 1,* 199–281.

Turner, V. (1974). *Dramas, fields, and metaphors: Symbolic action in human society.* Ithaca, NY: Cornell University Press.

Weick, K.E. (1979). *The social psychology of organizing* (2nd ed.). Reading, MA: Addison-Wesley.

Wood, B. (1988). *Dodger dogs to fenway franks.* New York: McGraw-Hill.

The Environment of the Oil Company: A Semiotic Analysis of Chevron's "People Do" Commercials

W. MARC PORTER
California State University, Chico

A widely used method of managing public perceptions is corporate image advertisements. Criticism abounds that such advertisements are merely empty rhetoric intended to make "us," key publics, like "them," the sponsors. The intent of image advertisements seems intuitively obvious: If "we" like "them," we will be nice to them by passing or not passing certain regulations—one does not wish harm to befall a socially responsible friend. Because they are often couched in simple, friendly terms, one may overlook the rhetorical sophistication of corporate image advertisements. This form of public relations is hardly "empty," but rather more often it is a rich and well-orchestrated crescendo of symbols.

Using semiotic and narrative theory, this study examines six of Chevron's "People Do" corporate image advertisements that focus on the corporation's contributions to the environment. It is argued that narrative theory is particularly relevant to the study of public affairs commercials because they rely heavily on storytelling as a form of persuasion. Semiotic theory and method, furthermore, provide a means for describing and interpreting how meaning is produced and constrained within these commercials. Few studies (if any) have conducted a thorough ideological critique of a major corporation's public affairs commercials in spite of their proliferation. Finally, this study demonstrates how critical methods contribute to our understanding of public relations.

A primary concern of this research is to understand how meaning is produced in television image advertisements. The distinction here is not what something means in a referential sense, for this implies that a single correct meaning exists within these commercials because of their description of a set of events. In contrast, the question "how does something mean" emphasizes the process of signification (the process involving the production of meaning through the play of signs and symbols). A semiotic understanding of meaning stresses the possibilities of meaning held within a "sign" (e.g., a word, picture, sound, or any image one experiences that invites a conception or experience of something).

Semiology and relatedly post-structuralism comprise a significant portion of this work's theoretical groundwork. This study borrows from Roland Barthes' (1970/1974) conception of codes and critical analysis and from Walter Fisher's (1987) insights on narrative theory. Also, this chapter relies on Richard Lanigan's (1988) semiotic phenomenology to aid the systematic interpretation of Chevron's six television public affairs advertisements. Lanigan (1988) suggested that Barthes' unique style of criticism is sensitive to both the structure of meaning (diachrony) and the experience of meaning (synchrony). This blend of structure and experience of meaning is as unique to public relations research as to the field of criticism. What it means for this analysis is that the semiotic researcher acknowledges the subjectivity of each critical work. This means that no message—in this case each image advertisement—contains only one meaning; rather, each reader finds subjectively his or her own meaning in each advertisement. By using semiotic theory, then, a single (not a universal or absolute) critical reading of the six Chevron environmental advertisements will stress how the content of the advertisements (both individually and collectively) fits into the national concern over corporate social responsibility and environmental issues.

SEMIOTIC AND NARRATIVE THEORIES

It is important at this point to make clear several conceptual definitions and theoretical assumptions that underpin this study. First, *corporate image advertisements* (including print and nonprint) advance a public's perceptions of a represented organization. One type of image advertisement, a public affairs commercial, enhances the sponsor's image (e.g., Chevron Corporation's persona) by addressing an issue that appears to advance a public interest (e.g., the environment). The six television commercials examined in this study were produced for Chevron Corporation by the advertising firm of J. Walter Thompson. All six commercials focus on Chevron's interventions for protecting the environment, and borrowing from the commercials' closing words, they are referred to collectively as the "People Do" campaign. Narrative theory represents a useful model for studying these commercials because each of the advertisements tells a story about how Chevron's "people" successfully contributed to the health of the environment.

The Appeal of Narratives

A *narrative* refers to any discourse that attempts to tell a story. Traditionally, a story involves a progression of events in which an enigma (i.e., a dilemma or problem) must be resolved. Fisher (1987) believed that *narrative rationality* subsumes all forms of human communication, including argument, making narrative rationality a universal condition of human speech. Thus, Fisher lifted narrative from a type of discourse (argument being another type) to the level of ontology. Narrative rationality is the logic of human discourse, a logic analogous to the telling of a story (Fisher, 1987). It can be understood as a rhetorical logic that even permits disputations to be mapped as stories. Narrative rationality views humans as sense-makers who tell stories, judge stories, and reason with stories: a *homo narrans*, as Fisher labeled human-kind.

According to Fisher, the two basic conditions of narrative rationality are narrative probability and narrative fidelity. *Narrative probability* or narrative coherence examines, in a diachronic sense, if the linear telling of the story (or argument) sequentially adds up: Does the story appear to work and is it free of contradictions? In other words, the standard of narrative probability helps the critic to determine if it is a good story. *Narrative fidelity* refers to the truthfulness and the reliability of the story: Does the story appear logically sound and reasonable? Narrative fidelity, thus, judges whether the story "rings true" in relation to what the person knows to be reality. Although I do not accept the ontological assumption of Fisher's conception of narrative (see Warnick, 1987), this study is based on the assumption that most PR image advertisements are narratively structured precisely because stories are a powerful form of rhetoric at least equal, if not superior, to the logic of argument.

If one considers narrative logic as merely a type—even a pervasive and persuasive one—then one can examine narrative structure as a form of rhetoric that appeals to human logic. The question becomes: What constraints are placed upon the rhetor and the critic when narrative logic is engaged? Narrative logic (i.e., storytelling) appears to constrain discourse in two ways: (a) it forces the rhetor to adjust the discourse to the "telling of a tale"; and (b) it restricts the reader from engaging in argument. One does not compete with a story; rather, he or she listens to it and evaluates its truthfulness in ways different than when witnessing or being involved in a debate. To an extent, the reader of a story is required to suspend judgment on the warrants used to make a story's case and focus instead on the plausibility of the tale. Thus, the reader becomes a receiver of a story, one who waits to experience the telling of the tale. The rhetor (in this case Chevron) must be skilled at telling stories, linking episodes, creating reasonable action among believable characters, and developing and remedying a dilemma. The conception of truth for a narrative is not "is the story true?" The question is more accurately one of verisimilitude: "Does the story appear to be true?"

In this regard, Chevron's "People Do" commercials have the power to be effective partially because they do not ask the viewer to argue for or against them. Chevron's 30-second stories (as is seen later) are unobtrusive and unoffensive because they are short tales about saving fish, bears, eagles, and butterflies. In other words, viewers are not called to arise from their couch to argue with Chevron about how to save the environment; rather, they are asked only to listen to a story.

In this analysis, narrative is viewed as a structural type that a rhetor may use as an available method for persuasion. Chevron's public affairs advertisements are therefore not conceived as less noble than other forms of rhetoric because they employ storytelling codes; instead, they are persuasive and informative precisely because they tell stories about how Chevron's people save the environment.

Semiotic Reading of Texts

Fisher cast much of his narrative theory along a diachronic or process view of human communication. For instance, narrative probability relies heavily on the linear (i.e., diachronic) telling of a story. The "telling" of a story involves the unfolding of events or the laying out of ideas. In contrast, semiotic theory emphasizes the synchronic nature of signification (i.e., the structure of meaning). It is the assumption of this study that one must consider both the process and structure of meaning in order to produce a thorough critical analysis of a text.

Semiology (the study of signs and the process of signification) is often used interchangeably with *semiotics;* the first term is attributed to the Swiss linguist de Saussure, and the second to the American logician Pierce. Because the basic posture of this analysis is cast in a Saussureian and post-structuralist view, it is perhaps more correct to refer to the theory as "semiology," although current usage permits the terms to be used synonymously. The Saussureian labels for the parts of a *sign* are used: *signifiers* (the acoustic image, the thing one senses) and *signified* (the conceptual image that one experiences in relation to the signifier). The signifier, for example, could be a phrase (e.g., "Once upon a time . . ."), a sound (e.g., the score to the movie *Jaws* or *Rocky*), or a color (e.g., sky blue or forest green). The signified is what one thinks about, such as a children's story, suspense, accomplishment, clean air, or an old growth forest.

Codes are the system of conventions or rules that serve to organize signs (i.e., signifiers + signifieds) into clusters of meanings. For instance, the signs: crystal blue water, exotic fish, and a cruise ship on the horizon, collectively form a code of a tropical ocean. Whereas signs represent the basic unit of description, codes represent the basic unit of meaning production. A single sign cannot be interpreted without a code, for at its most elementary level a code is a rule that links the signifier to its signified. Groups of codes form the basis for *myths.* Myths operate at a deeper level of meaning and work subtly to hold a system of codes together. A myth is not something that is false, but rather something that is thought to be true. Both codes and myths are conventionally understood rules or truths.

Myths and, to a larger extent, ideologies permit contradictions between codes by concealing and neutralizing differences among competing codes. For instance, many television situation comedies present families (whether nuclear families as found on "The Cosby Show" or "Rosanne" or less conventional mixtures as in "Kate & Allie" or "My Two Dads") that face one or two dilemmas in each 22-minute segment. The codes of family would include a matriarchal and/or patriarchal leader(s), a nonchanging setting—usually a house in which an informal living room is the central location of action, and dependents (children, grandparents, or relatives who have nowhere else to go). The code of comedies requires that viewers suspend some judgments about the realness of the problem or dilemma in order to permit humor. The fact that no one has a family whose mother is continually rolling off one-liners does not make "Rosanne" any less believable. The mythic level makes the two codes—the code of family and the code of comedy—appear congruent. In another example, we find a recoding of "blackness" in the Huxtable family; on "The Cosby Show" the family's wealth permits viewers to suspend their judgments about the more pervasive code for poor Blacks. We are left with the myth: Those who are financially secure would act the same regardless of race. The prevailing myth for "Rosanne," a situation comedy about a White and struggling middle-class family, is not that they are able to laugh in the face of adversity, but rather that a close-knit family can find happiness and humor without over-reliance on material wealth.

The object of a semiotic analysis is a "text" (a printed or nonprinted image that forms a community or system of related signs). The analysis of a text requires the systematic breaking down or "deconstruction" of the codes (structures, rules) in order to determine the fundamental structures that produce a meaning. The "interpretation" or "reading" of the text is actually not the deconstruction of it, but rather the reconstruction that produces another text or "parallel text" (i.e., the written work produced by the critic). The reconstruction of a text requires that the critic attempts to rebuild relationships between signs by testing particular relationships among signs and then defining what is and is not essential to a reading. Barthes (1970/1974, 1973/1975) believed that the "critic" is different from a "reader" because the critic begins with an intent to produce another text—a text whose entire purpose is to cast light across much of the meaning of the original text.

Semiotic theory holds as its central tenet that texts represent possibilities of meaning and invite multifarious readings (Barthes, 1957/1972a, 1970/1974, 1973/1975; Miller, 1987). Formalist critique, in contrast, characteristically stresses "the meaning" of the thing, and the critic's design is to discover the ultimate meaning of a work. As interpreted by post-structuralist semiotics that values multiplicity, an interpretation of public affairs commercials constitutes one attempt at describing codes and ideologies found within the six Chevron commercials. A close reading of each advertisement respects multiplicity and simultaneously seeks a critical analysis of significant codes and ideologies that produce and constrain meaning in the six commercials.

When a text is believed to hold multifarious possibilities for meaning, one may assume that all meanings are possible. The assumption of multiplicity is often criticized, not surprisingly, because it appears that a semiotic critic can "make" a text mean anything he or she wants it to mean; nothing could be further from the truth (Miller, 1987). One cannot read an advertisement on preservation of an ocean environment and interpret it as a rendition of Captain Nemo's dream—unless the text contains signs from the Jules Verne's fiction. In other words, although "subjectivity" is inherent in semiotic method, the semiotic critic is ethically bound to avoid misreading or misinterpreting a text (Barthes, 1973/1975; Miller, 1987).

Another assumption of semiotic theory is that the text maintains a life of its own apart from its creator. Barthes (1972b) asserted that the critic is not required nor remiss in failing to acknowledge the role of the creator's life and health in the production of text. Barthes argued that without the author, the argument regarding intentionality becomes mute. In contrast, formalist critics held that the only meaning that counted was the one that the author intended, and (the logic followed) that if one understood the text one could subsequently understand the author. The pervasiveness of this attitude toward a text is exemplified by the common belief in a direct correspondence between the author's life and all those characters and events that the author writes about.

The rejection of the creator's intent is particularly important when studying television commercials in which the authors/creators are not only unknown, but rarely limited to a single individual. This assumption provides a rationale for excluding from this analysis the creators, producers, graphic artists, and script writers of the "People Do" commercials. Neither knowledge of their private lives nor of their collective intent are necessary for understanding these texts. The six commercials can be studied apart from the aggregate of their creators and more directly in relation to how the character of Chevron is portrayed.

SEMIOTIC PHENOMENOLOGICAL METHOD

In general, semiotic method assumes that because meaning relies on signs for its production, meaning may be realized by systematically tampering with the process of signification. Pearson (1987) observed in his analysis of print advertisements that often what is most interesting is not what is said, but what is not said. The semiotic critic must be able to uncover the structures or system of relationships in order to sufficiently manipulate them. In turn, the critic is able to identify those relations that are fundamentally necessary to a meaning. Derrida's (1978) *différance* and Burke's (1964) *perspective by incongruity* are similar critical strategies for examining what the text is and what it is not by analyzing the absence and presence or similarities and dissimilarities among sign relationships.

John Fiske (1982) used a technique called the "commutation test" for identifying important signifiers. Fiske suggested that in order to understand a text, the critic must take out and substitute signifiers. The missing signifier or its substitute presumably alters the meaning of the message significantly only when the original signifier was essential to the critic's fundamental experience of the text. This method of analyzing relations among signifiers and their signifieds has a similar counterpart in phenomenological analysis called "imaginative free variation" (Lanigan, 1988). Lanigan suggested that the researcher reflectively plays with the possibilities of meanings contained in the signifieds; imaginative free variation asks the critic to experiment systematically with a text by moving, substituting, and discarding signifieds.

To accomplish the criticism of the Chevron advertisements, this chapter follows the three-step procedures typically found among phenomenological analysis (Ihde, 1986; Lanigan, 1988): steps include description, reduction, and interpretation. *Description* involves a thorough reporting of signs; a significant portion of what follows is detailed description of what this critic sees and hears in the six Chevron advertisements. *Reduction* begins to cluster, by using imaginative free variation, important signs into codes; in this step, the critic asks, "how does something mean?" *Interpretation* requires that the critic infers "why something means" based on "how it means." In other words, the interpretation reaches beyond the text to determine those structures that create a particular experience for the reader. Whereas description focuses on signs and reduction on codes, interpretation identifies myths and ideologies that undergird a text.

This research attempts to extend critical public relations theory in two ways. First, this study using semiotic and narrative theory examines a public affairs campaign by a major multinational corporation. Second, this study extends previous critical semiotic work that has examined print advertisements (Williamson, 1978), print issues advertisements (Pearson, 1987), and television culture (Fiske, 1987). Chevron's "People Do" commercials were selected because they represent a systematic attempt by a multinational corporation to associate itself with a major public issue. In this case, Chevron's environmental theme could be examined across multiple commercials, providing for its own intertextuality. Although Chevron has reproduced print versions of the "People Do" commercials, television image advertisements were chosen because little critical public relations research has been completed in this area. Further, because of the storytelling structure of the six advertisements, the "People Do" campaign permits a narrative analysis of a public relations effort.

DISCUSSION

The discussion organizes the analysis into six separate descriptions, reductions, and interpretation. In theory, it is far easier to define the distinctions among description, reduction, and interpretation; in application, it is important to recognize that these steps are synergistic. Each description includes the script from the 30-second commercial. The critical discussion of the commercials uses Chevron's titles for six advertisements, which are as follows: "Reef," "Eagle," "Butterfly," "Kit Fox," "Gorge," and "Bear."

Any of the stories in these commercials could be told to a child with little or no variation in the script. Each commercial begins with the enigma (e.g., the threat of technology) and ends with its resolution (e.g., human intervention saves some endangered place or species). The stories' simplicity makes the six commercials highly persuasive. Using Fisher's (1987) terminology, Chevron's advertisements are "good" narratives because they maintain narrative probability, or coherence (the stories hang together), and because they preserve narrative fidelity (they appear true).

Reef

This first public affairs story, "Reef," begins at sea level with a white fishing yacht mooring in the distance. The viewer begins to dive, air bubbles rise toward the surface, and the viewer is taken "104 feet down." The narrator's voice is calming and paced exactly with the rhythm of violins and piano music. As the camera's eye enters into a cylinder, which we learn is a gas station storage tank, the music crescendos to a heavier beat, more threatening, only to lighten again as the camera moves from the sunken tanks and back into the open water. Until now, one has only watched white fish flutter past, but when the camera exits the cylinder a diver wearing a blue suit and yellow tank swims along with an underwater light. He or she swims on, and eventually joins four other divers—two of whom appear to be women due to their waving hair. The divers are holding a Chevron emblem that appears to glow when the divers' lights are held in back of it. The divers appear to be sitting atop one of the gas station storage tanks apparently left there by Chevron. The narration to this commercial is as follows:

> Two and a half miles off Florida, 104 feet down is a unique housing develop-ment. In an area once virtually empty of life, families now live and prosper. These coral-covered cylinders were once gas station storage tanks, sand-blasted clean to form environmentally approved artificial reefs. Algae forms, fish gather, and a food chain begins. Do people really do all that so that fish can have a population explosion? People do. (Chevron, "Reef")

In order to understand this text, one must begin to question what is and is not present. First, the story begins with the location; although not specific in nautical terms, the distance from the state and to the ocean floor is sufficient to carry the viewer off the coast. The visual effects also move the viewer from the surface and then, like a diver, into the depths of the darkening ocean. The comment about the "unique housing development" where "fam-ilies now live and prosper" does not at first appear to be about fish. The code becomes one of mystery created by the language and expanded by the full mystery of the ocean (a code that could also be considered a myth). As the Jules Verne novel foreshadowed, a viewer may consider that a human habitat has been created in the ocean's depth. Instead, the viewer is pre-sented with rusted, coral-covered cylinders with half-open ends. The first shot of these metal objects leaves the viewer uncertain about their identity and purpose. The mystery of the tanks is solved as the narrator describes them as "gas station storage tanks." Each word is a significant qualifier for what these apparently steel (due to the rust) cylinders once did. Further, a contradiction immediately exists between the fact of what a gas station signifies and what the ocean and fish signify. The "gas station storage tanks" are quickly associated with a code of authority through the signifiers that the tanks were "sand-blasted clean" and were "environmentally approved." Sand is natural enough, common to the ocean, and associated with fairly thorough and abrasive cleaning. Although it is not stated who "environmentally ap-proved" the artificial reefs, one would infer that it was the United States Government, probably the Environmental Protection Agency. The word "artificial" seems lost in the next line, which is uniquely chained with rhythmic action and sounds poetically like the food chain of which it speaks.

The music increases as the divers wave enthusiastically at the camera, and the narrator concludes with the question which again personifies the fish. Fish are typically not considered to have "population explosions," to live in "housing developments," or to be "families" who prosper like suburbanites.

This advertisement about the artificial reef appears to include a code of purity, represented by the clean, white deep sea fishing or diving yacht, the air bubbles (signifying life and healthy water), crystal blue water, and white fish. The characters include the fish as well as the arm-waving divers; the fish appear, however, to take center stage. The next code, suspense, builds the threat from the enigma by having the viewer dive into an area "once empty of life;" the code of suspense is supported by the music that begins to crescendo to a Jaws-like tempo as the camera enters the cylinders. Fish move in and out of the scene depending on the degree of implied threat. When the camera dives into the tank, the fish disappear and the string instruments thunder. All is safe in a matter of seconds when the light appears at the end of the cylinder, white fish swim in the sunlight, the camera exits, and another diver (i.e., the viewer has assumed the role of a diver) swims past. The camera angles form another code that gives the viewer his or her perspective as a diver. Beginning with the descent into the water and ending with a swim to meet the other divers, the viewer moves from apparent isolation in the depths to membership in a diving team.

To test how important particular signifiers are to the meaning, one can substitute signifiers, what Fiske (1982) called the commutation test. To begin, does it make a difference whether the boat is a white deep sea fishing yacht? In terms of the codes of orientation (the distance and depth) it would make little difference if the boat was a rusty shrimper. Yet, in terms of the code of purity a rusty fishing troller would have appeared unpleasant—not environmentally healthy. Likewise, a cruise ship would have given the viewer perspective regarding ocean depth and distance, yet would signify a party or vacation. A cruise ship violates the code of mystery or suspense that makes the viewer as diver experience the ocean's isolation and foreignness to air-breathing humans.

The narrator's voice is also a rich signifier understood as an all-knowing observer who speaks with precise intonations, and although his voice sharpens at suspenseful moments, it brightens when safety is apparent. The narrator sounds like a grandfatherly reader of a child's favorite story of which the grandfather knows the conclusion; so, perhaps, does the child, but the soothing voice encourages one to listen and not to ask too many questions. The narrator answers the final question with "People Do," delivered not with a rising voice, but a sinking inflection as if to say, "People do" because they care. Within two words, the narrator's knowledge of the simple truths of the world is grasped by the listener. This is what is meant by narrative fidelity.

The narrator is singularly important to these stories; his voice is clear and rich. Voice tone is not harsh and nasal like Hal Holbrook's narration of National Geographic, nor overly chipper or poorly inflected like Barbara Walters and Mike Wallace. The flavor is neither hokey like that of a Walt Disney animal film or objectively detailed with controlled enthusiasm like a National Geographic Special on animals. Instead, the narrator sounds like a great story-teller, and nearly alone, without visual support, his smooth dramatic voice could support the storytelling code in each of these advertisements.

Finally, the gas station's storage tanks represent the closest the viewer gets to the oil company that paid for this 30-second spot. It should be noted that Chevron's name never appears in the script although it regularly appears in the visuals—in this case a sign is held up. What does the viewer learn about these tanks? Foremost, we know that they are not part of nature—the codes of nature being the fish, the water, the coral reef—but that they presumably become part of nature. This is important to recognize. Gas station storage tanks do not generally call forth pictures of purity, but rather pictures of oily grime and dirty corner gas stations. Quite a different picture would have been created had Chevron chosen to show the viewer the rusty storage tanks being dug up, cleaned off, and dumped in the ocean. Instead, Chevron builds an association between that thing that is not natural and that contained chemicals lethal to the food chain and those things that are natural and delicate (the white fish appear at times to be nearly transparent). Moreover, Chevron's reef is not only added to the ocean, but the viewer is led to believe that the reason life flourishes 104 feet down is because of the steel tanks. In order to make this part of the story believable, Chevron chose not to film storage tanks that had been recently dumped and still exposed shiny metal sides; rather, the tanks have been submerged long enough to be fully covered in growth and to have turned a rich orange, probably from rust.

The interpretation of this advertisement leads to the myth of a benevolent company that gives back to the environment those things that it has taken. Why is it significant that old gas station storage tanks are being dumped off the Florida coast? One interpretation requires recalling why the tanks were most likely removed. Several years ago, contaminated ground water became a major concern in U.S. cities. In several northeastern cities, it was discovered that rusting gas station storage tanks were part of the problem. Although nearly all gas station storage tanks that are buried in the gas station lots are now covered with fiberglass, most tanks installed over 20 years ago were only steel. The commercial ignores the history that connects foul water to rusted tanks. Chevron's advertisement can be understood not only as a story about how the old gas station storage tanks saved the fish, but how the story supports an ideology of the happy environment where everything old can be safely returned to the environment for the slow and natural process of decay after people finish with it.

Eagle

The second advertisement involves a simple plan for saving the life of an eagle. In this case, the critical analysis should begin with the script and then describe the visuals and music. The narrative runs as follows:

> This eagle could land in trouble. The high point he might decide to rest on could be dangerous. Unaware that 13,000 volts await him, he heads toward it—and lands, unharmed. Wooden platforms above the power lines now keep him above the danger. They were developed and put there by a lot of people whose work brings them to this remote area. Do people really reach that high to protect a natural wonder? People do. (Chevron, "Eagle")

This story begins with an aerial shot of a golden eagle soaring above a valley with mountains outlining the background. This advertisement is the only one analyzed that does not mention the location in reference to a state. After a few seconds of soaring, the narrator picks up the story and begins to create suspense. Although the view shows the wooden platform above the power line, it does not come into relief until the eagle lands. The danger seems more immediate. The danger is not the beauty of these western U.S. mountains, sharply carved and ominously cloud-covered; rather the danger is technology—"13,000 volts of electricity" traveling through, unnaturally, this "remote area." When the eagle lands, the camera angle changes as the narrator states "unharmed" in the most reassuring way, and four people (three White men and one White woman) are simultaneously brought into the view. The man on the far left taps the arm of the man on the far right as the latter man puts down his binoculars. The group stands close together with the woman (dressed in green ranger-type clothing and hat) standing slightly in the background. But all of them appear pleased that the eagle landed safely or perhaps (more simply) that they were able to view the eagle's flight. Whatever the cause, the camera zooms in toward voiceless people smiling and talking about something; this portrayal would lead one to infer (because of the linear progression of events) that the eagle perched high above was the reason for their excitement. The story closes again with the question about the "natural wonder," and the camera zooms in to the white plastic shell safety hat worn by a clean-shaven, healthy looking young man in his early 30s. Clearly visible on the front of the safety hat, as the narrator asks the final question, is Chevron's logo with its royal blue and majestic red sargent stripes.

The codes of nature are once again apparent in this advertisement as they are in all of the "People Do" commercials. Without a word, the viewer soars with a golden eagle against a backdrop of snow-laced, gray rock mountains. The sky is both bright blue (almost Chevron blue) and filled with white puffy clouds that hug the mountains in the distance. The eagle is the primary carrier of nature, for "he" is not likely to be found soaring above cityscapes. Codes of technology are represented by the power lines and the close and zooming shots of the gray power cables, metal couplers, and insulators. Technology is again portrayed in contradiction with nature; this contradiction maintains narrative coherence in all six commercials. The harmony between technology and nature is dependent on "people" who through simple know-how nail together a few boards that reach above dangerous technology and save the noble eagle.

The story requires a happy ending—a resolution to the enigma of technology. It is not a story about how several eagle carcasses were found entangled and electrocuted on power lines, but how this one male eagle (signifying greater strength and nobility, perhaps) lands safely on a 2' X 6' board. The viewer does not immediately question why four people are standing almost directly below the power lines and probably in soft soil given their proximity to a meandering run-off creek. We are not shown how they got to this remote area or why a man would be wearing a hard hat if he was out eagle-watching with three compatriots. The storytelling code (again largely dependent on the narrator's voice and script) limits us to a story about an eagle who lives to fly another day because forward thinking people placed wooden platforms above highly dangerous power lines. Although technology is first seen as unnatural, it is made more natural by using wooden power poles, not the highly expansive metal frame suspension types that are often found in remote western locations. Technology is made softer by the greenness of the grassy field behind and the richness of the soil beneath the eagle watchers, and, of course, it is made less forboding by the *wooden,* unpainted platform on which the eagle finally rests from its strong flight.

It should be noted that Chevron did not use an American bald eagle, but a golden eagle. The former, perhaps, was over-coding the issue of morality. The golden eagle with its brown feathers and silver-tipped wings still depicts the beauty of powerful flight. It is close enough to signify the nobility of the more familiar bald eagle, but unfamiliar enough that the bird does not distract from the greater message: that Chevron is an environmentally responsible company that finds even the simplest ways to protect "natural wonders."

Butterfly

The third commercial also depicts people as producing the balance between nature and technology. The first shot moves from an aerial view of a beach to a soaring jet reaching for the sky. Another link is made between technology and nature by metaphorically describing the jet "reaching for the sky" and a small butterfly (a fragile and natural flier that flutters and does not soar) "reaching for its dinner." This parallel goes further when one considers the large white jet signifies a technologically advanced flying machine; in contrast, the story is about a wispy butterfly called the El Segundo Blue that flutters, not soars, and is no larger than a fingernail. Visually the butterfly is depicted resting upon the fingertip of a healthy man who apparently has been tending the buckwheat that has been planted on this land just for the butterfly. The narrative is as follows:

> On the coast of California, while big jets reach to the sky, one of the smallest endangered species quietly reaches for its dinner. The El Segundo Blue lives on wild buckwheat, on land that is part of an oil refinery. It's not much bigger than your fingernail, yet people who work there protect the area and plant buck-wheat. Do people really do that so a tenth of a gram of beauty can survive? People do. (Chevron, "Butterfly")

The narrative shows close-up shots of the butterfly followed by a panning out to show the butterfly resting on a fingertip. The blue-clothed workmen speak and smile, although voiceless, while the narrator tells us that people plant wild buckwheat here. As the story ends and the narrator begins the final question, the camera pans, leaving the men in the background and revealing a sign that reads "Endangered Species Sanctuary." The Chevron label in the lower half of the sign then provides for a segue to the black background and white Chevron sign with the white bold words that answer the question.

The codes have become familiar after two previous advertisements. Codes of happiness are depicted with smiling faces or waving arms. The carefree myth of the butterfly is coded by showing it casually resting upon wild buckwheat or a person's finger and then watching it catch the wind to flutter away. In many respects, the jet soaring toward its destination stands directly opposed to what the aimless butterfly signifies.

Further, to overcome the interpretation of humans being intruders into nature, people are largely absent from these advertisements. In the first commercial only five people were present, the second included four, and this one just two. In the last three commercials, two people appear in the "Gorge" while no one is visible in either "Kit Fox" or "Bear." The environmental work of Chevron's people is done quietly and unobtrusively. The stories are not about people so much as they are about how animals and locations have benefited from what some people did—we are witnesses to environmental successes, not failures.

The message is simple like a fairy tale: People make a difference. It is the myth that humankind can alter the course of its environment. And no matter how seemingly insignificant or small the life, whether small white fish or an even smaller butterfly, people can make things better. Chevron never mentions the material cost for planting buckwheat, or building and installing platforms, or sand-blasting and delivering gas storage tanks. The material costs are left for arguments, not storytelling. In these stories it does not make a difference how much it cost to plant buckwheat or how many eagles were saved versus the cost of the platforms; moralistically nature holds value over all things material. To be sure, Chevron is a company that makes its profits by taking "natural" resources and creating products that can cause significant harm to the environment. To avoid this most blatant contradiction between the user of nature and the contributor to nature, Chevron's name is not mentioned in the script and only appears towards the conclusion within the visuals of the story in three of the commercials: "Reef," "Eagle," and "Butterfly." Chevron's logo is always seen at the end of these commercials, yet in "Kit Fox," "Gorge," and "Bear" one does not see any Chevron logos perched atop storage tanks, on hard hats, or on warning signs. The next three advertisements continue the theme of linking Chevron Corporation with environmentalism; each step is a small issue that attempts to demonstrate that Chevron does care. The answer is not simply that "people do," but more directly when read with the Chevron logo above the words, that "Chevron people do."

Kit Fox

This story is about a small western fox that is endangered. The kit fox in the story is female in order to make the animal's plight seem perhaps more difficult, the animal less strong. The story moves from the eeriness of a full moon and a hungry coyote to a rising sun and a still-safe female kit fox. The story is narrated as follows:

> On a moonlit California desert, a kit fox senses the prowling coyote. Caught in the dangerous open, she speeds to the edge of an oil field toward one of these curious mounds specially made for her by the people who work there. She shoots through the pipe—too small for the coyote—and into a cozy den that keeps her snug and safe. Do people really do these things just to help an endangered species make it through the night? People do. (Chevron, "Kit Fox")

The codes of action are more pronounced in this commercial largely because of a "chase scene" in which the coyote apparently chases the kit fox through the dark forest hoping to catch a meal. The chase begins with the fox sniffing the dark air and a coyote lurking in the bushes. The fox darts away, running over large stones across a creek (in the desert) and across a field where it appears that the fox is looking over its shoulder as it runs, as if to judge how close the coyote is. The camera follows the chase; in fact, within the last few yards to the dirt mound, the camera is actually moving against the grassline to provide the viewer with the fox's perspective of its destination and add a sense of urgency. The narrator's voice adds to the drama, and the kit fox somehow knows to run into a dirt mound through a pipe. The coyote is stopped at the entrance to the human-made burrow: Two vertical bars hold back the coyote's intruding snout as the fox curls timidly in the rounded center of the burrow. The next scene shows the kit fox inspecting the field as the sun apparently begins to rise.

Chevron takes advantage of the popular myths about wolves, and by extension coyotes, as vicious hunters of innocent animals. What is not stated is that western coyotes are also a threatened species and that they are largely scavengers who serve an important function by reducing populations of rabbits and cleaning the western ranges of carrion. But the telling of the story takes precedent over the facts, and the intervention of humans takes precedent over nature's food chain because a small kit fox requires saving. The kit fox serves two codes: first, "she" is in fact an endangered species that permits a code of protection to supercede any natural order, and second, the fox hunt contributes to the drama of the story because codes of fox hunting are well-known (even though they are not widely experienced). This second code could be missed due to the importance of the first. The fox and the fox hunt have long traditions of storytelling; foxes appear throughout children's stories as the smart, calculating animal who could match any human con artist. The fox hunt is equally legend: the English gentry riding forth with dogs howling, a fleeing red fox who stands little chance of survival, and the frightened animal collapsing from exhaustion before it dies.

The first point regarding the codes of endangered species is important enough to label it a myth. The myth may be understood that when an animal faces extinction—which is ultimately what is meant by the label *endangered*—then humankind should do everything in its power to keep that from occurring. The natural laws no longer apply when an animal is endangered. So the California condor was removed from its natural environment and into special care lest we lose the entire species. The irony of this logic is that people forget why the species is endangered. The kit fox is not endangered because wily coyotes eat too many of them; rather, the kit fox's habitat has been so greatly limited by human and technological growth that the propagation of the species has nearly ceased. The kit fox requires human intervention in order to survive because human intervention has significantly altered its chances of survival.

The Gorge

This story dramatizes the fact that a dam was not built in Colorado's Gunnison Gorge. The story implies that Chevron, as a morally responsible organization, freely decided not to build the dam because it would have upset the environment of the gorge. The narrative begins by using almost onomatopoeic language to sketch the full visual beauty of the gorge and the river. Then, the narrator's tone switches as he states that a dam would threaten the life of this gorge forever; the viewer may wonder if this commercial is part of a "save the gorge" campaign. The visual and musical effects also become dramatic as the commercial continues. The sky above becomes filled with grey clouds that disappear in the next scene when a blue sky is viewed from the eyes of two rafters who appear to be father and son. The script goes as follows:

> Through Colorado's Gunnison Gorge the river whispers and roars past cliffs carved by time. A dam would threaten the life and beauty of this canyon forever. But the right to build a dam belonged to the people who decided never to use that right. Now, what took nature two million years to make will still be seen by the eyes of our children's children. Do people sometimes care for nature by leaving it alone? People do. (Chevron, "Gorge")

The picture of the gorge moves from an aerial view in which a small Chevron-blue raft floats below, to a back view of the gorge's high rocky walls against the grey sky above, and finally to a view of the rafters passing on, birds flapping skyward, and the message that the canyon is saved for future generations.

The man and boy move quietly along the muddy river; the paddles barely disturb the water's surface as the man directs the raft slowly into the next turn. The boy's face is turned ever skyward—staring constantly above. The camera pans in showing the boy's uneven teeth and curious eyes, as the narrator speaks of saving the canyon for our children's children. The codes for heavenly beauty abound in this commercial. For instance, we find the journeying of the man and boy alone in a raft, the sun reflecting off rocks and muddy waters making both appear almost golden, and the birds rising above the gorge, pushing hard to ascend its high walls. The dam would have stood in contradiction to this scene. It would have been a false wall built to upset nature's balanced beauty. Instead, the implications are that Chevron did not build the dam for reasons not given in this story. And the silent trip of the bearded man in the Chevron-blue life jacket and the freckled boy in his Chevron-red life jacket signifies that they, like Chevron, do not disturb nature, but merely admire it.

The use of the man and boy to signify the father and son is revealing. The same meaning could not have been conceived if a group of tourists went crashing over rapids. The scene is intentionally somber and respectful of nature. A woman and girl would have broken verisimilitude; female rafters for conventional reasons would have distracted from the natural balance and invited people to debate whether a woman and girl could negotiate the river. The calmness is extended by the smooth flowing waters, not rapids. And although the rocks are jagged, they are softened by the lighting effects of glare, blackouts, and long camera angles. The myth for this commercial is consistent with the others: Human beings possess the right to rule or destroy nature, but because of our wisdom we can choose to respect nature. Life is to be enjoyed in most human societies, and although Americans are not entirely epicureans, they do value pieces of nature that can be visited to restore one's personal sanity. The theme of this advertisement, then, is that Chevron has placed the value of nature over a need for hydroelectric power, flood control, or irrigation water.

Bear

The last commercial involves a story about how oil exploration in Montana never wakes up the hibernating bear. The commercial begins with the sound of wind swirling and snow spiraling in almost surreal fashion (it is possible that artificial snow was used). The camera picks up a tree with a large hollow base; the next shot would lead one to believe that the bear is inside this hollow. The bear's long brown snout nudges the leafy floor as the narrator reads:

> In a den high in Montana's Black Feet Country, a grizzly settles for a long winter's nap, unaware that down below people with motors and machinery will explore for oil through deep winter. But before she wakes, the people will be gone. The explored land will be replanted so it will soon look as if no one had ever been there. Do people sometimes work through the winter so nature can have spring all to herself? People do. (Chevron, "Bear")

The visual signifiers include a scene of a field covered by snow, and one hears wind howling. Like the "Kit Fox," no people are visible in this commercial. We also see no signs of human intervention. The narrator tells us that machinery is working below (apparently further down the mountain and not geologically under the bear's den), but the viewer never sees any equipment. What is shown is a snowy field slowly becoming transformed into a mid-spring field with grass a foot high and snow still capping the mountains. A bear walks lazily through the grass; the camera zooms in on the animal's huge paws that methodically rise and pound. The same bear, perhaps, is then seen playing with a new cub; the inference is that the original female bear is now the same bear playing with her cub.

This commercial connotes the warmth of one's own den with a fireplace roaring in the winter. The bear's den seems warmly comfortable from one's home. No one questions how the camera was able to film a bear in its den falling asleep. The human codes for bears make most of us believe that these huge animals sleep in caves; although this is true, many bears do sleep in hollows. The space in this hollow seems greater than what the tree might have provided. Would the story have been different if we watched squirrels or chipmunks curling up to sleep? These small animals thrive near humans; nevertheless, the bear's rich storybook history as the king of the northern forest makes this animal, and its mythical hibernating habit, a useful signifier to represent all sleeping animals. The danger of bears to humans is overlooked by the somber music and sleeping bear, by the bear's slow walk in the spring, and by the cub jumping at her mother's feet. The state of Montana is significant because it places this commercial within the continental United States; and, more importantly, it turns the attention away from Alaska where the drilling for oil in cold weather may be considered commonplace. Montana represents a less well-known, and therefore less distracting, location for turning the viewers' attention.

Although this commercial does not include people or show technology, it is the only one that addresses directly a primary business activity for Chevron—oil exploration. This commercial sets up the narrator as the presenter of the technology—but only its verbal form. One never sees men in parkas bracing against cold winds trying to drop well pipes while standing in mud. This absence is significant because it would disrupt the story about the bear; it would make the uncleanliness of oil exploration too present, too real. The angle for the story is the sleeping bear all snug in its den; the link for Chevron is to take the signifier of the snugly bear and attach it to the responsible oil exploration. The interpretation is that Chevron is sensitive to all animals, including the stately Montana bear, and Chevron's employees will brave the bitter cold of a Montana winter to avoid upsetting nature. If there is any doubt, the narrator adds that "the explored land is replanted, so it will *soon* look as if no one had ever been there" (italics added).

A CRITICAL SYNTHESIS

In each of these six commercials, Chevron works diligently to tell a story about how some animal or aspect of the environment is protected by the work of "people." Protection is the salient theme. Whether a canyon river is protected or a population of fish or a sleeping bear, the protection is not natural, but rather humanly created: "People do" the protecting. People drop gas station storage tanks, build platforms for eagles, plant wild buckwheat for little butterflies, build houses for kit foxes, save a canyon from drowning, and protect the sleeping bear from summer intrusions. Nature is dependent on humankind. Because of people's recent superiority over nature (i.e., humankind's ability to destroy nature faster than nature can rebuild) Chevron's answer can be slightly turned to demonstrate the other side of the question. Who needs oil refineries, dams, and gas station storage tanks? People do. Who destroys most completely the El Segundo Blue's and kit fox's habitats? People do. Who strips top soil during mining operations and produces factories and products that pollute the environment? People do. This twist is not intended to be a critique of Chevron in particular. In fact, this critique is more leveled against a prevailing ideology about the environment: the ideology that Chevron's advertising consultants merely relied on to make these six stories ring true.

The prevailing ideology views the environment as a resource over which humans hold control. More specifically, nature is understood egocentrically as having been created for use by people. Because it is ours to use, it is also ours to misuse. Widespread abuse of the environment has resulted in many politicians and corporations (including Chevron) stepping forward and demonstrating their concern for the environment. People criticize Chevron for environmental insensitivity—a myth of the large corporation is that big business only feigns social responsibility in order to make more money. Yet, these same people sit comfortably in centrally heated homes watching television and microwaving dinner: None of these technologies could have been developed without some cost to the environment. The nurture model of the environment, then, sees humans as caretakers with almost god-like power to control the garden's growth. As promised to some cultures in Genesis, humans are "given dominion" over the earth.

Are there other perspectives of the environment? Devall (1988) argued that the anthropocentric view of the environment is only largely a Western perspective. Ideologically, westerners do not perceive themselves as being a part of or belonging to the land. For example, Nelson (1983), in his ethnography of Alaskan Indian tribes, described the people's kinship with bears and their reverence for nature—perspectives that would be entirely foreign to most Americans. Chevron is not at fault for using the available means of persuasion. It is also likely that Chevron's people (its advertising firm) did not believe that the public conceives of the environment egocentrically, and that Chevron itself conceives the environment the same way because of the ideological depth of the human's possessing dominion over the earth.

In the end, the ideology of the environment as resource and humans as the great protectors and manipulators of the environment becomes a foundational and deeply hidden structure upon which all six of these narratives were based. Individually they included different codes for depicting nature, building suspense, and resolving a dilemma. More similar among these commercials were their myths regarding the contradiction between codes of technology and codes of nature. This contradiction could only be resolved at the mythic level. Further, when the six commercials are understood collec-

tively, an ideology emerges that not only subsumes the contradiction between technology and nature, but more importantly deals with the deeply
hidden contradiction between humankind and nature. The narratives are
effective largely because they neither invite debate nor expose the myth or
ideologies of western environmentalism.

Although a person may have a gripe with Chevron because it represents a
large oil and chemical corporation, the person may actually believe that
Chevron is doing something "right." Rightness is measured as the degree to
which Chevron's ideology agrees with an individual's ideology regarding the
relationship between people and the environment. One believes that
Chevron is "helping" or "saving" the environment to the extent one believes
that drilling in winter, constructing fox dens, or creating sanctuaries for
butterflies saves the environment. Chevron's "People Do" commercials are
narratively excellent because they build stories that sound true and good—
that is, they sustain narrative fidelity and narrative probability. Thus, the
"People Do" commercials are superior forms of corporate rhetoric for at
least two reasons. First, because of their narrative structure, Chevron's
commercials circumvent argument by offering believable stories about how
to save the environment. Second, Chevron establishes its six stories on a
widely accepted understanding of the environment to such an extent that
few would argue against Chevron's environmental interventions—the ideology of western environmentalism makes, for example, establishing fish
sanctuaries from gas station storage tanks or building bird landing platforms
the right thing to do.

What we may learn from Chevron's "People Do" stories, then, is that the
simplicity with which problems are resolved and the places where people
are happy and nature is secure are the source of good stories. The lesson
from these commercials for the critical public relations theorists is not
whether Chevron's environmental position is "right," but rather how are
Chevron and the culture that maintains it constrained by a single ideological
understanding of the environment. In this case, Chevron appropriates a
dominant understanding of the environment in order to create a favorable
opinion of itself. There is no guarantee that the "People Do" commercials are
highly influential in shaping favorable opinions toward Chevron (a concern
that exceeds the scope of this study). Yet, critical theorists must wonder if
Chevron's depiction of the environment does not somehow confound, encourage, or affirm a limited environmental view for television viewers. What
is the more important question: that Chevron is viewed more favorably by
people who share its ideology of environmental interventionism? or that
Chevron itself and its viewers are constrained by an ideology which excludes
wholistic understandings of the environment? Certainly, for the public
relations practitioner, one must acknowledge that good narratives make

effective public affairs commercials, but public relations theorists should recognize how ideologies are concealed in narrative structures and how these ideologies constrain a public's understanding of its world.

ACKNOWLEDGMENTS

The author acknowledges the cooperation of Chevron Corporation and J. Walter Thompson Corporation for providing copies of the "People Do" commercials.

REFERENCES

Barthes, R. (1972a). *Mythologies* (A. Lavers, Trans.). New York: Hill & Wang. (Original work published 1957)

Barthes, R. (1972b). The death of the author. In S. Sears & G.W. Lord (Eds.), *The discontinuous universe: Selected writings in contemporary consciousness* (pp. 7–12). New York: Basic Books.

Barthes, R. (1974). *S/Z* (R. Miller, Trans.). New York: Hill & Wang. (Original work published 1970)

Barthes, R. (1975). *The pleasure of the text* (R. Miller, Trans.). New York: Hill & Wang. (Original work published 1973)

Burke, K. (1964). *Perspective by incongruity*. Bloomington, IN: Indiana University Press.

Derrida, J. (1978). *Writing and difference* (A. Bass, Trans.). Chicago: University of Chicago Press.

Devall, B. (1988). *Simple in means, rich in ends: Practicing deep ecology*. Salt Lake City, UT: Peregine Smith Books.

Fisher, W.R. (1987). *Human communication as narration: Toward a philosophy of reason, value, and action*. Columbia, SC: University of South Carolina.

Fiske, J. (1982). *Introduction to communication studies*. New York: Methuen.

Fiske, J. (1987). *Television culture*. New York: Methuen.

Ihde, D. (1986). *Experimental phenomenology: An introduction*. Albany, NY: State University of New York Press.

Lanigan, R.L. (1988). *Phenomenology of communication: Merleau-Ponty's thematics in communicology and semiology*. Pittsburgh, PA: Duquesne University Press.

Miller, J.H. (1987). *The ethics of reading*. New York: Columbia University Press.

Nelson, R.K. (1983). *Make prayers to the raven*. Chicago: University of Chicago Press.

Pearson, R.A. (1987, May). *Decoding corporate discourse: Semiotics and the analysis of organizational texts*. Paper presented at the meeting of the International Communication Association, Montreal.

Warnick, B. (1987). Narrative paradigm: Another story. *Quarterly Journal of Speech, 73*, 172–182.

Williamson, J. (1978). *Decoding advertisements: Ideology and meaning in advertising*. London: Marion Boyars.

"The Decision Is Yours" Campaign: Planned Parenthood's Character-Istic Argument of Moral Virtue

DENISE M. BOSTDORFF
Purdue University

In the mid-1980s, the Planned Parenthood Federation of America found itself the target of vocal attacks for its pro-choice stance on abortion. Pro-life supporters, those who oppose legal abortion, held public rallies and demonstrated outside abortion clinics, including those of Planned Parenthood. Frequently, protesters harassed patients who attempted to enter clinics; a few individuals even resorted to violent bombings of such institutions in order to make their views on the subject known (Beck, 1985). Meanwhile, a pro-life film, *The Silent Scream*, depicted an abortion via "ultrasound visualization" and drew widespread media attention (Adler, 1985; Spake, 1985). Public spokespersons like then President Ronald Reagan and New York Archbishop John J. O'Connor also added legitimacy to the pro-life cause ("Ronald Reagan on abortion," 1984; Woodward, 1984).

As the nation's largest family planning organization, Planned Parenthood was an especially tempting target for pro-life groups, and such outspoken public sentiment meant a political backlash, as well. In 1982, the Reagan administration attempted to block Planned Parenthood's participation in the Combined Federal Campaign, a charity drive among federal employees that annually contributed over $500,000 to the agency (Spring, 1982). Three years later, the White House backed a move by congressional conservatives to eliminate federal funding for Planned Parenthood and other family planning clinics that offered abortion as an alternative to unwanted pregnancy ("A new attack on abortion," 1985). Finally, federal departments subjected Planned Parenthood to unprecedented, frequent audits—audits that were costly for the organization in both money and personnel, but that failed to turn up any wrong-doing. According to Donald Devine, the head of Reagan's Office of Personnel Management, "They [Planned Parenthood] promote abortion . . . I think that's detestable" (Ashkinaze, 1984, p. 93). The public debate over abortion was a moral one; not surprisingly, the ethics or character of Planned Parenthood had become part of the controversy.

So it was in October 1985 that Planned Parenthood began a public relations campaign designed to counter its opponents' claims. In all, a series of eight, one-page ads were run over a period of several months in publications that included *Time, Newsweek, Ms., New Republic, Columbia Journalism Review, New York Review of Books, Atlantic Monthly,* and *Esquire,* among others. Each ad consisted of a black-and-white photo of an individual (i.e., a doctor, a teen-aged girl, a man in a park, a woman with a child), which was followed by text on the bottom half of the page. According to Douglas Gould, vice president for communications at the Planned Parenthood Federation of America, the public relations campaign was intended to reach educated audiences; thus, the organization felt its ads could use a great deal of text (at least 50% of the page) and still convey its message. That message, Gould claimed, was the importance of abortion rights (D. Gould, personal communication, June 4, 1986). Indeed, each ad asks readers to use an accompanying coupon, which includes a box for readers to check. The statement beside the box reads: "I've written my representatives in Congress to tell them I support: government programs that reduce the need for abortion by preventing unwanted pregnancy; and keeping safe and legal abortion a choice for all women." In addition, the coupon asks readers to send their "tax-deductible contribution in support of all Planned Parenthood activities and programs."

Although the ads may ask for political support and money, this chapter asserts that the importance of abortion rights per se is not the central focus of the campaign. Rather, Planned Parenthood makes its requests based on the goodness of its much-maligned character. In short, Planned Parenthood's ads establish the organization's character based on the ends it pursues and the social roles it assumes. This chapter examines "The Decision Is Yours" campaign as an exemplar of organizational persuasion that functions to establish moral virtue. By examining Planned Parenthood's campaign, this chapter should contribute to broader knowledge of public relations by shedding light upon how organizations can use public relations to demonstrate their morality. In the following, two ideas are discussed: first, the concept of character and how one's character may be ascertained, and second, the exemplification of such principles in Planned Parenthood's "The Decision Is Yours" campaign.

CHARACTER AND MORAL VIRTUE: THE VALUE OF ONE'S PURPOSE AND THE VALUE OF ONE'S ROLES

Etymologically, the word "character" is related to morals. According to the *Compact Edition of the Oxford English Dictionary* (1973), both *ethic* and *ethos*—terms that deal with morals or "character-istic" spirit—are derived from the Greek word for character or ἠθος. Indeed, *Liddell and Scott's Greek-English Lexicon* (1977) informs its readers that ἠθος means "accustomed place," "habit," or "mores . . . character." Thus, the posture one normally assumes or the way one habitually acts reveals one's moral character. Aristotle presented this idea in his *Nicomachean Ethics* (1956, II.i.1–2) when he said that "moral or ethical virtue [ἀρετῆς . . . δ' ἠθικὴ or one's goodness of character] is the product of habit . . . and has indeed derived its name, with a slight variation of form, from that word."

Aristotle was not the only individual to think of moral virtue and character as intertwined. Kenneth Burke (1969a, p. 231), for instance, said character corresponds with his own concept of agent or actor; as he put it, character "is 'what makes us ascribe certain moral qualities to . . . agents.'" In *Character, Community, and Politics*, Cochran (1982) claimed that the "center" of one's character is "his distinctive mark, the set of moral qualities which make him who he is" (p. 18). Even if character is considered to be synonymous with moral virtue, however, one might ask how a rhetor's character may be ascertained. The answer to this question seems to be twofold. First, an individual's character may be revealed by the ends he or she pursues, and second, by the social roles that rhetor assumes.

According to Aristotle, the ends one pursues are indicative of one's purpose and hence, one's character; as he explained, "for as is the moral purpose, so is the character, and as is the end, so is the moral purpose" (1959, III.xvi.8). Perelman and Olbrechts-Tyteca (1969) added support for this idea when they wrote that intention places emphasis "essentially on the person and his permanent character. Intention is closely bound to the agent; it is, as it were, an emanation, the result of his will, of his intimate character" (p. 301). Because we can never know the intention of others directly, we must make judgments about their purpose, based on the ends their actions achieve (Aristotle, 1959). Pro-life activists today, for example, cannot know George Bush's true intention when he argues against the federal funding of Planned Parenthood; such activists realize, however, that the end result of such a policy would be a decrease in monies available for abortion clinics. Because pro-life supporters place high value on this outcome, they perceive the President's purpose—and hence, character—to be good, as well. As Perelman and Olbrechts-Tyteca observed, "the relation between what must be considered the essence of the person and the acts which are but the manifestation of that essence is fixed once and for all" (pp. 296–297); thus, the values we attribute to particular acts prompt us to attribute those values to the person who performed the acts. This is not the only way in which character may be ascertained, however. We also attribute character to a rhetor based on the social roles that individual assumes.

According to Cochran, an important part of character is the set of social roles or "masks" one wears in society. These may include the role of parent, teacher, concerned citizen, unhappy tenant, devout church member, and others. The notion of social roles corresponds, interestingly enough, with the concept of persona. Originally, the Latin term *persona* referred to the mask an actor wore on stage; later, the contemporary word *person* developed from the term (Elliott, 1982). Thus, an audience may evaluate the character of a rhetor (person) through the value it attributes to the various masks or personae the rhetor publicly assumes. If the President portrays himself as the protector of the unborn, for example, and pro-life activists accept his portrayal, they will evaluate his character in a positive way because they support the role he assumes. In summary, one may evaluate rhetors' characters in two ways: first, by ascertaining the rhetors' purpose based on the value of their acts, and second, by assessing the worth and plausibility of the social roles the rhetors assume. Conversely, rhetors may attempt to establish their good characters by demonstrating the positive value of their acts and purity of their purpose, and by convincingly portraying themselves in valued social roles.

Although character normally is considered the essence of an individual, principles of character may be applied to organizational rhetors, as well. Organizations as diverse as General Motors, the American Cancer Society, and the National Rifle Association speak as distinctive entities in their public messages. Furthermore, these organizations have many of the same legal communicative rights that individual citizens have (Consolidated Edison v. Public Service Commission of New York, 1980; First National Bank of Boston v. Bellotti, 1978; Pacific Gas and Electric v. Public Utilities Commission of California, 1986; C. Vibbert, 1990). In the past 20 years, corporations and other organizations have taken advantage of this favorable communication environment in order to discuss issues of interest to them and to influence relevant public policy (Crable & S. Vibbert, 1985; Heath & Associates, 1988; Jones & Chase, 1979). These same organizations have sought to establish particular images with their publics (Botwinick, 1984; Day, 1980; Denbow & Culbertson, 1985; Foss, 1984; Gray & Smeltzer, 1985; Heath & Nelson, 1986; Sauerhaft & Atkins, 1989). Not surprisingly, some image campaigns have placed their central focus on the good moral character of the organizational rhetor. These companies exemplify Aristotle's (1959) principle that arguments of moral character ("$\eta\theta o s$") constitute "the most effective means of proof" (I.ii.4–5). One example of organizational discourse that typifies this concept is Planned Parenthood's "The Decision Is Yours" campaign.

THE MORAL CHARACTER OF PLANNED PARENTHOOD: "THE DECISION IS YOURS"

Since the early 1980s, pro-life activists have assaulted the moral virtue of Planned Parenthood and other pro-choice advocates on a regular basis; thus, the emphasis on character in Planned Parenthood's 1985 campaign therefore seems quite natural. Just as legal argumentation frequently deals with the moral virtue of an agent, these ads establish the good character of Planned Parenthood and subvert the assumed moral virtue of abortion opponents. Hence, the tag line of each ad, "The Decision Is Yours," makes the reader a judge in the courtroom of public opinion. In these ads, Planned Parenthood establishes its moral character in two ways: (a) by emphasizing the goodness of its purpose and the comparative evil of its opponents' intentions; and (b) by assuming positive personae and casting pro-life forces in negative social roles.

The Value of One's Purpose

The Purpose of Planned Parenthood. In each of the eight ads, a coupon clearly indicates Planned Parenthood's overall purpose: to "reduce the need for abortion by preventing unwanted pregnancy" and to keep "safe and legal abortion a choice for all women." Planned Parenthood acts on such intentions by providing counsel, contraceptives, and legal abortion to women who desire them. Although not everyone will attribute high moral principles to Planned Parenthood's stated intentions, the organization's campaign argues that such purposes are highly virtuous because the outcomes of Planned Parenthood's actions are highly virtuous. By offering legal abortion and family planning, Planned Parenthood provides three valuable benefits: the choice of when and whether to have children, the prevention of teen-age pregnancy, and the protection of women's health and lives. If readers place great value on such ends, they likely will evaluate Planned Parenthood's purpose—and hence, character—in an equally positive way. In addition, Planned Parenthood attempts to align its intentions with higher moral purposes related to these valued outcomes.

According to Planned Parenthood, one benefit of its family planning and abortion services is the genuine control these provide individuals over their lives. Two ads, for instance, tell the reader that abortion is a difficult decision, which each woman only can make for herself. By providing safe and legal abortions, Planned Parenthood protects the right of women to make their own choices and thereby, ensures women's other rights. As one ad explains it, "The right to decide when and whether to bear children gives women genuine control over their own lives. Not in the abstract. But in real, practical terms. Anatomy is no longer destiny" (Planned Parenthood, 1985f). Planned Parenthood's actions do not benefit only women, however; legal abortion and family planning services provide men with control over their lives, as well. One advertisement tells male readers that "the public controversy over keeping abortion safe and legal concerns your freedom as well. To marry when and if you want. To decide with your partner to have children when you want them. If you want them" (Planned Parenthood, 1985g). By demonstrating the positive outcome of its acts, Planned Parenthood subordinates its purpose of reducing unwanted pregnancy and maintaining legal abortion to a higher moral purpose: providing people with the right of self-determination.

In addition to this, Planned Parenthood argues that family planning and abortion services help prevent teen-age pregnancy. One ad states that Planned Parenthood provides birth control to teens with just such an end in mind (Planned Parenthood 1985h). Another explains that most teen-age mothers are single mothers "trapped in a cycle of poverty that costs billions extra each year. In malnutrition. Disease. Unemployment. Child abuse." Worse yet, the ad continues, each teenage mother is "robbed of her childhood and her hope." Such assertions are unlikely to provoke disagreement from any reader. The ad then goes on to state: "While we must do everything we can to help prevent unwanted pregnancy, we must also preserve the option of safe, legal abortion. A teenage girl shouldn't be forced to become a mother if she's not ready" (Planned Parenthood, 1985c). Again, Planned Parenthood's stated purpose seems much more virtuous when aligned with the worthy intention of eliminating such a troublesome societal problem.

Finally, "The Decision Is Yours" campaign claims that Planned Parenthood's desire for legal abortion and adequate birth control provides a third benefit: the protection of women's health and lives. In one ad, Planned Parenthood tells the reader that back-alley abortions are "painful, dirty, humiliating, and horribly dangerous" (Planned Parenthood, 1985g). In another, a physician explains:

> As a doctor I know that outlawing abortions doesn't stop them. It just makes them extremely dangerous. When abortion was illegal, I treated women maimed and crippled by self-induced and back-alley abortions. I remember vividly the gruesome suffering and needless deaths that resulted from this butchery.
>
> Women, throughout history, have had abortions whenever they felt it was their only option. Outlawing abortions won't stop women from having them. (Planned Parenthood, 1985e)

Statements such as these demonstrate that Planned Parenthood's actions result in the protection of life, rather than its destruction, as pro-life advocates so often allege. By explaining how legal abortion aids women, Planned Parenthood associates its intention to maintain legal abortion with a higher moral purpose of protecting life. In this way, Planned Parenthood attempts to establish the goodness of its character.

The Purpose of Pro-Life Advocates. In contrast to discourse about its own purposes, Planned Parenthood describes the intentions of its opponents and the outcome of their actions in very negative terms. Overall, "The Decision Is Yours" campaign makes it clear that pro-life forces have two purposes: to outlaw legal abortion and to restrict birth control information. All eight of the campaign ads mention the first of these intentions and question its morality. Seven of the ads, for instance, include the following passage or a passage similar to it: "They [pro-life activists] want to outlaw abortions for all women, regardless of the circumstances. Even if her life or health is endangered by a pregnancy. Even if she is a victim of rape or incest. And even if she is too young to be a mother" (Planned Parenthood, 1985c). When explained in this way, the purposes of pro-life advocates seem extreme and somewhat less than virtuous. Similarly, five of Planned Parenthood's ads point out that many pro-life activists want to restrict access to birth control by cutting federal funding for family planning services (Planned Parenthood, 1985c, 1985e, 1985f, 1985g, 1985h). This purpose also appears immoral, as well as contradictory because birth control is what prevents unwanted pregnancies and hence, abortion. According to one ad, easy access to birth control could eliminate the cause of abortion altogether. Unfortunately, however, "the same people who want to outlaw abortion also want to prohibit access to birth control, specially for young people" (Planned Parenthood, 1985e).

Beyond questioning the morality of pro-life intentions, Planned Parenthood also explains the negative outcomes of its opponents' actions and associates these with other, less virtuous purposes. Not surprisingly, these negative outcomes stand in complete opposition to Planned Parenthood's positive results. First, pro-life actions—if successful—will lead to fewer choices for men and women and therefore, less control for individuals over their lives. Men, for instance, will lose the right to decide when to marry, when to have children, and whether to have children (Planned Parenthood, 1985g). For women, the stakes are even higher. Legal abortion and birth control services give women the means to protect their educations, careers, and futures against contraceptive failure and unwanted pregnancy (Planned Parenthood, 1985a, 1985b, 1985f). If pro-life forces have their way, women's rights as a whole will be endangered. One ad claims that pro-choice opponents "believe there's only one place for women. At home, in the kitchen and nursery" (Planned Parenthood, 1985f). Planned Parenthood aligns pro-life advocates' intentions to outlaw abortion and to restrict birth control with the purpose of robbing women of their rights.

Another detrimental result of pro-life actions would be an increase in teenage pregnancies. One ad claims, "Forty percent of all girls who are now fourteen will get pregnant before they're eighteen. One million each year" (Planned Parenthood, 1985c). If pro-life forces succeed in restricting birth control, these statistics only will increase. Worse yet, if abortion is outlawed, the poverty, unemployment, and child abuse that results from teen-age pregnancies will grow, and these young mothers will be robbed of their futures (Planned Parenthood, 1985c, 1985h). Through such explanations, Planned Parenthood depicts the actions of pro-life advocates as contributing to a societal problem, rather than alleviating one.

Finally, Planned Parenthood shows how its opponents' actions could threaten women's lives. The public relations campaign indicates that women will continue to seek abortions, whether they are legal or not, even "at the risk of being maimed or killed with a back-alley abortion" (Planned Parenthood, 1985a, 1985b, 1985d, 1985e, 1985g). To underscore this point, Planned Parenthood (1985d) states that "millions of American women had abortions before they were legalized nationwide in 1973. An untold number were maimed for life. Thousands were literally slaughtered, packed off bleeding and infected to died in abject terror." Because pro-life supporters want to "turn back the clock" and outlaw abortions, their alleged purpose of protecting life loses much of its credibility in Planned Parenthood's ads. Thus, Planned Parenthood strips its opponents of their morality by questioning the virtue of pro-life intentions and demonstrating the ill effects pro-life policy would have. Emphasis on purpose is not the only means by which Planned Parenthood establishes its good character and denigrates that of its opposition. In addition, Planned Parenthood's campaign casts itself in helpful social personae and portrays pro-life forces in threatening social roles.

The Value of One's Roles

The Roles of Planned Parenthood. In "The Decision Is Yours" campaign, Planned Parenthood portrays itself in a variety of helpful social roles: counselor, educator, protector of life, provider of choices, defender of women's rights. Perhaps the cleverest aspect of Planned Parenthood's ads, however, is how they prompt readers to see Planned Parenthood as *their* counselor, *their* educator, *their* protector, *their* provider, and *their* defender. This occurs in a number of ways. First, readers' eyes immediately are drawn to the black-and-white photo that covers the top half of each ad. The photo is a picture of a person: a young Black woman deep in thought, a young White woman who looks as if she were about to cry, a man in a park, a doctor, a teen-age girl in a classroom, a mother holding her young son, an older woman sitting at her kitchen table with a cup of coffee, and a professional woman at her place of business. The visual impact of the pictures encourages readers to identify with the people shown. According to Burke (1969b), identification is integral to persuasive success; Burke claimed that a communicator persuades an audience only insofar as his or her language identifies the ways of the communicator with the ways of the audience. In "The Decision Is Yours" campaign, Planned Parenthood strategically used photographs to foster the perception of similarities between the organization and its publics. Planned Parenthood further reinforced such identification by frequently targeting particular ads to particular magazine readerships. *Esquire*, for example, published the ad that features the picture of a man in a park; the ad that *Ms.* ran, on the other hand, contains the professional woman's photo (D. Gould, personal communication, June 4, 1986). Taken as a whole, Planned Parenthood's identification strategy encourages readers to take the perspective of the person in the picture, a perspective which is revealed by the large headline immediately beneath each photo. In two ads, for instance, the headline reads, "Abortion is never the easy way out" (Planned Parenthood, 1985a, 1985b). Four other ads have the person speak to readers directly. The teen-age girl, for example, asks readers, " 'Do I look like a mother to you?' " (Planned Parenthood, 1985c); the professional woman claims, " 'The right to choose abortion makes all my other rights possible' " (Planned Parenthood, 1985f). Through the use of photos and headlines, Planned Parenthood guides the reader to assume the role of the person portrayed. The only exception to this is the doctor ad, the one ad in the series that identifies the person in its portrait by name. Although few people easily will assume the doctor's role, most can identify with the doctor–patient relationship. Because the doctor looks directly at readers, they are encouraged to listen to his medical advice on "How to prevent abortion" (Planned Parenthood, 1985e). In general, then, the graphics and headlines of the Planned Parenthood ads help readers take the perspective the pictured person represents.

Within the text of the ads, this perspective-taking continues. Reader identification with the pictured individual means that readers themselves serve as character references for Planned Parenthood, just as the person in the photo does. One ad, for instance, shows an older woman who claims that she nearly died over 40 years ago from an illegal abortion (Planned Parenthood, 1985d). Because Planned Parenthood offers legal abortion and thus assumes the role of protector for such women today, readers are led to view Planned Parenthood as their protector, too. In other ads, character references are more explicit, as in one that begins with the personal testimony of a young woman. The woman reveals that she became pregnant at age 15 and went to Planned Parenthood on the advice of a friend:

> They [Planned Parenthood] were so wonderful. They talked to me about what I could do. I knew I wasn't ready to be a mother. I wanted to tell my parents but I didn't want to hurt them. Planned Parenthood helped me talk to them. I had an abortion. Getting pregnant was the worst crisis of my life. But I know I made the right decision. I finished school, got married and now I have two wonderful kids. I don't know what I would have done if abortion wasn't legal. My only choices were a back-alley abortion, trying to do it myself, or being a fifteen-year-old mother. Planned Parenthood saved my life when I was fifteen. I got my future back. (Planned Parenthood, 1985h)

If readers identify with the woman in the picture, her testimony on behalf of Planned Parenthood becomes their testimony, as well. The ads therefore encourage readers to view Planned Parenthood in the social role of benevolent counselor for both the woman and themselves.

Planned Parenthood also leads readers to see the organization as a helpful persona for them personally through its strategic shifts in "person." Frequently, the text employs the third person to discuss how legal abortion and adequate birth control impacts on the individual in the picture or individuals like him or her (i.e., "a woman" and "men"); then, slyly, the text changes to second person or "you." In the ads headlined by "Abortion is never the easy way out," for instance, the text explains:

> The decision to have an abortion—or not—can be the most difficult decision a woman will ever make. It's never the easy way out. But for some women, it's the only way out. It certainly isn't a decision anyone else can—or should—make for you. (Planned Parenthood, 1985a, 1985b)

This subtle transition from third person to second person involves readers directly in the topic under discussion and reinforces the perspective the picture and headline provide. Other ads use the same strategy (1985a, 1985b, 1985f, 1985g, 1985h). Because Planned Parenthood portrays itself as the social persona who helps the person in the photo, the organization also casts itself in the role of helper for the reader.

The Roles of Pro-Life Advocates. Unlike Planned Parenthood's portrayal of its own personae, the organization casts pro-life advocates in very negative social roles: opponents of choice, harmers of life, enemies of women's rights, advocates of ignorance. Indeed, seven of the eight Planned Parenthood ads refer to pro-life advocates as an "increasingly vocal and violent minority" (1985a, 1985b, 1985c, 1985d, 1985f, 1985g, 1985h). Although one ad claims that some opponents hold public office—"men in the White House, in Congress, in the Courts" (1985g)—most ads treat pro-life advocates as part of an unrespectable fringe element: "fanatics," "anti-choice fanatics," and "these people" (1985a, 1985b, 1985f, 1985g). Planned Parenthood attacks the character of pro-life advocates further by describing the way they habitually carry out these social roles. In two ads, readers are told that abortion opponents will "stop at nothing—including harassment, physical intimidation, and violence—until they succeed" (1985a, 1985b). Other ads warn that pro-life activists will use threats, bombings, and even attacks upon the Constitution in their attempts to get what they want (1985c, 1985d, 1985h). In general, Planned Parenthood portrays its opponents as ruthless stormtroopers who carry out their acts in a manner consistent with that persona.

Finally, because Planned Parenthood encourages identification with the pictured individual in each ad, it also guides readers to view pro-life advocates in social roles that threaten both the photographed person and the reader. Once again, the text reinforces such identifications by demonstrating how abortion opponents affect the reader—"you." Two ads, for example, warn that "there's an increasingly vocal and violent minority that wants to take away your right to decide for yourself" (1985a, 1985b). Planned Parenthood casts pro-life activists as opponents of choice, a persona that poses harm for the reader, as well as the women in the ads. The other advertisements use similar strategies. In one, a professional woman claims that abortion opponents threaten all of women's rights; the ad asserts, "if you're not free to decide the important things for yourself, you're not free at all" (1985f). By portraying pro-life supporters as enemies of women's rights, Planned Parenthood attacks the character of the opposition and personalizes for female readers the threat such forces pose. Its campaign as a whole depicts Planned Parenthood in virtuous social roles and portrays pro-life activists in less-than-virtuous personae. By comparison, the character of Planned Parenthood shines.

A "CHARACTER-ISTIC" ARGUMENT OF MORAL VIRTUE

Throughout "The Decision Is Yours" campaign, Planned Parenthood established its good character and moral virtue through two means: First, by demonstrating the goodness of its purpose and the evil of its opponents' intentions, and second, by assuming positive personae and casting pro-life forces in negative social roles. When these ads were published, at least some pro-life activists seemed to realize the harm such arguments posed to their cause. An editorial in *America*, for example, criticized Planned Parenthood for portraying all pro-life advocates as violent fanatics. According to the essay, "The promoters and writers of these ads claim the moral high ground, but that claim is spurious. For in such presentations there is deplorable blindness or, more likely, dishonesty" ("Truth in advertising, please," 1986, p. 1). Today, pro-life groups continue to attack the morals of Planned Parenthood. Randall Terry, head of Operation Rescue, for instance, calls Planned Parenthood "the single largest child killer in the United States" (Szegedy-Maszak, 1989, p. 19). Nonetheless, Planned Parenthood has managed to convince millions of other Americans that the organization's character is virtuous, rather than vicious. Between 1977 and 1988, Planned Parenthood's income from its clinics, Title X grants to affiliates, and contributions from individuals, corporations, and foundations nearly tripled (Szegedy-Maszak, 1989). Planned Parenthood also began to run a new series of public relations ads recently that aims to subvert the morality of pro-life advocates (Planned Parenthood, 1989a, 1989b, 1989c; also see Olasky, 1987). Although the idea of ἦθος or character is as ancient as Aristotle, the rhetorical principles that underlie it are still relevant today.

Indeed, Planned Parenthood is not the only organizational rhetor whose discourse exemplifies such concepts. The National Rifle Association, for example, also employs such principles in its on-going "I'm the N.R.A." campaign. Each ad includes the photograph of a different person—a minister, a test pilot, a housewife, and so on—all of whom are holding guns of some kind. The pictured individuals tell the reader how they became members of the N.R.A., how the organization has helped them in some way, and other purposes the N.R.A. serves. Like "The Decision Is Yours" campaign, these ads establish the National Rifle Association's moral character, based upon the social personae the organization assumes and the good purposes it holds. Organizations, like people, develop and are responsible for their characters. Through the rhetorical principles of "character-istic" argument, organizations use public relations campaigns to convey their morality to others.

REFERENCES

Adler, J. (1985, January 14). Chicago's unsilent scream. *Newsweek*, p. 25.

Aristotle. (1956). *The Nicomachean ethics* (H. Rackham, Trans.). Cambridge: Harvard University Press.

Aristotle. (1959). *The "art" of rhetoric* (J.H. Freese, Trans.). Cambridge: Harvard University Press.

Ashkinaze, C. (1984, November). The battle against Planned Parenthood: Can it survive? *Glamour*, pp. 85, 92–94.

Beck, M. (1985, January 14). America's abortion dilemma. *Newsweek*, pp. 20–25.

Botwinick, P. (1984, November). The image of corporate image. *Public Relations Journal*, pp. 12–14.

Burke, K. (1969a). *A grammar of motives.* Berkeley: University of California Press.

Burke, K. (1969b). *A rhetoric of motives.* Berkeley: University of California Press.

Cochran, C.E. (1982). *Character, community, and politics.* University: University of Alabama Press.

Compact edition of the Oxford English dictionary. (1973).

Consolidated Edison Company of New York, Inc., v. Public Service Commission of New York. 65 L Ed (1980). 2d, 319–340.

Crable, R.E., & Vibbert, S.L. (1985). Managing issues and influencing public policy. *Public Relations Review, 11*, 3–16.

Day, C.R., Jr. (1980, May 12). Do companies have personalities? *Industry Week*, pp. 72–78.

Denbow, C.J., & Culbertson, H.M. (1985). Linkage beliefs and diagnosing an image. *Public Relations Review*, *11*, 29–37.

Elliott, R.C. (1982). *The literary persona*. Chicago: University of Chicago Press.

First National Bank of Boston et al. v. Attorney General Francis X. Bellotti of Massachusetts et al. 55 L Ed (1978). 2d, 707–750.

Foss, S.K. (1984). Retooling an image: Chrysler corporation's rhetoric of redemption. *Western Journal of Speech Communication*, *48*, 75–91.

Gray, E.R., & Smeltzer, L.R. (1985). SMR forum: Corporate image—an integral part of strategy. *Sloan Management Review*, 73–78.

Heath, R.L., & Associates. (1988). *Strategic issues management*. San Francisco: Jossey-Bass.

Heath, R.L., & Nelson, R.A. (1986). *Issues management*. Beverly Hills: Sage.

Jones, B.L., & Chase, W.H. (1979). Managing public policy issues. *Public Relations Review*, *5*, 3–23.

Liddell and Scott's Greek-English lexicon. (1977). Oxford: Clarendon Press.

A new attack on abortion. (1985, November 11). *Newsweek*, pp. 24–25.

Olasky, M.N. (1987). Abortion rights: Anatomy of a negative campaign. *Public Relations Review*, *13*, 12–23.

Pacific Gas and Electric Company v. Public Utilities Commission of California. 87 L Ed (1986). 2d, 1–28.

Perelman, Ch., & Olbrechts-Tyteca, L. (1969). *The new rhetoric: A treatise on argumentation*. (J. Wilkinson & P. Weaver, Trans.). Notre Dame: University of Notre Dame Press.

Planned Parenthood. (1985a). *Abortion is never the easy way out* (Photograph of a black woman).

Planned Parenthood. (1985b). *Abortion is never the easy way out* (Photograph of a white woman).

Planned Parenthood. (1985c). *Do I look like a mother to you?* (Photograph of teenaged girl).

Planned Parenthood. (1985d). *Forty years ago, I had a back-alley abortion. I almost died from it.* (Photograph of woman at kitchen table).

Planned Parenthood. (1985e). *How to prevent abortion* (Photograph of a doctor).

Planned Parenthood. (1985f). *The right to choose abortion makes all my other rights possible* (Photograph of professional woman).

Planned Parenthood. (1985g). *What every man should know about abortion* (Photograph of a man).

Planned Parenthood. (1985h). *When I was fifteen, Planned Parenthood saved my life* (Photograph of mother with child).

Planned Parenthood. (1989a). *Sex education classes in our public schools are promoting incest* (Photograph of Jimmy Swaggart).

Planned Parenthood. (1989b). *Should a woman's private medical decisions be made by a man with a bullhorn?* (Photograph of Joe Scheidler).

Planned Parenthood. (1989c). *Would you lie to a pregnant teenager?* (Photograph of a teenaged girl).

Ronald Reagan on abortion. (1984, April 30). *Newsweek*, p. 23.

Sauerhaft, S., & Atkins, C. (1989). Image wars: Protecting your company when there's no place to hide. New York: Wiley.

Spake, A. (1985, July). The truth about "The Silent Scream." *Ms.*, p. 92.

Spring, B. (1982, September 3). Planned Parenthood nearly disqualified from charity drive. *Christianity Today*, p. 84.

Szegedy-Maszak, M. (1989, August 6). Calm, cool and beleaguered. *The New York Times Magazine*, pp. 16–19, 62–64.

Truth in advertising, please. (1986, January 11). [Editorial]. *America*, p. 1.

Vibbert, C.B. (1990). Freedom of speech and corporations: Supreme court strategies for the extension of the first amendment. *Communication*, *12*, 19–34.

Woodward, K.L. (1984, August 20). Politics and abortion. *Newsweek*, pp. 66–67.

Epilogue: Visions of Critical Studies of Public Relations

ROBERT L. HEATH
University of Houston

Taking rhetorical approaches to the study of public relations is a developing aspect of the study of how organizations communicate with key audiences. In coming years, critical attention to organizations as rhetors may become widespread to complement the study of individual rhetors that has domi- nated rhetorical criticism for most of this century.

Critical studies of famous speakers abound. Mention of rhetoric brings to mind speakers such as Daniel Webster, Abraham Lincoln, Frederick Dou- glass, Susan B. Anthony, or Theodore Roosevelt. Modern examples include Franklin Roosevelt, John F. Kennedy, Martin Luther King, Jr., Jesse Jackson, Barbara Jordan, Margaret Thatcher, and Ronald Reagan.

Without doubt, people such as these contribute their thoughts to create the ideas that guide society. But in the scope of matters, examinations of the rhetoric that prevails in a society are inadequate if they miss or dismiss public relations. Many individuals are synonymous with the practice: Ivy Lee, Edward Bernays, Theordore Vail, Betsy Plank, and Herbert Schmertz. On a matter of substantial public policy implications, Thomas Edison and George Westinghouse each conducted public relations campaigns before the turn of this century to determine whether direct or alternating current would be the standard of the electric utility industry. Westinghouse won and alternating current became the standard. Many other examples could be noted.

Mobil's op-eds have attempted to influence opinions on activities and procedures of the oil industry, as well as to criticize unfair journalistic reporting. United Technologies features values basic to American society and the free enterprise system. Allstate Insurance campaigned for seat belts and other safety features for automobiles. The U.S. Council for Energy Awareness has kept readers and viewers up to date on the economic and political advantages of nuclear generation, as well as its safety features. Warner & Swasey has championed American representative democracy and free enterprise, and W. R. Grace and Company has warned of the perils of an increasing federal deficit. Public relations has been a powerful force in establishing an American mentality and lifestyle.

By way of this glimpse at the many public relations campaigns that are prominent in our society we lead into what can we modestly suggest as a research prospectus for the rhetoric and criticism of public relations. A few questions may be important to subsequent studies of public relations employing rhetorical and critical approaches.

What can a rhetorical approach to public relations contribute to the discussion of the ethics of public relations?

Rhetoric has long been associated with ethics for two broad reasons. Ethics give insights into the "good reasons" that are proposed as the substance of rhetoric and offered to influence judgment. Also, ethics is related to the choices of rhetorical strategies, as well as considerations of ends and means. This kind of analysis offers much promise for the continuing discussion of public relations.

This kind of perspective also brings us to realize many positive aspects of public relations we might otherwise overlook. Public relations has been used by consumer groups to draw attention to dangerous products, such as the annual list of unsafe toys published during the Christmas buying season. Public relations is a vital part of conservation efforts of an increasing cadre of organizations seeking to influence public policy, increase membership, and acquire contributions to protect endangered animals and preserve wildlife areas. Public relations has raised money for a wide array of diseases, such as cancer, polio, and muscular dystrophy. Colleges and universities use public relations to feature their unique academic programs, along with their athletic, scientific, and artistic accomplishments. Public relations lobbying by insurance companies has increased automobile safety.

What new and vital insights can a critical approach to the study of public relations give into its role in the formation of symbols and ideologies that influence society and individuals well beyond the scope of individual campaigns?

Organizations, especially corporations, have attempted to gain public acceptance for key concepts that are important to their operations. Utility companies such as AT&T helped win public acceptance for the advisability of *regulated monopolies.* Cities have sold citizens on the advisability of *public* (as opposed to *private*) mass transit, and the federal government gained acceptance for the advisability of a *volunteer, professional military force.* A wide array of companies and environmental groups have pressed the federal government to adopt a *national energy policy.* NASA has sold the concept of *space flight and exploration.*

By examining key symbols of our society, and locating the influence public relations has had over them, we gain insights into the potency of the profession.

Does a rhetorical approach to public relations produce a view that features a two-way asymmetrical model of public relations?

Some practitioners as well as scholars may be disturbed by the notion that public relations is used to assert self-interest. Carried to one set of conclusions, this paradigm brings up the specter of deceit, manipulation, and thought control. If these ends were inseparable from a rhetoric paradigm, it would be hard to justify even though it dominates the practice of public relations. Viewed this narrowly, there is reason to be concerned about the rhetorical underpinnings of public relations. Seen more broadly, less concern is justified in regard to this paradigm.

To make this point requires starting with a review of the systems paradigm that several leading scholars have championed because it features the symmetry of interests (Grunig & Hunt, 1984; Long & Hazelton, 1987; Pavlik, 1987). This approach to public relations aspires to establish understanding as the outcome that fosters a harmonious relationship between the parties involved in an issue addressed by public relations. The assumption is that the best means for establishing satisfying relationships is to be open, allowing information to flow into and out of the organization participating in public relations. Through this flow of information, interested parties can come to understand one another and make appropriate adjustments. This version of public relations assumes the inherent worth of openness and looks to achieve interdependency—a basic characteristic of systems—through an information-driven means for satisfying differences of opinion.

The assertion of self-interest paradigm is not antithetic to the symmetry paradigm. Indeed, because each public relations statement competes against other statements to be received, believed, and yielded to, the assertion of self-interest can only go as far as others are willing to allow it to do. Rhetoric assumes, in the context of our free enterprise and representative government systems, that each statement is part of a debate—the vigorous public contest of ideas. Each statement made in public is subject to be ignored, derogated, and challenged. Even given the fear that corporations have disproportionate influence because of their ability to engage in "deep-pockets" spending, they do not dominate the opinion arena, and may even be at certain disadvantages because of their apparent size and questionable credibility.

The history of public relations demonstrates that as corporations exert too much influence, therefore treading on the self-interests of others, they suffer constraints. Around the turn of the century and shortly thereafter, limited legislative restrictions had already been placed on many corporate practices including the formation of monopolies, unfair trade practices, manufacture and sale of unsafe or unsanitary products, and unfair labor practices. If deep-pockets spending is a fact and if rhetorical manipulation works to the exclusive advantage of corporations, how can we account for the increasingly tight regulations that have been placed on myriad corporate activities in this century?

Inherent in the systems rationale for the symmetry paradigm is the conception that the strong should not dominate the weak. Reflecting on biology, the source from which systems theory took much of its rationale, we can learn that the strong can dominate only to the extent that a balance exists. In nature animals that live by eating other animals become dependent on the health and stability of the population of their prey. Even herbivores can literally eat themselves out of house and home—goats for instance can overpopulate an island and thereby destroy the food supply they need to exist.

Systems by definition are self-regulating and self-correcting. The interests involved in any system—in this case those related to free enterprise and public policy—balance to the extent that each assertion of self-interest produces various counter assertions. The extent to which one self-interest is constrained occurs at the point that other self-interests say "No!" This "no" saying is the foundation of a negotiated self-interest model. Through open contest of ideas, the rewards, costs, privileges, and constraints of the self-interested parties are negotiated.

One value of public relations is its ability to contribute to the collective shared reality that brings harmony, a shared perspective that leads people to similar, compatible conclusions. To achieve its full potential in this regard, requires constant and aggressive critical reexamination of the rhetorical substance, form, practices, ethics, and strategies that are employed in public relations.

How can 2,000 years of studies of rhetoric be brought to bear to increase insights into the message selection and message design strategies of public relations?

Rhetoric has become a well-established and useful rubric for guiding the study of how people select, create, and execute messages. Thousands of discussions of this kind have provided insights into the substance and form of arguments, stylistics, tactics of definition, and the structure of messages. Now that tradition is moving to scrutinize the activities of public relations.

REFERENCES

Grunig, J. E., & Hunt, T. (1984). *Managing public relations.* New York: Holt, Rinehart & Winston.

Long, L. W., & Hazelton, V., Jr. (1987). Public relations: A theoretical and practical response. *Public Relations Review, 13*(2), 3–13.

Pavlik, J. V. (1987). *Public relations: What research tells us.* Newbury Park, CA: Sage.

Author Index

321

Subject Index

ACB-0669